AF662485

Bombay Modern

Bombay Modern

Arun Kolatkar and Bilingual Literary Culture

Anjali Nerlekar

SPEAKING
TIGER

SPEAKING TIGER BOOKS
125A, Ground Floor, Shahpur Jat, Near Asiad Village
New Delhi 110049

First published in USA by Northwestern University Press

Published in India by Speaking Tiger 2017

ISBN: 978-93-86338-33-4

10 9 8 7 6 5 4 3 2

Printed at Gopsons Papers Ltd

To my mother, Saraswati Kadekodi (1940–1984).
She is at the source of all I do.

My pencil is sharpened at both ends

. . .

what I write with one end
comes out as English
what I write with the other
comes out as Marathi

—Arun Kolatkar, "Making Love to a Poem"

Contents

Note on Transliteration and Sources

I have used the customary English spelling for Marathi and other Indian-language words and have tried to keep the spellings as simple and understandable as possible. When I quote from a source, I retain the transliteration and spelling of the source. Most Indian-language words are italicized, except where the word is easily recognizable in English.

There are a few Marathi words that are consistently used in the text and I give their pronunciations here:

> *sathottari* is pronounced as *sāṭhottari*
> *katta* is pronounced as *kaṭṭā*

Translations, when not attributed, are mine; I mention the source of another's translation.

I have interviewed people associated with the writing community in and around Bombay over the last eleven years and therefore do not list each interview I have recorded. Where I refer to a personal interview or to statements made, they are part of the series of conversations held over many years.

The names of a few sources require explanation:

Sarpa Satra: Sarpa Satra. Mumbai: Pras Prakashan, 2004 (to be distinguished from "*sarpa satra*," a long poetic sequence in *Bhijaki Vahi*; the quotes around an italicized title indicate it is a poem and not a book).

Kolatkar Papers: Unpublished papers, drafts of poems, and diary entries in Marathi and in English, including sketches by the poet, a musical score of "The Butterfly," the Balwant Bua book proposal for Penguin (1986), the manuscript of the long narrative *Balwant Bua*, the manuscript on Royan, newspaper clippings, and notes.

Clearing House Papers: Unpublished personal correspondence between Adil Jussawalla and Arvind Krishna Mehrotra, compiled by Jerry Pinto.

Adil Jussawalla Papers: Papers, including personal correspondence and magazine clippings.

Illustrations

Acknowledgments

I have spent over a decade engaging with the texts and the people related to Bombay *sathottari* poetry and I have found a community of friends, mentors, and supporters whom I will briefly acknowledge but who deserve more than I can say here.

I am grateful to have had the opportunity to present my research at various workshops and seminars where the discussions have helped hone the book's argument: the workshop "The View from Below" at Cornell in 2008; the Maharashtra Studies conference in 2011 and 2014; the Cornell South Asia Studies Seminar in 2012; the Center for Cultural Analysis, Rutgers, in 2012; the two-part Workshop on Indian Literature as Comparative Literature, held in 2013 at Rutgers and in 2014 at the French Institute, Pondicherry, India; and the Madison conference on South Asia in 2014. I am also grateful for the fellowship with the Center for Cultural Analysis in 2012, the Rutgers Council Grant in 2011, the Women of Color Initiative Grants in 2012 and 2013, and the AMESALL department that provided me with the time and the resources necessary for my research. My students (especially Jacob Meeks, Hanna Campbell, and Megha Patel) have also provided valuable insight into my readings over the years that I have taught Arun Kolatkar's poetry at Ithaca College and at Rutgers University and I am lucky to have had them in my classes.

My heartfelt thanks to those who gave me access to their valuable collections: Bhalchandra Nemade, Satish Kalsekar, Mangesh

Narayan Kale, Avadhoot Dongare, Pat Rodrigues, Michael Perreira, and Dhananjay Paranjape. Thanks in particular to Jerry Pinto for giving me access to the compilation of the Clearing House letters, the Bhandarkar Library in Pune for giving me access to Kolatkar's books and clippings, the SCILET library in Madurai for access to their vast collection of Indian English texts, the library at Cornell, and Bronwen Bledsoe. For their liberal sharing of time and memories, I am grateful to Gieve Patel, Vijaya Chitre, Bhalchandra Nemade, Eunice de Souza, Meera Kosambi, Sujit Patwardhan, Vilas Sarang, Ashok Kelkar, Satish Kalsekar, and Manohar Shetty.

I am profoundly grateful to Mrs. Soonoo Kolatkar and Ashok Shahane for giving me permission to reproduce writing from Arun Kolatkar's published books and unpublished manuscripts. Vrindavan Dandavate has unhesitatingly given me access to his collection of *sathottari* documents. He created the wonderful personalized cover illustration for the book and I am extremely fortunate to have his support in this project. To the members of the Military Café/Stadium Café *katta*, Ashok Shahane, Avinash Gupte, Vrindavan Dandavate, Ratan Sohoni, Dilip Bhende, and Michael Perreira, who allowed me to be part of the rambunctious group and considered me one of their own, my deepest gratitude. I also owe an immense debt to Kiran Nagarkar, who spent many weeks in the United States and India discussing literature and the *sathottari* period with me.

It is lovely to get the opportunity to thank so many friends who have contributed toward the book in tangible and intangible ways: to Prachi Deshpande for inspiration, scholarly support, and deep affection; to Aparna Balachandran, Kelly Dietz, Ujwala Samarth, Ashok Gopal, and Hartman De Souza, dear friends and collaborators in things scholarly as well as extremely silly; to Ann Volin, Jill Zasadny, Joan Wingert, and Paivi Giannios for long-enduring friendships and deep understanding; to Nahyan Fancy for neighborly chats and help; and to S. Shankar, Janet Walker, Sumit Guha, and Indrani Chatterjee for generous professional and personal support. I am incredibly lucky to have had amazing colleagues and friends in the original South Asian Studies reading group at Rutgers, Meheli Sen, Triveni Kuchi, Preetha Mani, Asher Ghertner, Mukti Lakhi Mangaram, Jessica Birkenholtz, and Nida Sajid, as well as in Philip Webb, Ana Laguna and Patricia Akhimie; they have all read parts of the book and provided valuable friendship throughout the years. Vinay Dharwadker has been an important interlocutor for my work and has aided in the writing of this book in more ways than I can mention. My sincere thanks to both Vinay Dharwadker and Aparna Dharwadker for their important work on Indian modernisms and for the personal and professional support. My deep gratitude also goes to Girish Karnad, who always inspires with his writing and his generosity; his decade-long friendship has sustained me in more ways than I can articulate here.

Yolanda Martinez San-Miguel and Alamin Mazrui, each in turn, have been my rock of support at Rutgers: this book sees the light of day because they were there. I have been extremely lucky in my second home at the Department of African, Middle Eastern and South Asian Languages and Literatures (AMESALL): my deep gratitude to the department chair, Charles Haberl, for ready help whenever asked; to Ousseina Alidou, wonderful friend; and to the rest of the AMESALL faculty for their innumerable acts of kindness and collegiality. I also want to thank the faculty at the English department at Ithaca College for making my stay there so memorable.

I started my work on Kolatkar's poetry in Kansas; my heartfelt thanks to Joseph Harrington and Byron Caminero-Santangelo at the University of Kansas, who gave me the initial confidence to work in this area. I am deeply indebted to Rajeev Patke, my literary guide for over two decades: I owe my modernist preferences to his amazing classes in Pune. At Northwestern University Press, Ed Dimendberg and Susan Gillman have been valiant supporters at the FlashPoints series, and Henry Lowell Carrigan, Gianna Mosser, and the editing team helped me with patience and care through the various stages of the publishing process. Special thanks also to Emily Polokoff for speedy and generous editing help and to the anonymous reviewers who gave detailed suggestions that have improved the book. I would like to thank the editors of *Perspectives, Studies in Translatology* for permission to reprint my essay "The Rough Ground of Translation and Bilingual Writing in Arun Kolatkar's *Jejuri*" in this book.

My never-ending gratitude goes to my perennially smiling brother and anchor in life, Arun Kadekodi, who continues to believe in my work even while disliking modernism; to my sister-in-law Meenal Kadekodi, who is a loving surrogate sister; to my nephews, Saurabh Kadekodi and Rohan Kadekodi; and to Gopal Kadekodi, Savitri Kadekodi, and Sita Bhat for their unconditional love. My wonderful friends Rajeev Panikath, Smita Rajeev, and Subrata Das assisted me on multiple Bombay trips and I value their lifelong friendship. I want to thank the extended Nerlekar/Lad family including Shobhana Nerlekar, Asha Nerlekar, and

Mugdha Lad; my deep gratitude goes to my father-in-law, Prabhakar Nerlekar, who always encouraged me in all my scholarly engagements.

To Shamim Mahadwala (Tasneem Bhavnagarwala), lifelong friend and a beacon of positivity, I wish I could say more to show how indebted I am. My heartfelt thanks also go to my gang of Symbi trekkers, whose relentless mockery and fun-filled encounters have kept me young beyond my years.

I give a brief introduction to Ashok Shahane as an editor and publisher within the book, but I want to acknowledge here the friendship of a decade with a man who has not only shared freely the enormous quantity of material available on Arun Kolatkar as a poet, and on the *sathottari* Marathi publishing scene, but also spent hours every month talking on the phone with me and sharing his memories, brainstorming with me about my book cover (the idea for the cover emerged from a joint discussion with Ashok Shahane and Vrindavan Dandavate). He accompanied me on a delightful walking tour of Kolatkar's Kala Ghoda one exciting evening and even cooked lunch for me himself one afternoon in 2008 (he makes exceptionally good rotis!). He is a mentor and friend, and I consider him a part of my extended family. My gratitude to him and the generous Rekha Shahane is beyond words.

Arvind Krishna Mehrotra and Adil Jussawalla each welcomed me to their homes and allowed me access to their incredible archive of material on Arun Kolatkar, on their own work, and on the *sathottari* period in English poetry. Adil's incredible archivist's mind and Arvind's extraordinary knowledge about Indian poetry have been my central resources, and both of them have guided this project throughout. They have also been generous partners with Bronwen Bledsoe and me in starting an archive on Bombay poetry at the South Asia Manuscripts Collection at Cornell University by sharing much of their collection of unpublished manuscripts, out-of-print documents and journals, and rare publications. I cannot believe my luck in having their unreserved support, and I give my deepest thanks to Adil and Arvind for making this project possible.

This book is dedicated to my mother, Saraswati Kadekodi (1940–1984), who, deprived of formal education herself, taught me to love reading and inspired me with her progressive thought. I learned my Marathi *barakhadi* from her as a child and remember her in everything that I do and think. In a way, reading Marathi poetry is a way of going back to my days with her. I wish my father, Madhukar Kadekodi (1932–1996), were here, too; his broad-minded politics are my inspiration (even if I have also inherited his love for singing songs off-key). He created a full life for his children with very little material resources.

And most of all, I would like to thank the three men in my life: my sons, Mukul and Aseem, who have uncomplainingly lived through the travails of writing this book—they are my windows to a world of wonder and are two of the most important reasons to live and to laugh; and Shashank, for his patient ways of sustaining me through countless writing emergencies and at all other times, for the rich life of twenty-nine years, and for the memories of Harishchandragad in 1985.

Bombay Modern

Introduction: Archiving the Ephemeral

Have our mother tongues lost poetry, or has poetry lost its mother tongue?
—Dilip Chitre

Kolatkar's poetry is at the heart of *Bombay Modern*. Despite the fact that this book *ends* with a series of close readings of Kolatkar's poems, the project itself is committed to finding the right critical tools to understand the work of this bilingual, multivocational poet. In order to accomplish this aim, Kolatkar's poetry forms the core of close readings in the second half of the book while the focus of the first half is to highlight the way in which bilingual and material readings of literature can reveal new pathways of interpretation, a new methodology of understanding Indian modernisms that are far too often parsed in only one language and only in the words on the page. Kolatkar best exemplifies the multivocational poet of the post-1960 (or the *sathottari*) period who as a poet wrote the poem, as a publisher generated the space for it to appear, and as an editor invented the readers for the new departure and created the conditions necessary for that poem's dissemination. The quintessential poet of Bombay, Kolatkar embodies in his poetry, like his contemporaries, a new way of knowing the urban space—not nativist, not internationalist, not global, not national. Kolatkar puts into practice a method of knowing that tunnels its way through these established posts of categorization.

Let us look at a short and quirky poem by Arun Kolatkar, one that names him in the very first line:

My name is Arun Kolatkar

I had a little matchbox
I lost it
then I found it
I kept it
In my right hand pocket

It is still there[1]

The poem frames a random everyday act—innocent because of the randomness, precious because it captures the transient moment, and gently mocking of the pomposity of poetry and poets by juxtaposing the naming act of possessiveness in the first line and the meaninglessness of the thing that is possessed. Kolatkar's persona declares with some contentment that the matchbox, lost earlier but now found, is in his right pocket, forcing the reader to ask, "So what?" What are we supposed to get out of this declaration or this poem? The act must have more significance since it was memorialized on the page. And yet it does not yield any deeper meanings easily. The poem uses the very act of writing and publishing, the means of making eternal something that is not, as its sparring partner in the fight for meaning. And there is no resolution for the reader; the poem sits down and says nothing. This attention to the arbitrariness of everyday and the incalculable paradoxes that can be teased out of it makes Kolatkar's poetry live uncomfortably in the hall of the canonical works that have been crowned as the most representative of the time. The literary fidget that all his works perform in such canonical contexts is what makes Kolatkar's poetry so difficult to classify and simultaneously fascinating. How are we to understand this poetry that repeatedly performs its own demise? *Bombay Modern* traces the textual pathways of the "excluded middle" of Bombay modernity,[2] a space that lies between the recognition of the canon and the discomfort of being part of it, by reading the poetry within the context of the history of the material practices that structure its existence in the post-1960 world.

I started working on Arun Kolatkar's poetry early in my career and first met the poet himself at the Military Café with his gang of friends, Ratan Sohoni, Avinash Gupte, Vrindavan Dandavate, and Ashok Shahane, in 2004 and later in the same month at the publication ceremony of his books at the National Centre for Performing Arts in Bombay (a few months before Kolatkar passed away in September 2004). But researching Kolatkar's poetry has also taken me to various people and different material and linguistic spaces: among them, to the other informal countercultural spaces ("*kattas*") frequented by Kolatkar's band of friends at Stadium Café; to the homes of friends, writers, and poets like Pat Rodrigues, Pavankumar Jain, Vilas Sarang, Eunice de Souza, Kiran Nagarkar, Ashok Kelkar, Arvind Krishna Mehrotra, Adil Jussawalla, Dilip and Vijaya Chitre, Bhalchandra Nemade, and, most often, Ashok Shahane; and to the multiple public and private archives, spaces like the Asiatic Society, Michael Perreira's home in Bakhtavar, the Bhandarkar Oriental Institute, and the office of Satish Kalsekar. As a result, it became clear to me that it was important to read Kolatkar against and within the contexts of bilingual writing and the material act of publishing that informs so much of the thematic concerns in his work. Kolatkar cannot be understood in isolation: he needs to be read within the framework of his fellow writers and publishers, to whom he was responding in his own work and who were themselves writing and publishing radical and avant-garde work elsewhere. An ethnographic examination of the fluid and the contingent period of emergence of the Bombay modern needs to complement the purely formal and textual reading of such poetry. Reading Kolatkar means reading his contemporaries, too, and, equally important, reading the new ways of circulation, publication, and dissemination that became semantically embedded in the poetic structures of these writers.

The period after independence in India was one of extreme experimentalism and, with the increasing literary and artistic contact with Anglo-America and Europe, one that shows an immense correlation between artistic and literary movements in India and in the West. With regard to post-1960 Bombay, however, it has become commonplace now to emphasize the intense crossover between India and the West. In the case of Bombay poetry this acknowledgment came early: the poets themselves (Dilip Chitre in 1967, Arvind Krishna Mehrotra in 1980, and Vilas Sarang in the 1990s)[3] as well as scholars such as Bruce King[4] have written about the international connections between Bombay poetry and international literature, as there was a need to shed light on this aspect at that time. These are important literary reminders to not segregate the local from the global and to acknowledge the interflows of each into the other. While recognizing the undeniable heterogeneity of influences for any literary text, however, it is perhaps more important in English scholarship today to recoup the multiple multilingual and regional language crossroads evident in the literary texts of the *sathottari* period. Dipesh Chakrabarty illustrates this gap when he catches a scholar on Rushdie cramming the regional literatures of India into a generalization while listing the Western influences on Rushdie's work in specific detail. Chakrabarty notes the "asymmetric ignorance" toward Indian languages and writing when he remarks that "the author is under no obligation to name with any authority and specificity the Indian allusions [in Rushdie]."[5] Similarly, Arun Kolatkar's Marathi writing outpaces his English in terms of sheer size, and it is not enough to read his work only in English or only within the context of his English contemporaries.

There are two facets to this discussion of modern Bombay poetry, and while poets in English and Marathi have always been conscious of the twin contexts of their writing (both global and regional/vernacular), scholarship on these poets has not kept up with the multilingual reaches of this poetry. Even a poet and scholar like Dilip Chitre, who earlier staked a claim for global amalgams in Indian poetry in his 1967 introduction to *An Anthology of Marathi Poetry, 1945–65*, felt the need in 2001 to examine the dire straits of vernacular knowledges and call to preserve the plurality of regional languages in literature in the face of the onslaught of global forces: "We should be continuously shaken by the erosion of local and regional colour, the dying of dialects, the termination of oral traditions, the withering of folklore."[6] The *sathottari* poets, in English and Marathi, engaged with these questions in their own individual ways. *Bombay Modern*, therefore, uses the idea of the *sathottari* (the post-1960) as a way to direct the reading gaze to multiple regional modernisms that were being articulated in both English and Marathi poetry in these years.

The project of *Bombay Modern* is modest: it limits its sphere of study to "Bombay" and to the *sathottari* period. It does this in an attempt to examine at close range the specific way in which this poetry redeployed the regional, the national, and the international to create a very tangible yet transient conception of the local. But what is the range of concepts like "the post-1960"/"the *sathottari*" or the concept of "Bombay" that marks here a more nebulous space than the city of Mumbai on the map? I define the personal compass of these terms first before discussing what important comparisons lie at the heart of the project of *Bombay Modern*.

THE POST-1960 OR *SATHOTTARI* PERIOD

The *sathottari* period (approximately 1955–1980) has been traditionally framed as a transnational whirlwind of influences and borrowings, with English, American, European, and Latin American movements taking center stage and where these transnational influences are framed as the muses for Indian regional and English writing. This indeed was a global moment in many ways: the influences of the Vietnam War, the aggressive presence of the United States through academic institutions in India, the opening up of book markets to international journals and literary texts, the easy availability of journals like the *Evergreen Review* and books published by Grove Press, the Beat writers' visit to India in 1962, alongside the Penguin anthologies of modern poetry that became available in Bombay, and the attempt by the United States to recruit Indian writers for its ideological battles and propaganda wars[7] all contributed toward an extension of the cosmopolitanism of Bombay evident since the nineteenth century. But this was a threshold of space and time, with the writer's gaze homeward as well as abroad, and the interconnection between the literatures of different languages is never studied fully when reading modern Indian poetry.

In this book, the term *sathottari* describes a certain rebellious worldview held by the writers at the time of the creation of the linguistic states and the establishment of Bombay as the capital of Marathi-speaking Maharashtra. It also marks a period indicating the emergence of the first significant magazines in 1954 and 1955 (*Quest*, edited by Nissim Ezekiel in English, and *Shabda*, edited by Arun Kolatkar, Ramesh Samarth, and Dilip Chitre in Marathi)[8] to the waning of the little magazine movement at the end of the 1970s.[9] I deliberately use the Marathi nomenclature *sathottari* but with a different and new emphasis to cover both the English and Marathi literature of the period in order to indicate the conjoined sense of the modern that is evident in the form of Bombay poetry. There are many sociopolitical events that indirectly influenced both English and Marathi writing of this period (foremost among them, the creation of the linguistic state of Maharashtra in 1960 and the Ambedkar movement for the Dalits), and these political events are integrally connected with the transgressions of the literature of this period. On the other hand, the term *sathottari*, which marks a post-1960 generation, also connects the multiple rebellions of this group of poets in English and Marathi to the worldwide agitations in the 1950s and 1960s (the Beats in the United States in the 1950s–1960s, the broader "vulgar modernism," as Loren Glass terms it, the New Poetry of the 1960s in Great Britain, the concrete poets in Europe and the Americas in the same years).[10] Even as it makes global connections to other world literary movements of protest, the idea of the "*sathottari* period" locates the literary readings in a specific local context of Bombay.[11]

The idea of the *sathottari* is used in a modified manner in *Bombay Modern*, different from its conventional use in Marathi criticism. Generally, Marathi literary criticism uses the term *sathottari* to characterize a radically experimental spirit in Marathi writing, but the term is also mired in simultaneous attributions of both nativism and the avant-garde. Sachin Ketkar sees it as a turn toward an indefensible claim of indigeneity: "It is often seen as a sort of 'nativist' reaction to the elitist, Westernized, urban middle-class, and upper caste social background of the early modernism of the forties and the fifties, as represented by literary magazines like *Satyakatha* (The True Story, 1933–82) and *Mauj*," and refutes the nativist description for these poets as whole.[12] Laetitia Zecchini interprets *sathottari* as "avant garde" and therefore refuses to accept this descriptor because she refutes the differentiation between modernism and the avant-garde with regard to Kolatkar's work.[13] The term is disputed in both Marathi and English scholarship, but *Bombay Modern* uses the idea of the *sathottari* to build upon the contentious nature of the classification of the post-1960 and to expand the scope of its application from a narrower avant-gardism in Marathi to a broader network of experimentations and rebellions that connect the multilingual literature and art of resistance emerging in Bombay with each other and to the world outside Bombay. In many ways, all such radicalisms of the period used similar linguistic, textual, and material means to get across a range of standpoints on self, society, and world and a common term for them highlights such convergence.

The concept of the *sathottari* also reminds us that there are multiple modernisms that converge on particular periods and locations. As Vinay Dharwadker shows in his long view of Indian literary history, the modern can be traced to the nineteenth century itself. He notes four dynamic elements of the various modernist waves in Indian literature:

> (1) Europe's longstanding critique of Indian society and culture, stemming from Europe's self-definition of its autonomous modernity; (2) India's counter-critique of Europe, which starts

> early in the nineteenth century; (3) Europe's self-critique, in response to the encounter in the colony; and (4) Indian self-critique, developed "outside the purview of the colonial state" and based on a Kantian "public use of reason" under a republican ideal, which accepts many points in the European critique and seeks responsively to transform Indian ways of life.[14]

This schema is a useful reminder to not singularize the post-independence moment as one of an originary Indian modernism, and it also allows us to mark several stages in the interactions between modernity and literary texts.

In Marathi, the early break toward the modern at the turn of the twentieth century is attributed to Keshavsut (1866–1905):[15] his well-known poems, like "*Tutari*" ("Bugle") and "*Amhi kon?*" ("Who are we?"), were a loud call for change in traditional Marathi poetic forms and idioms through a newfound individualism influenced by English Romantic poetry.[16] There are many other literary stances taken by poets between Keshavsut's early modernism and the midcentury modernism of Mardhekar (the Ravikiran school of poetry, Kusumagraj's poetry of revolutionary zeal, and so on). However, B. S. Mardhekar's poetry (part of the *Navi kavita* movement that induced a radical split from previous writing through its combination of high modernism and *bhakti* literature) is the clear inheritor of Keshavsut's mantle in Marathi literature.[17] In turn, the *sathottari* poets are conventionally seen as the angry young men in Marathi poetry who rebelled against the formalism of Mardhekar's poetry and reject him in their search for a yet another new idiom that reflects the ordinary everyday world. In this schema, *sathottari* poetry marks a second-level modernism in the post-independence period in Marathi poetry.

In *Bombay Modern*, I am redrawing the ambit of the concept of the *sathottari* in Marathi and expanding it (to the years 1955–1980) to mark the careers of both the cohort of naysaying young poets (such as Chitre, Kolatkar, Nemade) and the poets whose rebellion can be connected to a robust multilingual or translating consciousness that emerges at the same time that Maharashtra was formed (Dalit and Socialist poets in Marathi like Narayan Surve, Namdeo Dhasal, and Raja Dhale, as well as English poets like Nissim Ezekiel, Adil Jussawalla, Arvind Krishna Mehrotra, and others).

In English poetry, I use *sathottari* to cover Ezekiel and his generation of poets, as well as the younger poets like Jussawalla, Mehrotra,

Kolatkar, and Chitre. There are other ways to parse these modernisms: Engblom points out how high modernism came later to English (in Ezekiel's poetry) than in Marathi;[18] and from some other perspectives, there are obvious generational divides between Ezekiel's writing and that of the younger Mehrotra and Jussawalla.[19] But using the extended idea of the *sathottari* to read this literature allows us to highlight the common formal and linguistic rebellions made by these poets and the shared tools of literary revolt utilized by them. The term *sathottari* has the capability of including such regional, national, and international cosmopolitanisms through its global comparativism and its local articulation.

THE LOCATION OF BOMBAY

Throughout the book I use "Bombay" instead of "Mumbai" for several reasons. "Bombay" was the term that the English poets themselves used even after the name of the city was changed to "Mumbai" in 1995 by the political party Shiv Sena (this was part of the Shiv Sena's agenda to assert an aggressive Marathi identity in Bombay). Moreover, using "Bombay" also avoids anachronistic reference because during the post-1960 period that is the ambit of this book, the city was called Bombay.

"Bombay," in this case, marks a more nebulous configuration than what can be seen on the state maps. While there are mapped boundaries that delineate spaces in the national structure, I use "Bombay" here to signify mainly the city of *sathottari* Bombay but also its routine extensions through literary links into Pune and sometimes into Aurangabad. At other times, these links are restricted to the narrow space of a traffic island[20] in the southern part of the coastal colonial city. It is the urban location that beckons thousands from across the nation every single day, but it also connotes the access for writers to the processes of production and dissemination of books and magazines. Take, for example, the Marathi *kattas*[21] held in the Asiatic Library in the Churchgate area of South Mumbai, where new literary ideas and radical literary texts were discussed: "There used to be people from outside Bombay who came there regularly or on particular days to meet Ashok, like Chandrakant Patil, Ravindra Kimbahune, Dilip Chitre, or the ones from Bombay like Bhau Padhye."[22] According to many, Patil and Kimbahune belong to the group of the so-called Aurangabad split when one of the leaders of the Marathi little magazine movement, Bhalchandra

Nemade, moved from the city of Bombay to the more rural Aurangabad to create a native poetics and a novel writing practice. And yet, even when Nemade, Patil, and Kimbahune seemingly separated themselves from urban poetics, they were in close conversation with the leaders of the little magazine movement in Bombay and, in fact, wrote their texts in reaction to and in response to Bombay literary ecology.[23]

Similarly, in English poetry, Arvind Krishna Mehrotra lived much of his adult life in Allahabad and spent only a few years of his graduate study in Bombay. But the little magazines he started and many of his connections were centered on Bombay literary processes.[24] Melanie Silgardo makes a similar point about the location; she says, "The assumption of the time was that all the poets writing in English lived in Bombay."[25] As Anjum Hassan notes, "This assumption makes it possible to think of Bombay, when talking about Indian English poetry, not just as a place where the poetry was written"[26] but as something larger and less defined.[27] These examples illustrate the city as "the amalgam of disjointed processes and social heterogeneity."[28] To quote Ash Amin and Nigel Thrift's study of urban spaces: "The city has no completeness . . . [it is] a place of near and far connections, a concatenation of rhythms, always edging in new directions."[29]

This Bombay spread along two registers simultaneously: across the oceans into Euro-America and Latin America and across the state boundaries of Maharashtra into West Bengal, the Hindi heartland, and other regional spaces of India. In addition, on a third register, it ranged outside the cartographic lines of the city to encompass other spaces within Maharashtra as well. As Rushdie describes Bombay in his fiction, "It was an ocean of stories; we were all its narrators, and everybody talked at once."[30] That extended idea of Bombay has been eulogized as the cosmopolitan equivalent of Paris and New York in its nurturing of diverse talent and creativity during this period, and undoubtedly there was a sense of great upheaval in all spheres at the time.[31] This creative and restless spirit is one important aspect of the period that is crucial when studying Kolatkar's poetry, but it is only a partial perspective of a larger oeuvre. While persistently reading Williams or Apollinaire, Kolatkar was simultaneously interacting with and reading the work of not just older *bhakti* poets[32] but also contemporary Marathi poets like Lokakavi Manmohan and Durga Bhagwat. While publishing the Beat writers in his little magazine *Aso*, Ashok Shahane also featured contemporary poets from Kannada, Bengali, and other languages (such as Gopalakrishna Adiga and Jibanananda Das) in the

1960s. It is not just the ancient Indian pasts or the modern Western present that flowed through the poetry of the *sathottari* period; it was also the Bombay modern, the contemporary moment in Marathi and English, which infused the works of Kolatkar and other poets of this period. Seeing the resonance between, say, the worker's world from the otherwise unrelated Marxist Marathi poetry of Narayan Surve and the street dwellers from the poetry of Kolatkar[33] is as important a literary exercise as that of tracing Kolatkar's connections to Baudelaire. Similarly, a study of Mehrotra's angry English poetics alongside that of Namdeo Dhasal's violent Marathi Dalit poems is equally fruitful and revealing of the larger poetic world of Bombay from which both emerge.

In her essay on nineteenth-century Bombay, Meera Kosambi differentiates between "Bombay" and "Mumbai" by highlighting the dual provincial-cosmopolitan influence on Bombay's sociopolitics and history from the very beginnings of this port city.[34] Since the international cosmopolitanisms of Bombay are repeatedly highlighted in most studies of both Indian literature in English[35] and in Marathi, *Bombay Modern* takes the entanglements of the international world in Bombay writing as a given and moves toward uncovering regional/vernacular links within the English and Marathi poetry of Bombay. Even while today's cityscapes are inveterately globalized, "Urban dwellers experience their globally situated and connected urban space as decidedly local lifeworlds, thick with specific experiences, practices, imaginations, and memories."[36] This book examines those "local lifeworlds" of English and Marathi poetry writing in Bombay, thus presenting an alternative literary cartography for *sathottari* Bombay poetry and for the poetry of Arun Kolatkar.

MULTIPLE LANGUAGES

In her 2012 essay "How to Do Multilingual Literary History? Lessons from Fifteenth- and Sixteenth-century North India," Francesca Orsini questioned "research models based on single languages" and showed how the "long fifteenth century" could be fruitfully studied across multilingual archives and practices to reveal new ways of understanding that period. Her project is a crucial reminder, especially in literary studies, where monolingual readings have been the norm despite repeated attempts by a few poets and scholars to defy the trend.[37] For instance, in 1990, Philip Engblom wrote about six Bombay poets, both English and Marathi, under the title of "Bombay Modernisms" and asked, "Can one reasonably suppose a coherent culture that (even across linguistic lines) encompasses this apparent diversity of Bombay poets?"[38] *Bombay Modern* seeks to answer that question with a look at the combined Bombay poetry of Marathi and English.

As chapter 3 demonstrates, this *sathottari* period was a multilingual world by all accounts. Ramachandra Guha notes in his essay "The Rise and Fall of the Bilingual Intellectual" that "between (roughly) the 1920s and 1970s, the intellectual universe in India was—to coin a word—'linguidextrous'. With few exceptions, the major political thinkers, scholars and creative writers . . . thought and acted and wrote with equal facility in English and at least one other language."[39] He notes the steep decline in "intellectual bilingualism" in the next generation, a point reiterated by Francesca Orsini (with regard to Hindi writing) when she highlights the "lack of linguistic awareness and cultural sensitivity between Indian traditions, mirroring that of the West towards India as a whole."[40] Like Guha in his essay, Orsini also delineates the incremental sidelining of the issue of linguistic diversity in Indian literary contexts. Many *sathottari* writers have consistently engaged with the multiple languages of Bombay and of India, but among scholars, there have been only a few (Vinay Dharwadker, Philip Engblom, Rajeev Patke, for instance) who have shown such bilingual reading of the texts of Bombay literature.[41] *Bombay Modern* builds on this previous bilingual scholarship on *sathottari* poetry by adding the print-cultural materialisms to the ambit of study in order to excavate the sense of the "local" that was constructed by the poets. The multiple linguistic environments diversify the ecology of the text, and the criss-crossings of internal cultural allusions locate the text in a time and place. As Ramanujan insists,

> After the nineteenth century, no significant Indian writer lacks any of the three traditions: the regional mother-tongue, the pan-Indian (Sanskritic, and in the case of Urdu and Kashmiri, the Perseo-Arabic as well), and the western (mostly English). Thus, Indian modernity is a response not only to contemporary events but to at least three pasts. Poetic, not necessarily scholarly, assimilation of all these three resources in various individual ways seems indispensable.[42]

Such a focus on multiple linguistic backgrounds allows for a heterogeneous perspective on texts that would otherwise seem singular and monolithic.

This insistence on multiplicity is certainly evident in Kolatkar's poetry. Kolatkar's long draft of the unfinished "Making Love to a Poem" is included in the posthumously published volume *The Boatride & Other Poems* (2009). There, after writing about the possibility of being misunderstood because of his bilingualism, he describes the two-in-one existence of the bilingual poet:

> You need a double barreled gun to shoot a bilingual
> poet
> for I'm two beasts
> you're hunting / tracking not one but two beasts
> though our tracks may crisscross
> and we may come to the same waterhole to drink
> and to the same saltlicks
> there are two distinct scents we use
> to mark the boundaries we hunt in different parts of the
> jungle
> though our territories may overlap
> or sometimes when our paths cross we may pass through each
> other
> exchanging some of our characteristics in the process[43]

Kolatkar will not reduce himself to just one poetics, or in this case just one "beast."[44] Sometimes he is two, at other times the two merge into one. This is a poem overtly about his bilingual writing and it raises the issue of how to comprehend these multiply voiced aesthetics of Marathi and English. The poet himself insisted on registering his bilingualism in all his brief introductions in anthologized sections or in the opening pages of each Marathi and English book by Pras Prakashan. For instance, on the first verso page in Kolatkar's Marathi book *Chirimiri*, in the list of his previously published books, there is the English *Jejuri* in Roman script and *Arun Kolatkarchya Kavita* and *Bhijaki Vahi*, the two Marathi books, listed in Devanagari script. It is clear that the poet urges you to read both his languages in order to get a complete picture of the combined oeuvre.

GENRE, REALISM, AND *SATHOTTARI* LITERATURE

Bombay Modern explores the possibility of understanding *sathottari* Bombay through its poetic practices rather than its more publicized fictional representations. Poetry reveals a site that stages the inexpressible contemporaneity of Bombay; it complicates the understanding of the modern sensibility of Indian literature by showing its incommensurable local articulations in Bombay across Marathi and English.

Indian literature is often analyzed in terms of competition between a Western center and a native periphery, with English always occupying the center and the regional languages always trapped in the margins. But a multilingual reading of these literatures allows us to question the fixed notion that equates privilege with anything written in English and subalternity with all Marathi writing by showing how the poets in English shared a peculiar sense of invisibility with the Marathi poets. In "Fullstoppers and Semi-colonials," Vilas Sarang attributes the invisibility of English poetry to what is seen as its "derivative English" and says:

> Indian English poets may be privileged as compared to their native counterparts, but they are also "under-privileged" from the perspective of the Anglo-American, English language world. . . . [They] are not at the Center of *their* world; they are on the periphery. So they, too, are subject to the schizoid feelings of their Indian language counterparts.[45]

Bombay Modern does not subscribe to the evaluation of English writing as derivative. Instead, in alignment with Jahan Ramazani's statements about the genre of poetry,[46] I suggest that the marginal status of the Indian poets in English is because of their choice of genre; poetry was, and continues to be, insignificant in the critical calculations of English literature in India and in postcolonial studies. On the other hand, the Marathi poets are, and continue to be, prominent in their own Marathi literary culture but are unknown and unheard of outside that linguistic sphere, on the national scene. It is a complicated habitation of privileged invisibility that poets on both sides of the boundary occupy, "privileged" because, when compared with each other, each set of poets has a disproportionate cultural advantage (the metropolitan privilege of English versus the relatively wider readership of Marathi poetry) that is then canceled out by symmetrical lacks that make each invisible (the lack of metropolitan cachet for Marathi poets, the lack of regional/local acceptance for English poets).

The choice of the genre of writing is one means to explain this contradictory space. In the *sathottari* period, despite stray exceptions, challenges to the normativity of the national perspective and the interrogation of the capitalist world appeared predominantly in this newly constituted poetic genre. And "where, and how, then do contemporaneous idea systems and sociopolitical statements get expressed in a given poem's linguistic and rhetorical strategies? Answer: *In any poetic function that can be made visible:* genre, line break, placement of words, rhyme, diction, sound, or syntax."[47] Studying the structures of Bombay poetry of the *sathottari* period, especially in its distinctive usage of various realisms, will therefore provide new avenues for exploring contemporary settings and bring to light practices and lives that otherwise lie in the shadows of urban studies of Bombay.

While "realism" is not a respected term in mainstream modernist studies, it makes a comeback in postcolonial readings of literature in an emphatic manner. More than a decade ago, Laura Moss cautioned against throwing out the form of realism with the combined discursive baggage of colonialism and stated that "discussions of postcoloniality [can] be advanced by the inclusion of realism as a possible mode of resistance."[48] In art criticism, Geeta Kapur predated this warning with her note about the tilting of "the definitional balance of Indian modernism"[49] by art that was simultaneously realist and progressive. More recently, Priyamvada Gopal, Ulka Anjaria, and Toral Gajarawala have shown how realism indeed has tremendous powers of resistance as a literary tool in the hands of postcolonial and subaltern writers.[50]

None of them, however, looks at the disruptive potential of the combination of realism and poetry in India. In fact, over the years, poetry has been viewed as inherently antithetical to the realist project. At the end of her study of realism and the Indian novel, Meenakshi Mukherjee states how the intense "tension between individual and society" that developed necessitated a form like the realist novel but that if such a disparity had not been powerful enough, "creative expression may have turned inward, towards solipsism and away from realism—perhaps poetry would have been a more suitable genre in such a situation."[51] Poetry is positioned explicitly against an active engagement with the "real world" here. Dipesh Chakrabarty also writes about the split in Tagore's work into the realistic work of fiction that critiqued his society and the more imaginative work of poetry that expressed his love for the same world.[52] According to Chakrabarty, the classification of poetry as imaginative writing persisted for a long period after Tagore because of the towering literary presence of the poet.[53] If insurgent postcolonial writing is identified with realism, then because poetry gets categorized as imaginative, it loses any claims to value in most contemporary postcolonial studies.

This equation of the poetic and the non-real is one explanation for the larger absence of the genre as a whole in discussions of postcolonial literature, but it also indicates the nonintuitive and new combination (at least in the Indian context) of a particular brand of realism and poetry that the *sathottari* poets were attempting to create. *Sathottari* writing saw many correlated realisms advocated by the poets: social realism (that depicts the material conditions of the lived world in a forthright manner), Dalit realism (that combined the social realism with a linguistic directness that was shocking to readers), and the seemingly apolitical realism (of the poets who focused on the language of the street, of the everyday, but refused to align themselves with any overt political ideology).[54] While these might be simplistic definitions of the multiple realisms, the thread connecting all these different approaches to realist poetry is the emphasis on the revisioning of the poem's language and an insistence on using the registers of the workaday world. Most writers with this literary agenda congregated in the little *sathottari* magazines and shared the principle of foregrounding the languages of the quotidian in their own contexts.

There are distinctions, for sure, within this capacious category of *sathottari* realism. For instance, Nissim Ezekiel states, "I look about me now, and try / To formulate a plainer view" and declares the intent to take the larger realist turn in literature.[55] But while his poetry attempts to inject the world of everyday into the as-yet-sterilized halls of poetry (witness his famous Indian English poems), overall he still retains the outer form of the poem, visual and aural, that one associates with more traditional poetry, a form that also connotes the barricading of the spheres of life and art. On the other hand, there is the next generation of poets, represented by the Clearing House poets who broke with the imagery and sometimes the format of the older poems and thus present a radical formal politics of poetry. As Mehrotra says, in short lines that are syllabically uneven and unrhymed:

> Just two days ago
> the poet traded all
> the rare lines
> in his collection
> for common ones.[56]

And one sees much more of the brashness of the colloquial in many of Mehrotra's poems, especially in his Kabir translations that demonstrate how American slang can represent the feel and intonation of modern Indian urban life:

> To tonsured monks and dreadlocked Rastas
> To idol worshippers and idol smashers,
> To fasting Jains and feasting Shaivites,
> To Vedic pundits and Faber poets,
> The weaver Kabir sends one message:
> The noose of death hangs over all.
> Only Rama can save you
> Say it NOW.[57]

The assertive counterbalancing of polar images, the use of capitalization in the last line that indicates the brazen and forceful style of street speech, and the dissonant insertion of contemporary global references ("Faber poets" and "Rastas") in the writing of the Indian past indicate a more sweeping reworking of the conventions of poetry in order to reflect the discordant real world of contemporary modernity. Even if the references could be criticized as Anglicized or class based (how many common readers of Indian English understand the context of "Faber poets"?), the poem breaks the traditional mold of writing poems with its forcefully juxtaposed contraries; in that sense, it opens a door to the quotidian outside art. Or as Namdeo Dhasal says in "My beloved poem" in Marathi: "I do not want to settle this life on a separate island / you keep walking holding the hand / of the commonest of the common man."[58] When reading this poetry, one is forced to expand the idea of literary realism to include the larger world it springs from, and in different ways, the poetry participates in the multiple conversations about the ownership of the public sphere of Bombay.

The poets combined disparate elements of their lived worlds into their poetry, but they all tried to reflect the palpability of that experience and the materiality of their world through a linguistically violent wrenching of poetic conventions to suit their content. Whether it was Narayan Surve, who used the workers' spaces and the irreverent language of their lives to write poetry, or Namdeo Dhasal, who rejected the niceties of literary conventions in an effort to highlight the injustices of the Dalit world in the streets of prostitution in Kamatipura in Bombay, or Arun Kolatkar, who focused on the poor female pilgrims of

Pandharpur or the homeless population in Kala Ghoda in Bombay, or Adil Jussawalla, who wrote about the frustration of an English poet in the urban precincts of Bombay, all attempted to incorporate some element of their experienced world in their poetry. Some of these would be comfortably identified as realist (Surve) while others (like Jussawalla) would be an important part because of the realism of their language in its approximation to everyday tones of speech.

One such philosophy of the "real" that started in the mixed venue of the little magazines but increasingly moved into its own individual sphere of writing was evidenced in the poetry of the Dalit poets. By the end of the 1960s, there was a rising public consciousness of Dalit lives and a perceived need to represent with honesty their specific and overwhelming reality. Explaining the need for a Dalit periodical, Gangadhar Pantavane, the editor of *Asmitadarsh* (The Mirror of Identity), one of the first significant Dalit magazines of the period, says that they needed a space and a language to express what "they lived, they experienced, they treasured, they fought against, the misery and grief that their entire lives was."[59] The Dalit world seemed to be a separate and unseen space to upper-caste society. In fact, when Namdeo Dhasal asked the most famous Marathi playwright of the day, Vijay Tendulkar, to write an introduction to his book of poems, *Golpitha*, Tendulkar was surprised by the number of words he did not know and could not understand. He asked Dhasal to explain this long list of words that were incomprehensible to a middle-class, upper-caste man like him:

> This was his world. He had noted every turn and line of this lived world and therefore he was authorized to own it. I was the ignorant. What is *chandrabindi*, *dobari*, *sadalaleli jhade* hundreds of such words. I was ashamed of my own ignorance. I realized how unaware I was of the lived world so close to me and it was a thorn in my side.[60]

It is this life, and the inflicted oppressions in this world, that finds expression in the poems of the Dalit writers who for the first time used the vocabulary and the language associated with their lived experiences in the caste-discriminating life of Bombay and elsewhere in Maharashtra. Here is part of a poem from "Arsefucker's Park" by Dhasal (translated by Chitre, 2007):

> I am a venereal sore in the private part of language.
> The living spirit looking out of hundreds of thousands of sad,

pitiful eyes
Has shaken me.
I am broken by the rock exploding inside of me.
There's no moonlight anywhere;
There's no water anywhere.
A rabid fox is tearing off my flesh with its teeth;
And terrible venom-like cruelty
Spreads out from my monkey-bone.[61]

The ferocity of the images is both in the content and in the terrible speed at which they multiply and overwhelm the reader: a venereal sore, an explosion, darkness, thirst, a rabid fox, tearing flesh, venom, and the tailbone ("monkey bone"). Like the rest of the poetry of this period that wanted to show the unadorned universe of the poor and the ordinary, this poetry aimed at representing specifically the Dalit world of nonprivilege or, as Shanta Gokhale puts it, "the stink of bodily functions, the anguish of hunger and a compassion for lumpens (his word) like himself."[62]

The Dalit writers birthed a short-lived yet separate and powerful literary movement in the early 1970s, creating distinct little magazines and starting a Dalit Panther activism inspired by the Black Panthers in the United States. But in the early *sathottari* years, when the little magazine movement was just gaining foothold, one of the creators of the later Dalit Panther movement was also part of the relatively broad-based anti-traditional rebellion against the establishment at the time. Raja Dhale, poet, artist, and Dalit activist, started the Marathi little *Atta* in 1964 that was distributed as a free adjunct to the little magazine *Aso*. Namdeo Dhasal's little magazine *Vidroha* (The Revolt) and the Pantavane-edited periodical *Asmitadarsh* published articles by non-Dalit as well as Dalit writers. *Bombay Modern* focuses mostly on the output of those early years of the little magazine movement when the nativists (like Nemade), the leftists (like Satish Kalsekar), the Dalits (like Raja Dhale), and the internationalists (like Ashok Shahane) worked in tandem and in consultation with each other. The *sathottari* period exhibits a creative confusion of sorts in this diverse mixture of influences; Vilas Sarang characterizes the *sathottari* writers as a kind of rowdy cabal of boisterous street youth who are more than likely to unite if only to hurl a renegade rock to disturb the peace of a traditional gathering of people.[63] The rebellious refusals and angry structures of writing were the shared writing forms of this period.

THE MATERIAL OF POETRY

Sathottari poetry hinged itself upon the revitalization of the language of poetry—it sought to bring the demotic language into the elite halls of poetry. This counterhierarchical movement centered itself on the materialization of the body as a rebellious move, one that diverted the reader's attention toward considerations of physicality: this was achieved through the imagery of the body, through using so-called obscenities that highlighted bodily functions, and through the insistence on visualizing the lives of the poor that were predicated on manual, physical labor. In multiple ways, these poets refuted the earlier romantic hermeneutics of poetry and asserted one predicated on an equation of the real with the material or the physical. One important way in which they manifested such emphasis was by making the materialisms of the text a part of the semantics of the poem. The poem became a locus of a new reading method created by the different mode of publication, format, and dissemination of the little magazines. Self-reflexivity, the "what" of the text merging one with the "how" of it, became an important part of the poetry of this period and the poetry reclassified notions of the inside and the outside of social interactions and literary texts. Among the names that Jussawalla, Mehrotra, Kolatkar, and Patel considered for their publishing collective (before settling on "Clearing House" as their final choice) are suggestions such as "Lines," "Off Print," "The Index," "Narrow Margin," and "Printer's Devils."[64] Every one of these indicates the moving of the craft of book-making and of the architecture of the page into the discussion of the words on the page and in the book. *Sathottari* literature therefore requires a reading of the poetry as it would be "the subject of bibliographers, sociologists, economists, and tradespersons of various kinds."[65] Reading *sathottari* poetry requires the conceiving of a poem as a material construct and the writing of it as a craft rather than an art. The emphasis is on the "making" of a poem.

The influence of the concrete poetry movement on the *sathottari* poets was formative, and the poetry movement that flourished simultaneously in Brazil and Switzerland starting in the late 1950s also energized these writers in India. Concrete poets aimed to create a "poem-product," and as Stephen Bann notes in his compilation of the preeminent concrete poems from this period, concrete poetry "deals with the communication of its own structure-content and thus involves a process of metacommunication."[66] The revolt of the little magazines needs to be placed in this sphere of "metacommunication": through the format, the material that went into the making of the magazine, the handmade unevenness of many of these issues, and the smallness of the product, the little magazines declared a different poetic aesthetic in keeping with their artistic and social philosophies.[67] Among the poets, Mehrotra in English and R. K. Joshi in Marathi could be seen as the vanguard in this respect,[68] but many other poets of this period also exhibit distinct traces of this movement in their work. As R. K. Joshi puts it, they try to write texts that "cross the literary limits of word-meanings/such poems."[69] *Bombay Modern* looks at the contexts and paratexts of translation, community, and publication that manifest themselves in the process of making material the literary beings of poetic texts. It enables "a socializing [of] the study of texts at the most radical levels,"[70] as McGann puts it, and presents a conception of the text as "a laced network" of linguistic and material practices.

What is the method for such examination of the material existence of texts? McGann presents a framework for such a reading by proposing a separation between the "linguistic code" of the text (the traditionally read text as merely the words on the page) and "the bibliographic code" of the text: "the symbolic and the signifying dimension of the physical medium through which (or rather as which) the linguistic code is embodied."[71] The dimension of the "bibliographic code" includes "typefaces, bindings, book prices, page format, and all those textual phenomena usually regarded as (at best) peripheral to 'poetry' or 'the text as such.'"[72] This is a conception of the poetic text that looks at the conventionally understood "vehicle" of delivery or the externalities of the poem as an integral element of the meaning of the text, a unity of the material and the linguistic: "Body is not bruised to pleasure soul."[73] The majority of literary criticism focuses only on the linguistic code, but *Bombay Modern* examines the cover image of Arun Kolatkar's books and the architecture of the pages to show how Kolatkar rejects the traditionalisms of the older writing as well as of religious ritualisms.

But there is more to the materialisms studied in *Bombay Modern*. In his study of Anglo-American modernist poetry, George Bornstein adds a third code to McGann's two by creating a "contextual code" that also includes the physical environment of the text:

> Placement of a poem within a collection occupies a middle ground between its linguistic and bibliographical codes. On the one hand, such a contextual code is bibliographic in that it

> pertains to the physical constitution of the volume; on the other, the contextual code is linguistic in that it is made up of words.[74]

Thus the physical context of the poem also determines the range of its meanings. Chapter 1 examines the revolt of the little magazines against *Satyakatha*, a Marathi journal of legendary authority at the beginning of the *sathottari* period. *Satyakatha* had a widely admired editor in S. P. Bhagwat (also known as Shri Pu.), who published translations (Chitre's French translations appear along with some of Shahane's translations from Bengali literature) as well as the creative work of other progressive writers who later congregated in the pages of the little magazines. One could easily ask, then, where was the necessity to rebel against this periodical? The move to the impermanent spaces of the little magazines makes sense only when one looks at the contextual code of *Satyakatha* publications and realizes that these writers appeared in a long list of mixed company that was not of their literary or philosophical heft. Or take the interpretation of Kolatkar's poem "The Butterfly" in chapter 5. Reading the images and the lines of the poem in Kolatkar's English poem "The Butterfly" means attending to the linguistic code of the poem; examining the use of white space on the page (which makes the butterfly literally disappear from the reader's eye) shifts the focus to the bibliographic code; and tracing the connection of this butterfly image to the contemporary collection of folklore by the Marathi anthropologist Durga Bhagwat, from whom it was inspired, indicates the opening of the contextual code of the poem. Such material reading enables *Bombay Modern* to trace the entangled relations of English and Marathi poetry in the *sathottari* urban landscape.

Reading the jacket of the book, the design of the page, the placement of the poem in the book, and the process of publishing are all elements of the reading process that are conventionally bifurcated from the textual reading of a poem. It is therefore "time for . . . kicking our nicotine-strength addiction to privileging ideas and content over structure and form," as Clifford Siskin asserts.[75] As creators of the little magazines in the period, the *sathottari* poets experimented with the creation of a material/textual continuum that posed semantic questions of transience and eternity through the architecture of the page and the book. Capitalizing on the easy equation of "the material" with "the real," they attempted to catch the ephemeral moment through the physical attributes of the format. The little magazines and the books from small presses aimed to get

> the reader over our shoulder—the eyes for which the item first appeared; the living glance that scanned the paper even as we scan it. . . . You become, as you read, an intimate part of the detail of their experience—not just overhearing them, but momentarily being *within* them.[76]

It is the erotics of the reading act that comes to the fore in many of the *sathottari* texts. Kolatkar explicitly makes this connection in one of his unpublished fragments in Marathi. The paratexts of the poem or the book are enveloped into the sensuality of the reading act when Kolatkar ponders over the open bookcase versus one with glass doors. He tried out two parallel stanzas to say this (the English translations are mine):

hat pudhe karava
va hatat pustaka yava
itki sopi hi prakriya asavi
itki sopi hi prakriya asavi
asa mala nehemich vatata alay

hat pudhe kela ki
pustaka rangetun
bot pudhe kela ki
ki pustakachya kanyala
sparsh karta yava

to extend your hand
and the book appears in it
it should be that simple
it should be that simple
is what I have always felt

when you extend your hand
the book from its row
when you extend your finger
you should be able to touch
the backbone of the book[77]

Here the Marathi word for "backbone" is the "spine" of the book, a word that becomes catalyzed through its English/Marathi pun into a sensual shiver because holding a book is seen as an erotic encounter instead of a merely intellectual interchange. He further plays with the book and the idea of it in half-formed lines of a poem that demands that there be no barriers (like shelf doors) between the speaker and his books:

tari apala avadata pustak gonjarayala tyachyavarun hat firavayala
apalya ek nimitta hi milata kuravalayala
ani ~~prastavik~~ prastavane itaka
kinva foreplay itaka mahatvacha ahe
asahi mala vatata asava
ratikriye purvichya hastasparshadi
prastavane itakach mahatvacha ahe

still to caress our favorite book to run our hands over it
we will find an excuse   to fondle
and like the ~~prelude~~ foreword
    or foreplay it is as important
        i must think so too
    the touch of the hands before sex
            it is as important as the foreword[78]

It is tantalizing to think about the poem that could have been, but it goes to show the self-consciousness of the poet's writing act and the configuration of the engagement with the reader as a physical exchange in the world of the "real."

Kolatkar is not alone in this. Reviewing the collection of essays by Adil Jussawalla, *Maps of a Mortal Moon*, Arvind Krishna Mehrotra zooms in on one of the essays therein, "The Joy of Sensuous Writing," where Jussawalla agrees that "the physical act of writing becomes an analogy for love-making ('The envelope was plump with the letter I'd fed it and the fine tip of the pen I was using sank into it as it formed the letters')." Mehrotra also notes that this essay "was, with fine discernment, written for a tits-and-bums magazine, the short-lived Allahabad-based *Fantasy*."[79] The incongruity of the placement of this essay, and the presence of this high-literary poet musing on the act of writing in a "tits-and-bums" magazine, as Mehrotra describes it, is important in comprehending the project of capturing that eternally elusive "everyday" that these writers tried to make visible in their work. These complex and interwoven poetic modernisms are best explored through an equally catholic interdisciplinary reading of the poem that goes beyond the word-marks on the page to study the book as object, publishing as a practice, and the page as a textual and visual field.

THE GENDER OF POETRY AND WOMEN WRITERS

There are only a few women writers at the center of the little magazine movement. The women writers and intellectuals were part of the *sathottari* world but, with few exceptions, their work came into prominence only in the 1970s and 1980s. These years (toward the end of the *sathottari* period) were more evenly divided between men's and women's projects, with younger writers like Melanie Silgardo starting the Newground Press at the end of the *sathottari* years and several younger women writers in Marathi appearing in the 1970s and after. The little magazine movement at its nascence was more or less a masculine space (with supreme exceptions like Durga Bhagwat and Gauri Deshpande).

A brief look at the composition of the *kattas*,[80] the informal social gatherings that generated the new *sathottari* literature, indicates the homosocial nature of the meetings. There certainly were some women in these gatherings, more so in Marathi contexts: Durga Bhagwat in the regular meetings at the Asiatic with Ashok Shahane and Bhalchandra Nemade; Tara Reddy with the groups of Keshav Meshram, Shashi Pradhan, Narayan Surve, Baburao Bagul, and Tulsi Parab; and Rajani Parulekar with the group of Satish Kalsekar, Vasant Gurjar, Chandrakant Khot, and others. But there were few such women writers/editors; the ones that were there did not get central roles in the literary counterestablishment (with the exception of Durga Bhagwat in these *kattas*, who was prominently participant in her own right in these meetings). In English, there was Kamala Das holding her famed literary salons (but she is not seen as part of the Bombay poets because she was not part of the same publishing circuits, nor did she interact with them closely). Later in the 1970s, however, women started making their presence felt in the little magazines, in periodicals, and in book publishing. An example is the 1978 issue of the Marathi little magazine *Rucha*, published by a woman (Sushila Panse), edited by a woman (Anjali Kirtane), and one that had several women poets listed in the contents. In the 1960s, however, it was more difficult for women to be seen at the forefront of the writing revolt.[81]

This is not to say that the leading writers and editors of the time were consciously exclusionary. Note the close professional and personal association that people like Shahane had with Marathi women writers like Kamal Desai and Durga Bhagwat or that of Arvind Mehrotra and Adil Jussawalla with English poet Eunice de Souza. In many cases, they critiqued each other's work, helped publish the writing, and publicly claimed writerly camaraderie.[82] Moreover, Durga Bhagwat herself repeatedly rejected the categorization of herself as a "woman" writer and Shahane narrates an amusing episode to illustrate this behavior. When Durga Bhagwat was contacted by a magazine asking for a submission of a piece as a woman writer, she was extremely angry and snapped: "I didn't sell my womanhood then when I was young—why would I do it now?"[83] Bhagwat was closely associated with some of the most important works of the period, and contemporary writers openly credit her work as the foundation for theirs. Durga Bhagwat's study of folklore is at the basis of Bhalchandra Nemade's novel *Kosla* (Cocoon), which is widely acknowledged as the marker of the *sathottari* change in Marathi fiction. In the article by Nemade on the fiftieth anniversary of the publication of *Kosla*, he states that Bhagwat's studies are the source of the last section of his novel. Ashok Shahane also states that Bhagwat was closely connected with the creation of one of the first Marathi littles, *Atharva* (founded in 1961). She found the folk stories for Shahane's little magazine and helped select the cover image for the singular issue of the important little magazine. Kolatkar also references her anthropological work in his own poetry (see chapter 5).

The lack of a broader participation of women, however, and some of the gendered compositions of the manifestos and editorials associated with the little magazines attests to an overall masculine worldview of the littles, at least at the beginning of *sathottari* period. Gauri Deshpande, the bilingual poet, editor, publisher, and novelist, has a revealing exchange with the editor of the reputed periodical *Satyakatha*, S. P. Bhagwat/Shri Pu.[84] In one of her many letters to Shri Pu. Bhagwat, Deshpande writes,

> You have praised me so much in your letter that I am embarrassed! The plus point is that it helped remove the writing block that had plagued me for the last month or so. But I am curious about one thing. Do note, it is not a complaint but just an observation. You men give so many different talks and keynotes at various literary occasions and conferences, but you do not even mention the work done by women in literature. There is the usual triumvirate of Vibhavari, Durga Bhagwat (and as an also ran, Kamal Desai!) The rest of us get relegated to a parenthesis or a footnote (Nemade or Chitre don't even allow us that much!) So why is it that I get such unrestricted praise only in private?[85]

This could be read as a complaint of the younger writers against the historical pressure of the predecessors (after all, Deshpande does concede that some women writers are visible in the setup, only not the younger ones of her generation), but a close look at the writing of the little magazines also demonstrates a figuration in writing that is masculine, for example, the editorial in *ezra* that talks about "fathering" the magazine or the "statement" of *damn you*, 4: "damn you telling malay roy choudhury 'look here, ginsberg is a nice fellow. we are happy you are a friend of his. but don't go on postering [*sic*] the world, our tiny invisible world . . . there is more than wishing to see the earth thru someone's hymen." Similarly Santan Rodrigues, the editor, wrote in the very first issue of *Kavi* (1976): "In fact, KAVI is as unsympathetic to the 'new' poets as we are to effete and the established ones. KAVI worships at no particular poetic shrine, least of that of menopausal 'masters', poets who died several years ago but still carry on writing out of sheer habit."[86] The use of words like "menopausal" and "hymen" as derogatory descriptors, as equivalents of the ineffectiveness of the work of the other poets, points to a subtext of gendered viewpoints that appears at various stages in this movement.

This subtext reinforces Dipesh Chakrabarty's observation about the homosocial nature of the *adda* and, by extension, that of the physical conversations over a cup of tea or *katta* that helped fuel the formation of the littles, and also of the figurative literary *katta* that the little magazine declared itself to be. To quote Chakrabarty,

> Bengali modernity, for complicated reasons, never quite transcended the structure of opposition between domestic space and that of adda . . . literary modernity and its attendant spaces of the school, university, coffeehouse, bookshops, and magazines did indeed help to expand, deepen, and modernize the homosocial space of adda and even allowed for women's participation in it. But its male character was never erased, and it often left the heterosexual men involved in literary endeavor with a sense of—this is where I register my debt to Lefebvre's coinage—"phallic solitude."[87]

Chakrabarty modifies the notion of "phallic solitude" from Lefebvre but the extended usage explains well how, despite the relatively progressive nature of the writers in this movement, the writers still tripped at the threshold of gender representation.

And yet, some of the aforementioned poets were the same writers who addressed the issue of women's freedom in multiple ways in their work. For instance, Ashok Shahane says, "Our cohort acknowledges the relationship we have with Lakshmibai.[88] The relation is that of mother-son. Of course the son is the wastrel here. We sons ended up ignorant and as a sign of our defeat at the hands of [Lakshmi] Bai, we are even ready to wear bangles."[89] It is a far-reaching statement because unlike his predecessors, Shahane acknowledges a woman writer as his ancestor, and his defiant willingness to wear women's bangles demonstrates a mitigation of the aggressive domination of the male point of view, even if the willingness to be feminine (wearing bangles) is coded as a sign of defeat. Similarly plays, such as Girish Karnad's *Hayavadana* (1971), and films, such as Satyajit Ray's *Charulata* (1964), addressed the increasingly visible issue of women's liberation from traditional mores. Both Karnad and Ray were associated with the Film Institute of India in Pune during this period and were connected in a sense to the larger cultural moment of Bombay and Pune.[90] In *Hayavadana*, Karnad asks why Padmini cannot love two men and actually have physical appetites like a man. But in the end, Padmini commits suicide/sati because she cannot have what she wants—her death is not submissive like that of a traditional wife but defiant because she chooses to die because she cannot get what she desires; the fact remains, however, that she *dies* and that she is not allowed to live her desired life. Likewise, in Ray's *Charulata*, the memorable image is of Charulata, the heroine of the film, watching the world pass by through her dainty binoculars from her prosperous Victorian home—the rebellion is there but curtailed. Neither narrative ends with freedom for the woman even though these characters strain at the bonds. All these artists, writers, and poets declare failure of some sort in creating a narrative of the completely liberated woman. In the work of several *sathottari* writers and artists (as in Arun Kolatkar's *Bhijaki Vahi*), there is a move by the men toward an androgyny of sorts—either in terms of ventriloquizing the female voice or of self-consciously adopting traditionally designated female roles for the male speaker—but the writers and artists also admit that this move does not result in a complete unshackling of the woman's self in the work. They are aware of the need for a deeper inclusion of women's worlds but are unable to do so themselves. The discussions in the rebellious *kattas* as well as in the little magazines show a new destabilizing of gender narratives but they leave the central patriarchal structure of literary authority intact.

In juxtaposition, I take the example of two women writers, Gauri Deshpande, who published in the first decade of the little magazines (the 1960s), and Eunice de Souza, who published in the next decade of the little magazines (the 1970s), to show how the poetic voice of the female speaker came to be expressed in the period. Gauri Deshpande's first book of poems, *Between Births*, was published in English in 1968 by the Writer's Workshop in Calcutta. Her work also appeared in the *Dialogue* publications edited by Pritish Nandy in 1971 (who is associated with the Calcutta group of poets), and because of this publishing relationship, Bruce King associates her mainly with the Calcutta group of poets despite her stay in Pune/Bombay throughout her life.

However, if she is considered a bilingual writer, Gauri Deshpande's alignments do not appear so black and white. She worked at the *Illustrated Weekly* in Bombay and was also closely associated later with the feminist periodicals in Marathi in Pune and Bombay (like *Stree* and *Milun Saryajani*). Her poetry appeared in Bombay's *Contemporary Indian Poetry in English* (1972) edited by Saleem Peeradina even as she was also writing short stories in Marathi. In 1974, she was literary editor at the influential little magazine *Opinion Literary Quarterly*, which despite its name that seemed to promise periodicity survived for only four issues. But within that span, it had the poetic vision of publishing Kolatkar's *Jejuri* and Keki Daruwalla's "Crossing of Rivers," and is considered a significant little magazine. Deshpande wrote complex novellas and short stories in Marathi that highlighted the internal life of modern urban women, and she also needs to be part of any discussion of little magazines if only for having been a prescient literary editor of the *Opinion Literary Quarterly*.[91]

In English, besides Deshpande, there is also the visible presence of poets like Eunice de Souza within Bombay in the *sathottari* generation. Eunice de Souza (b. 1940) held her own in the midst of writers with powerful personalities like Mehrotra, Jussawalla, and Kolatkar; younger than the first generation of poets like Kolatkar, she is still part of the group of writers that shaped the poetry of today (although she belongs more to the years of the small presses, run by the same little magaziners in the 1970s). As a poet and editor of anthologies of poetry and of interviews of the *sathottari* poets, Eunice de Souza has created a unique space for her ironic, concentrated, and laconic utterances in English poetry of the Bombay of this period; she also mentored and influenced other women poets like Melanie Silgardo from the next generation. While not overtly as rebellious as Deshpande in her writing, De Souza has biting poems that insist on the private separateness of her self from the patriarchal groupthink of her time:

> Nothing is ever still:
> Rocks move. Rivers move.
> Time passes.
> Allow me my tailspin.
> One day I'll find my axis
> and revolve around the sun.[92]

The refusal to follow the sun is her assertion of her feminine life and self (or "the tailspin," as it is interpreted by the rest of the society). At the same time, the poem is a grim statement of her knowledge that this rebellion will eventually be snuffed out by forcing her to follow the sun (which represents the commonly accepted patriarchal traditions). Compare this to a poem by Sally Stern, who is from the Beat generation in the United States:

> I know that I shall be the sea
> And the mother
> And never me.
> Wait
> I am here
> Under the sea
> Recognize me.[93]

Stern also protests the invisibility of women, but while her speaker waits to be heard, De Souza's speaker actually is rebelling against being heard in accepted ways and therefore rebelling against being slotted in conventional categories.

When Deshpande and De Souza wrote in the latter part of the *sath-ottari* period, the female voice is not that of a victim; it reveals the rich inner and outer lives of the women, many times embattled, but always resourceful and defiant. *Bombay Modern* focuses much more on the earlier years, the period of the birth of the little magazines, and presents the result of the unsettling of gender normativities in this period in one complicated portrayal of male authorship and the lives of women in the reading of Kolatkar's Marathi book of poems, *Bhijaki Vahi* (The Soaked Notebook).

PART ONE

The Context

Overview: The *Sathottari* Period

From among the multiple political upheavals that took place during the *sathottari* period in this region, two of the most significant were the various outcomes of the Ambedkar movement, including the mass conversion of the Dalits (the so-called untouchables) to Buddhism by Dr. B. R. Ambedkar in 1956 in Nagpur, Maharashtra, and the creation of the linguistic state of Maharashtra, after a long agitation, in 1960. These momentous political events and their ideological fallout impacted the day-to-day life of the people living in contemporary Maharashtra, especially in Bombay, and the connection of the little magazines and their writers to these events shows the manner in which they reworked and wove the social and historical moment into the literary content and form of *sathottari* literature.

Sharankumar Limbale, a Dalit Marathi scholar and writer, asks with agitated passion in his novel *Akkarmashi* (The Outcaste): "Do we belong to Maharashtra or Karnataka? It's the same about our language as well . . . which is our real language? My mother is Mahar and my father is Lingayat; mother in the hut and father in the mansion; father landlord and mother landless: I am the outcaste. Village, language, mother, father, caste, religion—in all cases, I am broken apart."[1] If Limbale wrote this in 1984, almost a quarter century after Maharashtra was formed in 1960 (and fifteen years after the renewed agitation for the border towns between Maharashtra and Karnataka),[2] it is safe to conclude that the impact of the violent agitation for the (politically) monolingual state must have been felt even more in the immediate aftermath of 1960. The little magazine movement, the small presses, and the writers associated with these should be seen in dialogue with or in dissent against these political and social events, even though it would be incorrect to read an indexical relation between an event and a piece of writing. Always reacting but not just reactive to historical events, the *sathottari* poets and the small publishing movement cleared ground for new ways of writing the world around them.

In 1956, Dr. Ambedkar led the Dalits to free themselves of the oppressive caste system of Hinduism by converting to Buddhism. This conversion was the single most important event in the post-independence period for the Dalit writers, but it was also a significant event in the life of non-Dalit writers, who were energized by the revolt of the Dalits against entrenched societal practices and their resounding "no" to the traditions of the past. Some of the anger and refusal seen in the writings of the little magazines can be sourced to the complete rejection of the casteist mode of thinking and the resultant fury that was unleashed by this conversion in 1956.

There were poets from this movement who were also intensely agitated by caste discrimination and who wrote about it in the new brutally realistic, physical register of the body that was popularized also by the Dalit writers. For instance, in *Chirimiri* there is the savagely funny poem by Kolatkar about the casteist priest from the main temple of Pandharpur in Maharashtra, a place of pilgrimage for Marathi people all over the state: "*shthatipranapra*" (a nonsensical word formed by writing backward the word "*pranapratishtha*," which refers to the ritual of installing life into the inert stone image in temples). Here, Kolatkar refers to an incident after Independence in 1947, when caste discrimination was criminalized by law yet the temple of Pandharpur was still closed to the Dalits. Sane Guruji, an activist-writer in Marathi, led a protest that resulted in governmental intervention and to a legal directive to open the temple doors to everyone. The resident priest of the temple at that time was extremely offended by what he viewed as a diktat from the government and, in retaliation, performed in reverse the prayers of the idol-installation ceremony of the temple deity, thus symbolically taking "the life" out of the idol so that it is left as nothing but stone.[3] The priest then proceeded to preserve this godly essence in a *lota* (a multipurpose brass container that usually stores water). In his poem, Kolatkar narrates this incident and then brutally addresses this god who is now made to reside in the *lota*:

go seek cover in the *lota*, god
the *lota* now is your measuring rod

having put him in this lota shut
now use this god to wash your butt[4]

so utterly small, god, is your purview
What else is there I can ask of you?[5]

In Marathi, Kolatkar uses the word *dhungan* to refer to the "butt," a harsh word of obscenity that shocks twice: because of its use in the structure of a poem and, worse, because the usage here is equivalent to cursing God himself. The anger embedded in this usage aligns itself closely with the kind of linguistic breakdown of the language of civility that the Dalit writers tried to effect in their own writing. The language of bodily frankness, and of so-called obscenities, is something that is shared across the Dalit and non-Dalit writers of this period.

If non-Dalit poets evoked the Dalit cause and the resultant anger in their writings, it is equally important to note the involvement of people like Raja Dhale in the little magazine movement in Marathi because he represents the presence of the Dalit writer in this seemingly non-Dalit textual and material space. Raja Dhale started the Dalit Panther activist movement in the 1972 along with the writers Namdeo Dhasal, Arjun Dangle, and Daya Pawar, and in its brief life span of five years, the Dalit Panthers garnered a huge following and represented the aspirations of the awakened Dalit youth. It also made Dhale and Dhasal key figures in the Dalit renaissance in literature. But their roots lie equally in the little magazine movement as in Dalit activism. Dhale started his little magazine, *Atta* (Now), in 1964, a pamphlet-like "unperiodical," which was distributed for free alongside the more established *Aso*, started by Ashok Shahane in 1963.[6] Shahane served as a mentor to Dhale (as Dhale himself claims in multiple interviews), and Dhale later aligned himself with the Marxist Satish Kalsekar to start other little magazines like *Tapasi* (The Enraged) and *Chakravarti* (The Emperor), as well as other short-lived little magazines in the 1960s. The movement benefited greatly from the irrepressible energy of Raja Dhale as he created several new venues for emerging, new writers, and he also gained experience in articulating literary rejections, something he put to great use in the next decade of Dalit activism. Dalit literary history notes the role of the little magazines in the social and literary awakening of the Dalits, but that history of Dalit resurgence in writing starts in the late 1960s and early 1970s, with little magazines like *Vidroha* started by Dhasal in 1968 and periodicals such as *Asmitadarsh* in 1967, both with an explicit focus on the Dalit experience. It is clear, however, that the connection between Dalit literature and little magazines is spread over an older and a more mixed literary space that precedes the predominantly Dalit magazines by almost a decade; it starts with the less clearly focused but more wide-ranging revolt of the little magazines of the post-1960s, themselves inspired by the Dalit political rebellion of the 1950s and that brought together a disparate group of activists and writers who only later expressed distinct and separate ideologies by moving into a more defined space of writing and work in the 1970s.

Along with the conversion of the Dalits, an equally significant happening in and around Bombay in the late 1950s was the agitation for a separate state for the Marathi-speaking people that culminated in the creation of the state of Maharashtra in 1960. The agitation was violent, prolonged, and disruptive even as it tried to ensure the political dominance of the Marathi-speaking population within the new creation of the state boundary. The writers and editors of the little magazine movement were young twenty-something rebels at this time, and their lives were witness to both a multilingual and noncategorized colonial state, the Bombay State, and later to a monolingual and proudly parochial Maharashtra in the 1960s. The writing and translation practices of these writers should also be seen against this contestation of linguistic and regional/national identities.

On the regional scale, 1960 was the year when the state of Maharashtra was created as a Marathi state with Bombay as its capital; on the national scale, it was also the birth year of the national institution of the Sahitya Akademi and its strong push for translation as a mode of nationalist reformation of regional identities. The period of 1955–60 had seen two brief attempts by the national government to retain the cosmopolitan character of the state and of Bombay city, first through a plan that tried to create a tripartite structure of Maharashtra, Gujarat, and Bombay city (which kept Bombay city governed by the center), then when the people rejected it soundly, by creating a bilingual state of Gujarati- and Marathi-speaking areas along with the city of Bombay. After various strikes and massive disruptions of city life, the state of Maharashtra, with a Marathi-speaking population, was formed in 1960. It was an extremely disruptive time in the life of the city and the state, with periodical political strikes by the agitators and the ensuing violence, riots, and police action.[7] The next several years, 1964–71, saw two wars with neighboring Pakistan and the death of Jawaharlal Nehru, the first prime minister of India. The nationalistic chauvinism that was the necessary accompaniment of such events must be seen alongside the regional chauvinism of the monolingual state, a pride that was used later to violent ends by the political party that emerged during the same time, Shiv Sena. The formative little magazines of Bombay and Maharashtra, with their multilingual insistence and their refusal to be boxed into one language or form or region, emerged in this very environment: *Aso* in 1963, *Poetry Review* and *ezra* in 1967, and *Vacha* in 1968. Arun Kolatkar captures the bilingual refusal to be reduced to just one language. Soon after winning the Commonwealth Poetry Prize in 1977 for his English book of poems, *Jejuri*, he was interviewed by the *Indian Literary Review* in 1978, and Kolatkar refused to be categorized as an only English or only Marathi writer: "Since poetry is what I do with language and I know two languages, I wrote in two languages. If I knew three languages, I would have written in three."[8]

CHAPTER I

Little Magazines and the New Space for Literary Writing

These writers, like cattle tethered to the [establishment] posts of *Mauj*, have now forgotten how to graze in distant pastures.

—BHALCHANDRA NEMADE

damn you used to things. damn you used to seeing neon signs replace the stars. the village reduced to the bone. generations evaporating and being replaced by the same, with a new name. damn you without questions or answers.

—ARVIND KRISHNA MEHROTRA

The period of 1955–80 is that of the little magazine movement in Bombay, a movement that manifested itself in many of the regional writings in the various Indian languages in the post-independence period after 1947. This *sathottari* period in literature is first and foremost defined in Bombay by the rapid emergence and the equally quick disappearance of the little magazines. Within the brief period of their sway, they created the modern poetic canon of English and Marathi poetry. The little magazine is not a form of writing invented in Western modernism but "a world form."[1] But it is not an empty abstract global container to be filled in with local/regional content. Instead, the magazines examined here show that the paper used, the format chosen, the visual and textual forms of the contents within, and the distribution and circulation of these magazines were dictated as much by the social and political realities at that time in Bombay and India as by the distant examples of Western little magazines at other places and times.[2] The little magazine (and with it the translations it encouraged and the genre of poetry it showcased) instituted a material local and, with it, locus-specific practices that resulted in a poetry that repurposed the past in unexpected ways and announced a new set of questions regarding the nature and identity of English and Marathi literature in the globalized, modern, post-independence world. In this chapter, I survey the *sathottari* scene in English and Marathi in Bombay to demonstrate why a formal and historical analysis of the little magazines should be an integral part of any critical reading of the work of the *sathottari* poets from Bombay (and, by extension, of any other such multilingual spaces and literatures in India). The little magazine movement introduced a multilingual and material modernism that presents a unique way of coding the interrelation between the local and the global in Indian literature.

Many of the *sathottari* poems were engaged in capturing the peculiarly contemporary historical, social, and cultural moment, and these transient publications of the time, the little magazines, provide an important and unerring guide to that obsession with the "now" of the *sathottari* period. In their pages rises a unique picture of Bombay, different from the state-mapped urban space and separate also from the city that emerges in the received poetry of previous decades. In their ephemerality and relative invisibility in historical archives, the little magazines perhaps resemble the cockroaches and bugs that infest the lives of the poorer Bombay residents, creatures that became adopted as the symbols of the ordinary life of the street that the poets wanted to transmit in their art. As the bilingual poet Dilip Chitre wrote:

> Bedbugs[3] bite me. Cockroaches hover about my soul.
> Mice scurry around my metaphysics,
> mosquitoes sing among my lyrics,
> Lizards crawl over my religion,
> Spiders infest my politics.
> I itch. I become horny. I booze. I want to get smashed.
> And I do. It comes easy at Chinchpokli
> Where, like a minor Hindu god, I am stoned
> By the misery of my worshippers and by my own
> Triumphant impotence.[4]

Not surprisingly, this is the same image that the authors of *A Secret Location on the Lower East Side* use to depict the nature of the concomitant literary rebellions in the United States:

> New York was where a counterpoetics flourished in what Richard Schechner spoke of . . . as "a resistance and alternative to the conglomerate . . . that exist[s] only in the creases of contemporary society, and off leavings, like cockroaches . . . [but]

> run[ning] through the actual conceptual center of society, like faults in the earth's crust."[5]

The little magazines of Bombay could be seen similarly as the De Certeau-like "tactics"[6] of the marginal writers who undermined the cartographic reach of the institutionalized gaze and created underground or guerilla tactics in order to be heard. They did not go out into the periphery, at least not immediately.[7] Rather, they stayed at the center and burrowed from within in order to reformulate that institutional center.

WHAT IS A LITTLE MAGAZINE?

It is difficult to give a narrow definition of a "little magazine,"[8] but there are two statements about little magazines that might help us understand, even if not pin down, the elusive nature of this mutating mode of writing, publishing, and circulation. The first is by Eric Bulson, who writes about localized forms of literary rebellions in little magazines around the world: "The form of the little magazine, which we identify with the birth of modernism, was already in place in non-Western countries around the world, including Japan and Argentina. It does not belong to the West, even if it was the vehicle that carried so many modernist texts in and between England, the United States and Europe."[9] And Bulson reminds us, tongue in cheek, about the eclectic nature of their appearance: "When it comes to the little magazine, one size does not fit all."[10] Indeed the term "little magazine" covers publications big and small in size, relatively periodical to not at all, and magazines that were highly visible as well as ones that were hardly known. The second statement is by Chandrakant Khot, one of the prolific editors of Marathi little magazines and a respected *sathottari* writer, and was published in the Marathi little magazine *Abakadaee* (ABCDE), which published eleven issues between 1969 and 1972[11] at the end of the first *sathottari* decade and saw the birth as well as heyday of the little magazine revolt in Marathi literature. Khot published an index of the Marathi little magazines in the second issue, and he writes about the difficulty he experienced in collecting this data:

> The majority of opinionators are those who voice their judgment without having read a little magazine. Hence this thankless task of making an index. . . . What is the exact definition of a "little

> magazine"? [This task is] extremely annoying. Some of them seemed like little magazines. We contacted them. They wrote back: we were never little magazines. We grew old trying to get hold of all the little magazines. Each such experience deserves an individual novel. Therefore there are some gaps in the index. But the attempt is honest.[12]

If Bulson dislodges the form of the little magazine from its visible Western location, Khot shows that there is in fact no definitive form (or format) for this publication in Bombay.

Khot's statement is instructive because it sheds light both on the effort to define what little magazines are and on the way in which these magazines were archived in public memory. So, if it is difficult to locate the national boundaries or the definitional limits of this form, or if the crucial history of this form is retrievable mainly through the indexes and descriptions of the creators of the little magazines themselves, then it might seem like the little magazine is the quintessential never-to-be-caught snark of literary publishing—without a home, without a form, undefinable, and therefore unknowable. However, even if we cannot define the limits of this form, maybe it is possible to follow the example of Wittgenstein's theory of family resemblance and language games, where even if we cannot find the essential definition of a term, we can recognize it through a series of crisscrossing similarities. Just as the members of a family might not have one common physical trait but share similar traits, little magazines, while impossible to corral in one strict definition, have a series of commonalities that can be seen across a range of individual publications. Thus a few of them might share an emphasis on the unperiodical nature of publication, most might share an anticapitalist stance, and still others might consciously aim at ephemerality. But there is not a clearly defined group of publications that can be said to share *all* such characteristics at the same time.

In Anglo-American literary studies, the form has been called different things by different people. Pound called them "small magazines" in his essay by the same name; Scholes and Wulfman explain the "little" in terms of its connections to "literary" and to the notion of "cuteness": "In the world of periodicals, little magazines were perceived as handsome little Davids confronting ugly big Goliaths."[13] There has not been much disagreement about the name in Indian magazines in English ("little magazine" seems to be an accepted term there), but Marathi writers have tried to name this form in different ways: *aniyatkalika*

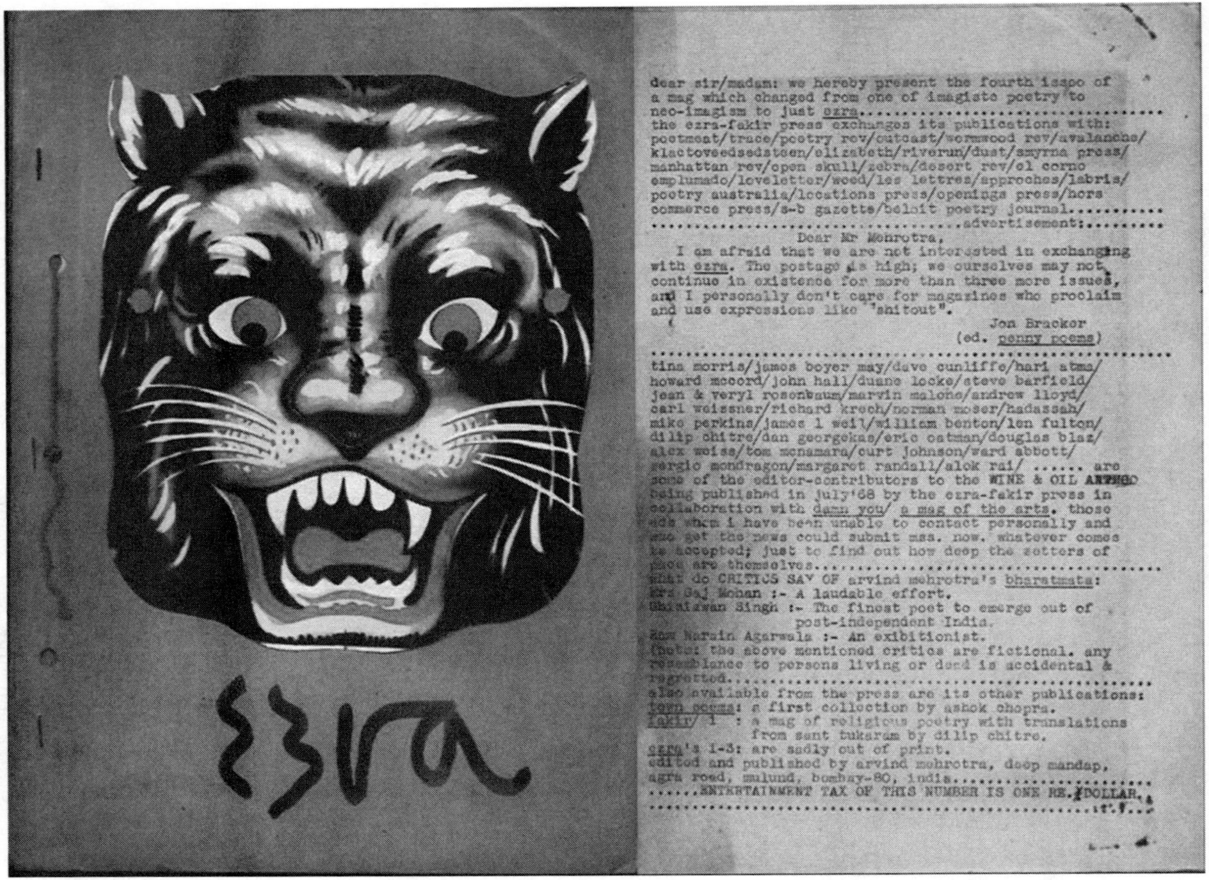

Figure 1.1 The striking cover of Arvind Krishna Mehrotra's little magazine, *ezra*, 4, and the first page with the editorial statement. Mehrotra went to the local toy store and bought about fifty such masks and hand-glued each individual mask onto the magazine covers (with permission from Arvind Krishna Mehrotra).

(unperiodical), *laghu-aniyatkalika* (little unperiodical), *laghupatrika* (little magazine), and *laghuniyatkalika* (little periodical); *aniyatkalika* is what is widely used in Marathi.

In their appearance and format, many of these magazines broke with conventional ways of representing themselves like other serious periodicals, an indication of their repudiation of the establishment. The little magazines came in many different shapes, sizes, and formats.[14] The formative and much-respected *Aso* (So be it) introduced the square page format of the concrete poetry publications into the world of Marathi publication, and it was noted and commented upon by its readers. On the other hand, *Sa. Na. Vi. Vi.* (RSVP) was published in the format of a mail envelope. *Tornado*, started by Pavankumar Jain in English, had human hair on its cover (not an image of hair but actual human hair) to simulate human genitals. *Atta*, published as a free addition to Shahane's little magazine, *Aso*, looked like a brochure in style and format. *ezra* sported a cheap paper mask glued to the cover page, a demon mask that is commonly available at local toy stores. Others, like *Poetry India*, on the other hand, had a look similar to that of respectable academic journals,[15] classically conventional in format, and yet unlike such respectable magazines it lasted only six issues. There are magazines that lasted three years (like *damn you*) and others like *Kavi* that lasted longer.[16] They were all "little" in different ways, sometimes in size and mostly because of their non-market philosophy, while at other times they were small because of the brief time they existed as little magazines.

Similarly, the little magazines adopted the deliberate oppositional stance of rejecting the standard practice of regular periodicity. As David Bennett reminds us in his discussion of the interwar American magazine, "It was against the 'tyranny' of historical imperatives . . . that modernity and the avant-garde turned their backs."[17] This description fits the Bombay *sathottari* little magazines as well. On the back page of the first issue of *ezra* is the editorial and publishing policy of the magazine, where the editor of the magazine, the poet Arvind Krishna Mehrotra, says, "price and format will vary . . . number of copies printed is a secret the stationer unknowingly shares with me." That this issue of *ezra* is the first one is evident from its opening editorial statement and a handwritten (not typed) "ezra/I" at the bottom of the first and second pages of the eighteen-page magazine. There is no other bibliographical information—no volume or issue number or year.

The protest against periodical regularity can be seen in unique ways in each magazine. The Marathi *Aso* carries the following information for readers on its back page:

in 1965
only
6 issues
each issue
24 pages
each page
9.5 square inch in size
the cost of 1 issue
1 rupee
together for 6 issues
5 rupees
1st issue
will come out
in February
Aso.

It purports to note every single detail of periodicity, format, and cost, but the visually poetic format of this description (and the intentional placement of different numbers—6/24/9.5/1/6/5/1—very near each other on the page) is meant to deliberately obfuscate the clarity of such details.[18] And finally, there is the little *Atta* that advertised its forthcoming issue on the back cover of the little magazine *Aso*: "We will publish this whenever we damn well please." It is a brazen repudiation of any form of compliance with the establishment.

The creators and editors of these magazines intentionally rejected the business model of the bigger journals, especially their appeasements and compromises with the voices of money, power, and popularity, as these editors saw it.[19] Many little magazines did not charge their readers any subscription fee, while others survived their brief life cycle on the basis of a small, loyal band of subscribers.[20] For instance, *Aso* started publishing on the expected support of a group of interested readers who promised to fund the enterprise. Shahane relates how he left Bombay and went to Pune when the magazine he was editing then, *Rahasyaranjan*, closed down:

> But the others like Prabhu, Nemade, even Kakatkar, said, "Why are you wasting your time in Pune? Come here to Bombay and we will do something." So then I returned there and went to Sangam Press and asked how much it would cost to publish a magazine. They said Rs 120 for the setting, printing, binding, paper, all of it

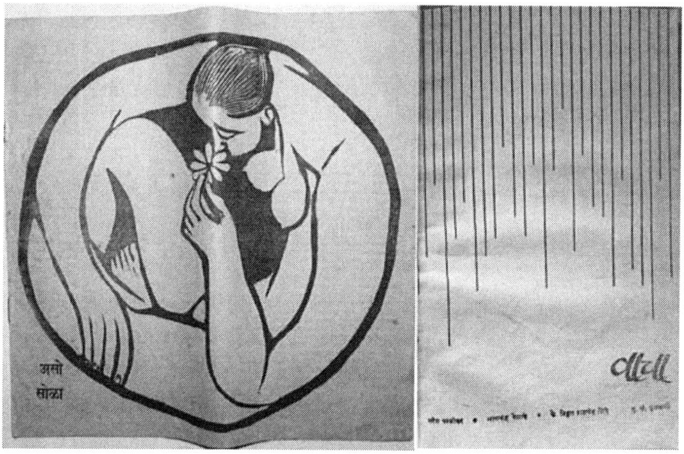

Figure 1.2. On the right, the little magazine started by Bhalchandra Nemade, *Vacha* (1968). On the left, Ashok Shahane's *Aso* 16. Along with *Aso*, *Vacha* was one of the two most influential Marathi little magazines in the *sathottari* period (with permission from Bhalchandra Nemade and Ashok Shahane).

> together, for 500 copies of a 16-page magazine. Then these friends of mine collected 12 people who were willing to pay Rs 10 each for each issue. When we collected Rs 120, we used to bring out an issue. And it used to cost 15 paise for book-post in those days. The decision was to bring out 12 issues. And 12 X 15=180. So who ever paid Rs 1.80, we would mail a copy of the mag to them as well. No cost for the magazine itself, they only paid the mailing charges.[21]

Yet others, like *Vacha* (started by the poet and novelist Bhalchandra Nemade), chose to have a limited circulation of five hundred copies every month despite the demand for more copies because, according to Nemade, they were satisfied with their readership and did not see the need to get bigger. *Abakadaee* offered the first five issues for free, and as with the earlier *Aso*, they asked for Rs. 1.50 to cover the cost of mailing the magazine. In that sense, we can say about these Bombay little magazines what Ian Hamilton says about the Western little magazines: "all 'little magazines' have been small in one or another of these ways, and usually in both. They have had small resources, small respect for the supposed mysteries of 'how to run a business,' small appeal outside a very small minority of readers."[22] The smallness of the Bombay little magazines had diverse physical and social manifestations, but they shared a common literary purpose: discovering a way to write about the unique sense of the post-independence modern that had enveloped the *sathottari* Bombay world.

THE *KATTA* OF MODERN INDIAN POETRY

The *sathottari* period was a time of radical interrogation of the increasingly market-oriented lifestyle of Bombay, and the writers of the period confronted the consumerist world in multiple ways to counter such anonymizing of the individual. Much of Bombay literature, poetry in particular, documents the impoverished life of the individual in which the consumerist world of urban dystopia divests a person of his social and cultural ties to the community. The novelist Kiran Nagarkar, part of this group of bilingual writers, gives a particularly chilling account of the insane rush of urban living that dehumanizes each person's world:

> There is another way of keeping your self-awareness alive in Bombay. Through those red and green lights. Screaming at every crossing. Your eyes glued to them as if your life depended on them. And when the green light comes on, whether you want to go in that direction or not, whether you want to cross the street or not, whether your father pops it or not, whether you want to go to the toilet, whether the war in Vietnam ends . . . what does it matter what's on the other side of the street, get out of my way, you mother fucker, you son of a bitch, out of my way, can't you see any moment now the light will turn red and we will all get left behind on this side of the street.[23]

One reaction to this degraded sense of life in urban locations was a version of critical regionalism, broadly expressed by the writers of the little magazine movement, who opposed the invisibalizing of global modernity by presenting a complex of spaces and experiences that highlight the local *within* its entanglements with the global. Bombay emerges as a changed space in the *sathottari* period when studied through the writings and the materialisms of the Marathi little magazines that juxtapose the spontaneous and informal spaces of the literary *katta* or *adda* against the imagined community promised by the nation. Through the interaction spurred by these informal exchanges and through the symbol of this subversive communal structure that was replicated in the anti-structure of the little magazines, there arises a picture of the city that lives within the fissures of the institutional and the national.

The story of the Marathi little magazines usually starts with the story of the monumental periodical *Satyakatha* (1933–82), which the little magazines rejected stridently on various platforms. By the 1960s, *Satyakatha* (The True Story) had become a one-stop publishing location for writers to gain literary acceptance and respect in the Marathi world. The little magaziners rebelled against this monolith: while many of them initially appeared in the pages of *Satyakatha*, and a few continued to publish in both *Satyakatha* and the little magazines, their overt target was what they perceived as the authoritarian and aestheticized editorial policy of *Satyakatha* that was seen as overly demanding and intrusive by the newer writers. In more ways than one, the *sathottari* writers wanted to be in a like-minded cohort; they wanted to write and be read and understood by their peers and to be in a literary environment sympathetic to their ideas and creativity; they wanted to be a community of their own. In his influential essay of literary revolt, "*Ajakalachya Marathi vangmayavar 'ksha' kiran*" ("An X-Ray of Contemporary Marathi Literature"), Shahane says: "It is important to clarify that we do not consider Shankar Patil, D. M. Mirajdar, Aarti Prabhu . . . Madhu Mangesh Karnik etc. as part of our generation. They are of the same age as us but they do not share our tendencies,"[24] thus declaring clearly who are his literary colleagues and who are not. Robert Creeley, the Black Mountain poet, makes a similar point about the little magazines in the 1950s in the United States:

> The "little" magazine is for me first of all a meeting place, and that's not in the old sense of it at all. It's again in Olson's sense of those who live their lives decently in print, but properly in print. And the way you meet people, not simply to say, "Gee, Harry, it's good to know you," but you find all manner of actuality and occasion for your life.[25]

Clearly the idea of the little magazine as a meeting place of like-minded writers moves across national and cultural borders.

These literary groupings are based figuratively on conversations on the stoop, or a *katta*, as it is called in Marathi. A *katta* could be a spontaneous and unstructured meeting at a streetside café, a street-corner hangout, or any other unceremonious meeting place, something informal and unmoored to established practices and therefore by nature transient (there is no goal of producing anything institutionally as a result of this coming together of bodies).

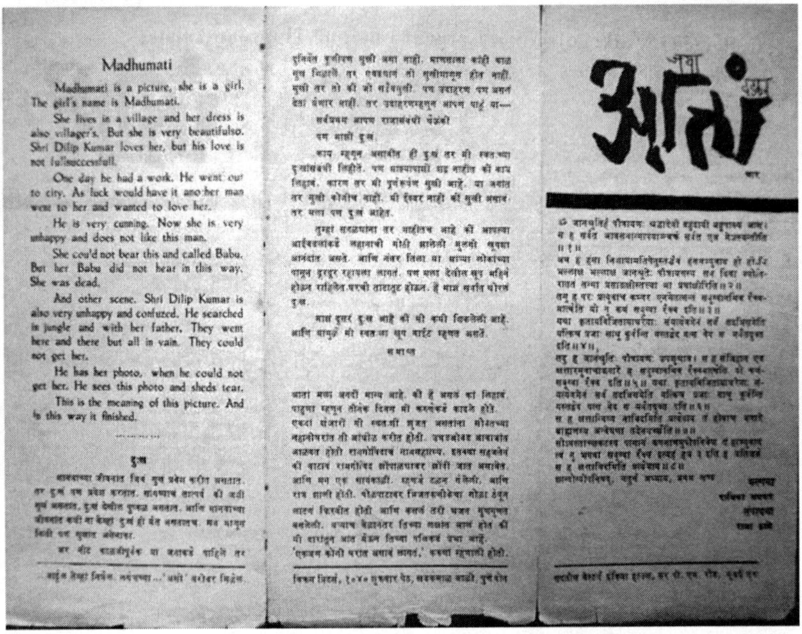

Figure 1.3. The Marathi little magazine *Atta* (Now), started by Raja Dhale and appended to the issues of Ashok Shahane's *Aso*. Note the presence of different languages and scripts in this brief space (with permission from Raja Dhale; image by Mangesh Narayan Kale).

In form and format (denying chronological structure and predictable periodicity) and in content (focusing on marginalized existences), the little magazine replicated the typical structureless spontaneity of the *kattaladda* that Dipesh Chakrabarty analyzes in his essay "Adda, Calcutta: Dwelling in Modernity." As he says of the *adda*, "Roughly speaking, it is the practice of friends getting together for long, informal, and unrigorous conversations."[26] The *adda* was the injection of the personal and of an anti-profit-making activity in the impersonal capitalist world; Chakrabarty goes on to say, "What made the word *adda* respectable in the twentieth century was its association with the spaces for the production of a modern Bengali reading public."[27] It is this investment in the not-for-profit element and the focus on the organic and the personal that explains why the little magaziners objected so vociferously to the existence of monumental *Satyakatha*. Or as Tulsi Parab writes in, "literal(ly) poems from earlymorningquartertothreeofthreedecembernineteensixtyseven,"[28]

before three one,
two:
me
you
the basic source

It is the relation between "you and me" that is the crucial one for the writers of the little magazine movement. As the representative of the literary establishment, *Satyakatha* did not offer the same camaraderie or the sense of belonging to a discriminating group as did the various little magazines (the *Satyakatha* was generally more conservative in its editorial policies), and that could be one explanation for this revolt.

The little magazines were frequently planned and executed among a group of people who met in informal spaces (this is the story of *Aso*, *Vacha*, *ezra*, and the small presses like Clearing House and Pras Prakashan)—they were the fruit of the excitement and passion of a handful of writers. In his essay in *Khel* in 2012, Pradeep Nerurkar relates how youthful cross-generational friendships of Bombay little magaziners in Marathi created the various nodes of the movement. It is a veritable who's who of the movement in Marathi: "N. V. Kakatkar, Ashok Shahane, Arun Kolatkar, Sadanand Rege, Sharad Mantri, Bal Thakur, Sudhir Kolatkar, Krishna Karwar, Manohar Oak, Bhau Padhye, Raghu Dandavate, Vrindavan Dandavate, and Keshav Meshram."[29] They used to meet at a restaurant called Cellar to drink tea on Saturday afternoons (or have "a poet's *adda*," in Nerurkar's own words) where everything literary under the sun was debated and imagined. Another such instance of a *katta* is that of Nerurkar himself and Raja Dhale, who used to meet up after college with Satish Kalsekar, Manohar Oak, Chandrakant Oak, and Ashok Lachke near the VT train station and chat for hours over cups of chai at a local Irani café. Camaraderie, youth, and idealism characterize the anticapitalist relationship that is the basis of most of the little magazines.[30]

In fact, this Marathi concept of *katta* became the very title of a little magazine, *Katta*, created by the students of Fergusson College in Pune, which appeared at the end of the *sathottari* period. When I was attending Fergusson College I remember waiting eagerly for every issue of *Katta*, not knowing when the next issue would be published because it was an "unperiodical." In the second issue of *Katta*, the student editors explain the rationale for publishing this little magazine:

> Some people say to us, what a wasteful way to pass your time, but they do not know that in Pune, the real culture happens in Pune's restaurants. . . . You will see people of all kinds from all kinds of background here. Take a stroll by "Triveni" (in front of Lakshminarayan)—Sudhir Gadgil, Mahabal and some *khadi*-wearing person will definitely be there. . . . if you go slightly ahead and go to "Apsara," you will meet Pradeep Sidhye, Anil Gogate, etc.

The editors go on to map the restaurants in the vicinity of Fergusson College based on the kinds of people who go there and the activities they foster. They list college students of the time (Dhanya Paranjape), drama critics like Shanta Gokhale, playwrights like Satish Alekar, and politicians and activists like George Fernandes and Mrunal Gore. This list is a good indicator of the richness of such informal places and the conversations that happened there.

The "unperiodical" *Katta* itself might not seem like a serious literary little magazine (and it does not claim to be one), but it nevertheless achieves in a lighthearted manner what Kolatkar practices in the long poem "Breakfast at Kala Ghoda" in *Kala Ghoda Poems*.[31] There, Kolatkar lists all the restaurants in the vicinity of the neighborhood of Kala Ghoda in Bombay, classifying them by the kind of breakfasts they serve, and he indicates the diverse patina of this crowded space in poem 7:

> They are serving khima pao at Olympia,
> dal gosht at Baghdadi,
> puri bhaji at Kailash Parbat,
>
> aab gosht at Sarvi's,
> kebabs with sprigs of mint at Gulshan-e-Iran,
> nali nehari at Noor Mohammadi's,
>
> baida ghotala at the Oriental,
> paya soup at Benazir,
> brun maska at Military Café,
>
> upma at Swagat,
> shira at Anaṇd Vihar,
> and fried eggs and bacon at Wayside Inn.
>
> For yes, it's breakfast time at Kala Ghoda

as elsewhere
in and around Bombay.

—up and down
the whole longitude, in fact,
the 73rd, if I'm not mistaken.[32]

This list seems pointless on the surface because of its serious attempt to document all the dishes in these everyday spaces. Why would a poet give an exhaustive list of the breakfast dishes served at these various restaurants? Each dish mentioned here evokes a different communal presence: *shira* and *upma* are found in traditional Marathi/Brahmin homes; *baida ghotala* makes the Parsi and Irani expatriate communities visible; and "fried eggs and bacon" references the Christian/Anglicized groups. Written in the period when religious parochialism was fanned by political parties like the Shiv Sena, the poem is a counterexample of the mixed nature of Bombay city.[33] Similar to the way in which *Katta* bases its aesthetic on the informal, seemingly pointless conversations engaged in over a cup of chai, Kolatkar wrote many of his poems sitting in the Wayside Inn in Kala Ghoda, Bombay, where he met his longstanding friends from the little magazine days—Ashok Shahane, Vrindavan Dandavate, Raghu Dandavate, Avinash Gupte, and Ratan Sohoni—as well as a changing population of visiting friends and acquaintances.[34]

Such a spirit of informal community also explains the radically oppositional tone taken by Shahane in "*Ajakalachya Marathi vangmayavar 'ksha' kiran*," which came on the literary scene with a deafening outcry.[35] He rejected most of the accepted greats of Marathi literature, because although they belonged to the same period, they were not part of his cohort:

> Lakshmibai, Balkavi, Tukaram, Namdeo, Dnyaneshwar . . . Shri Chakradhar, Vinoba, Manmohan. . . . Jibanananda Das, Sudhin Datta, Anandshankar Rai, Kamal Mujumdar, Gopalakrishna Adiga, Rajindersingh Bedi, these Indian folks, plus Kierkegaard, Dostoevsky, Ortega, Thomas Mann, Camus, Beckett, Ionesco, Genet, Artaud, . . . this is our world. Each one of these lent a hand to make this world.[36]

These were the minds that were the topic of conversation at the various *kattas* of the *sathottari* writers, a chosen like-minded group of people within whom they saw themselves and whom they discussed in their exchanges in the café.[37] The pages of the little magazine were also such a literary stoop for these writers: just as in real life they met at a café and shared ideas, in these pages they appeared together and had their works talk to each other.[38]

But it is more than that. The idea of the throwaway transience embodied in the notion of the *katta* unites imagery, format, content, and material practices of publication and circulation of the *sathottari* littles. In fact, Vilas Sarang, the bilingual younger writer of this generation, compares the *sathottari* writers' meetings to the casually formed roadside groups of young men (seen as dropouts of middle-class society) who join together in a game of three-card poker in the street.[39] The unpredictability and the anarchist nature of these spontaneously formed streetside assemblies constitute the threat these writers posed to middle-class morality of the period. If the format of the little magazines emphasizes the irregularity and the spontaneity of the publishing act, the material practice of meeting at a café for a spontaneous exchange of ideas is premised on a suddenness of emergence and disappearance. It is the non-permanence, the expendable nature, and the unmonumentality of the passing moment that is of the essence—as are the subjects of these poems: the spent people of Bombay (Chitre), the disillusioned intellectual (Jussawalla), or the homeless (Kolatkar).

THE *SATHOTTARI* "NOW"

The little magaziners believed that there were different and novel ways of seizing the fluid present of their lives. The aim was as follows, to quote Mehrotra from his editorial "statement" at the beginning of *damn you* 6: "when a crow in flight scratches its paws over a desert it's a canvas we try to get hold of, before wind and sand pile in. we . . . [make] sporadic and silent appearances. we're on the prowl." Here the poet stalks that elusive "now" of the age that many artists of the time were also trying to capture in their own separate ways. As Jack Spicer asked in San Francisco, "What I mean is can a poem ever / Take accidentals for its ultimates?"[40]

As an example, here is R. K. Joshi, the poet, calligrapher, and typographer,[41] popularly known as Ra. Kru., introducing himself in *Punha Ekada Kavita* (Poems Once Again), an anthology of contemporary poems by the poets N. D. Mahanor and Chandrakant Patil:

> My name [is] Raghunath Krishna Joshi. *I am Ra. Kru./R.K.* Birth was in Sangli in 1936. *My ophthalmologist is A.* School Education Satara, Kolhapur, Sangli, and other places. *[My] Nose ear throat specialist is B.* Art education 1952 to 1956 in J.J. School of Arts in Bombay. *Dentist is C.* Joined Bensons Ltd as a commercial artist in 1960. *[My] Cardiologist is D.* Since then [I] have been Art director at Ulka Advertising. *The blood belongs to the pressure.* First letter poetry [*sic*] from the study of calligraphy. *The hands belong to the aches.* Then [I] got typographic poems, sound poems, formal poems and poster poems published in *Satyakatha* at various times. *The legs belong to the street.* These were the first attempts at concrete poetry in Marathi. *The brain belongs to the office.* Manuscripts, explorations in Roman and Devanagari calligraphy, research in typography, these are the preferred focuses. *Half the salary belongs to my wife.* Reading and writing barely moderate. *Half of me belongs to Delhi.* [I] Lectured in an hands-on manner in Art Institutes. *The phone belongs to the neighbor.* [I am] Credited with two travels abroad to read papers at conferences. *The TV and fridge belong to the mechanic. . . . The poem belongs to the letters.* [I] Tried to start a movement regarding the idea of the beauty of letters and their practical reach but regretfully was unsuccessful. *Only mine, just one piece of wealth.* For the last 12 years [I] have more or less worked as poet artist graphic designer calligrapher typographer word-event creator student of numerous styles of transcription and letter art. *Every minute that I experience/live.* Collection of poems lectures notes about letters yet unpublished.
>
> 16/10/78[42]

If one were to separate the italicized self-description from this passage, the note would appear trite and a little bit like the content of a Hallmark card: “Only mine, just one piece of wealth. . . . Every minute that I experience/live.” But R. K. Joshi cleverly intermingles the emotional with the factual in the typical form of the biographical note one finds in books. The result of this deliberate and unruly mixing of registers and content is that the picture of the man refuses to be of a single facet and of a singular ability. The person appears contradictory and fluid, and steps outside the prescribed limits of sterile biographical sketches. More important, the crux of the piece is not his achievements in the world but “every minute that I experience/live,” in the uncatchable “now” of his present moment that the words are trying to trap in a linguistic grid. That "now" seems inextricable from the messy details of the person's existence, both the mundane ("The phone belongs to the neighbor") and the noteworthy (like being the "Art director at Ulka Advertising"). By contaminating the genre as well as the visual format of the biographical note, Ra. Kru. tries to wedge the "now" of the contemporary moment into his own work. Each of these writers and editors of little magazines was trying to capture the fast-moving present of the lived experience by employing an individual combination of writing approaches: it was an assault on literary, textual, and printing conventions all at once in the hopes of getting through to some other, inexpressible side of things.

Take the concept of the throwaway, and the concomitant randomization of the inflexible, for instance, that explains the composite worldview of the writers and editors of these little magazines. The notion of the throwaway connects several disparate writing practices, like those of Dilip Chitre, the imagery of the poems of Kolatkar, the visual appearance of the little magazines, and the practices of circulation of these magazines. It is one point of entrance for these writers into the world of "now." Consider, for example, Dilip Chitre, also an artist, filmmaker, critic, and translator. He refused to edit his work in the sense of managing his appearance as a poet for the eyes of the world and published a huge corpus of writing, not all of it of uniform quality. As he said,

> My output tells a story by itself. My collected poems in Marathi from 1954 to the present day occupy nearly 1000 pages. My English poetry is about 50 per cent of that volume; and my translation of poetry would fill another 700 pages. This is embarrassingly large; but since poetry is what I principally do in life, I can hardly apologise.[43]

This tendency to document his poetic thoughts, all of them, is in keeping with the nature of the man and poet, who valued the momentary significance of the ephemeral gesture or word or poem. A particular poem or phrase or word could be forgotten later, as the poet himself did, or maybe thrown aside for something more timely, but these poems document in a democratic fashion and without prejudice the passing and the impermanent. Or as Arvind Krishna Mehrotra wrote in his poem in his little magazine *ezra* 4 (1966): "i never tear what is created / nor use birth control while writing."

The throwaway is the ephemeral "now," but it is also prominently the garbage and waste that is evident in the poetry of the major poets of the day. There is Mehrotra's "Bharatmata" ("you are in the world's slum, the lavatory") and Chitre's "The View from Chinchpokli" about a neighborhood in Bombay:

> A fouled Sun rises from behind the textile mills
> As I crawl out of my nightmares and hobble
> To the sink. Then I luxuriate in the toilet
> While my unprivileged compatriots of Parel Road Cross Lane
> Defecate along the stone wall of Byculla Goods Depot.[44]

But garbage is the very center of the poetry of Kolatkar's *Kala Ghoda Poems*, a book that elevates the piles of garbage collected daily outside the steps of the monumental Jehangir Art Gallery in Bombay as the true art installations of the city. Kolatkar demolishes the veneration of the art museum here by equating the art inside with the garbage piles outside. He airs the stuffy definition of art by opening the door to the ordinary and the material life of the everyday Mumbaikar. In the third poem of the series titled "Meera," Kolatkar describes the "fresh new installations" that go "on display / in front of the Jehangir Art Gallery":

> in the form of modest piles of rubbish
> all along the kerb
> . . .
> and consisting of dry leaves, scraps of paper,
> prawn shells, onion skins, potato peels,
> castoff condoms, dead flowers . . . [45]

This is the litter and garbage that the street sweeper has collected at the curbside and will put in her cart. Kolatkar says:

> These installations might as well have been
> titled "Homage to Bombay, one,"
> "Homage to Bombay, two" and so on
> since a good bit of city stands
> on sweepings such as these.
> All of Colaba, for example, or Khetwadi.[46]

Here the viewer is made to cross the thresholds of the art gallery with its canonized painters and elite clientele and is forced to notice the work of the lowly sweepers who are considered less than human—in fact, not "considered" at all in the structure of bourgeois Bombay life. It reveals a geographical reality of Bombay, which stands partially on land redeemed from the sea: the city that stands on reclaimed land becomes also the city that stands on the backs of these poor, lower-caste sweepers' work and life. The so-called permanence of art and science is relocated to the ephemeral piles of rubbish of the sweepers, and museum art suddenly becomes less enduring; instead, the street scene and life become more memorable.[47] Thus the monuments of colonial and neocolonial establishment that flank the street life of the homeless—the imposing Victorian buildings that house the David Sassoon library or the Rajabhai Clock tower—all become hollow symbols of power in this poetry. The seemingly permanent structures of power are emptied of their value and become accessories to the lives of the homeless that they overshadow at the intersection of the Kala Ghoda square. And while it is true that the poems in *Kala Ghoda Poems* by Kolatkar were not published in any little magazine, this focus on garbage and on the transient nevertheless shows the impact of the philosophy of the movement on the entire corpus of the poet who worked in the arena of the little magazines and small presses all his life. The throwaway piles of garbage in Kolatkar's poetry, the attempt to capture life in art through seemingly unedited poetic responses in Chitre, and the breaking apart of the visual format of the printed page and of the magazine format are all of a piece with the urge to arrest the present of urban *sathottari* Bombay in the little magazines. By emulating the passing moment in its transient value, the little magazines were an archive of that "now" through the material practices of the *katta* that they emerged from and through the throwaway subjects of their poetry that they made visible.

THE GEOMODERNISMS OF BOMBAY

In the last issue of *Poetry India*, there is an advertisement for the little magazine *Klactoveedsedsteen* (published by Panic Press in Heidelberg, Germany) where the editor, Carl Weissner, states that he has been impressed by the Bengali poetry published in the City Lights journal *Kulchur*, and asks for more Indian poets to submit to his little, *Klacto*:

> During the past few months I have established contact with several poets, writers and editors in your country, and out of a genuine interest in the new writing that is coming out of India . . . I

> would now like to offer the pages and facilities of this magazine to you, the new generation of India poets [*sic*] . . . O.K., feed me your silver X-Rays / Brainwaves / Orgones / semantic soulgear / Blue panic!!![48]

This unlikely advertisement asking for Indian poetry from a magazine in the Western world is just one instance of the worldwide connection made by the little magaziners during this period; there are many such connections that have been excavated. This Anglo-American and European connection is well-documented by various scholars.[49] The English poets were clearly looking westward, as Mehrotra says about his early years in Allahabad in *Partial Recall*: "In 1964, the year Nehru died . . . I was sitting in darkness's heart, in a bungalow in Allahabad, in a railway waiting room in Bilaspur, as scores of Indian poets—from Henry Derozio to Srinivas Rayaprol—had done before me, I was taking my bearing from distant stars. The two I took mine from were e. e. cummings and Kahlil Gibran."[50]

The opening of the market to paperbacks and the ready availability of journals like the *Paris Review* and *Evergreen Review*, the availability of anthologies of English and American poetry like Donald Hall's *Contemporary American Poetry* (1962) and *Penguin Modern Poets 5* (1963),[51] and the rise of travel from and to the West meant that the Indian poets in English, many of whom visited the United States or Europe, were participating in the same larger literary movements as those in Anglo-America.[52] This was true of most urban spaces in India as it was in Bombay. Bruce King documents the many ways in which Indian poets in English were influenced by American literature and were publishing in venues in the United States: besides visiting the United States, many of the poets benefited from the close political connections between the two countries after India's independence and the institution of resources like the American Studies Research Center in Hyderabad in 1964. King also notes the close association between Indian poets like Srinivas Rayaprol and American greats like William Carlos Williams and e. e. cummings, and he further notes the publication of the *sathottari* poets in American little magazines as well as larger journals like *Wormwood Review*, *dustbooks*, *Sewanee Review*, *Kenyon Review*, and *Atlantic Monthly*.[53]

There is an undeniable give-and-take between the American and Indian poetic *sathottari* worlds. As Mehrotra says in his excellent introduction to Kolatkar's *The Boatride & Other Poems*, Kolatkar brought about an amalgamation of the Blues' aesthetic with that of *bhakti* poetry. When Kolatkar writes songs and poems in the style of Bob Dylan,[54] he confirms the influence of the Western modernist history of radical internationalism in the location of Bombay.[55] Mehrotra himself published a book of concrete poems at almost the same time as when the concrete poems were becoming the rage in Brazil and Europe. The Marathi poets manifest the influence of such global modernisms as well. Besides Kolatkar and Chitre, Manohar Oak translated Spanish poets into Marathi in various Marathi littles, and several Dalit poets translated the black poets and the speeches of Dr. Martin Luther King into Marathi.

While there is no doubt that there was an intense cosmopolitanism in *sathottari* Bombay, several previous generations of authors in Bombay can also claim to have crossed national boundaries in writing Indian literature. During the 1940s and 1950s, in Marathi literature, B. S. Mardhekar wrote his famous modernist poems and domesticated Eliot and Pound to Marathi tastes.[56] This was also when millworkers, directly inspired by Marxist thought, agitated for their rights and created oral, theatrical, and literary texts in Marathi to counter the mill owners' disregard of their working conditions.[57] All of this happened *before* the *sathottari* poets inserted themselves into the literary sphere. Cosmopolitanism was not new to *sathottari* Bombay—what was new was the specific kind exhibited by the *sathottari* poets through their material practices and their networks of publishing and circulation. Or as Laura Doyle and Laura Winkiel say in their discussion of "geomodernism," "in both the creation and the interpretation of modernisms, that is, so much depends on *which* modernism, written when and why and from what place—which city, which hillside, which seat on the train, which new nation or colony, and before, after, during which war."[58]

The writers and editors of little magazines in Marathi and English not only moved in a shared cultural and literary space but were aware of the work done in the other Indian literatures by the little magazines. One way to examine these interlinks is to look at the network of pathways at the core of any poetic text to see the collaborations of writers and the connections of regional, national, and international influences. A good example is the publication of "Bharatmata," a long cult poem by Mehrotra. Formally, the poem leads us to Ezra Pound as well as the Ginsbergian "Howl" in its incantatory denunciation of the post-independence nation. Not coincidentally, Mehrotra's first little magazine was titled *ezra* and it claims clear ancestry to Pound in the editorial of the very first issue:

"what do you want me to do with you. rather, what do you expect to follow. images. poems. plagiarisms from that butler of poetry, ezra pound."

Even this American ancestry offers a limited perspective on a poem that energized such a large portion of the youth in Bombay when it was first published as a mimeographed copy by Mehrotra's own ezra-fakir press and then by Nissim Ezekiel in his little magazine *Poetry India* (April/June 1967).[59] Ashok Shahane was working at the Mohan Mudranalaya press in Bombay when the issues of *Poetry India* were sent to be printed there. Excited about the new poem and its radical stance on literature and language, Shahane made about a hundred chapbook copies of Mehrotra's poem as a stand-alone text and gave them to Mehrotra for distribution among his friends. The two editors/writers, along with Adil Jussawalla, have collaborated on publishing Kolatkar's poetry since then.[60] "Bharatmata" proved to be the introduction between the Marathi publishing world of Shahane and the English writing world of Mehrotra, and between the works of the other poets associated with the two.[61]

A connection of common influences arcs across the English-Marathi divide between many of these poets. If Mehrotra brought Pound and Ginsberg to bear upon the newly independent Indian society in his English poem, Kolatkar also translated Ginsberg's "Kaddish" into Marathi for Shahane's *Aso* in 1963 (a poem that could be thematically and formally related to Mehrotra's work, too). Moreover, in *Bhijaki Vahi*, one of the last books Kolatkar published before his death in 2004, there is a magnificent poetic philippic against the nation and the world that harks back to these Ginsbergian poems. And there is more. Three prominent examples from the period will illustrate this interconnection across the two worlds. The first is the close literary collaboration between the Beat writers and the Bombay poets. It is a known fact that Ginsberg and Peter Orlovsky read their poetry on Alkazi's terrace in 1962 on their visit to Bombay,[62] but the Beat poets were also interacting with both the English writers and the vernacular writers in Bengal and in Maharashtra, like Ashok Shahane and Kolatkar in Bombay. Shahane published Ginsberg's poetry in English and in Marathi translation[63] in *Aso* as well as the work by Orlovsky in its original English. Shahane also wrote a poem in the little magazine *Timba* where he mocks the rabid fervor generated by religious personalities like the Shankaracharya. Shahane trivializes such religious zeal with a seemingly frivolous comparison and connection with the Beats and with Hollywood:

> the world is a dream
> the Shankaracharya has said

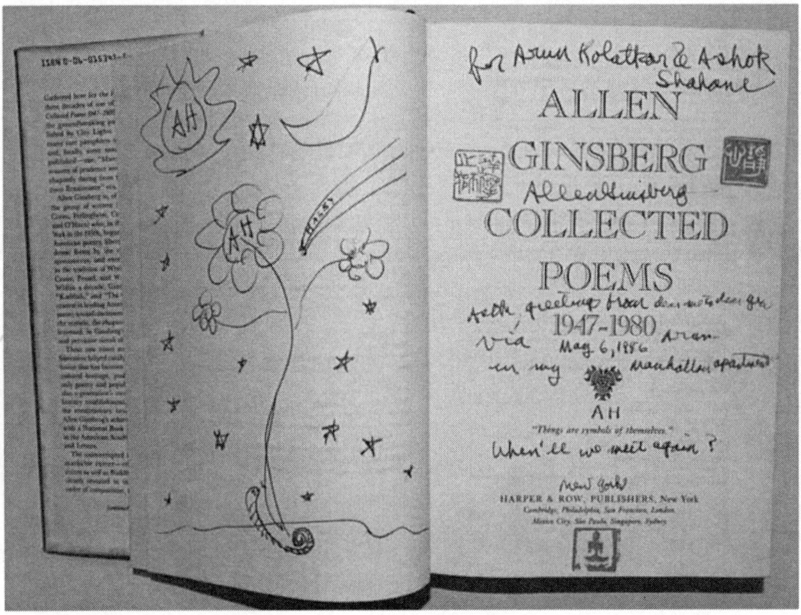

Figure 1.4. The copy of Allen Ginsberg's *Collected Poems* given in 1986 to Arun Kolatkar, inscribed with the poet's sketches and best wishes for both Arun Kolatkar and Ashok Shahane ("with greetings from dear me to dear you") and a question for both: "When'll we meet again?" (with permission from Soonoo Kolatkar and Ashok Shahane).

as Allen reported[64]
Arjun was the last man
and maybe also Burt Lancaster[65]

"Allen" here refers to Allen Ginsberg, and in this poem, Shahane self-confidently accepts the long way home when he states that he learned Shankaracharya's teaching through hearsay from Ginsberg. It shows the defiant refusal to accede to claims of monolingual affiliations. It is also a little-known fact that Ginsberg's poem "September on Jessore Road" first appeared in Bombay, published by Ashok Shahane. When the Bangladesh War began in 1971 and Ginsberg wrote the poem, Shahane printed and distributed copies of it and gave the proceeds to the Bangladesh aid committee set up in Bombay (see figure 1.5).[66] Followed closely, such circuits of the global invariably lead to the space of the local.[67]

The second example is Arun Kolatkar's *Jejuri*, which includes poems that traverse repeatedly across linguistic lines. The poem "The Priest"

Figure 1.5. "September on Jessore Road," a poem by Allen Ginsberg first published as a poster-poem/broadside by Ashok Shahane, and designed by R. K. Joshi, in Bombay, 1971. The "sun" in the middle of the black-lettered word "Jessore" is bright red on the original broadside (with permission from Soonoo Kolatkar and Ashok Shahane).

from *Jejuri* appeared in Marathi on pages 88–89 of the 1977 special issue of *Rucha* on Kolatkar even as the book of poems in English, published by the small Clearing House Press, won the Commonwealth Poetry Prize that year. The history of this book of poems manifests the entangled nature of the multilinguistic *sathottari* worlds. Initially one of the poems from the *Jejuri* collection appeared in the English little magazine *Dionysus* (edited by Abraham Benjamin and Shirish Pradhan), which promptly lost the manuscript of the collection of poems. It was then rewritten in English and appeared in full in A. D. Gorwala's *Opinion Literary Quarterly* in 1974, then was apparently shown to Arun Khopkar (who published a poem from it in *Rucha* in 1977, when the English book of poems was published), and eventually appeared as a Marathi book of poems posthumously in 2011. Dilip Chitre's work demonstrates a similar catholicity in its publishing spaces: his translations from the French poets appeared in the Marathi *Satyakatha* (December 1963), his translations of the Marathi poet Mardhekar in the English little magazine *Poetry India* (1966), and translations of the Marathi Tukaram in Mehrotra's English little magazine *fakir* (1968).

A crucial third way in which the little magazines provided a mixed space for writers emerges when one considers the presence of Dalit writers and editors in the *sathottari* years. The iconoclastic philosophy of the little magazines borrowed its energy from the foundational rage of the Dalit writers in its refusal of tradition in most of its manifestations, be it in vocabulary, imagery, poetic structure, or representative realisms. The little magazine movement was clearly influenced by the Ambedkar revolt in the 1950s and the subsequent Marathi publications of writers like Shankarrao Kharat and Baburao Bagul in the early 1960s when the first Marathi little magazines started appearing at the same time (*Shabda* in 1955 and *Aso* in 1963). The little magazines also provided a space for many rising Dalit writers to showcase their work. There is a synergy between the two movements that is important to note. The *sathottari* poetry is notable for the emphasis on the material as well as the textual. The angry materialism seen in the poems of Chitre or Kolatkar is comparable in terms of literary technique with much of Dalit literature's emphasis on the body.

Take the discussion of modernism and Dalit poetry. When Aniket Jaaware lists the characteristics of the modernity of Dalit poetry (with reference to Namdeo Dhasal, who started publishing in the late 1960s), the descriptions seem uncannily applicable to the poetry (Dalit and non-Dalit) that was published in the little magazines in the late 1950s and early 1960s. For instance, Jaaware says of Dalit poetry: "The poetry is filled with the truth of the body, which works as a very powerful contrast to the generally soulful nature of main-stream Marathi poetry. If there is any single source of expression, it is the body. It is as if the body speaks."[68] The non-Dalit poets of the post-1960s were rebelling against precisely the "soulful" nature of Marathi literature, as can be seen in the essays by Shahane and Nemade. It can also be seen in the criticism leveled against the *sathottari* poets of the little magazines, where these poets were castigated by readers specifically for their so-called overly obsessive focus on the body.

The "meta" nature of Dalit literature, as Toral Gajarawala states in her book, is also a reiteration of what Jaaware emphasizes in his essay: "The poet is now reflecting not so much on social conditions, as on how to speak of it. Dalit poetry has now a tradition of production, circulation and consumption."[69] The little magazine movement was based on a similar premise: to reformulate the poetry of the time by restructuring the format, publication, and dissemination of the poems themselves. The mode of delivery was a semantic element in the content of the poem. This movement focused on getting the street language into poetry,[70] getting ordinary lived experience into literature, and as Kolatkar shows in *Kala Ghoda Poems*, getting art from within the walls of the Jehangir Art Gallery into the outside pedestrian world by seeing the piles of "dry leaves, scraps of paper, / prawn shells, onion skins, potato peels, / castoff condoms, dead flowers" as the newest art installations in Bombay. The connections between Dalit and non-Dalit literature appear, therefore, in the "production, circulation and consumption" of the little magazines and in the poetics formulated by the writers of the movement.[71]

The *sathottari* period is one in which the Dalit writers were writing with non-Dalit writers in English and Marathi little magazines and also running predominantly Dalit magazines themselves in which non-Dalit writers also appeared regularly. For instance, while early Marathi Dalit writers like Baburao Bagul appeared in translation in the English little magazine from Delhi, *Vagartha*, the poets also appeared in Bombay little magazines in Marathi that were not exclusively Dalit, for example, Baburao Bagul, Raja Dhale ("*ratra*"), and Anant Tawade ("Dr. Martin Luther King") in *Vacha* 3. Raja Dhale was also involved in editing Marathi little magazines: *Atta* in 1964; *Yeru* (1967) with poets Tulsi Parab and Vasant Gurjar; *Tapasi* (comprising just one issue, in 1968); and *Chakravarti* (1969) with the Marxist-oriented Satish Kalsekar. In 1972 he founded the Dalit Panthers along with the now-canonical Marathi poet Namdeo Dhasal, an organization modeled on the Black Panther movement in the United States. Thus the origins of Raja Dhale as a writer are clearly rooted in his experience of writing, publishing, and organizing in the little magazine movement.

It is also interesting to examine the contents of the very influential Dalit periodical *Asmitadarsha*,[72] which continued the conversation with the Bombay writing world even as it challenged the urban focus of Bombay writing. *Asmitadarsha* is not a little magazine; it had an annual Diwali issue that was a literary symposium where Dalit and non-Dalit writers from Bombay and elsewhere would discuss important social and literary issues. For instance, in the 1976 Diwali issue of the magazine, a discussion about the little magazine movement of the previous decade showcased participants ranging from editors and writers of Bombay little magazines to those of more established magazines; the discussants were Bhalchandra Nemade, Satish Kalsekar, Chandrakant Khot (all editors of Marathi littles), M. T. Madkholkar, and several Dalit writers and critics, like Daya Pawar, Keshav Meshram, and Sudhir Rasal. In other words, the little magazine movement features Dalit and non-Dalit writers working together, influencing and being influenced by each other, and creating this messy but energetic period of writing from which emerged the separate and distinct identities of several strands of literature (like Dalit literature and regional/nativist literature) in the 1970s. While it is true that there were exclusively Dalit *sahitya sangh* (literary meetings) beginning in the late 1950s and that a distinct Dalit voice began to emerge in the 1960s, what we associate with a separate and individual Dalit identity in literature today started emerging clearly at the end of the 1960s in the magazines and bloomed mainly in the next decade. In the 1960s, most of the radical writers were acting in tandem in their various refusals.[73] As Raja Dhale says in his interview to the Marathi newspaper *Lokaprabha*, "I am a man of the little magazines. That is my identity. People do not know whether I am a Dalit or not."[74]

Finally, the presence of other languages in these little magazines (there are far too many to document) shows the variegated nature of Bombay modernism. This appears in the translations so actively encouraged by the editorial policies of magazines across the divide; in the use of other regional languages in their poems (Hindi and Sanskrit in Kolatkar's English poetry; English in Nemade and Kolatkar's Marathi poetry; regionalized English in Ezekiel); and in the visual presence of the scripts on the pages and covers of the little magazines. For instance, in the Marathi little magazine *Timba* (The Dot), the sound "Ti" of the Marathi word *Timba* starts with the Roman letter "T." Similarly, the title of the Marathi little magazine *Abakadaee* is a riff on the first five letters of the English alphabet. And Adil Jussawalla's poem in *Missing Person* not only incorporates the Devanagari script but also integrates the script, the use of the language, and the hybrid location of the poet when he writes:

> an अ's an er . . . a cough
> once spoking your valleys with light.
> But the a's here to stay.
> on it St. Pancreas station,
> the Indian and African railways.
> That's why you learn it today.[75]

The gap between the "अ" of the Devanagari script (pronounced "uh") and the "a" of the English Roman script (with the awkward, audibly duplicating "er" in between, representing the sometimes uneasy, at other times seamless, coexistence of the two languages) represents the gap between the contemporary vernacular realities and the Anglophone lives in urban Bombay, both meeting on this page and, even if opposing, still occupying the same space. The page establishes a relation between the two, visually, architecturally, and linguistically, and shows in a compact way the complex world of the *sathottari* Bombay.

The rebellions in English and Marathi by the editors and writers in Bombay were fused in terms of strategy and public manifestations even if their motivations sprang from separate literary impulses. They read some of the same texts, they disrupted the material format of the magazine in similar fashion, they focused on the visual arts in related modes, they twisted the habitual modes of articulation in connected ways, and they emphasized a robust multilingualism in their content, format, and worldview.

"CERTIFICATES FOR GRAND REBELLION": AN EVALUATION

The little magazines created the new radical space for literary conversations and exchanges in the 1960s, but they were also short-lived (barely two decades for the two *sathottari* generations), and they have been variously judged by many writers within and outside the movement. The English little magazines have not received the same readerly attention or analysis as have the Marathi littles. In terms of the English little magazines, Nissim Ezekiel can be seen as one of the most influential poet/editors of the generation because of his seminal role in starting several magazines, little or otherwise, at the beginning of this movement as well as in his role as mentor to so many English poets of his generation and the next. *Poetry India*, more than any of his other journals, left an indelible stamp on modern Indian poetry through its publishing of some of the great poets of several Indian languages. But the younger generation of writers has had varying opinions about the older little magaziners. Kersy Katrak stated that "Arvind Krishna Mehrotra's *damn you* replaced Ezekiel's *Poetry India* as the dominant of our little magazine culture,"[76] while Lawrence Bantleman had a more forceful review of the new little magazines by Mehrotra in 1966:

> Anybody cheesed off [at] the literary establishment in India will welcome these two magazines, if only for the revolt of these students. The Illustrated-Ezekiel-Lal axis, if they are not already awake, ought to beware. If "damn you" and "ezra" do not come to produce some of the "best" of Indian writing in English, it will not be for lack of effort.[77]

However, Ezekiel's work does not seem to be as much of a rejected model as this review might suggest. Not only did it feature much of today's canon in regional languages as well as that in English, but it also paved the way for others in the following years: Ezekiel's acknowledged pupil Santan Rodrigues started the influential *Kavi* expressly in the line of *Poetry India*, and it was enthusiastically received by other younger poets as a welcome publication for poetry.

In English literary criticism of Indian poetry, Bruce King was one of the first to document the little magazines exhaustively and give them credit for their role in the making of today's canon. But besides his work, and some other brief overviews of the little magazine movement, the preface to the anthology *Another India: An Anthology of Contemporary Indian Fiction and Poetry* by Ezekiel and Meenakshi Mukherjee,[78] and Mehrotra's essays in *Partial Recall* (2012), there has not been a major evaluation of or commentary on the little magazines in English. Both Jussawalla and Mehrotra have a long-abiding interest in and a comprehensive collection of little magazines in English as well as associated literature of the time (and of course documents related to Clearing House, the small press they started in 1976). Thus Mehrotra and Jussawalla, between them, hold the archives of the little magazines, in their collections of publications and in their own work in publishing, editing, and writing that has been crucially important in the creation of the modernist canon today. As Mehrotra bemoaned this situation in a recent interview, "This is where the academic comes in, to sift through the material and make it available to a new audience. It means hunting down fugitive magazines, and it is hard work, which no one's willing to do."[79] Mehrotra rightly notes that the work of canonization and archivization has fallen onto the shoulders of the poets themselves. The poets during this period wrote reviews of each other's work, anthologized the poems of their contemporaries, and helped publish each other's work.[80] While this has sometimes been seen as "inbreeding" or the work of a closed, elite group, it cannot be denied that the English poets in Bombay (and probably other parts of India as well) kept their work afloat through their own efforts.

At the end of the 1970s and into the 1980s, in Bombay, the little magazine movement in English transitioned into small press publishing; in addition, the energy also moved outward to places like Delhi (where Meenakshi Mukherjee started *Vagartha*) and Orissa (the home of *Chandrabhaga* by Jayanta Mahapatra). The exception was *Kavi* in Bombay, resolutely kept afloat by Santan Rodrigues for several years. *Kavi* blends the rebellious attitude of *damn you* with the more conventional format of magazines in its selection of content and in its presentation. For instance, here is the editorial of the first issue of *Kavi* by

Rodrigues, which in its aggressive and defiant tone reminds the reader more of the iconoclasm of *damn you* than of the more sedate *Poetry India*. Rodrigues claims that descent openly:

> KAVI comes at a time when poetry in India survives in some occasional corner of the magazine as a "filler" or, at best, on a patronizing a "Poetry Page". Following the demise of Nissim Ezekiel's "Poetry India" there has been a vacuum which yet remains to be filled. KAVI, hopefully, will attempt just that.[81]

On the other hand, in its systematic presentation of Indian poetry in English as part of the larger landscape of Indian literatures and in its publishing a mix of reviews, essays, poems, and editorials, it seems to follow the methodical lead of Ezekiel's *Poetry India*. The magazine bravely continued despite revenue shortfalls and was one of the important little magazines in the latter part of the *sathottari* period. The English little magazines came and went in this time but without much ado; they have been largely invisible in the contexts of literary criticism.

The narrative of the life and legacy of the Marathi little magazines is different in Bombay. There were more little magazines in Marathi, a more sustained effort to archive them in public memory, and a more vigorous debate about the efficacy and usefulness of their work. To name just a few, little magazines like *Chakravarti* (volumes 2, 5, 9) and *Abakadaee* (volume 2) took stock of the movement from within; poet and editor Chandrakant Patil published a scathing comment on the little magazines as a whole in the last issue of *Vacha* (volume 6, 1969).Vijaya Rajadhyaksha wrote an essay about them in 1975 criticizing them for their directionless iconoclasm;[82] *Navakshar Darshan* (volume 5, no. 2) included a comprehensive review of the movement in 2009; and Sharankumar Limbale's anthology of Marathi literary criticism evaluates the efficacy of this movement vis-à-vis the Dalit writing movement in the 1970s. The latest anthology of little magazine literature is *Nivadak Abakadaee*, an exciting collection of the best of the little magazine/annual periodical edited by Satish Kalsekar and Arun Shevte. All of this is in addition to the considerable and detailed online archiving of the period and of the movement by Avadhoot Dongare,[83] the new bibliography of little magazines (compiled by Rafik Suraj),[84] the broad overviews of the movement in histories of modern Marathi literature, and a much larger, still unpublished study funded by the Indian Foundation for Arts (IFA) by Mangesh Narayan Kale (a study of the periodicals and the little magazines from the beginning of the twentieth century until the present). In general, the Marathi literary world has taken much greater cognizance of the movement and also showered greater criticism on the movement.

Today's younger readers of Marathi literature hold the little magazines in Marathi responsible for bringing an end to the much-respected and monumental periodical *Satyakatha*. This magazine had various stages under different editors who left their mark on the literature published there, but the period of relevance for us is the *sathottari* years. By this time, *Satyakatha* had become a one-stop publishing location for writers to gain literary acceptance and respect in the Marathi world. This was because of the publishing empire overseen by Shri Pu. Bhagwat, the editor. In addition to publishing this massive, historically significant periodical, he also oversaw the publishing of the Mauj Press and ran a weekly magazine, also called *Mauj*. Therefore, even though there were other significant periodicals in the field,[85] *Satyakatha* was seen as having a stranglehold on literary publication either in magazines or, by extension through Mauj Press, in the book business. The little magaziners rebelled against the so-called domineering editorial policy of the established journal and made this revolt the hallmark of their movement.

Satyakatha ended its long run in 1982 for multiple reasons: the lack of incoming money, the changing social and literary landscape (it could no longer retain its role as literary arbiter), and mainly because its cultural and literary standing was severely compromised by the incessant attacks by the many *sathottari* little magazines. Some of the most damaging attacks included a public burning of an issue of *Satyakatha* in 1969 and the famous and widely read critique penned by Raja Dhale, the Dalit activist/writer and one of the earliest little magaziners, titled "*Satyakathechi satyakatha*" ("The True Story of *Satyakatha*").[86] But by the time *Satyakatha* closed its doors, the little magazines that had launched these attacks had also disappeared. For instance, the little magazines started by Raja Dhale himself (*Atta*, *Chakravarti*, *Tapasi*) had long since stopped publishing any issues before *Satyakatha* ended in 1982, as did the innovative and early little magazine by Shahane (*Aso*) and the much-respected little magazine started by Nemade (*Vacha*).

Many younger Marathi writers have argued that the permeable boundary between the little magazines and *Satyakatha* blunted the rebellious edge of the otherwise revolutionary message of the little magazines. Some of the important figures in the movement—poets like Dilip Chitre and Vasant Abaji Dahake—continued to publish both in *Satyakatha*, the periodical of the establishment, and in little magazines. Younger poets of today, such as Pravin Bandekar and Mangesh Narayan Kale, rightly ask about the efficacy of the little magazines in the face of such publishing history. As Bandekar points out, the poet Dahake published in the little magazine *Trishanku* in 1971 at the same time as he published his poem "*Sarvatra pasarleli mule*" ("The scattered roots all around") in *Satyakatha*. He therefore asks, should these poets be considered "rebellious poets from the little magazine movement or progressive poets from the *Satyakatha* cohort?"[87] To the younger poets, it seemed a case of split loyalties on the part of the older poets.

Finally, there is the interrogation that comes partly from the writers and editors of the littles themselves, a question about the lack of political engagement leveled at the earliest practitioners in the movement. Dalit activists like Raja Dhale, one of the earliest creators of little magazines alongside Ashok Shahane, later moved on to the politically charged writing of the Dalit literary movement and into Dalit activism. Dhale openly accepts his literary debt to the pioneering work in the little magazines done by non-Dalit writers like Ashok Shahane, calling Shahane his "guru." However, he also criticizes this group of writers for being apolitical and not striving for social justice: "His fight was not with the system, but just with the literature of the time. His rebellion was against a handful of white-collar writers while we want to end the slavery imposed by traditional life on us."[88] Satish Kalsekar, from his Marxist perspective, voices similar disappointment with the perceived lack of activism on the part of such writers as Shahane and his cohort.[89] While the early little magazine creators like Shahane and Nemade focused on clearing the language of its cobwebs of tradition and conservatism,[90] the younger and later writers asked for a more direct involvement in the social and political world around them and found the older little magazine writers wanting in that regard.

The little magazines of the 1960s did not have a united agenda or a singular focus, and even the practitioners in retrospect regretted the lack of any overt political direction to this *sathottari* movement that burst onto the scene with such force but lasted for such a brief period of time. Several writers also look back nostalgically at the passionate energy with which the literary endeavors were undertaken and the sense of determination with which they resisted the establishment.

These contradictory reactions are brought together in an iconic poem by Bhalchandra Nemade on the *sathottari* writers, titled "*Kavi lok*" ("The Poets"):

> Like bees we came together, like bees we were dispersed
> no sooner with workmanlike drawl did we sit on our
> honeycombs
> torched by the billowing smoke we dropped off in bunches
> swarms and swarms of sacrificed bees we fell off the honeyed
> combs
> the surviving ones kept coming back drawn by each other's
> agony
> being disinherited, forced to dangle upside down again
> elsewhere on some ridge
> repeatedly beaten back we left behind with extreme zest the old
> building new homes with renewed energy
> manufacturing the wax from our own being we kept creating
> sweet hexagons
> it was our very own after all
> buzzing we came restlessly agitatedly we slept impotently calling
> out blind love
> balancing the demands of the invisible world
> holding the hope for an ambrosial dawn, hanging on
> in this complex setting whose fate was it to be the indolent male
> and whose luck to be the female?
> humming through a million mouths in the first sunrays,
> to take your life on your wing as you bring back feverishly bit by
> bit
> frivolous or deep philosophy, aestheticism or naturalism,
> homegrown or foreign
> no schools of thought were taken into account
> the certificates for grand rebellion were fake.
> What was real was the flower-rooted intoxication
> it did not matter for which queen bee it was
> this living practical daily jihad[91]

On one level, the poem can be read as a straightforward rejection of the theories of insurgence that are often put forth as a rationale for the little magazine movement. For instance, the central trope of the buzzing bees in this poem might remind one of Samuel Taylor Coleridge's dismissive account of his critics in *Biographia Literaria* (1817). There, Coleridge writes about "the present mode of conducting critical journals during his time": "Gnats, beetles, wasps, butterflies, and the whole tribe of ephemerals and insignificants, may flit in and out and between; may hum, and buzz, and jarr; may shrill their tiny pipes, and wind their puny horns, unchastised and unnoticed."[92]

Nemade's poem, while not quite as dismissive, is not flattering of the flamboyantly stated ambitions of the little magaziners: "The certificates for grand rebellion were fake," it says. And it asked the question Susan Sherman posed in 1971 of the Beat generation of literary activists: "I believe when you talk about liberation, you talk about liberation from and liberation for. What are we trying to be liberated from and what are we trying to be liberated for?"[93] Nemade's poem indicates no such common goal or purpose for the writers. Yet unlike Coleridge's damning evaluation, there is something heroic about the energetic travel and anger of the bees in Nemade's poem. In English, Mehrotra also writes similarly about his poetic agenda:

> Must pick up an axe
> reach the forest
> chop down an elder tree
>
> Move steadily on my raft
> burn myself
> at every port[94]

"Chop[ping] down an elder tree" reflects what the English and Marathi poets were attempting at the time, and the "daily jihad" of the Marathi poets is another way of describing the English poets' desire to "burn myself / at every port." As Nemade says, they were not discriminating in their rebellions: "frivolous or deep philosophy, aestheticism or naturalism, homegrown or foreign," all were part of the movement. And Nemade's "flower-rooted intoxication" indicates a youthful and abundant idealism, while the "daily jihad" shows the relentless and dynamic anger toward the establishment of these metaphoric heroic deaths. As Nemade's poem shows, this was a movement that was messy in the details, mixed in its ideals and membership, and diverse in its goals, but it ushered in a new genre at the canonical center of literature, even if it lived only for a brief period of time.

CHAPTER 2

Small Presses and Stabilizing the "Littles"

People like you keep asking me to write and leave something behind for posterity. And I tell them I make beautiful books. Isn't that enough?
—Ashok Shahane

There is both the desire to be seen but also the desire to not be mistakenly seen.
—Adil Jussawalla

The separation between little magazines and small presses that I am making in this book is an artificial differentiation. The same people who operated the little magazines also published a small number of books during this period: Ashok Shahane, who edited *Aso* (1963–65), also published Pras Prakashan[1] books; Bhalchandra Nemade, who brought out *Vacha* (1968), also started the press Vacha Prakashan in the 1970s; and Raja Dhale, the creator of various Marathi littles like *Atta* (1964), *Yeru* (1967), *Tapasi* (1968), and *Chakravarti* (1969), also founded the publishing outfit Atta Prakashan. In English, Arvind Krishna Mehrotra, the editor of the little magazines *ezra* and *damn you*, began the ezra-fakir press in the 1960s and later, in 1976, was the one of the four founding members of the now legendary Clearing House (along with Adil Jussawalla, Arun Kolatkar, and Gieve Patel); and Santan Rodrigues, the editor of the English little magazine *Kavi*, was one of three poets who started Newground Press in Bombay. The publishing chops of the small book publishers were developed in the rough and exciting contexts of little magazine production. For example, Mehrotra, the editor/publisher of *damn you* and *ezra* in Allahabad in the 1960s, brought his magazine experience to his literary collaborations in Bombay. Describing how he and Amit Rai planned to start a magazine inspired by the American little, *Fuck You/A Magazine of the Arts*, Mehrotra recalls:

> Amit's father, a publisher, had converted a part of the front verandah of his house into an office. In it, among the wooden tables and chairs, stood a Gestetner mimeographing machine, covered in dust and seldom used. We had it cleaned and learnt how to operate it. After applying ink from a large tube to the roller, we rotated the drum a few times to let the ink spread evenly. We then fastened the stencil, fed the paper and watched nervously as the sheets rolled out.[2]

Such experiments formed the foundation of future book publishing in the context of small press books. As Loss Glazier notes very simply in the American context, "Small presses are noncommercial publishing operations that publish books; little magazines are their serial counterparts."[3] This chapter both connects and separates the workings of the twinned operations of the little magazines and the small presses: the origins are the same, and the people working in them are the same, but the operation of the ventures and the structure of the products are vastly different. In that sense, they are separate even if they belong to the same literary family.

Like the transatlantic modernists, the *sathottari* Indian publishers in Bombay started their careers as writers and editors of little magazines, which defined the nature of their work throughout.[4] The independence of the small presses was linked to the rebellions of the little magazine movement, and the individuality of their books stemmed from their extremely close connections with the writers. Having already been the editor of avant-garde writers' work in the little magazines, the small press publishers were intimately conversant with the cultural and historical contexts of their own era and cultivated unique ways to read a poet's work, as well as the aesthetic and textual preferences of the given writer. Two such collaborations are discussed in detail later in the chapter: the first among Arvind Krishna Mehrotra, Adil Jussawalla, Gieve Patel, and Arun Kolatkar in English poetry (in Clearing House Press) and the second between Ashok Shahane and Arun Kolatkar in Marathi poetry (in Pras Prakashan). For the editors and publishers, being a close associate of the poets while also having a small publishing house with its traditionally noncommercial interests meant that there was less overhead, more flexibility in design, and a greater potential for textual experimentation.

A general enthusiasm for poetry flourished during the *sathottari* period, an interest that was fueled greatly by the push of little magazines that highlighted the genre in its pages. With the demise of many of the initial little magazines at the end of the 1960s and the increasing cultural visibility accorded to the poetic genre, there was a sense of excitement and the expectation of artistic success expressed in the creation of the small presses. These were presses that yearned for the independence of the little magazines but within a more semipermanent context. As the poet/publisher Melanie Silgardo states:

> Bombay at the time had a burgeoning poetry life. There were readings, and poetry groups that met, magazines like *Kavi*, publishing ventures like Clearing House. . . . Everyone was a poet, there were one-poem poets and ten-poem poets, one-volume poets and several-volume poets. Impossible to deny that there was a writing culture that was enabling.[5]

This sentiment is echoed by the poet Eunice de Souza, who was closely associated with the generation of poets that included Mehrotra and Jussawalla:

> We had some very well-attended poetry readings in the canteen area of St Xavier's College. Arun's [Kolatkar] songs which were taped were played at one of them. Santan organised readings in other colleges, as I recall, and Kamala Das held her "salons."[6]

With the quick demise of each new little magazine that had helped showcase their work, the poets struggled to find a good, relatively stable way to tap into this general interest in poetry that they had managed to generate through their own efforts.

SMALL PRESS, LONG POEM

The small press expanded the possibilities of writing for the modernist poets and allowed them to write long poetic sequences and thus extend the scope and size of their craft. The transition from the modernist lyric to the long poetic sequence is considered the impetus for the rise of the signature form of Anglo-American modernism.[7] This model of modernism can serve as a point of comparison with the *sathottari* indigenous eclecticisms in Bombay.

In Bombay, after the initial burst of the little magazines at the beginning of the *sathottari* period, there was a clear urge felt among the writers to both highlight the methodological extremism of their work and conserve the sense of literary innovation developed in their association with the little magazines. While the poets of the little magazine movement espoused a robust individualism and literary autonomy at the outset of the period, in his drafts, Kolatkar was already musing on how he was "afraid / this poem of mine has sprung a leak / history has a way of catching up with us."[8] His poems were insisting on a longer engagement with the productive physical world outside. The seemingly autonomous life of the poem could not be sustained for long, and the eventual frustration of the poets was akin to that of the American poet Jack Spicer, who only a decade earlier described his own short lyrics in memorable language:

> The poems belong nowhere. They are one night stands filled (the best of them) with their own emotions, but pointing nowhere, as meaningless as sex in a Turkish bath. It was not my anger or frustration that got in the way of my poetry but the fact that I viewed each anger and each frustration as unique—something to be converted into poetry as one would exchange foreign money.[9]

The long poem stabilized the fleeting and monumentalized the transitory in the short lyric, demonstrating the desire to hold a mirror up to sociopolitical and literary life. As Kolatkar wrote in one of his many unpublished drafts, the poet wanted "to pin [his] paper down" not merely by the "lack of wind" but by the weight of the poetic line and the poetic text.[10]

Yet in the search for weight and ballast for the poems, and in the attempt to add weight and longevity to their poems, there was also the need to avoid "tumbling into the trap of master-narrative," as Brian Mchale puts it.[11] So too with the poets of the little magazines when they moved to the small presses. As Jussawalla put it in his notes on the birth of Clearing House Press, "I would like neither preciousness nor any weighty sense of permanence to be associated with the scheme. There have to be standards, naturally, but set within the context of work being done in India."[12] These poets coveted a way to avoid the imprisoning universalization of a singular narrative, to retain the banal and the quotidian while making it also tell the larger story of the *sathottari* period. Several poets, in both English and

Marathi (Jussawalla, Kolatkar, and Chitre, among others) resorted to the poetic sequence to expand the representation of their lived experiences in poetry; others (Nemade and Oak) connected the poems in a book by having loose thematic and stylistic threads running through the individual poems.

Thus even while the poets valued the ephemerality and the unpredictability of the little magazines, they needed to do more to consolidate the initial impact of their work; the book as a unit seemed to provide that stability for them. The long poem became, in fact, an increasingly used form by some of the poets of this period, and the space available in a book housed these poems more easily than did the smaller number of pages of the little magazines. Kolatkar wrote long poems from the beginning; "The Boatride," written in 1963, was published by Mehrotra in *damn you* 6 (1968), and he also wrote the poetic sequence of *Jejuri* in the 1960s. One early example illustrates the problems faced by poets who continued to write such long works. The first appearance of any of the English *Jejuri* poems was in *Dionysus* in 1965. Because of the physical constraints of the little magazines, however, Kolatkar initially had to agree to split the long work and publish separately one poem from the *Jejuri* sequence because the editors, Abraham Benjamin and Shirish Pradhan, could not publish the complete long poem in their little magazine.[13] Publishing the entire poem in a book seemed to be the only viable solution to this problem.

However, despite the excitement from younger readers, there were not enough presses that were willing to publish the poetry books of these writers.[14] So the former editors of little magazines stepped in and became the publishers of the newly formed small presses. The small presses adapted the available technology of printing and publishing to the needs of this group of experimental writers and, through the subversion of the market structure of publishing, tried to stake a claim simultaneously for a volatile literary radicalism and a stable literary home.

In the West, the 1950s and 1960s saw a series of new printing technologies bursting their way into the market. Len Fulton describes in detail how the new technology enabled "the experimenter and his editor (often one and the same)" to be "wholly free in point of technological fact." With the advent of the larger offset machines, the smaller ones ended up in the hands of the small press editors and writers: "in 1960 some 78 per cent of little magazines were letter press-printed, 17 percent were offset; by 1969 only 31 percent were letter press, 54 percent were offset."[15] The situation was different in Bombay in terms of what was available to all, both for mass printing and for smaller, specialized publications. The letterpress was the mainstay of printing in India after independence up until the 1960s. Offset machines that were used to print textbooks or packaging material (like wrappers and cartons) had limited use because these used the much rougher zinc plates, could not be used in small quantities, and did not allow for high-resolution printing that was required for more well-designed material. The letterpress machines were slowly eased out of the larger market and replaced by the offset machines (which were faster and hence could potentially garner larger profits). However, because of the inflexibility of offset-printing, the letterpress continued to be used in such situations into the mid-1970s even as the offset machines were used by the larger publishers for mass-printing projects.

In India, the small presses and the little magazines used the letterpress technology to publish their smaller print runs and more intricately structured projects. Sujit Patwardhan, the owner of Sangam Press and the printer for all Pras Prakashan books for a long time,[16] has an interesting comparison of the *sathottari* printing technologies with those in Anglo-America:

> I remember in London in the mid-1960s many small budget literary magazines were being brought out with hybrid technology—typewriter composing (IBM golf ball typewriter or Justowriter, Varityper) with facilities for multiple fonts—small offset machines like Rataprint using thin metal and even paper-plates—all to save cost as conventional offset printing was expensive and letterpress was being phased out/had died. There was no equivalent phase of hybrid technology in India to any significant extent. People like P Lal's Writers' Workshop in Calcutta continued to print by letterpress and concentrated on special cloth binding to give their products their own USP.[17]

Today the remaining small printers all use offset printing machines with phototypesetting facilities, but in the *sathottari* years the small printers' and publishers' experience differed dramatically from that of the larger ventures: the small presses printed fewer books and had smaller profits but made the process a labor of love and excellent design through the control they exerted over the printing technology.

THE MATERIALISMS OF SMALL PRESSES

The small presses also brought to the forefront the intimate connections between the visual arts and the textual medium by affording the editors and poets much greater control in decisions about design, textual presence on the page, and the material impact of their writing. The small presses became the logical destination for the poets and editors of the little magazines who had a passionate interest in visual arts and who tried to marry the visual and textual in their work. Amit Chaudhuri writes about how the poets "poached and encroached upon the territory of the painters,"[18] but in reality this "encroachment" went both ways. Painters like Gulammohammed Sheikh and F. N. Souza published prose pieces, and the poets attempted to bring the visual dimension into the otherwise mainly intellectual approach to reading poetry. The Marathi little magazines are notable for the sketches of Raja Dhale, while English little magazines like *Tornado* can boast of illustrations by the famed modern artist Bhupen Khakhar. Dhale himself edited several Marathi little magazines and then started a small press himself, Atta Prakashan. Bhupen Khakhar, along with Gulammohammed Sheikh, started a little magazine in Baroda, *Vrishchik*, which featured a cross-genre roster of painters and writers, many of whom had close connections with Bombay, and Mehrotra, Kolatkar, and Patel, among others, appeared in *Vrishchik* in its medieval poetry issue. Much of the creative impulse of the time passed through Rampart Row in Bombay, where artists, poets, and writers exchanged ideas and artistic influences. Dilip Chitre, an artist and poet himself, maps out the geography of this area in South Bombay that was the mixed bag of artists, writers, and cosmopolitan give-and-take:

> The *Artists' Aid Fund Centre* was located on this street. . . . M. F. Hussain, K. Ara, F. N. Souza, [H. A.] Gade, S. H. Raza, V. S. Gaitonde, and many others were regulars at the Centre just diagonally across the street from the Jehangir Art Gallery. In the vicinity were the David Sassoon Library, the Army and Navy Building, the Elphinstone College, the Institute of Science, the Cowasjee Jehangir Hall, and of course the Prince of Wales Museum.[19]

Similarly, in his essay on street music in *Partial Recall*, Mehrotra states how he first heard Kolatkar read in the Gallery Chemould in Bombay,[20] where Khakhar's paintings were also being exhibited and painter Jatin Das was reading his poems. Among the Clearing House poets were two artists, Kolatkar and Patel, and each in his own way created new material and textual pathways across the disciplines of poetry and visual art. In one of the several animated letters between Jussawalla and Mehrotra from the Clearing House Papers (May 7, 1976), Jussawalla informed Mehrotra that

> Gieve is leaving tomorrow for a painters' camp in Kasauli—at Vivan's. He has taken some of your poems and mine to educate the painters. He will also get at least 40 orders for CH or be compulsorily sterilized. You can then shoot me for making a joke about compulsory sterilization. Arun can compose and sing a song at the funeral.

There was a distinct synergy between the painters and poets during this period. This collaboration is reflected in the way that many of the books published by small presses arrest the eye at the level of the page before the reader's eye grasps the textual words and goes beyond the surface of the page. Through the abandonment of accepted ways of writing (being seen and being heard), these writers were trying to pin down the present in all its disparate and complex manifestations.

One way to understand this effort is by using Jerome McGann's ideas of the linguistic code and the bibliographic code. In *The Textual Condition* (1991), he set forth a theory of the social text that has since become the center of textual studies in Anglo-American literature, "that the meaning of works committed into language is carried at the bibliographical as well as the linguistic level, and that the transmission of such works is as much a part of their meaning as anything else we can distinguish about them."[21] The text is made up of not just the linguistic code, or the words of the text, but also the paratextual elements, "typefaces, bindings, book prices, page format, and all those textual phenomena usually regarded as (at best) peripheral to the text."[22] In the *sathottari* literature in Bombay, the bibliographic code is not just an accessory to the "meaning" of the text but, in its variable exchanges with the linguistic code, is frequently constitutive of it. The texts of the small presses (and the little magazines before them) necessitate precisely this kind of a reading of their material productions because they make the work's paratextual elements a part of its semantic field through their integration of the material/visual into the textual work.

The *sathottari* poetry was written at a time when technological modernity was coming into people's lives at a faster pace than ever before; when the millworkers' unions agitated publicly for better wages and the unions, in turn, were increasingly targeted by state power; when wars were being waged against Pakistan (1962) and China (1965) to secure the country's borders; when refugees poured in from Bangladesh during the Bangladesh War of 1971; and when the Emergency years (1975–77)[23] took away people's basic political rights. Beyond the country and the region other wars were being fought (the Korean War and then the Vietnam War with the accompanying protests). In the face of such overwhelming events of the immediate and distant world, the *sathottari* poets chose to go back to the small and the basic in search of answers. They looked to the handmade and the personally crafted: initially in the little magazines and later in the relatively more stable small press publications, writers searched for a place to materialize their poetic explorations.

The nature of the production of the poets' writing, the circuits of distribution, and the reason why the small presses (and the little magazines) came into existence coexist with a personal, handcrafted, market-circumventing mode of writing in this *sathottari* literary ecosystem. In his public talk in Bombay on June 21, 2011, Ashok Shahane noted that most publishers are usually happy to deliver a writer's manuscript to the printer and consider that the end of their part of the job; the resultant books are consequently indistinguishable from each other. But, he says,

> we do not create such multiple Ganeshas out of a singular mold. In reality, the publisher needs to create a mental image of the published copy of the book in his mind first. . . . The process of getting the manuscript to the printed stage is a long chain of events. And at every stage the sharpness of the image of the book in your mind gets a little hazy. Like our printer-friend Krishna Karwar used to say, one needs to birth a book, put some of your own life into it along with the ink.[24]

Similarly, Marathi poet Lokakavi Manmohan says that his "poetry presents no copybook lines for the good sense of the capable reader . . . to trace over and over again. . . . It is very much the 'hand' of one man."[25] Allen Ginsberg offers a parallel sentiment:

> The very private nature of your activities, and some of mine, the hand activity of it—the very privacy of that activity—is what

> keeps it down to the human scale. And maintains a human tradition. And though the world has gone completely, mechanically mad and robotic so that our own efforts sometimes seem totally inundated . . . in the apolitical machine world, the continuation of a solitary love prophetic home-made, hand-done tradition is in the long run the only safe, reliable healthy media that as artists we can work with—is an old, old tradition and shouldn't be despised at all.[26]

The role of the handmade and the emphasis on materiality of the literary output of this period thus need to be studied simultaneously across the genre of poetry, the production of the little magazines, and the later emergence of the small presses and the circulation of their books in this period.

This emphasis by the presses on the corporealization of the writing act was aided by the international influence of the concrete poetry movement that molded both English and Marathi poetry of *sathottari* Bombay. The concrete poetry movement started simultaneously with Ernst Gomringer in Europe and the Noigandres groups in Brazil in 1955. They wanted to get rid of the logocentrism of poetry and reconnect poetry to a sense of performance and to the very "act of perception," and specified how each such act translated into its corresponding form: "The optic or visual poet offers the poem as a constellation in space; the kinetic poet offers it as a visual succession; the phonetic poet offers it as an auditory succession."[27] This poetry materialized the letters and words to the extent that the white space, the black marks on the page, the letters themselves, and the words coagulated and became solid; the words on the page did not allow a transparent pass-through for the reader. To quote from the pilot plan of the Noigandres group:

> concrete [poetry] communicates its own structure: structure-content. concrete poem is an object in and by itself, not an interpreter of exterior objects and/or more or less subjective feelings . . . with the concrete poem occurs the phenomenon of metacommunication: coincidence and simultaneity of verbal and non-verbal communications.[28]

The concrete poem was eagerly adapted by the Indian poets to their own literary context not only because it was revolutionary in a stark and unmistakably visual way (what can be more striking than the ultimate disruption of not only the meaning/sense of the words but the very composition of the letters that make the word?) but also because of its implications for manufacturing and craftsmanship.[29] It was a "made" product, an object crafted in the way an artisan crafts useful, everyday things, but here it was done by the mind and the hand of the writer. The concrete poem for the *sathottari* writers expressed the poem's own rejection of tradition and history in the way it lived visually on the page.

One can trace the influence of the concrete poetry movement in Bombay through the little magazines into the small press productions. These initial forays into concrete poetry and the utilization of the page—as an arena for the eye as well as the mind—were done by some of the same editors and publishers who later supported experiments with the white space of the page in their book productions. In English publications, one of the biggest proponents and practitioners of concrete poetry was Mehrotra. He published a booklet on concrete poems in 1967 and a concrete poem called "Culture and Society" in the special issue of *Vrishchik* focusing on his poetry. It appears visually like a material construction made of words on the page; the words are placed one above the other and mimic the appearance of an official monument. The larger, horizontal bottom of the structure is composed of lines that are just one vowel: aaaaaaaaaaaaa / eeeeeeeeeeeeeeeee / ooooooooooooo and so on. The layers of lines shorten to a gradual "a . . . aha . . . haaaa . . . o . . . haaaa . . . h . . . ooo . . . haaa . . . . hee" so that while visually it imposes its structure on the page, the words that make up the sounds mock that monumentality by trivializing this solidity with disrespectful and manic laughter.[30] Though not a concrete poem per se, another poem by Mehrotra in *ezra* uses some of concrete poetry's disorder to unsettle the typography and create new ways of signifying:

> the earth
> wears such a dumb
> look
> maybe in me the
> sparrows
> have stopped
> chirr   rrp   purr   U
> ping

The poem demonstrates what its words both belie and confirm at the same time. And in an irreverent fashion, this poem states what

Coleridge says at the beginning of "Dejection: An Ode": that the world outside does not match the emotions inside the poet. In the poem, Mehrotra uses an enjambed line to create tension between a melancholy finished statement ("the earth wears such a dumb look") and a new, perkier interjection ("look") that hails the reader to imagine the sparrows indicated by the poetic voice, to actually see and hear them on the twittering lines that follow. The word "look" then becomes a repository of multiple meanings and a container for creative tensions that remain unresolved. The poetic voice laments the loss of creative vision because he is unable to hear the simple, everyday sparrow in his world, while the poem itself, through the misaligned placement of words and letters, re-creates for the reader what the poet misses in his life. The livelier sentiment in "look" (as the word stands by itself and points to this materialization on the page of the sparrows that have disappeared in the poetic persona's worldview) demonstrates a complex gain-in-loss, a re-creation of dramatic irony in the poem where the reader can hear and see the lively twittering of the birds that the poetic voice declares missing. The lines and the letters show energy and sparkle while the poet himself bemoans the inner loss of joy.

The range of materializing the word and the page can run from concrete poetry's extreme of solidifying words into objects to a lighter manipulation of the page in the Marathi little magazines of this period. Manohar Oak translated e. e. cummings into Marathi in the little magazine *Rucha* (1976), and Arun Kolatkar famously unsettled the letters of his page in *Jejuri* to indicate a field of dancing fowl. But the real concretist in Marathi poetry was R. K. Joshi.[31] He edited the tenth issue of the little magazine *Rawa* (November 1972) to include several strictly concrete poems that revel in the design and structures that the letters of the Devanagari script make on the page. Along with his attempt to write poems that "cross the literary limits / of word-meanings," he also stated his philosophy of concretism in the pages of this magazine, in the poem "the abbreviated nature":

> a lot in a little the television on the wrist
> the line instead of the context
> the letter instead of the word
> half a letter instead of a letter
> such a stepping down
> in order to reach a more powerful meaning
> such poems
> like a telegraph extremely compact extremely necessary

chosen / fitting / certain
the transport of extremely swift meanings

like the headlines of advertisements, acronyms etc
the l.c.m of language
what solidifies the essence of language in the precise location
such poems[32]

One of the striking examples of such poetry is his "*Ratricha ek*" ("The One in the Night") in the little magazine *Vacha* (see figure 2.1).[33] Most conspicuous here is the literally handmade quality of the poem: it could not be printed in conventional font because of the nature of the poetic exercise, and therefore the poem appears in its handwritten form in the little magazine. Nor can the poem be read in full because the writing gradually descends into illegible scribbling as it travels down the page—this is the poem of the sleep-deprived traveler on the railway platform who can't help but fall asleep. Thus the entirety of the poem has to be imagined from some lines and words that can be deciphered:

one in the night
on the morning's platform
. . . white
the yellow bitter moon
the parting in the hair of some woman

. . . winds

let me lie beside you
. . . thighs
the sleepy footfall
. . . a mirage
such bitter traps
. . .
lovely rest

The words available for perusal seem conventional enough: bitter moon, the parting of a woman's hair, sleepy footfall, a mirage—they all recall traditional romantic verse. What differentiates this poem is the embedding of that content in a form that indicates a sloppy, careless attitude toward the content, the semiarticulate words dragging the lines behind

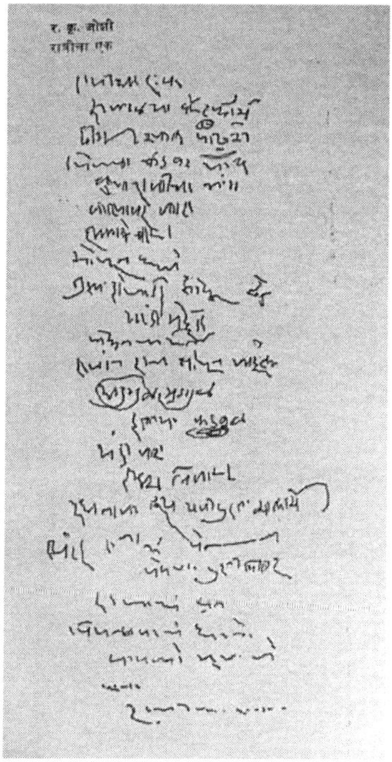

Figure 2.1. "*Ratricha Ek*" ("The One in the Night") by R. K. Joshi, in Bhalchandra Nemade's little magazine *Vacha* 3 (1968): 65. Image reproduced with permission from Mrs. R. K. Joshi.

them, the lines of the poem merging into graphic fans and curves, and all of it moving from a somewhat readable curvilinear Devanagari script to the almost-straight lines of the anti-script of the dozing passenger. The impact of this content changes because of the format of its delivery, and it now becomes something that the half-asleep man speaks as if in rote, as if from a script. The destruction of the script on the page is unraveling the scripted nature of poetry writing. What is on his mind is sleep, more than the so-called love he is professing to some woman. Or is it indeed the desire for the woman that becomes overpowered by the reality of sleep? The poem leaves the tantalizing answer unknown, and the reader is forced into repeated encounters with the mesmerizing page of this text that through its partial illegibility preserves the accidents of the hand and the elusive movements of the mind.

The freedom and the smaller size of the publishing project in little magazines and the books of small presses meant that small publishers had room to experiment with manuscript design. And because the poet was an editor and writer himself in other contexts, the book being published became a close artistic collaboration between the two. What follows is a closer look at two small presses from Bombay, one that published in English and the other in Marathi, both of which were legendary for the books they published and both of which were instrumental in creating a large part of the canon of modern poetry in English and Marathi today. They are also the two small presses that are closely linked to the publication of Arun Kolatkar's books, and the poet himself was intimately involved with the workings of both presses.

CLEARING HOUSE COLLECTIVE (1976–82): "THE SUCHMUCH PRESS"

The point of forming the Clearing House Collective is clearly articulated in the opening statement of the book published by a small press that followed it.[34] The Newground Publishing collective, started in 1978 by the then younger generation of poets (Melanie Silgardo, Raul D'Gama Rose, and Santan Rodrigues), was an attempt similar to that of the slightly earlier Clearing House Collective to find readers for the Bombay poets, and it had the support of the more senior poets from Clearing House: Arun Kolatkar designed the cover for the first book, *Three Poets*, and Adil Jussawalla wrote a striking preface to the book.[35] In it Jussawalla clearly states the purpose of the small presses and the reason why they came into existence. After noting that "the extent to which they [the poets] have relied on themselves to find their readers has gone unremarked" and listing the small ventures of the various poets, he reveals a crucial fact about modern poetry in Bombay: "the phenomenon of poets publishing themselves and other poets is not a secondary feature of Indian publishing, but the chief one. We are not and never have been poor cousins of big publishers. We have been the only means by which poetry has been kept alive while the big publishers slept."[36] Jussawalla ends the preface with a rebellious call to readers, welcoming them to the "conspiracy" of the poets. Jussawalla isolates the nub of the problem for poets in the *sathottari* years in this preface: the readers for the new poetry could be found, but the big publishers were not willing to take the risk of publishing their work.

Enter the small presses run by the poets themselves. Clearing House was one of the most distinguished of the small presses publishing in English because of the high quality of every book it published in its short life.[37] The Clearing House Collective started as a collaboration among four leading poets in the 1970s: Adil Jussawalla, Arun Kolatkar, Arvind Krishna Mehrotra, and Gieve Patel.[38] Each poet performed crucial tasks to run this project and brought with him diverse experiences in different aspects of book writing, publishing, and dissemination.[39] Three of them had previous editorial experience: Jussawalla edited the landmark Penguin anthology *New Writing in India* (1974); Mehrotra edited three little magazines (*ezra*, *fakir*, and *damn you*) and had contacts with the little magazines and small presses abroad; and Kolatkar was involved in the editing of and writing in one of the first Marathi little magazines, *Shabda* (1955), and worked with multiple English and Marathi little magazines. The poets slipped into their editorial roles with ease in the new venture.

In addition, Mehrotra had studied bookmaking and typesetting at the University of Iowa's International Writing Program in 1971–73 and had connections with the American little magazine/small press scene, where his own publications were known.[40] Jussawalla was the self-appointed custodian of the poetry of the period, mentored younger writers (Manohar Shetty fondly remembers Jussawalla reading through his manuscript), and provided the crucial space of his home in Cuffe Parade, Bombay, for storing the books of Clearing House and making it the unofficial office of the group. Kolatkar brought his experience in the advertising world and his art education to design extraordinary book covers and the eye-catching publicity for Clearing House (see figure 2.2). And Patel coedited the manuscripts for the press and created a meaningful bridge between the worlds of visual arts and poetry through his own second vocation of painting.

Each of the four poets had manuscripts of poetry books but no publisher. Therefore Jussawalla, with startup capital from his father in the amount of Rs 5,000, launched the Clearing House with the other three. They endeavored to wrest the publishing means from the big market publishers and give the poet near-complete autonomy over how his/her book was published,[41] and to make the books economically accessible to all readers and not be part of the staid classicism associated with traditional literatures: "I still insist the emphasis should be more on the service, the possibilities of new readers, discussions etc. than on publishing 'quality' poets."[42] In fact, keeping in mind their antipathy to the principle of longevity, one of the several names suggested for the collective was "Throwaway." They also envisaged a collective that had porous boundaries and would accommodate other poets, based on their willingness to put in the effort for self-publication, with no desire to become a full-fledged publishing venture at the expense of their own writing:

> I see CH as a kind of co-operative run almost exclusively by the poets who get themselves published through it at any given time. Otherwise we might as well be fulltime publishers, of a foolishly altruistic kind, helping to publish other poets, exhausting our time and energies doing so.[43]

The idea was to publish the books of the initial poets in the collective and then provide the expertise and any possible accessory help to others who would take up the huge burden of running the publishing operation themselves for their own publications. It is clear from the correspondence of Jussawalla and Mehrotra that although this was the original intention, things did not happen as they had expected and Mehrotra and Jussawalla increasingly found themselves becoming publishers when they wanted to be writers.[44]

The first four books published by the collective were by the four poets themselves: *Jejuri* (Arun Kolatkar), *Missing Person* (Adil Jussawalla), *Nine Enclosures* (Arvind Krishna Mehrotra), and *How Do You Withstand, Body* (Gieve Patel), all in 1976.[45] Kolatkar's *Jejuri* won the Commonwealth Poetry Prize in 1977 and catapulted the poet to literary fame in Bombay; Clearing House Press also gained added visibility in the process. The print run of each book was a modest 750 copies and initially they sold well. The poets advertised the set of four books at Rs 25, a sum that was extremely modest in comparison to the more expensive and ornate books brought out by Writer's Workshop Press in Calcutta by P. Lal. But

> when the time came to publish a new set of books, a new flyer with the same terms was sent out, but Clearing House found that this time there were very much fewer takers. . . . Printing further titles was only possible if a sufficient number of pre-publication offers could be sold and since they were not, Clearing House had to eventually fold up.[46]

Jussawalla worked out all the possible aspects of such a publishing project in a list:

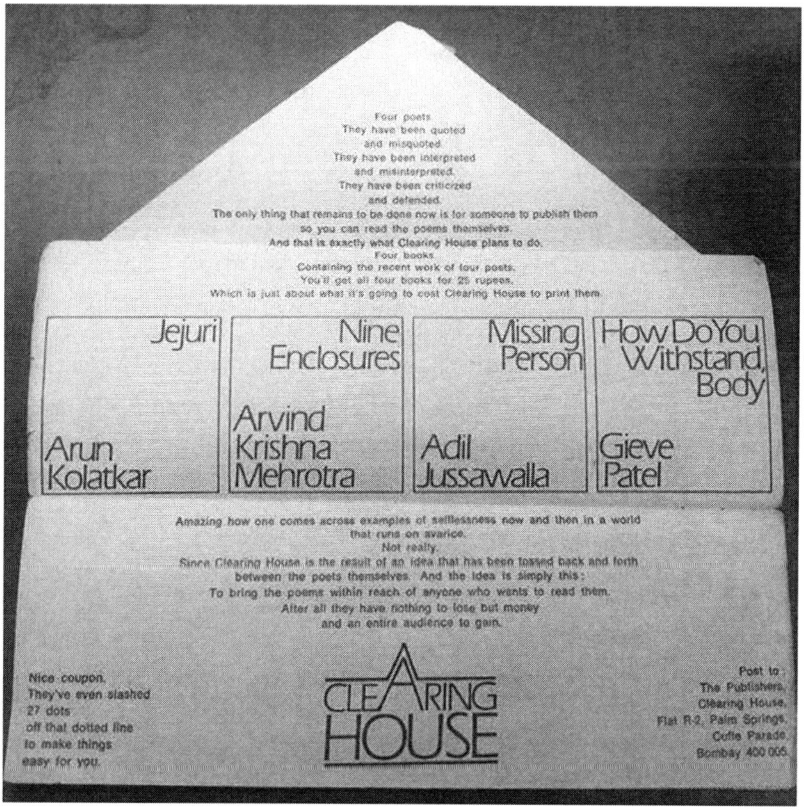

Figure 2.2. The publicity material designed by Arun Kolatkar to advertise the books soon to be published by the Clearing House Collective (with permission from Adil Jussawalla).

THE ADVANTAGES OF THE SCHEME:

A number of pamphlets of long-standing work can be published quickly and got out of the way.

The low price should help sales among students and lower middle-class readers.

The poet loses no money; profits on sales (if any) are largely his.

The poet surrenders no rights to the work. He is free to publish the same work with any other publisher. All that will be required is that the interested publisher pay a permission fee which again will largely go to the poet.

> The poet has complete control over the production of the book. If he wants professional help in designing etc. he can approach whoever he likes.
>
> Apart from his subscribers, and the sales from shops, the poet has control over who he wants the books sent to—for review, universities, etc.
>
> THE DISADVANTAGES:
>
> Attempts will be made to distribute books throughout India through the help of friends in different cities. But a thorough all-India distribution is clearly impossible right now.
>
> It will equally impossible or perhaps just difficult to get pamphlets recommended for university courses. Established publishing houses have a monopoly in this regard.
>
> For those poets for whom it matters, there is no prestige to be had by getting published in this way.[47]

The poets planned ahead meticulously and worked hard to circumvent the market and to reach the reader directly, but their model was sustainable for only a few years.

It is also remarkable to see the collegial and collaborative spirit of the poets throughout this venture; they designed, edited, and publicized each other's work selflessly and were united in their fight against the big publishers who wanted to take advantage of their fledgling operations.[48] After Kolatkar's book won the Commonwealth Poetry Prize (both Kolatkar and Mehrotra had submitted their books for consideration),[49] Jussawalla wrote to Mehrotra on August 20, 1977, stating what they reflected in their work at the collective: "A hurried note to let you know that Arun has won the Commonwealth Poetry Prize. We heard yesterday. A pity the result wasn't a tie with NE [*Nine Enclosures*] but still, one of us made it and we're all very happy."[50]

Clearing House books were extraordinarily distinct, and one important difference from traditionally printed books was their unique design. The collective used a very different aesthetic than that of the Writers' Workshop: the books were much more sparse and modern, with the now iconic square-shaped pages of small press books like those of City Lights, an abundant use of white space on the page, and unique covers crafted by Kolatkar.[51] What follows are two examples of Clearing House books that demonstrate the facility with which the editors could mold the design of the book to the poetry being published within them.

Arun Kolatkar was the "prize-winning" design expert in the group. Working at the advertising firm MCM in a magnificent pairing with Kiran Nagarkar, the two won multiple Communication Artists Guild (CAG) awards, and Kolatkar was inducted into the CAG Hall of Fame in 1988. He had the final word on designing the format and appearance of not only a book but also its marketing plan. As Adil Jussawalla set forth in his letter to Jayanta Mahapatra regarding the publishing of his book with Clearing House, "Arun doesn't like CLEARING HOUSE on the spines of our books and we generally follow his wishes on matters of design."[52] But it was also a collective effort whereby the poets could give their own input about the overall appearance of the press's books. For example, Mehrotra writes to Jussawalla,

> Adil: While you're working on the choice of paper and format I wanted to remind you that my preference is for a uniformity in these four, and also in succeeding volumes. The quality of paper might differ slightly, and this is something beyond our control, but we can certainly stick to the same size. . . . The other advantage is that it will make CH editions look straightforward and businesslike, whereas tailormade formats will make us look like one of those precious limited edition clubs.[53]

The distinctive size of the books seems to have emerged out of the principles put forth by Kolatkar. As Jussawalla wrote to Patel,

> Arun had the radical idea that no line in a poem should ever be broken. So if a manuscript had a single poem with a single line that ran over fifteen or sixteen words, the book would become longer to accommodate that.[54] The size of the Clearing House books was based on "Between Jejuri and the Railway Station", specifically the cock and hen dancing sequence. But when you look at how the poem works on the page, you see why it needed to be that way. And once that book was created to fit in that line, the others also took on that shape.[55]

In the end, this format garnered much praise from all readers and distinguished the books with their eye-catching appearance from those published by the Writers' Workshop.

Kolatkar was also responsible for the cover designs of all of the Clearing House books. The poets described what they wanted on the cover, and after reading the poems in the book Kolatkar designed the cover to fit the required vision as well as his own interpretation of the text. These designs were iconic and captured the reader's mind and eye through their apprehension of the given text's essence. One of the most arresting covers is the one for Gieve Patel's *How Do You Withstand, Body* (1976). The cover is a composite image in umber (a color requested by Patel) of the torso of a man and a kite that is striking in its multiplicity (see figure 2.3). The cover is almost completely filled with the geometrical shape of the kite, with the bamboo sticks that hold the kite taut in both directions prominently visible. The rest of the visual space of the kite is taken up by a man's torso, his two nipples in hyperrealistic effect on two sides of the kite and the chest indicated by a hint of chest hair. The bottom of the diamond shape is the man's navel, and along with the nipples on the top and the tapering shape of the kite, the image also looks like the face of some anxious creature, the nipples serving as eyes and the navel as the puckered mouth. The reader is forced to stop in his tracks and examine this amalgamated image of a man's torso, a vulnerable creature, and the upward-flying kite. Besides its arresting excellence, it raises questions about the body and its manifestations—how can a solid body fly up like a kite? Whose eyes are those, embedded in the torso, looking out with some fear? The realism of the torso and the kite clashes with the union of the two in this picture, and the surrealistic combination of the real and the imaginary infallibly points to the style of the poems within the book.

Within the book, Patel has the eponymous poem:

> How do you withstand, body,
> Destruction repeatedly
> Aimed at you? Minutes
> Seconds, like gun reports,
> Tattoo you with holes.
> Your area of five
> By one is not
> Room enough for
> The fists, the blows;
> All instruments itch
> To make a hedgehog
> Of your hide.[56]

Patel meditates here on how the human body gets beaten up in the daily routine of living, and the language of torture and violence is prefigured in the cover design. The reader is forcefully reminded of the kite-shaped torso on the cover, with the bamboo sticks that hold the kite taut now seeming like the rack on which the body is stretched and punished. In most of the poems, Patel shows the magnitude of the "five by one" body and the extent to which it still remains a mystery:

> My body constituted of organs.
> Their limits prescribed
> By me, I say I have a liver,
> A heart. Heart and liver
> Do not feel exclusively. Yet
> Before I die I should like
> To have known me each way[57]

The body is vast yet fragmented, and there seems to be little chance of grasping a sense of its wholeness, says the doctor-poet who routinely peers into the organs and the parts of that body in another poem from the book:

> Between pleasure and pain
> The subterranean splinterings;
> And then sensation
> Pitched out of the body's boundary
> To the air around! I walk today
> An integral man.
> Yet suspect I am
> Battered and ground[58]

This body is made up of materially solid organs, the body, and is grounded in that sense, and yet when the poet ponders the vast unknown of its insides, it seems nebulous and imaginary, an airy nothing to which the poet's mind gives a local habitation of a unified self and identity. The self-reflexive gaze on one's own insides as the solidity of flesh melts into air is perfectly pictured with the exposed nipples that would be eyes and that hail the reader into an interpretive act.[59] The cover of the book not only presages the thematic structure of the poems within but also adds its own layers of associations.

The second example of the brilliant design of the Clearing House books is in Mehrotra's *Distance in Statute Miles* (1982). Designed by

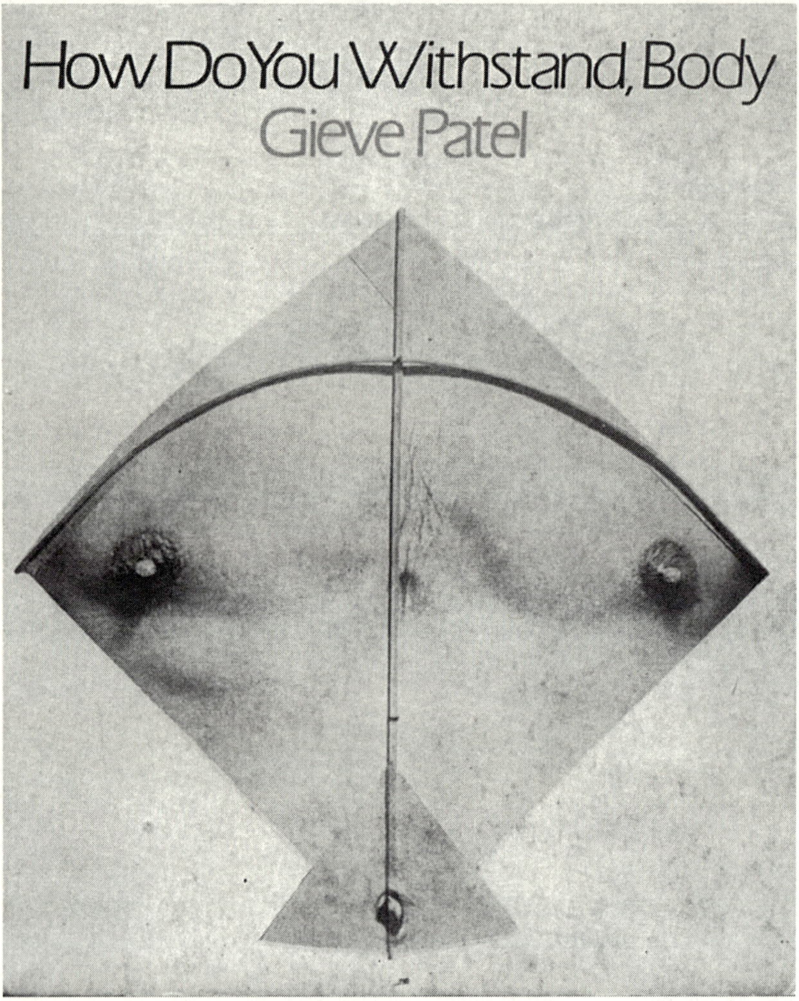

Figure 2.3. Kolatkar's cover image for Gieve Patel's book, *How Do You Withstand, Body* (Bombay: Clearing House, 1976). Image reproduced with permission from Gieve Patel.

Kolatkar, the cover of the book depicts a rising surf, a wave with white froth at the crest half engulfing the entire page. The image indicates the fluidity of all distances and the erasures of lines and borders through the rising wave that wipes out all such reckonings. As Mehrotra says:

> On maps it always takes
> The same position: away from the coastline,

> Two inches below
> The mountain range. But the man
> Who is turning the page doesn't know
> That it is flat as a blade. . . .
> It is in front of me.[60]

There is a hidden image on the cover, and it is the graphic designer's conspiracy of meaning here: the edge of the wave with the white surf also delineates a particular line, the silhouette of the bearded poet himself. In fact, once the face is seen, one cannot unsee it. But this other image, doubling with the fluid picture, demarcates the line of a profile and contradicts the first one of molten distinctions; the dualism of this holographic image suggests the complexity of measuring, delineating, and drawing boundaries that is the theme of the book in many ways.[61] The Clearing House books reveal hidden treasures of meaning at every reading, sometimes years after the initial encounter with them. This freedom to experiment with book design, the close dovetailing of the design and the contents of the book, and the experimentation with the relation between the visual and the textual are possible mostly in the small presses where the publisher was also the editor and poet himself and therefore understood the novelty of the writing act in such instances. This liberty is also possible only in projects of limited size where the small output allows the designer and poet to test new ways of engaging with the readers on the page without having the market's whim dictate the form of the writing.

Clearing House Press published only a few more books after the first four: in 1980, Dilip Chitre's *Travelling in a Cage* and Jayanta Mahapatra's *The False Start*; Mehrotra's *Distance in Statute Miles* in 1982; and H. O. Nazareth's *Lobo* in 1984. But almost every book has become part of the Indian poetry canon today (rivaled in canonicity only by the poetry books of the other big publisher, Oxford University Press and its Three Crowns series edited by R. Parthasarathy during this period).[62] Much of the canonization is due to the tireless efforts of the poets themselves to make this poetry available to readers and to the intense cooperation between them. For instance, Jussawalla remembers how he coaxed out, helped edit, and finally published Chitre's *Travelling in a Cage*. And Jussawalla and Mehrotra continued their collaboration with Kolatkar when, near the end of his life, Kolatkar decided to publish *Kala Ghoda Poems*: both Jussawalla and Mehrotra were the final readers of the manuscript before it went into print. Similarly, Mehrotra was entrusted with the responsibility of editing Kolatkar's self-translations from Marathi along with his first long poem, "The Boatride," in *The Boatride & Other Poems* (2010). This book added more than a hundred new poems to Kolatkar's English corpus and included the early songs and some important drafts of his poems. After the Clearing House publishing effort, Jussawalla went on to start his own press, Praxis, which published five books: three in 1988 (Gieve Patel's *Mister Behram*, Eunice de Souza's *Women in Dutch Painting*, and Manohar Shetty's *Borrowed Time*) and one each in 1990 and 1991 (Menka Shivdasani's *Nirvana at 10 Rupees* and Cyrus Mistry's *Doongali House, a Play in Five Acts*). Praxis ceased operations after the last book was published. Today all the Clearing House books have become collector's items because of their rarity, the excellence of their contents, and their design.

PRAS PRAKASHAN: "THE POETRY OF FRIENDS"

Ashok Shahane[63] is the founder of Pras Prakashan, the small Marathi press, and the person who has nurtured Kolatkar's publications. Seen as comparable to Lawrence Ferlinghetti (of City Lights Press in San Francisco), who oversaw the publication and the rise of the Beat writers' works, Ashok Shahane works alone, and he has published many of the *sathottari* Indian writers, most prominently Arun Kolatkar. Pras Prakashan is one of the few small presses that sprang up in the *sathottari* years to cater to the writing needs of a group of experimental writers in Bombay who would not have easily found a publisher for their work.

Other editors of little magazines in Marathi started similar small presses. The editor of *Atta*, Raja Dhale, started Atta Prakashan and published Vasant Gurjar's *Godi* (a book of poetry) and his own collection of poems *Sthitichi Kavita* (The Poetry of Circumstances). The editor of *Bharud*, Shashi Pradhan, along with some of his associates, published *Arambh*, an anthology of the poetry of ten new poets as well as *Udya Jevha Vietnam Ek Hoil* (Tomorrow When Vietnam Will Be One Again). The editor *of Akshare*, Ramesh Joshi, published Sudhir Kolatkar's poetry in book form. The editors of *Hema*, Satish Kalsekar, Pradeep Nerurkar, and Bandekar, started Sanhita Prakashan and published *Martik* (Made of Mud), a book of poetry by Chandrakant Khot, and Kalsekar's own poetry, *Indriyopanishad* (The Upanishad of the Senses).[64] *Rucha*, a little magazine edited by Ramesh Panse and Sunil Karnik, also published some poetry collections through its

Dnyan-Vidnyan Prakashan. Most of these presses closed down when the little magazines ceased operations; Shahane's Pras Prakashan resolutely stayed alive after the closing down of his little magazine, *Aso* (almost a decade earlier in 1965), despite his insistence on unconventional and non-market means of distribution and publication.[65]

Today Shahane runs Pras Prakashan from his tiny apartment in Malad, Bombay. There are books stored in all possible nooks and crannies in the space—in the living room, under the bed, under the chairs. Storage has always been a problem for Pras, as Shahane stated in an interview, and he used to lean on his friends to help him out in dire situations: "I used to live in Kandivali then and the roof of the house collapsed. Where to store the books now was a huge problem—they were scattered among friends, etc."[66] It is a one-man project most of the time; various friends (like Arun Kolatkar earlier and the dramatist/artist Vrindavan Dandavate now) lend a helping hand as needed.

In addition to publishing books by other canonical writers, Pras has published all of Arun Kolatkar's books of poems from 1977 until six years after the poet's death in 2011 (when the Marathi version of *Jejuri* became available). Shahane was Kolatkar's close friend for more than forty years and has taken upon himself the task of publishing the poet's remaining unpublished manuscripts. Kolatkar might yet appear as a prose writer as well if Shahane publishes Kolatkar's magnum opus on Balwant Bua, Kolatkar's irascible friend, which has yet to be published.[67] The book was described by Kolatkar himself as "a picaresque novel, a collection of stories, literature, biography, words of a ghati Casanova, a subaltern study, some kind of a secret history of Bombay, a one-man survey of the sexual behaviour of the citizens, and a report on the values they live by. All at the same time."[68]

The history of Pras Prakashan lies in the history of Ashok Shahane as a little magazine editor and publisher; he is frequently hailed as the father of Marathi little magazines and thus it is necessary to briefly discuss Shahane's career as a little magaziner. The story of this small publishing starts with Shahane being out of college and out of work. Penniless and living with friends in Pune, Shahane then moved to Bombay in search of work and found it at the printing press of Mohan Mudranalaya in the 1950s.

At the request of Mr. Kakatkar, the owner of the press, Shahane edited a landmark special issue of the Marathi magazine *Rahasyaranjan* on Rabindranath Tagore. The issue received glowing reviews from readers and critics, and Kakatkar, as a token of his appreciation, sponsored Shahane's new little magazine, *Atharva* (1961), which had a well-received first issue (which would sadly be the only issue because of a sudden lack of funding). Between his stints in Pune (where he went when he was out of work) and Bombay, Shahane developed a group of friends, mostly young writers who would eventually become part of the Marathi canon. Talking about literature, art, cinema, and life in these *kattas*, these young people were part of the angry rejection of the political, social, and literary solutions put forward by the older traditionalists.[69] Shahane had taught himself to read and write Bengali a decade earlier in Pune, and he visited Calcutta several times and befriended many writers there. This was also the period during which the Hungry poets in Calcutta, influenced by the Beats, walked a path of anti-tradition and created a new poetics of offense and rebellion. Shahane is the link between the modernist movement in Bengal and Marathi literature in Bombay.

In 1963 Shahane started *Aso*, which today is considered the foundational Marathi little magazine, all the while continuing to work at the printing press and gaining valuable experience in the process of printing magazines and books. In *Aso*'s final issue, Shahane included Kolatkar's untitled Marathi poem (in English it is translated as "Three Cups of Tea"), which was radical in its departure from traditional poetics. As Mehrotra points out, Kolatkar

> wrote the poem ("Three Cups of Tea") in 1960, at the beginning of the revolutionary decade that we associate with Andy Warhol's 1964 Brillo Box exhibition and the music of John Cage than with Kolatkar's poem; more with New York than with Bombay. Yet the impulse behind their works is the same, to erase the boundaries between art and ordinary speech, or art and cardboard boxes, or art and fart.[70]

However, the poem was not appreciated in Marathi literary circles then or by the printer of *Aso* at that time, Madhavrao Patwardhan, who refused to publish the final issue of the little magazine before relenting. This encounter with censorship strengthened the desire of Shahane and his friends to create an independent publishing venue that could bypass such social controls on expression, but Pras Prakashan came into being only many years later.

Editing *Aso* and the special issue of *Rahasyaranjan* brought Shahane into contact with Krishna Karwar (of the Karnataka Printing Press), and Karwar asked Shahane to join his new press (which ended its operations in the late 1970s). During this time Shahane was printing issues of *Poetry India* at Mohan Mudranalaya press where he encountered Mehrotra's powerful long poem "Bharatmata." Impressed by the new poetics of the then-emerging poet, Shahane printed a hundred offprints of the poem and gave them to Mehrotra to distribute among readers. Then came the Bangladesh struggle and Shahane became the first publisher of Allen Ginsberg's poem "September on Jessore Road," printing it as a broadside and collecting money donated by readers of that poem for the Bangladesh Aid Committee (see figure 1.5).

The first book published by Shahane and his friends was a volume of Marathi poems by Kolatkar, *Arun Kolatkarchya Kavita* (1977). But soon after, when the Karnataka press closed its doors, Shahane decided to keep the publishing of Pras Prakashan going on his own. Pras published 500 copies of the first book and the publishing expense turned out to be about Rs 20 per copy. Shahane says, "At that time, it was deemed expensive. But I don't know how, it got sold."[71] Starting with Kolatkar's books (Pras Prakashan brought out both of them in the 1970s, including the second edition of *Jejuri*, in English), Shahane also published a series of books by writers of the little magazine movement like Chitre, Nemade, Manohar Oak, and Raghu Dandavate, as well as others from Bengal.

In utter contrast to Adil Jussawalla, who meticulously documented the publishing activities of Clearing House, Shahane has no documentation of the workings of Pras Prakashan and has not even kept for himself a complete list of the books and editions of books published by Pras. In this respect, Shahane continues many practices of the little magazines in his small press publications of books, particularly the refusal to fit into any documentary structures of established literature. The initial books of Pras Prakashan were dated according to the Marathi/Sanskrit calendar, and for most non-Marathi readers, it is difficult to put them in chronological sequence. For instance, *Mayalu* by Vrindavan Dandavate, published by Pras Prakashan, is dated 1904.[72] Also, Shahane uses the unexpected Marathi word *khep* for "edition," explaining that the Marathi word is used to describe the time when a married woman returns to her mother's house to have her baby. There is a deliberate disregard of accepted forms of chronology and naming even here.[73]

Like the books of Clearing House in English, Shahane's books are valued for the rebellious nature of the literature as well as for the careful and artistic craftsmanship seen in their design and layout. A simple example of this artistic rebelliousness comes from Kolatkar's magnum opus in Marathi, *Bhijaki Vahi* (2003). The book collects women's stories from all over the world and from different spheres: journalism, legend, literature, art, and myth, among others. (For a detailed reading of the book, see chapter 6.) *Bhijaki Vahi* consists of poetic sequences on each female character, and one significant set of poems is on Cassandra, the sister of Hector and daughter of Priam in Homer's *Iliad.* Several poems in this sequence portray how she brokenheartedly demonstrates her visionary power that warns her of the impending destruction of Troy, foresight unheeded by the Trojans because of a prior curse upon Cassandra by Apollo. She therefore watches with deep horror as events unfold in front of her eyes that she is able to foretell with heartbreaking accuracy and that she is forced to watch helplessly, unable to avert the disaster.

In one of the poems on Cassandra she provides the reader with a holographic image of the Trojan city—bursting with energy and activity in front of her but buried under dead bodies in her premonition of catastrophe:

> Where you see
> paved, bustling broad roads,
> rumbling with the sounds
> of the hurtling chariots
> echoing with the booming
> hooves of horses
> there I see
> a surfeit
> of corpses
> bodies languid in death
> having lost their desire for food
> awaiting the vulture[74]

Cassandra gives another close-up of this double vision:

> where you can see the steps
> leading to the temple
> marble tiled, flying high,
> made shinier by the feet
> of women who pray daily
> that their husbands may live forever

their long tunics swishing at their feet
and sweeping the steps all hours of the day,
there I see
a disabled dog
licking blood
splattered on the marble
of my lover who came rushing
to protect me[75]

These lines paint a picture of the now and the tomorrow of the city (happy and lively now but almost immediately darkened with future death), and in her mind Cassandra can foretell with terrible precision what is going to happen soon. Each stanza contains a dual image, as if the citizens of Troy (and the reader of the poem) can entertain two possible scenarios. But on the next page, Cassandra ferociously takes away the choice and gives only one possible ending for it all:

where you see two
possibilities tumbling around
like two pebbles thrown
into a helmet
there I see only one
empty piece of armor
lying in the dust
alone[76]

The poem becomes doubly intense because of the layout of this poem on two facing pages: the left page has both visions, while the page on the right gives a singular one, representing Cassandra's foretelling of the disastrous future.

This effect[77] is further enhanced by the deft use of the white space of the page; on the left side where the city is active and full of life (the present condition of Troy), the page is full of text and has two long stanzas showing two related pictures of the scene. On the right side, which shows Cassandra's vision of the violent end of the city and its people, the two scenes collapse into one picture of gory death; the stanza that is at the bottom of an otherwise blank, white page signals visually the reduction of the multiple choices of life to the solitary end of death in the few words at the bottom. This manipulation of the reader's eye as well as mind is a signature move by Kolatkar and Shahane; they

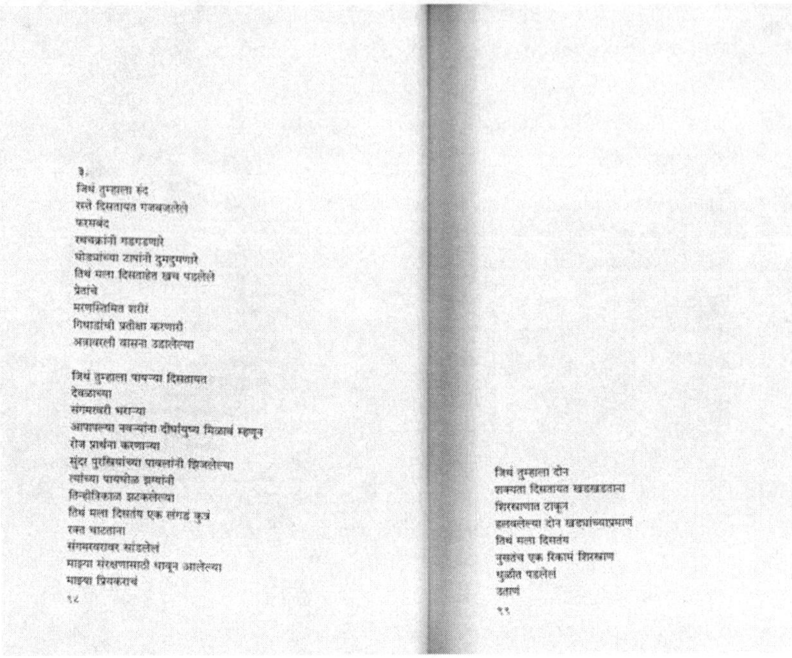

Figure 2.4. Poem 3 from the "Cassandra" sequence in *Bhijaki Vahi* (Mumbai: Pras Prakashan, 2003), 98–99. Image reproduced with permission from Soonoo Kolatkar and Ashok Shahane.

planned these pages together. Many Pras publications reveal such deft use of the bibliographic code and deserve close attention from readers for the content as well as the material format: *Majhi Kahani* (My Story, 1978) by Ustad Allauddin Khan and *Dubuk* (Plop, 2011) by Raghu Dandavate both reveal the flawless and meaningful cover designs and the matching of visual and textual content.

The spirit of rebellion remains strong in Shahane. He has published a number of texts and writers who have been seen as outside the pale of middle-class acceptability. Besides printing the work of Ginsberg, Kolatkar, and the "obscene" Bhau Padhye in *Aso*, Shahane also published the broadside of Vasant Dattratraya Gurjar's poem "*Gandhi mala bhetla*" ("I met Gandhi"), which was attacked as offensive by a fundamentalist organization, Patit Pavan Sanghatana, and challenged in court. The case is still being tried in various courts in Maharashtra as *Bombay Modern* goes into publication. In 2013, he took the formidable and well-established Marathi newspaper *Sakal* to court because of a violation of copyright laws regarding Kolatkar's poetry and won the initial case against the newspaper conglomerate against all odds, thus sensitizing the Marathi literary world to issues of copyright that were not acknowledged to the same extent before.[78] Shahane did not want monetary compensation for the violation: "The printed word is currency for me. I don't want money," said Shahane, "and by not asking for copyright [permission], they are in effect taking away our right to say no."[79] The case was eventually settled in December 2013, with the paper issuing a rare apology to the publisher and the poet.

Both Clearing House and Pras Prakashan were crucial vehicles for Arun Kolatkar's poetry, and the workings of the presses are embedded in the textual exertions of the books produced. But beyond Kolatkar, similar studies of other independent small publishers will reveal a vital cross-cultural material influence on the poetry and literature published in such venues.

CHAPTER 3

Translation and the Local Nexus of the Global in *Sathottari* Indian Literature

Dreaming in four different languages
And of continents of silence
    A man is fucked up by the nagging problem of meaning
—Dilip Chitre, "The Translator"

When Vijaya Rajadhyaksha, the noted critic of B. S. Mardhekar's poetry, asked of the *sathottari* little magazines in Marathi, "Here the question arises, why did these little magazines place so much importance on translated poetry? [Was it] because they felt Marathi poetry was meaningless?"[1] one could say she was being disingenuous about the long history of translations that permeates the chronology of Marathi writing of the entire twentieth century, or of all of modernist literature. Translations have an irrevocable relation to modernities around the globe,[2] but while "cultural form, social practices, and institutional arrangements surface in most places in the wake of modernity . . . , at each national and cultural site, those elements are put together (reticulated) in a unique and contingent formation in response to local culture and politics."[3] It is necessary to historicize the translating process, the translators themselves, and the texts they choose to transfer across languages to examine "this man [or woman], this language, this island, this background, this school, this time"[4] and see who translates, from where, in what context, and what the achieved result is. This is the narrative of how the *sathottari* writers had their own unique connection to the practice of translation and how they employed it to their own local ends in Bombay.

It is important to note that it was no easy glide across the various *sathottari* languages and cultures when the poets translated with equal fervor from Western literatures (English, French, and Latin American being the most prevalent) or from South Asian literatures (Urdu,

Bengali, Hindi, Punjabi, Marathi, English, Gujarati, and Tamil were just a few of the many). As Emily Apter states, "The term 'translation' has been compromised by its association with the metaphor of fluid borders."[5] Sometimes a facile statement of internationalism is made about the *sathottari* poets, an easy hybridity that rolls off the tongue, the pages, and the minds of the readers who assert the smooth crossing of all boundaries by the poets who apparently had a smorgasbord of international literature and only had to choose what to consume. A closer look at the material conditions and contexts of the creation of this literature instead shows frictions, resistances, and a move across boundaries that is deliberate and hard-earned, a narrative of the *sathottari* years in which translations became both a possibility and a necessity. The cosmopolitanism of the urban space and the literary cross-fertilization of the poetry of this period reflect an unequal world of international politics, local agitations, riots, and activism where, besides being a bridge across separated spaces, the presence of translation and multilingualism was also a tool of protest and a pathway to infuse new life into old forms.

The *sathottari* writers were routinely going across regional boundaries in search of a modern way of narrating the post-independent urban condition. The international boundary crossing is always mentioned, but it is notable how much transregional travel the literary texts were accomplishing through translations. It reveals the deep cosmopolitanisms of this indigenizing project of Bombay poetry in English and in Marathi, where the poets created a peculiarly unique sense of the local through such travels. That contemporaneous moment was reached through the harnessing of regional and international energies in the case of both English and Marathi *sathottari* poetry. If the English poets proceeded to find indigenous connections through their translations, the Marathi poets found transregional and international cosmopolitanisms through them.[6] In the end, even if the road leading up to the *sathottari* literary culture in Bombay might have been distinct for English and Marathi literatures, they assemble together at the meeting point of the contemporary local of the Bombay modern that they crafted together.

ENGLISH POETRY AND *POETRY INDIA*

Nissim Ezekiel is universally seen as the mentor and the earliest English poet-practitioner of the modernism associated with *sathottari* Bombay.

In his introduction to *The Oxford Anthology of Twelve Modern Indian Poets*, the editor and poet Arvind Krishna Mehrotra declares that "the origins of modern Indian poetry in English go no further back than the poets in this anthology," and the list begins with Nissim Ezekiel.[7] Gieve Patel, of the Clearing House four, states that "there is a whole trajectory of values that Nissim promoted from the 1960s to the 1980s. They changed over the years as his own poetry changed."[8] Ezekiel was a lifelong supporter of the practice of translation and an advocate of multilingualism (he helped publish translations in many print venues), and his editorial practice reveals the dense overlays of multilingual processes in what would otherwise be seen as monofocal English writing. Bruce King has traced the lifework of Ezekiel as editor and as poet in his 2001 book, *Modern Indian Poetry in English*, where he notes the various stages in Ezekiel's journey as editor of literary magazines until he started *Poetry India* in 1966, the little magazine that sutured literatures in English and the regional languages of India together in one literary space. Ezekiel was assistant editor at the *Illustrated Weekly* in Bombay before joining the Indian PEN[9] in 1955 and later starting the review *Quest* (1955–57). As King notes, *Quest* was a "general intellectual review associated with liberal democratic politics."[10] Wanting a literary space that would be devoted to the genre of poetry and that could give him the needed independence to frame it as he wished, Ezekiel started *Poetry India* in 1966.

One could say *Poetry India* was dedicated to translations and, through them, achieved its double goal (inventing a new heritage for Indian poets in English and entrenching English poetry amid the diverse regional poetries of India) in its brief life of six issues. In later years, Ezekiel said that "to be a westernized Indian through the education received, to think and feel in English and yet to relate not only to contemporary India but the whole Indian heritage is a self-conscious task which has to be systematically undertaken."[11] Ezekiel purposefully set about doing just that in *Poetry India* through its policy of specifying the languages of writing and translation in its contents. The first issue in January 1966 featured translations from Sanskrit, Marathi, Tamil, and Punjabi, as well as writing in English from India and, in a separate section titled "International," English poetry and poetry criticism from outside India. The separation between English poetry from India and that from outside the country was a clear indication of the effort to show the homegrown nature of this English verse. Furthermore, little magazines like *Poetry India* and *Kavi* broke down any separations between writing in English (in the original) and writing in translation by featuring the same poet both as the author in one issue and a translator in the next. For example, Gieve Patel appears as an English poet in the first issue of volume 1 and as a translator of the Gujarati poet Suresh Joshi in volume 1, issue 4.[12]

Even the visual ideology of the cover of the magazine (which had the table of contents printed on it) indicates the importance of translations: the language from which the poems were translated is printed in uppercase letters while the title of the poem and the name of the poet/translator are in lowercase letters. Within the pages of the magazine, translation appears in many forms: there were calls for contributions to anthologies of poetry that accepted translations into and original poetry in English (e.g., one for "An Anthology of Indian Poetry" to be edited by Howard McCord from Washington State University); there were translations published from soon-to-be-printed anthologies of translations (Chitre's translation of a Marathi poem by B. S. Mardhekar has a footnote that acknowledges the permission of the "Committee for Cultural Freedom" that commissioned the translations for an anthology of modern Marathi poetry); and there was one footnote to Ramanujan's Tamil translations, which briefly describes Sangam poetry that was part of the famous translations published by Ramanujan almost simultaneously with the magazine, in 1967, as *The Interior Landscape: The Love Poems from a Classical Tamil Anthology.*

Another important feature of *Poetry India* is the easy housing of English poetry next to poetry from other regional languages. With obvious flair, Ezekiel tried in this manner to establish the "native" element in English poetry of *sathottari* Bombay: when the original English poems of R. Parthasarathy and Gieve Patel appear next to the translations from Marathi and Tamil in English by Chitre and Ramanujan (both of whom were poets in English as well as writers in Marathi and Tamil, respectively), the reader is left with a set of poems that deliberately erased the difference between the supposed nativism of Marathi and the purported foreignness of English. Similarly, the Penguin anthology edited by Adil Jussawalla, *New Writing in India* (1974), is still considered a landmark effort for its paradoxical achievement of both discriminating literary taste and inclusivity. This anthology also included, and muddied, the difference between translations and originals by selecting well-known poets as translators and featuring them in both of their roles. For instance, several pieces of the Hindi poet Muktibodh appear in this volume, translated variously by Jussawalla and Mehrotra among others, while Mehrotra also appears in English as a poet; Kolatkar's poems are present both in the original in English and in translation from Marathi (by Chitre).

The impact of this push to indigenize English can be seen in 1976, a decade after the inception of *Poetry India*, when Santan Rodrigues, who had been mentored by Ezekiel, started a little magazine of his own called *Kavi* (The Poet), defiantly stating in the editorial of the very first issue, "KAVI is a journal of *Indian* poetry by which we mean poetry written by Indians in an Indian language, including English in which KAVI is published and into which Indian language poems will be translated."[13] This is reemphasized by the appearance of the title of the little magazine on the cover page: "Kavi" is not only a Hindi and Marathi word that graces this English magazine, but it is also visually a hybrid on the cover (the vowel sound of "ī" in the "vi" of *Kavi* is indicated by the use of the typical Devanagari ligature and vertical conjunct, thus creating a visual fusion of the Roman and Devanagari scripts). Such close examination of translations in *sathottari* writing and publishing (which presents a vibrant and energetic prospect of linguistic exchange) counters the grimmer perspective of "postcolonial" translations on the national level. M. Asaduddin notes that the "translation scene [in India] even in English was fairly desultory in the first three decades after independence." He mentions the UNESCO collection of representative works that sponsored translations but states that "the absence of any dialogue among translators about their craft and the lack of any tradition of documentation of problems encountered by individual translators meant that they worked in a kind of vacuum, depending mainly on their instincts and their own resources."[14] A study of translations in Bombay *sathottari* literature on the other hand demonstrates that this community of little magaziners, poets, and writers was invested in translations as a community, supported each other's projects, and created a new poetry and a new literature through the interconnections fostered by such translations. The linguistic travel as well as the localizing work done by Ezekiel and the *sathottari* poets is evident in the translation of the Marathi poems by B. S. Mardhekar published by the bilingual poet Dilip Chitre in the first issue of *Poetry India*. In highlighting the entangled lineages, histories of the texts, the poets, and the location, this example captures precisely the manner in which the poets tried to articulate the postnational sense of the present that lay at the crossroads of the nation and region, the local and the global, the metropolitan and the marginal. In 1966, six years after the creation of the linguistic state of Maharashtra (the result of many years of agitation, some of it violent and destructive) and the year in which the first issue of *Poetry India* was published, Bal Thackeray, the son of Prabodhan Thackeray[15] and a cartoonist at the Marathi journal *Marmik*, started an extremist political organization, the Shiv Sena, that demanded Bombay for Maharashtrians and, over the years, has whipped up xenophobic sentiments and frequent violent reprisals against various "outsiders" to Bombay and Maharashtra.[16] But

> if the right to be Maharashtrian had to be wrested by force from the federal state against the centralizing designs of Nehru (105 [people] actually did die in the course of the agitation leading to statehood), the desirability of statehood was sometimes not very obvious in the commercial and industrial metropolis of Mumbai (four million inhabitants in 1966, ten million by 1995). Maharashtrians, limited to manual labor and domestic service, carried no weight compared to Gujarati, Sindhi, and Parsi entrepreneurs, Marwari and Punjabi merchants, Tamil administrators, qualified labor from Kerala, or even in comparison to artisans and restaurant owners (Muslim and Hindu) from Andhra Pradesh and Karnataka.[17]

In an attempt to impose a monolingual worldview upon a linguistically diverse society, the Shiv Sena declared the political and geographical space of the city of Bombay as exclusively for the Marathi-speaking population in the same year that the little magazines (in Marathi and English) highlighted translation as the core of their literary agenda. In the face of a mounting social and political push toward a monolingual state identity, the little magazines thus insisted on a multilingual engagement with the world and with literature.

This is the larger backdrop for the translation of the Marathi poems of B. S. Mardhekar into English in the first issue of *Poetry India*. Mardhekar was a Marathi poet who wrote during the period of Indian independence (1947), and he brought a radically new, anglicized, and high-modernist aesthetic into Marathi poetry. Philip Engblom points out that "a Modernist 'dislocation' affected Marathi poetry considerably earlier than Indian English poetry. This is true at the very least in the sense that Mardhekar (born 1909) . . . preceded Ezekiel (born 1924) in generational terms."[18] By the time of the *sathottari* period, however, Mardhekar's work was set aside by the leading poets and editors of the day (like Ashok Shahane and Bhalchandra Nemade)[19] because it did not engage enough with the registers of the quotidian. Well aware of Shahane's stance on Mardhekar, Chitre (who was, after all, a member of their informal group of poets) nevertheless translated Mardhekar's poem into English for *Poetry India* in 1966, just three years after it was rejected by the Marathi poet rebels of the time.

Mardhekar's poetry might have seemed tired to the *sathottari* Marathi poets at that point, but the changed linguistic context of the poem (from Marathi to English) bestows a renewed radical stature to the translated poem in the transposed literary environment of *Poetry India*, specifically within the literary aesthetic furthered by Ezekiel. Regardless of the reputation of the poems in their literatures of origin, the poems in English translation get charged with an additional frisson of the other cultural world of Bombay. Mardhekar himself had effected such a transfer in his work in the previous generation when he replenished the then-Marathi literary world with the high modernism of Anglo-American literature in the 1940s and 1950s. What was old in Anglo-America became transmuted to the new and insurgent in the Marathi poetry of the 1940sand 1950s; and in 1966, in Bombay, what was considered dated by then (like Mardhekar in Marathi) became newly momentous when moved to the pages of the English little magazine *Poetry India*. The two-way transfer across English to Marathi (in Mardhekar) and then across the boundary again, from Marathi to English (in Chitre's translation), demonstrates clearly that translations became the "site[s] of interpretive communities that . . . challenge[d] current canons."[20]

Chitre's translation of Mardhekar's poem thus completes a fourfold maneuver: it declared Chitre's literary progressivism in his deliberate crossing of the linguistic border toward regional languages; it bolstered Ezekiel's own poetic project of rooting English poetry in the environs of Bombay; in its satiric demolition of traditional poetics and its status as a cross-border linguistic migrant, the translation ridiculed the monolingual political demands of the Shiv Sena; and it placed one more foundational brick in the construction of a new literary lineage for English poetry in the *sathottari* moment, creating a genealogy that rooted itself in both the Marathi literatures in Bombay and the English literatures of Anglo-America.[21] These are the dense pathways through which Ezekiel's *Poetry India* restages the social, literary, and political debates of the *sathottari* years through its translating focus.

TRANSLATION AND *BHAKTI*

The English poets faced a chorus of accusations of using the colonial tongue to write about the newly independent national life. Many anthologies of Indian poetry in English published in the second half of the twentieth century deal with the issues of the outsider status of English writing in India.[22] In fact, in his Association for Commonwealth Literature and Language Studies talk in 1986, Jussawalla illustrates how the English poets themselves were conflicted about writing in the language:

> So, in a poem, R. Parthasarathy writes of his "tongue in English chains" and of speaking "a tired language". Meena Alexander, in an essay, speaks of being "exiled by a dead script". Arvind Krishna Mehrotra, in another essay, shows the language to be honeycombed with traps, any of which the unwary writer may sink into. Keki Daruwalla sees the language he uses as an exasperating mistress. And English language and literature are subjects of attack in my poem "Missing Person," in which the colonizer himself joins in the attack, asking his creature to get back to his (own) language.[23]

Most English poets were concerned about this alien status that was foisted upon them, and they reacted by creating an individual heritage for themselves that was separate from that of the English writers in the West, an indigenous cosmopolitan lineage that spoke to their distinct position in English/Indian writing. The translations were the main method through which the *sathottari* poets constructed such a lineage that reflected their rejection of the conventional literary chronology of Tagore/Aurobindo/Sarojini Naidu and replaced it with that of "Kapilar, Paranar, Basavanna, Allama Prabhu, Kabir Tukaram, Nirala, Faiz" and "Browning, Yeats, Eliot, Pound, Auden, Williams, Stevens, Lowell, Ginsberg."[24]

A large part of that anti-tradition was the translation of the Western modernists into Marathi, which coalesced seamlessly in *sathottari* poetry with the widespread translation of the *bhakti* poets into English: "It is the coexistence of these literary lineages—medieval *bhakti* poetry and modern Euro-American poetry—and the complex interplay of translations, affiliations and languages that have fashioned literary modernism in India, at least when it comes to the linguistic traditions

(English, Hindi and Marathi)."[25] The significance of *bhakti* literature to the writing of this period, both English and Marathi, cannot be overestimated. While the term *bhakti* has a very long and complex history in religious studies (*bhakti* means "devotion" or "faith"), "*bhakti* literature" here refers only to the medieval Indian religious literature that has been seen as radically reformist of traditional caste-ridden Hinduism and that represented the anti-institutional, anti-Sanskrit, "democratic" movement in culture and literature since the beginning of the twentieth century.[26]

The *bhakti* poets, especially Tukaram for the Marathi poets, loom large in the imagination of this period: Bhalchandra Nemade wrote a book on Tukaram declaring him the singular poet to read; Kolatkar and Chitre translated the saint-poets' *abhangas*; Chitre worked his entire life on translating the enormous oeuvre of Tukaram (published in 1991 as *Says Tuka*);[27] Kolatkar asserted a direct lineage to him in his own poetry;[28] Vilas Sarang's book of literary criticism is titled *Aksharancha shram kela* (loosely translated as "The Labor of Writing"), which is a phrase from Tukaram's poetry; R. K. Joshi developed a new Tukanagari font to transcribe Tukaram's *abhangas*. Besides this focus of the Marathi poets on Tukaram's poetry, Mehrotra translated the North Indian *bhakti* poet Kabir; Gieve Patel translated the Gujarati *bhakti* saint-poet Akho; and, even outside the genre of poetry, the novelist Kiran Nagarkar, of the same generation of writers, used Mirabai, the female *bhakti*-poet from North India, as a centrally important figure in his novel *Cuckold* (2001).

The *bhakti* tradition, however, has been understood and utilized in multiple and asynchronous ways over the centuries.[29] Assessing the impact of *bhakti* is a fraught project because there are rival claims of the extent of the iconoclasm of the composite *bhakti* tradition with relation to the period of vernacularization as well as the "laicization" of religion in medieval India.[30] Scholars have shown that the *bhakti* tradition, which is related to the wave of vernacularization in medieval India, was partly in response to the advent of Islam at the same time.[31] Naregal shows that while the *bhakti* tradition worked at removing the hierarchical strata in society through the popular performance spaces where the poems spread, the texts themselves were sanctioned by those in power and therefore mediated by this relation to the center. Naregal and Deshpande also show how the tradition has been used by different people at different historical junctures to further very specific political and cultural agendas: the *bhakti* tradition was used effectively by the nationalists in their anticolonial struggle and at various times has been cast as the placeholder for the indigenous, the national, and the marginal.[32] The *sathottari* poets have yet another take on this *bhakti* tradition of many interpretations. As Chaudhuri notes, "the rejection of indigenous culture and religion, relegating them to the realm of superstition and irrationality, would be an important act on the one hand; as would, on the other, its recovery of that very culture as a life-giving, if perennially problematic, part of itself."[33] Translating the *bhakti* poets became a way of introducing folk culture (as opposed to the classical or the institutional) into the cosmopolitan poetry of the city. It represented for the poets a direct connection to the larger life of rural regions[34] and that of the impoverished sections that were not represented in the spaces of urban India's poetry.

There has been substantial scholarship (Dharwadker, Mehrotra, Patke, and Zecchini, among others) on the relation between *bhakti* poetry and its demotic manifestations in the lives of the poor, *bhakti* writing and forms of musical compositions, and the radically irreverent poetry that was at the center of Kolatkar's work. But it is also instructive to embed *bhakti* literature within the broader realm of religion as it is represented in *sathottari* poetry and to frame religion as a larger discussion of which *bhakti* forms one subset.

The poems of the *bhakti* saints are notable for their use of the vernacular, for language that connoted the anti-hegemonical struggle against the brahmin hold over religious practices. Most of the *bhakti* saint-poets were of non-brahminical caste, of vocations that ranged from potter to goldsmith to dancing girl. Being of the working class, they used the language that was used in their households and in their neighborhood in their poem-songs. What was seen as subversive and valuable by the *sathottari* poets was this particular use of the vernacular by the *bhakti* poets for disseminating religious ideas and concepts, an activity that was strictly associated with the "high" language of Sanskrit in medieval India. In thus rebelling against the traditional mode of religious expression, "it undoubtedly defied Sanskrit's monopoly in interpreting and ordering the world, and articulated the idea of the equality of all *bhaktas* [devotees]."[35] For the *sathottari* poets this was the most significant relation with their contemporary concerns: they sideline the religious search for the One that also forms part of the *bhakti* beliefs and instead look at the language and imagery of the poems by the saint-poets as their greatest contribution.

The Bombay poets asserted a right to this *bhakti* literature and its languages by accessing the revival of linguistic realism through the frank language and imagery of the everyday practices used by the saint-poets. Chitre's Tukaram, Mehrotra's Kabir, and Kolatkar's Janabai[36] and Tukaram all speak in a language that is terse, corporeal, and street-smart:

> To hell with knowledge
> To hell with wisdom
> let my feeling settle
> On the feet of Vitthal[37]
>
> To hell with decorum
> To hell with discretion
> let my mind stand still
> At the feet of Vitthal
>
> To hell with repute
> To hell with fame
> Let my mind be absorbed
> In Vitthal[38]

These translations of the *bhakti* poets repossess *bhakti* literature for contemporaneous *sathottari* realities, and through such reworkings the *sathottari* poetry creates a space for a distinctly separate social and political project in the history of the region.

It is instructive to note the difference between the poetry of the Beats like Ginsberg and that of the *sathottari* poets in their use of religious literature and beliefs. While both emphasized the corporeal, the quotidian, and the passing moment of contemporaneity, there were essential differences in the overall projects. As Susan Bassnett and André Lefèvre state in their essay, "There is always a context in which the translation takes place, always a history from which the text emerges and into which the text is transported,"[39] and these disparate contexts deserve close scrutiny.[40] For instance, Beat poets like Ginsberg consciously reverted to Eastern religions (Buddhism, Hinduism) to find recourse to what they perceived as the war-crazy, materialistic culture of the 1950s in the United States. Ginsberg uses Buddhist religious practices as a formal element to create "ecstatic language" that would bridge the chasm between the perceived world of material reality and the poet's desire for a new world. Ginsberg even chanted the "Om" in Lincoln Park, Chicago, at the Democratic Convention in 1968 and is thought to have quelled a possible riot that day.[41] On the other hand, such appropriations of religious literature in the modern Indian context would be seen not as radical politics but as a confirmation of the conservative agenda in politics and literature in the Bombay *sathottari* world: it would be understood by the readers as validating the majoritarian Hindu right-wing views on religion.

As an example, Adil Jussawalla is terrified about the desires of his dreams:

> You do not know how I fear you my dreams.
> At times I am quite terrified of you
> In case you lead me far from sinew, fibre.
> I have seen thwarted wrestlers go that way,
> Bloat themselves on transsubstantial food
> And plug Religion, while women wailed about them.[42]

Giving in to the temptation of religious belief is equated with gluttony here. Similarly, there is Gita Mehta's *Karma Cola* (1979), the book of fiction that delineates the ironic contact between the West and the East in the form of the religious Godmen who became so popular in society in the *sathottari* period:

> As the sitar wiped out the split-reed sax, and mantras began fouling the crystal clarity of rock and roll lyrics, millions of wide-eyed Americans turned their backs on all that amazing equipment and pointed at us screaming,
>
> "You guys! You've got it!"
>
> Well, talk about shabby tricks. We had been such patient wallflowers and suddenly the dance was over. Nobody wanted to shimmy. They all wanted to do the rope trick.
>
> The lines were kept open in spite of the political static.
>
> "Excuse me, operator, what did they say? What have I got?"
>
> "Hello, India, my party is saying you have the Big Zero."
>
> Mao had lost out to Maya. The revolution was dead.[43]

Mehta creates a modern voice in her Indian novel precisely by mocking the search for the mystic religious truth and the orientalizing practices of Western thought. As Vinay Dharwadker states, "Indian modernism's anti-traditionalism does not necessarily reproduce the anti-traditionalism of Europe's modernism."[44] Because religion and faith were the biggest sources of social and political divide in the country, Indian writers could be non-ironic about it in their work only by risking their connection to the world of modernity.

Instead, then, the *sathottari* poets picked up the *formal* elements of *bhakti* poetry rather than its emphasis on finding the Godly beyond. The seriousness of the religious/spiritual quest in the American Beat writers is countered in the Indian poets with an insistent search for an iconoclastic modernism that aimed to resist the religious traditionalism of Indian society. Kolatkar's real-life muse and the central character in his book *Chirimiri* (Petty Theft) is Balwant Bua, "the pimp of Vitthal," who takes 101 prostitutes to the pilgrimage of the holy temple in Pandharpur; Chitre's Tukaram speaks in a terse modernist idiom of the body; Mehrotra's Kabir employs American slang. These poets mobilize different elements from the *bhakti* repository and thus approach religious writing from an angular position. Therefore, despite the intertextuality of the writing of the *sathottari* poets and the Beat generation of writers, the indigenous modernisms they create are uniquely different. The *bhakti* poetry enabled the *sathottari* poets to set their stake in both worlds, that of folk traditions as well as countercultural linguistic innovations. The filiation to *bhakti* poetry roots their work in local worlds and it provides a fruitful lineage of indigenous contexts to both Marathi and English poetry.

Religion might have differing valence in the *sathottari* poets and the Beats, but the alchemy of the colloquial can equally be seen as the product of Beat literary influence as of the *bhakti* poets. The Beats espoused a local, small, handmade, and language-based poetry that challenged the elitist housing of poetry in the ivory tower of the arts and brought it into the filth and messiness of everyday life. The clutter of that life can be seen in the long lines of Ginsberg's "Howl" and in their shocking use of so-called obscenities, as well as in the frank depiction of sexuality that changed the face of writing in the United States and around the world. Ginsberg's visit to India, along with his fellow Beats, gave a dramatic boost to the burgeoning interest in their work in Bombay. They were most visible on the landscape of Bengali modern poetry, where they had close personal associations with the Hungry poets,[45] but their presence can be seen everywhere: in the translations in Marathi little magazines (such as Kolatkar's 1963 translation of Ginsberg's "Kaddish" in *Aso*) and in English little magazines (see Mehrotra's invocation of Ginsberg's "Howl" on the back cover of *ezra* where Mehrotra advertises his other little magazine, *damn you*):

> damn you/a mag of the arts
> the only platform offered by a bitched up society
> from where you can really
> HOWL

It is not coincidental that Allen De Loach, integral to the Beat movement in the United States, published both Kolatkar and Mehrotra, along with other poets, in volume 10 of *Intrepid* in 1968, an issue that was devoted to Indian poetry. Beat poetics provided liberation from literary proprieties regarding poetic language, and the *sathottari* period demonstrates a burst of writing that is sexually frank and unblinking in the representation of the harsh reality of urban life, a frankness that has its source in both the forthrightness of *bhakti* saint-poets and the anarchic Beat poets.

TRANSLATION AND THE MARATHI LITTLE MAGAZINES

There are many points of overlap between the formal, thematic, and literary concerns of the English poets and the Marathi poets of Bombay, but in the case of the Marathi poets, there is a more direct correlation between the creation of the state of Maharashtra in 1960 and the literary standpoint of the Marathi little magazines. The carving out of the linguistically structured state of Maharashtra (and the creation of Bombay as the state capital) happened simultaneously with the advent of the little magazines and their rebellious worldview. Gyan Prakash writes about the background of the creation of the Maharashtra state in *Mumbai Fables*:

> The Bombay State, which emerged from the colonial Bombay Presidency and included Gujarat and the Deccan princely states, was multilingual. While Marathi people constituted 44 percent of the population, Gujarati and Kannada speakers accounted for 32 and 12 percent, respectively. Creating a single state for Marathi speakers, who had never been historically unified, meant dealing with their scattered distribution and the multilingual nature of the Bombay State.[46]

This agitation was bisected by the related demand for a Marathi Bombay city (throughout the protracted negotiations of the late 1950s, there were proposals to keep the multilingual Bombay city separate from the proposed Marathi state of Maharashtra).[47] The demand for political and social monolinguality was momentous for the people of Bombay and of the state because this movement to make Maharashtra a predominantly Marathi state affected both the Marathi and the non-Marathi population: everyone had to change their conception of who they were and how they related to the society around them.

The movement was spearheaded by a motley group of leaders ranging from members of the Communist Party to those of the future Marathi right wing: S. N. Dange, Acharya Atre, S. M. Joshi, M. R. Dandavate, and, later, Keshav Sitaram Thackeray. Although the leaders of the Samyukta Maharashtra, "the unified Maharashtra" as the movement came to be called, had various political ideologies, they advocated for a singular Marathi identity for the Marathi-speaking population, which they wanted to materialize and represent in a new political state. There were repeated agitations in support of the idea of a linguistic state throughout the latter half of the 1950s, including a public bonfire (to burn the directive of the state) on the Chowpatty beach of the government, which reportedly did not award the city of Bombay to the proposed new state of Maharashtra; a strike by 600,000 workers in November 1955; and, as a result of the street violence, a death toll that reached as high as 100.[48]

Even as this movement was fighting its battles in the street, there were little magazines like *Shabda* (in Marathi, edited by Ramesh Samarth, Chitre, and Kolatkar among others, 1955) and *Quest* (in English, edited by Nissim Ezekiel, 1954–57) that attempted to ignite a new poetics in Bombay. As Sudipta Kaviraj notes, "Linguistic identity is not formed by the simple objective fact of some people having a common language; it lies in a more deliberate choice to see this fact as the essential criterion of their identity."[49] While the agitators of the Samyukta Maharashtra movement chose the monolingual Marathi identity as their own, the poets of the little magazine movement refused such categorization and showed their opposition to such delimitations through their translations. As Emily Apter states, we need to treat translation "as a set of performative and politically volatile interactions that happen at checkpoints."[50]

To take just a few examples of such translations, the little magazine *Aso* (1963–65), in its second issue, had Hindi poetry in Hindi,

Bengali poetry in Marathi translation, and English poetry by Peter Orlovsky and a letter in English about poetry writing by Allen Ginsberg. The magazine was also known for its excellent translations of Bengali poetry by the editor, Ashok Shahane. The little magazine *Atta* (1964) featured different languages on the cover of different issues: Punjabi, Sanskrit, Urdu, and English. Another little magazine, *Chakravarti* (1969), published several Hindi translations plus a bibliography of Hindi little magazines. And alongside interviews of the founders of the Marathi little magazine sphere, *Abakadaee* (1969–72) printed a bibliography of little magazines in Marathi as well as in Hindi, Gujarati, Telugu, and other Indian languages. This trend continued right to the end of the little magazine period: in its July 11, 1979, issue, *Rucha* presented a contents page that had "Today's Urdu poetry" on the left side and "Contemporary Marathi literature" on the right. Clearly the intention was to force a comparative lens on the writings that looked across and beyond the regional/parochial boundaries.

It was not just intraregional translation and multilingualism on defiant display in the *sathottari* little magazines. The Marathi little magazines also translated with equal fervor from international literature. *Aso* published translations of Ginsberg's English poetry (by Kolatkar) in Marathi. *Vacha* (1968) published translations (by Chitre) from French of Stéphane Mallarmé's poems. And in various spaces, Marathi poets like Tulsi Parab, Manohar Oak, and Satish Kalsekar translated Paul Celan, Cesar Vallejo, and Rafael Alberti, among many others. The unfolding to the outside that characterizes Marathi poetry in this period is an expansion to other regions in India as well as to countries worldwide.[51]

In the context of the struggle for a unified Maharashtra, the two wars with Pakistan (especially the Bangladesh War of 1971), the opening up of the book market,[52] the sudden availability of radical foreign literature, and the push toward multilingual engagement fostered by the Sahitya Akademi created a juncture in Bombay that could not be bridged by the regional/parochial "local" formed by the Samyukta Maharashtra movement, the national "local," with its push toward unity in diversity that was the project of the Central Government of India, or the facile "global" usually seen as the internationalizing of Indian writing. It is the selective emplacement of the Marathi writing at the intersection of all of these trajectories that needs to be acknowledged.

Arun Kolatkar has a deceptively simple poem in *Jejuri* that can serve as an image for the work of translations:

That's no doorstep.
It's a pillar on its side.
Yes,
that's what it is.[53]

The alienated traveler to the temple town of Jejuri pauses at what seems like the threshold to some space and looks closely. He realizes that it is the ruin of a temple, a pillar fallen down that is acting as a doorstep. Translation makes possible the movement across spaces and languages by creating that contact zone of the fallen pillar of the traditional/old and delineating a new threshold where none was before. These are the contact zones, as Susan Friedman points out, that generate transgressive border thinking. The translations published in the little magazines should be seen as functioning at an angle to both the monolingualism propagated by the Samyukta Maharashtra movement and the nationalism of the state-backed translation project. Featured within the format of little magazines that attempted to reject all institutionalized perspectives, these translations helped deconstruct unitary spaces of both regionalism and nationalism.

I want to end this section with a personal encounter related to this discussion of the little magazines and the creation of a vernacular local. Starting in 1979, the dying days of the little magazine movement in Marathi, a little magazine appeared in Pune, created by the students of Fergusson College, called *Katta*. This "unperiodical" *Katta* emerged as a rebuke to an established weekly journal, *Swarajya* (Self-rule), that published very poor jokes contributed by the readers. The cover of the first issue of *Katta* sports an epigraph in Sanskrit, a children's lyric in Marathi, and, in the center of the cover, the statement of the cost of the magazine (see figure 3.1). It reads in Marathi: "Price of issue: the equivalent of one Wills Packet of cigarettes (that is, 30 paise)." This is followed by a "note" in Gujarati (which is also translated in Marathi in the same line). The Gujarati line, with incorrect grammar, reads: "*sigaret piniye arogyana ghatak chhe*" ("It is dangerous to your health to smoke cigarettes"); the line ends in the typical Gujarati verb "is," which is pronounced as "*chhe*." The Marathi translation of this reads: "*sigaret odhane arogyala ghatak? chhe*"("Cigarette smoking injurious to heath? Is not!"). This is a play on the Gujarati verb "*chhe*" or "is" that is also used here at the end of the line—only in Marathi, the same sound means "what nonsense." The magazine is seemingly foregrounding the national project of unifying languages through translation by

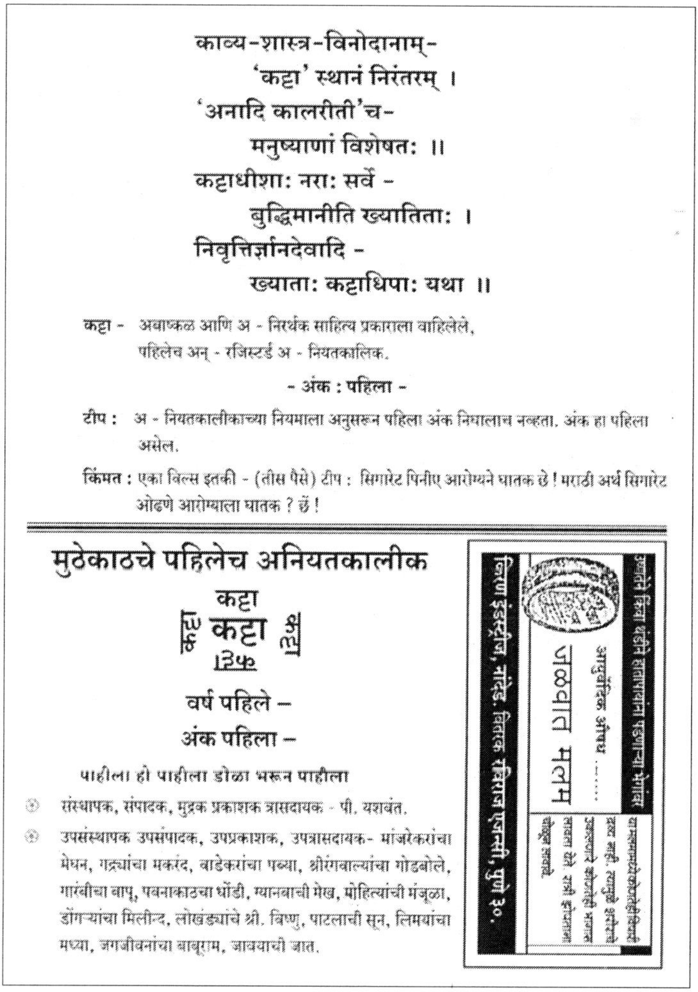

काव्य-शास्त्र-विनोदानाम्-
'कट्टा' स्थानं निरंतरम् ।
'अनादि कालरीती'च-
मनुष्याणां विशेषत: ।।
कट्टाधीशा: नरा: सर्वे -
बुद्धिमानीति ख्यातिता: ।
निवृत्तिर्ज्ञानदेवादि -
ख्याता: कट्टाधिपा: यथा ।।

कट्टा - अबाष्कळ आणि अ - निरर्थक साहित्य प्रकाराला वाहिलेले,
पहिलेच अन् - रजिस्टर्ड अ - नियतकालिक.

- अंक : पहिला -

टीप : अ - नियतकालीकाच्या नियमाला अनुसरून पहिला अंक निघालाच नव्हता. अंक हा पहिला असेल.

किंमत : एका विल्स इतकी - (तीस पैसे) टीप : सिगारेट पिनीए आरोग्यने घातक छे ! मराठी अर्थ सिगारेट ओढणे आरोग्याला घातक ? छें !

मुठेकाठचे पहिलेच अनियतकालीक

कट्टा

कट्टा

वर्ष पहिले –

अंक पहिला –

पाहीला हो पाहीला डोळा भरून पाहीला

संस्थापक, संपादक, मुद्रक प्रकाशक त्रासदायक - पी. यशवंत.

उपसंस्थापक उपसंपादक, उपप्रकाशक, उपत्रासदायक- मांजरेकरांचा मेघन, गद्र्यांचा मकरंद, वाडेकरांचा पब्या, श्रीरंगवाल्यांचा गोडबोले, गारंवीचा बापू, पवनाकाठचा धोंडी, घ्यानबाची मेख, मोहित्यांची मंजूळा, डोंगऱ्यांचा मिलीन्द, लोखंड्यांचे श्री. विष्णु, पाटलाची सून, लिमयांचा मध्या, जगजीवनांचा बाबूराम, जावयाची जात.

जळवात मलम

आयुर्वेदिक औषध ......

Figure 3.1 Cover page of the little magazine from Fergusson College, Pune, *Katta*. Image reproduced with permission from Dhananjay Paranjape.

showcasing multiple languages on its very cover; it can also be seen as giving the lie to the Marathi-only projects of political outfits like the Shiv Sena at the time. But the Gujarati "is" becomes the Marathi "is not" on the magazine cover even as both share equal space on the page. This confounding and confounded sense of the vernacular local is the new result of the translating project of the little magazines, which itself deserves further inquiry.

Such transitory publications can be found today in the possession of the very people who started these magazines in most cases. The small publishers (of magazines as well as books) themselves function as the local archiving agents of these ephemeral publications and of the translations within them just as the Sahitya Akademi was engaged in archiving the nationally visible, institutional literatures. These archives of the little magazines and books from the small presses reveal a more nuanced and somewhat different glimpse of that moment. To quote Karuna Mantena from a different context, "This is an alternative way to think about the distinctive nature of 'Indian reality,' namely through the forms of contestation specific to Indian democracy, rather than by recourse either to a continuous Indic tradition or the cultural projects of high nationalism."[54] Featured within the format of little magazines and coterie books in English and Marathi that attempted to reject all institutionalized perspectives, the translations helped simultaneously deconstruct unitary spaces of regionalism, nationalism, and cosmopolitanism.

TRANSLATION AND LOCATING THE NATION

The presence of repeated and multiple translations in post-independent India during the *sathottari* period is largely due to the constitutional backing of the project by the nation's leading institution of literature and languages, the Sahitya Akademi. The Sahitya Akademi was formally instituted in 1954 and actively encouraged translations across the Indian languages and into English as part of this nationwide effort. The Sahitya Akademi was modeled on the idea of the academy of letters in Europe, and the Akademi was also projected as the support as well as the monitor of the world of letters within India. However, India had fourteen officially recognized languages in its constitution in 1954 (many more were added later on), and the Akademi was also entrusted with the task of supporting the literary and linguistic project of unification amid the proliferation of separate linguistic identities. Therefore the Akademi commissioned histories of these languages, bibliographies of literature within each vernacular region, and monographs on writers from all fourteen languages. Most important, the Akademi's proposal included state support for translations across the Indian languages.[55]

Prime Minister Jawaharlal Nehru, the first prime minister of independent India and the first president of the newly formed institution of letters, states the fundament on which the Akademi was based in his foreword to the *History of Bengali Literature*:

> One of the principal functions of the Sahitya Akademi is to encourage all these great languages of India and to bring them closer to each other. Their roots and inspirations have been much the same and the mental climate in which they have grown up is similar. . . . It may, therefore, be said that each of these languages is not merely the language of a part of India, but is essentially a language of India, representing the thought and culture and development of this country in its manifold forms.[56]

In the first three decades of its existence, the Akademi published 284 translations of works by Indian writers and 159 translations of books by non-Indian writers. The support and the encouragement provided by the Akademi created a network that made more intraregional linguistic and literary contact possible through its various bibliographies, histories of languages and literatures, and monographs on individual writers from around the country.

The *sathottari* poetry in Bombay, in the translations as well as in the English and Marathi poetry, has a curious relation to this nationalistic push by the Sahitya Akademi to actualize Nehru's call for "unity in diversity."[57] Much of the literature of this period rejects the patriotism that becomes part of such a nationalist push; most of the major poets are bitterly critical of the society that they live in and the political realities of post-1947 India. And yet there is still an intermittent engagement with the idea of the nation even in the rejection of what it has become. For example, we see the presence of the prime minister in two different literary spaces. Nehru's presence was visible in the Sahitya Akademi publications exhorting Indian writers to rise above local differences, but he also can be seen in the Marathi little magazine *Aso*, which published a translation of Gopalakrishna Adiga's Kannada poem "*Nehru Nivruttaraguvudilla*" ("Nehru Will Not Retire") by A. R. Nadig. This poem openly satirizes the first prime minister's love of power and the use of humbug in his speeches: "the eternal youth who refuses to leave the stage even after the curtain has fallen."[58] In fact, the translations need to be understood within the "contextual codes" established by the rest of the translated and untranslated poetry of this period that appeared in the little magazines. The translations share the textual environment and the associated meanings of their surrounding texts.[59] In 1989, Arun Kolatkar dismissed the obsession with "Indianness," saying, "What makes you Indian should really take care of itself. It is an evolving concept."[60] Amit Chaudhuri develops this further, saying that "those who write in the languages of India, whether that happens to be English or one of the modern 'vernaculars', do not necessarily write about 'India' or a national narrative (that narrative, anyway, wasn't present in any clear way before Independence), but about cultures and localities that are both situated in, and disperse the idea of, the nation. . . . they extend our idea of what 'Indianness' is, while opening that idea to question."[61]

The textual contexts of the translations of this period were not nationalist even if they engaged with the concept of the nation. On the surface, there is ample evidence of such national connections: in 1966–67, Nissim Ezekiel called his little magazine of translations *Poetry India* (how much more patriotic can a title be?), a magazine that nevertheless published Mehrotra's equally nation-referencing and nation-subverting poem, "Bharatmata," in the sixth and last issue in 1967. This poem is a bow to Eliot's "Wasteland," as well as a loud call for change from Eliotic literary adherence to a more Ginsbergian aesthetic (as can be seen in Mehrotra's own little magazines, *ezra* and *damn you*). After the mock address to the new nation (which is in caps in the original), Mehrotra excoriates the smugness of the ruling class and the complacence of the institutionalized, debunking the dream of hope and change in the newly minted, independent India:

> O BHARATMATA
> O SOCIALIST MOTHER INDIA
> O BRIGHT STAR
> O LAND OF THE PEACOCK AND THE LION
> LAND OF THE BRAMHAPUTRA AND THE HIMALAYA
>   OF THE BRAVE JAWAHAR
>   OF THE MIGHTY GANDHI
> HOMAGE TO THEE
>
> India my beloved country, my motherland
> you are in the world's slum, the lavatory . . . [62]

The juxtaposition of the capital letters that mark the victorious, self-satisfied patriotic celebration of the nation and the small-lettered jolt of reality that shows the disappointment of the common man is also reiterated in the false romanticism of the diction in the first part ("bright star," "land of the peacock and the lion") versus the hard reality of its poverty and the dispossession of its millions ("the world's slum," "the lavatory"). The ending of the poem is even more brutal:

> then i am once again ready to hold
> the Indian by his armpit
> to bite into his adamsapple
> to tug in my teeth the hair on his chest
> to lick round his navel
> to enter his bowels
> to deurinate him completely
> to violently wrench his penis off
> and use it for a pen
> to write these prayers
> jai hind
> jai jawan
> jai kisan
> jai bharatmata[63]

The poem has the invocation to the nation as the shell of the poem; the address to "Bharatmata" opens and closes the text and within is a violent, disturbed, and disturbing rending of the nation's body.[64]

The rejection of the patriotic chronicle of the nation went further: there was a dismissal of the grand narrative in favor of the smaller, both in size (the fragment) as well as the marginal (that is, life on the street). The registers of everyday living made a noticeable appearance in all of the literature of this period (including the translations by the *sathottari* writers), and the contrast between what translations received state support and which translations were favored by the writers of the little magazine movement might hold the key to the difference between the national and the postnational of the little magazines. The foreign translations published by Sahitya Akademi were canonical texts, age-old classics. Among them were Al-Biruni's *Kitab al-hind* and *One Thousand and One Nights* (Arabic); from English, Milton's *Aeropagitica*, Whitman's *Leaves of Grass*, and Thoreau's *Walden*; Goethe's *Faust* from German; the works of Confucius and Lao Tze from Chinese; and Machiavelli's *The Prince* from Italian. On the other hand, the international authors and texts that the Bombay poets read and translated were more current in the West in the 1950s and 1960s and were regarded as more subversive in their own social/national spaces as well; this exposure came through the opening up of the book trade and the easing of global travel. While the Sahitya Akademi published Milton and Shakespeare in translation, the little magazines in Marathi published translations of Paul Celan (by Tulsi Parab); Stephen Mallarmé (by Dilip Chitre); e. e. cummings, Cesar Vallejo, and Luis Carlos Lopez (by Manohar Oak); and Allen Ginsberg (by Arun Kolatkar).

Even when the poets did translate the widely accepted works (like the *bhakti* poets, translated by Mehrotra, Chitre, and Kolatkar, among others), it is the anti-establishment stance that is the common factor: the language that was employed in the translations was radically disruptive of the canonical expectations of the text so that the translating act represented rebellion even in the midst of popular or institutional backing. For example, the hard sarcasm of Mehrotra's afternote to his Kabir translations (first published in the little magazine *Vrishchik*) explains the drastic departures of the register from the traditional language used in such situations. Mehrotra published the Kabir translations as a book only in 2011, but he had been perfecting them over the previous five decades:

> I hope there's a scholar/reviewer who is already snooping around these recastings, smacking his lips, all set for the kill. I hope someone rushes excitedly to Kabir's oeuvre and comes back with the headline: THESE DAMN THINGS DON'T EXIST THERE. In all probability they don't. Yet. Between Kabir and me stand five centuries, and any number of vulgar translations of his poetry—mainly Tagore's and Banke Bihari's. All these had to be melted, purified, and cast again. So Kabir begins living in the nineteen seventies, I in the fourteen hundreds.[65]

The mutinous juxtaposing of a popular Americanese with poetry that is part of the religious traditions of India reworks given wisdom regarding these texts and makes the poems converse with the contemporary global nexus of the Bombay local.

This literature thus engages with the nation at various points but refuses to be defined by this concern and provides the tangent on the artificially constructed linear "nation-to-globalisation narrative";[66] it is the "postnational" that is defined by Nivedita Menon. In the case of the translational *sathottari* culture, it is possible to think in binaries and interpret the international connections of translations as the Parisian glory of modernism that has shed any connection to national concerns, or the intraregional "Indian" translations as certification of a new nativism that draws black-and-white lines between inside and outside. The work of these translations does not "lin[e] up with narratives of triumphant post-nationalism rendering national borders obsolete," but neither do they "[retreat] to a reconstituted national space in the face of this triumphalism."[67] The translations were shared, written, and published in informal spaces and practices (*kattas*) that burrow under the large ideas of national communities in their relative invisibility while the translations themselves fly in from beyond regional and national boundaries. There is a refusal to vacate the location of their material existence even as there is intense interrogation of all aspects of that space and that existence.

TRANSLATING THE *SATHOTTARI* MOMENT

Common literary wisdom states that Marathi literature hybridized in the *sathottari* period when it accepted literary and artistic influences from Anglo-America and Europe. But here is an example that shows how a Marathi and English *sathottari* contemporaneity was evidenced on an unlikely stage in Naropa, Colorado, in May 1986.

Rejecting the national perspective as well as the monolingual directive, the unaccommodatingly bilingual Kolatkar (along with other Hindi poets) performed the *sathottari* contemporaneity of Bombay in front of an American audience of the Beat poets and other poetry lovers at the Jack Kerouac School of Disembodied Poetics at Naropa, Colorado, on May 20, 1986. The Indian poets read their poems in their regional languages—Kedarnath Singh and Ashok Vajpeyi read their poems in Hindi and Arun Kolatkar read his work in Marathi. The poems were simultaneously translated onstage into English for the American audience. Each poet read several of his poems, and it is worth noting the sequence of the poems with which Kolatkar chose to end his reading: the last three "Marathi" poems were "Three Cups of Tea," one of the "hospital" poems, and "Fire." In fact, "Three Cups of Tea" is not Marathi at all but really in Bombaiyya Hindi and, along with extremely rough language of the street, has the notorious contra-patriotic statement "prickface i said / what's there in india."[68]

The last three poems increasingly up the ante against the national story. The second poem was part of the set of hospital poems from his 1977 Marathi anthology, *Arun Kolatkarchya Kavita*, where the poetic persona is a recovering patient in a hospital room. Describing the intense feeling of impotence and meaninglessness that pervades the patient, the poem notes the presence of the patient's brother interested in the cricket match being played between India and New Zealand at the time. When the brother comes rushing in at the end of the poem declaring that India has beaten New Zealand in the cricket test match, the poet says in the very next line: "i feel like i want to pee."[69] Not only is the national obsession *not* interesting to the poet but he actively juxtaposes it with a scatological image to demonstrate his disdain of the seeming momentousness of such narratives. And the final poem of the reading, "Fire," asks for a bonfire that will engulf the colonial and national monuments of Bombay like the Gateway of India. The fire can also be seen as a reference to the violent agitations that engulfed the city just before the monolinguistic state of Maharashtra was formed:

> you are hearth   neighboring fire
> scatter the city   make them wait
> rajabhai tower the gateway the taj the majestic hotel churchgate
>   station
> the town hall   the victoria terminus   the regal the eros,
> detached   immobile
> keep burning please   for my sake
> keep me warm   terrify this city[70]

There on the stage was a poet who made both Marathi and English visible side by side as well as the process of translation between the two. And the map of Bombay (Rajabhai tower, the Gateway of India, the Taj Hotel, the Majestic Hotel, Churchgate Station, the town hall, the Victoria Terminus, Regal Cinema, the Eros) appears in the context of his representation as an "Indian poet" in the United States at that moment and also gets erased by the fire in the poem that burns all of the city.

"The everyday [always] escapes," according to Maurice Blanchot,[71] and translations and multilingual writing practices were an attempt to capture that elusive essence of the ordinary in *sathottari* literature. Translation captures the double bind of this moment: the rejection of the past in so many ways yet the embrace of the *bhakti* poets, the rejection of authorized narratives in the social, literary, and political world coupled with the desire to impact these same worlds in a decisive and lasting manner, the look internationally as well as internally. Through the reconstitution of the context of interpretation and unsettling the originary immovability of the text, "we are exploring the undefined possibilities of verbalization, which are also undefined limitations. Translations tell us what we would otherwise not know; they make us question everything we might have thought we knew."[72]

This was a time when multiple contradictions elbowed each other to structure the world of *sathottari* Bombay: a reluctantly masculinist movement that was very sympathetic to several women writers, a multilingual opposition to the parochialism of the time, a window into the invisible regions of India as well as an opening to the larger global presence, a movement that was anti-authority and anarchist in many ways that is surely becoming the orthodoxy of today. The role of the translations in this period cathects each one of these "local" social, political, and literary situations, and through a study of these translations, we can examine "the construction and deconstruction of texts, the unpredictable courses taken by two interactive semiotic systems both operating, in different ways, outside their usual verbal and cultural orbits."[73] In his poem "The Translator," Dilip Chitre's speaker says he is "fucked up" by the silences between and among multiple languages in the multilingual urban space of Bombay caught up in monolingual squabbles in the *sathottari* years. The large-scale recourse to translations in *sathottari* Bombay could be seen as one common instrument used by English and Marathi poets to counter that "nagging problem of meaning."

PART TWO

The Texts

Overview: Arun Kolatkar's Life and Work

Arun Kolatkar was born on November 1, 1931, in Kolhapur, a large heartland city of the state of Maharashtra. There was English and Western art in his world through his father's influence and exposure to Indian art through the company he kept as a young adolescent in Kolhapur, and the young Arun Kolatkar grew up in a multilingual context. After finishing high school in 1947, Kolatkar moved to Bombay to join the J. J. School of Arts, Bombay's premier college for the study of art, but did not complete his coursework there (without attending class, he completed his final year of study on his own in 1957 and finished at the top of the class anyway). These were also the years when he met and befriended the young writers in Marathi literature, namely Dilip Chitre, Ashok Shahane, and Bhalchandra Nemade. Nemade was taking graduate classes in Bombay and would often meet up with Kolatkar and Shahane at the Asiatic restaurant and discuss their common interest in Tukaram, among other things. These were financially tough times as Kolatkar moved from one job to another, but they were happy years, according to his friends, especially since he married Darshan Chhabda, the sister of the famous painter Bal Chhabda.[1]

They wed in 1954, but the fourteen years of their marriage were marked by poverty and later to a two-year bout of heavy drinking on Kolatkar's part before they divorced in 1969. This period was also one of the most formative periods of his life, during which Kolatkar wrote many Marathi poems (that were later collected in *Arun Kolatkarchya*

Kavita in 1977). Ashok Kelkar, a close friend, recalled how Kolatkar used to write to him from time to time and include poems in his letters; Kelkar saved them and later, when *Arun Kolatkarchya Kavita* was being published, the letters came in handy as drafts of some poems for which the originals were missing. Kolatkar initially published a few poems in larger periodicals (six poems in *Satyakatha* in 1955 and one, "Ghoda," in 1956; he also published in English in Ezekiel's *Quest* in 1955). However, with the start of *Shabda* in 1955 and later through his association with Shahane, Nemade, and Mehrotra, Kolatkar resolutely avoided big publications and presses and dedicated his efforts to the small publishing world.

Not only did Kolatkar make the acquaintance of Shahane and Nemade; he also met Ginsberg and Orlovsky in 1962; traveled to Jejuri, the temple town in Maharashtra, with the poet Manohar Oak and his brother, Makarand; finished writing the first version of *Jejuri* (which was lost by the editors of *Dionysus* in 1966); and participated closely in the little magazine world in English and Marathi, along with Shahane, Mehrotra, and many others.

The 1960s and 1970s were rocky years in professional terms. Kolatkar joined several advertising firms as a graphic artist; he later teamed up for almost two decades, on and off, with Kiran Nagarkar, and individually and together they won six CAG awards for their advertising campaigns, the highest honor in the industry. The advertising world also brought him into contact with the fiery and unpredictable K. T. Royan, printer and biker, who had a creative yet devil-may-care attitude toward the world, and many of his lifelong friends (Vrindavan Dandavate, Dilip Bhende, and Ratan Sohoni) were from this industry. This was the time when he met Mehrotra, Jussawalla, and Gieve Patel. Equally important, he started taking *pakhawaj* lessons from Arjun Shejwal and through him met the irascible, funny, irreverent Balwant Bua, who became the subject of multiple writing projects for Kolatkar. In Kolatkar's unpublished manuscripts, which include a play, a musical score, bilingual drafts of poems, and prose, there are two large narratives, one on Royan and the other on Balwant Bua. The latter is the more finished work and Kolatkar even wrote a book proposal for it to be submitted to Penguin in 1986. Royan and Balwant Bua, in their lives as close friends of Kolatkar and as subjects of Kolatkar's writing, represent the two sides of Kolatkar's art and world: Royan, the Malayali Christian printer who might as well have been a "gunslinger in a Wild West film stepping into a saloon," refracts Kolatkar's interest in American film and arts; and Balwant Bua, "the pimp of the god Vitthal," as Kolatkar describes him in Marathi,[2] who connected Kolatkar to *bhakti* literature and music through his passionate *bhajan* sessions, reveals Kolatkar's intense relations with Marathi *bhakti* literature and art forms.[3]

The late 1960s, the period during which Kolatkar and his first wife separated, was clearly a difficult time, as it also coincides with his heavy drinking phase; the "drinking songs" are from these years of turmoil. In a folder titled "Loose Ends: Late fifties/early sixties," there are fragments where Kolatkar's writing reflects the troubled times:

you never know it then yes I guess I guess but you don't realize it then do you
you only realize it later you realize it long after it has happened

long after you've parted separated gloomily you look at the books in the shelf
you tell yourself she will be back

And in a small, pink notebook titled "early sixties," Kolatkar titled an incomplete draft "House Collapse," which has the following lines:

the moment for

the house of man
is now, to drop
on the hands
and the knees
of a self
made debris.

And then Kolatkar married Soonoo Katrak in 1969 and completely gave up the smoking and drinking of his previous years.

Also during this period, Kolatkar's interest in American jazz and blues peaked, and in 1973 he made some recordings of his own songs for Avinash Gupte to take to London to sell. Kolatkar's passion for the blues and for Bob Dylan can be seen in the many songs he wrote[4] and in poems like "*Kay danger wara sutlay*" ("What a 'danger' wind is blowing"), which is clearly a take on Dylan's "Blowin' in the Wind." The project of selling his songs did not succeed, and Kolatkar never went back to this ambition again. But his interest in music continued—he had weekly *bhajan* singing sessions with Balwant Bua, and he learned to play the *pakhawaj* from Arjun Shejwal. He also took several trips abroad for various Festival of India events: he traveled to England, Yugoslavia, Germany, France, the United States, and Sweden between 1978 and 1987.

The 1970s were an important decade in Kolatkar's life, as this is when he joined the Clearing House Collective, started by Adil Jussawalla, along with Arvind Krishna Mehrotra and Gieve Patel. Besides having *Jejuri* published by Clearing House, Kolatkar designed all the covers for the books they published and engaged with other writers (Eunice de Souza and Kiran Nagarkar) who were publishing in small presses by designing covers for them.

Even before Kolatkar had published any books of poems, he was already known within artistic and literary circles. Nagarkar notes that when he met Kolatkar in 1968, "he was already something of a mythical figure."[5] One of the important elements in the making of that myth was the grand opposition of immense poetic and artistic talent combined with a reputation for reclusive behavior (or, in Dilip Chitre's words, "he was a no-comment person. He lived a no-comment life").[6] Kolatkar won several awards for his writing, starting with the Commonwealth Poetry Prize in 1977 for his English *Jejuri*; the H. S. Gokhale award for *Arun Kolatkarchya Kavita*; the Kusumagraj award in 1994; the Bahinabai Chaudhuri Kavya Puraskar in 1995; the Bank of India excellence award in 1999; and the Keshavrao Kothavale Paritoshik for *Bhijaki Vahi* in 2004. But he always remained wary of accepting awards as one can see in his somewhat reluctant interview with Sunil Karnik in 1977:

> [Karnik]: You have won the national award from the "Commercial Artists Guild" many times. And now you have won the Commonwealth award for poetry. Do you finally feel that you have achieved all that you had set out to do so?
>
> [Kolatkar]: I accept awards as an occupational hazard. There is very little relation between these awards and whatever I have wanted for myself. I certainly do not want to stake down my tent on *this* plateau.[7]

Kolatkar also wrote about this discomfort and the lifelong dread of being canonized in his song "Been Working on this Statue":

been working on this statue for close to forty years
it's going from bad to worse and now I'm close to tears
. . .
i'll find a rope and tie the damn thing to the top of my jalopy
i'll go for a drive to the pier I'll drive right on into the sea
yeah we'll go for a ride the two of us just me and him
we'll find out what's what and who's who for one of us can
swim[8]

Kolatkar did not want to become cast into bronze with public recognition because, as he says, in "awards have many uses" (an unpublished draft he wrote in 2004 that was included in *Boatride* posthumously): "awards are also like silver nails in the poet's coffin" but that his "best was yet to come."[9] He was absolutely right in expressing that sentiment as there are many boxes full of unpublished material in Ashok Shahane's possession that reveal many more aspects of Kolatkar's writing than what is apparent in his published work.

After a gap in publishing of twenty-six years, Kolatkar published *Bhijaki Vahi* and *Chirimiri* in 2003. He was diagnosed with stomach cancer in March 2004 and, after attending the publication event for his books in Bombay (for *Kala Ghoda Poems*, *Sarpa Satra*, and *Dron*), Kolatkar passed away in Pune on September 25, 2004.

CHAPTER 4

The Book as a Little Magazine: The Cosmopolitan Localism of *Bhijaki Vahi*

Let the cat of the visual purr and lick
The milk of your sight.
—ARUN KOLATKAR, KOLATKAR PAPERS

Bhijaki Vahi (The Soaked Notebook) was the biggest poetic project in Marathi that Kolatkar published during his lifetime (and it also secured the Sahitya Akademi award posthumously for the poet in 2005). Even more than his other books of poems, *Bhijaki Vahi* is one of the notable achievements of Kolatkar's writing career because it binds together some of the persistent concerns of the poet over the six decades of his writing career.[1] In the book, there are nineteen poetic sequences, each named after one woman, hailing from India and from all over the world, appearing in mythology, religion, and modern-day history, who restate and rehistoricize world politics and local stories with women's perspectives that have been frequently overlooked. They are Helen, Isis, Hypatia, Cassandra, Laila, and Rabia, from the mythological and real worlds of Greece and the Middle East, Mutayakka from the *bhakti* traditions of South India, Hadamma from Native American tales, the three Marys from the Bible, Apala (from the Sanskrit *Rig Veda*), Kim (the young "napalm" girl fleeing the Vietnam War in Nick Ut's famous photograph), Dora Maar (Picasso's girlfriend, well known in the Euro-American world), Susan Sontag (American activist, writer, best known for her work that theorized photography and trauma), Nadezhda Mandelstam (the wife of Russian poet Osip Mandelstam), Maimun (a young Muslim girl from Haryana, India, who was killed in 1997 for marrying someone outside the community), Kannagi (from ancient Tamil narratives who is lamenting her husband's death), and Rajani (the poet's sister who lost her son in an airplane disaster).[2] We hear the bemoaning of Isis for Osiris and of her heroic yet futile attempt to resurrect his dead body; of Hypatia's murder for her "prideful" attempt to master mathematics and philosophy, both considered to be the bastions of male privilege in ancient Greece; and of Laila's uncharacteristic rejection of her soppy but famous lover, Majnun. Each poetic sequence contains several poems that examine and extend the account from different perspectives. Some poems show the woman's voice intermingled with the poet's own, others present the woman as the addressee, and yet others reveal the men as the narrators of the named woman's world.[3] There is a sense of a novelistic expanse in these poems, despite the genre constraints,[4] because of the heteroglossic presentation of women's stories where the world around each character gets enough material imaging as the lives themselves. All the stories reveal women who fight for their lives, and for a voice, but in the end get beaten down by the patriarchal world.[5]

Collecting the stories of women around the world and across the ages seems like a recipe for the worst kind of superficial cosmopolitanism that characterizes much popular fiction today, but Kolatkar finds a way to ground the diversity of the world in enduring local contexts. Instead of the local being served on a platter of exotic otherness to the rest of the world, the world itself comes knocking at the doors of Marathi literature. Kolatkar demonstrates the gap between the representation and the real, and between the closure of a book and the openness of a little magazine through the narration of women's disparate stories. In the end this leads him to a spectacular rejection of the "visual honey" and the empty words of representation in a Beat poetry–influenced as well as *bhakti* literature–infused denunciation of self and world:

> let all this dirt be washed away
> from your eyes
> keeping only the limpid tear
> only one left
> in the end
> preserved in your eyes
>
> that tear will help
> in creating
> a new world
> o
> mother-soul of the universe[6]

Thus ends the last poem in the book. The front cover has a stylized Egyptian image of a weeping eye while the title of the book and the epigraph on the back cover allude to the writings (from seventeenth-century Maharashtra) of the *bhakti* poet Tukaram. *Bhijaki Vahi* takes a radically different poetic route from the previous works of Kolatkar: it is not in the same ironic or sarcastic mode as *Kala Ghoda Poems*, for instance, nor does it reveal the same level of detachment of observation as *Jejuri*. The book shows a stark emotional and involved poetics; the poet has an overt stake in this project, and the ultimate cry of despair (that is a prayer for an apocalyptic end to the world as it is now) runs very close to a deep personalization of the poetic project. It also marks the ability of the poet to re-create himself anew so late in his career.[7]

But, in some ways, *Bhijaki Vahi* is not an easy book to read. It is based on three concurrent pathways of thought (the materialism of the world, patriarchal structures of society, and meditations on time, past and present), and they can all be brought together by uncovering the philosophy of the little magazine that runs beneath the surface of this book. The ephemeral and relatively disjointed structure of the little magazine clashes with the monumental, Grecian urn-like nature of the book. This confusion becomes part of the topos of the text because the multiple thematic strands get entangled in this disjuncture at the heart of the textual structure.

THE BOOK AS LITTLE MAGAZINE

In his essay "Periodical Fragments and Organic Culture," David Bennett studies the American magazine *transition* in the context of modernism and the avant-garde and notes the connection between little magazines and modernist texts: "Literary composition, for the authors of *The Wasteland*, *Ulysses*, *Paterson*, and *The Wake*, was virtually synonymous with the scissors-and-paste labor of magazine editing and the editorial forging of provisional links between disparate materials."[8] This model is also true of texts such as Kolatkar's books of poems that grew out of his passion and his work for the little magazines.

As shown in chapter 2, the little magazines of the *sathottari* period were unperiodical publications that attempted to capture the fleeting present moment through a rebellious and alternative vision of the literary and the artistic. This unconventional approach was possible because of the business model and the structure of the little magazines, which allowed the editors/poets complete control over the format and sequencing of the pages and texts. Little magazines are usually comprised of semiseparate contents/narratives that are frequently not related to each other outside the published space of the magazine; the reader is asked to consider these unlikely combinations of separate narratives together because of the editor's hand that visualizes the connections. There is also an air of contingency about the contents because of this tenuous connection—any text from the magazine could easily be taken out, or one more text could be added if the editor so desired. The revision of and addition to the structure (of the magazine) were part of the core philosophy and part of the possibilities of the form of the little magazine.

This sense of unlimited possibilities was also embedded in the logic of discontinuity of the little magazine, which premised itself on the intermittent publication of issues and a defiance of conventional readerly expectations of the notion of everlasting art; the little magazine could and would appear whenever it was possible for the editor to publish an issue. It replicated the freedom of the magazine reader who could open the magazine on a whim and read any piece or article in a little magazine out of sequence and at staggered periods of time. The fragmentary approach, the oppositional perspective, and the espousal of the ephemeral mark the production of most of the little magazines of this period. The book, on the other hand, is more "complete" in the sense of being integrated and cohesive. It has a stronger hold on the contents, a unified vision where, in the best of the books, the contents all seem inevitable and necessary.

Of course, this is not to impart any false monolithic status to the structure of the book in general. Most books exhibit the play between completeness and separateness, and each discrete poem in a text has a relation of affinity and distanciation with the book as a whole. There is indeed an individual structure to the poem that declares its integrity as a unit, and yet the book conveys a different sense of incomplete meanings when it subsumes the poem in its structure. Authors negotiate this relation according to the needs of work and the market; but most of Kolatkar's books of poems, especially *Bhijaki Vahi*, deliberately walk the tightrope between a book and a little magazine and use this structural precariousness as one more tool to expand the semantic content of the work. The book does archival work as it organizes and presents narratives of women from all ages and from all parts of the globe within the halls of Marathi poetry and forces an interaction between the two on Marathi ground.

It is important to note that none of the poems in *Bhijaki Vahi* appeared in a little magazine, nor were the poems written in the *sathottari* period when Kolatkar was an integral part of the world of both English and Marathi little magazines and small presses. It would perhaps be more logical to read his English book of poems, *Jejuri*, as a little magazine, for instance, since it first appeared in part in *Dionysus* in 1965 and in full in *Opinion Literary Quarterly* in 1974. However, I contend that because of Kolatkar's close involvement with multiple aspects of the production, design, and contents of the little magazines as well as small presses, his later work still evidences the impact of the literary philosophy of the little magazines on his work. Kolatkar had a long-lasting loyalty to the principles of small publishing and refused to publish his work in either the very commercial periodicals or the very big presses.[9] Therefore, reading any book in Kolatkar's oeuvre as a belated little magazine will not only reveal new and rich layers of meanings in the text but also will show the pervasive influence of the little magazine movement on Kolatkar's lifelong work.

This can be seen in *Bhijaki Vahi*, which becomes a signature textual vehicle that holds Kolatkar's career investment in little magazines. The book achieves this by containing stories of variable origins, having a textual space that waxes and wanes with different literary practices, and including radically heterogeneous linguistic, national, and artistic influences. The separate long poems, like the ones on Kannagi, Dora, Kim, Hypatia, Isis, Mary, Helen, and Rajani, are so disparate in point of origin, cultural background, and chronology that in a way the book seems a loosely bound collection of poems, with local unities fighting against larger discontinuities. The best example is the pair of the long poem "*sarpa satra*" (in Marathi) and the book *Sarpa Satra* (in English, 2004). *Sarpa Satra* consists of a long poetic sequence that rewrites and revitalizes the story of the snake sacrifice from the epic *Mahabharata* by contemporizing the mythical references to current political and social events. Even though the poetic sequence was written by Kolatkar simultaneously in both its versions in English and Marathi, "*sarpa satra*" first appeared as one of the several poetic sequences in *Bhijaki Vahi* in 2003. But because Kolatkar deemed the comment of the poem especially pertinent for the times, he published *Sarpa Satra* separately as an independent book the next year. In addition to erasing rigid translational ideas of the original and the duplicate, this act of publication also emphasizes the variability of the structure of the work—it can float away on its own or have its umbilical cord connected to the larger book.

The two lives of this long poem create two related but distinct possibilities for understanding the meanings of the text: in *Bhijaki Vahi*, because of the resonance from the other poems around it, "*sarpa satra*" is seen as an additional instance of a woman (Jaratkaru) in legend who is oppressed by irrational and violent state power; but in the poem's stand-alone avatar as the book in English, the comment on current society and state takes center stage, with the woman's role taking a seat further back, because it becomes a single voice of a woman when separated from the community of female voices that live in the larger Marathi *Bhijaki Vahi*.[10] The same poem lives in two different languages, in two separate contexts, and is read in distinctly separate fashions. The overarching unity of *Bhijaki Vahi* strains under readerly encounters with such fugitive elements of the book that slough off and reappear in other forms.

Yet another instance of the volatility of *Bhijaki Vahi*'s contents is in the shedding of four poems from the original corpus. The book was initially planned in two volumes but was then shortened and collated into one large book of poems. It comprises narratives of various women—real, mythical, and literary—and from various sources (art, journalism, literature, folk stories, oral narratives, and photography). The common thread among them is the subject of the poems (women/woman) and the insistent concern of the writing with the issue of representation. Therefore, when selecting the content for the book, Arun Kolatkar and his publisher, Ashok Shahane, left out four poems that addressed the issues of politics and culture of spaces—"Jerusalem," "Paris," "*Asmita*" (identity), and "*Parampara*" (tradition)—because they did not fit well into the thematic unity of the rest of the poems. Shahane brought out these poems posthumously as a separate booklet titled *Arun Kolatkarchya Char Kavita* (Four Poems of Arun Kolatkar), and there is an undeniable link of tone, method, and context between these poems and the ones in *Bhijaki Vahi*. The spaces referenced in *Arun Kolatkarchya Char Kavita* are connected to the narratives of the women in *Bhijaki Vahi*, and the connection between these poems and the longer book is fairly evident.

There are, thus, two separate books of poems that were originally part of *Bhijaki Vahi* and that form an intriguing and volatile continuum in the reader's mind despite their separate existence. It is important to keep this history of poetic fragments in mind when reading Kolatkar's books because it shows the multiple rebellious possibilities inherent in these supposedly separate yet interconnected texts. It also firmly connects *Bhijaki Vahi* with its uneven and changeable structure with the layout of the equally inconsistent little magazines, which also showcased a variable format and encouraged fluid structures of writing in *sathottari* Bombay. *Bhijaki Vahi* veers between monumentality (it has the whole world in its eyes) and transience: because of the disparateness of the narratives and the different contexts of the characters and stories and the self-enclosed nature of each story, there could be more or fewer stories or even different ones.

Just as the labile narratives of women within the book provide the experience of disjointed reading that echoes the structure of the little magazines, the front and back covers of the book, along with the opening and closing poems, perform the task of stitching together the different stories with the thread of a related voicelessness enforced by the combined power of patriarchy, nation, and religion. The covers hold the divergent narratives together both literally as well as literarily. The book is bracketed by the poem "*tipa*" (tear drops/water drops) and the final monumental lament for the world racked by violence and injustice. These poems, along with the cover image and the epigraph (that appears before the title page as well as on the back cover of the book), need to be studied together because they perform the task as editor of a little magazine here: they hold the individual pieces in one space and bring incongruent narratives together in one particular meaningful relation.

Although the original plan for *Bhijaki Vahi* had been to release it in two volumes, Kolatkar wrote the opening poems in the book at the very end of the writing process. This clarified the structure of the work because it brought the overall theme of vision and weeping together. The first three poems of the book are an exploration of tears and the act of weeping. The poems do not sentimentalize tears here; rather, they are repeatedly compared to hard substances like material elements (gold, silver, lead, oil) and to daily tasks (cooking, carving, writing). Through such pairings, Kolatkar implies the use and significance of the women's tears, which are neither futile nor meaningless:

> Drops fall from the eyes
> Drops
> Drops of tin
> Of lead

Drops
Drops of oil
Of ghee
Drops
Drops fall from the eyes
Drops
Drops of milk
Of honey
. . .
Drops
Drops fall from the eyes
Drops
Drops of wine
Of vinegar
Drops
Drops fall from the eyes
Drops
Drops of petrol
Of turpentine
Drops
Drops of ink
Of acid[11]

These drops are also those of ammunition ("drops / of .35") and of "sulphur," thus merging violence, anger, and grief in one singular contradictory image.

The last poem of the book takes this further: it is a howl of frustration and anger against the world and self for failing the women and their imposed voicelessness in multiple situations. As stated earlier, the last poem revisits both Beat poetry in its incantatory line and the twelfth-century Marathi saint-poet Dnyaneshwar's *bhakti* poetry in the form of the closing prayer (*pasayadan*), a formal feature common to much of the subsequent Marathi literature.[12] It is addressed to the "*vishwatmaka*" ("the female soul of the world"), a transgressive verbal gesture that is equivalent to addressing the traditional male god as a woman. The poem asks the tears to wash away the dirt of the world from the poet's eyes even as he lists the attributes of that infection: among other things, "brotherhoods, family deals, all the mahabharatas, crusades, jihads."[13] The book-ending poems then connect to the weeping eye of the cover when they ask for a deluge (from the tears of

Figure 4.1. The various sketches made by Kolatkar for the cover design of *Bhijaki Vahi* (2003); the different metaphors of the weeping eye refer to the different images of the eye/gaze in the book (with permission from Soonoo Kolatkar and Ashok Shahane).

the women) to cleanse the filth of cruelty, violence, and patriarchy from the world and, as I will show later, from the poet's own work.

There is, thus, a repeated approach both toward and away from the sense of wholeness in the book, and this is one important way in which potential unities are dispersed across the ages and around the globe in

Bhijaki Vahi. In their wide array of origins, the stories represent the fruit of Kolatkar's lifelong objective as he stated it to Eunice de Souza:

> I want to reclaim everything I consider my tradition. I'm particularly interested in history of all kinds, the beginning of man, archeology, histories of everything from religion, to objects, bread-making, paper, clothes, people, the evolution of man's knowledge of things, ideas about the world or his own body, the history of man's trying to make sense of the universe and his place in it which may take me to Sumerian writing. It's a browser's approach, not a scholarly one, one big supermarket situation. I read across disciplines, and don't necessarily read a book from beginning to end. I jump back and forth from one subject to another.[14]

Bhijaki Vahi also encourages the browser's approach as it performs the curatorial job of collecting the world's stories and events in these Marathi poems. What is the connection between Laila and Majnun and, say, Osip and Nadezhda Mandelstam? Nothing in terms of their history, but everything in Kolatkar's book of poems because they live adjacent to each other. One can also imagine more poems added or some taken out without affecting the overall unity of the book or the significance of its theme.

The recurring topos of the battle between the transitory and the monolithic that lies at the heart of this book can be best understood by exploring three networked themes: the gaze of the poet, the artist, and the reader; women and their voices; and the lasting legacy of the seventeenth-century Marathi *bhakti* poet Tukaram.

VISION, REPRESENTATION, AND TEXTUALITY

In "Cartographies of Silence," Adrienne Rich writes:

> If at the will of the poet the poem
> could turn into a thing
> a granite flank laid bare, a lifted head
> alight with dew
> If it could simply look you in the face
> with naked eyeballs, not letting you turn
> till you, and I who long to make this thing,

were finally clarified together in its stare.[15]

Here Rich articulates the yearning of poets of all ages and spaces: the desire to spring across the gap between the word and the world and actually, magically touch the object through words. "If it could simply look you in the face / with naked eyeballs," says Rich, craving a direct relation with written work. And her poetry offers the positive and uplifting vision of a goal achieved after a hard-fought poetic battle with words. In Arun Kolatkar's poetry, on the other hand, while we see a similar fight to open a window to the world in his poetry, in the end Kolatkar is not as optimistic about the achieved results. In Kolatkar's unpublished manuscripts that reside in Ashok Shahane's modest apartment in Bombay, there are multiple drafts of unfinished poems and stanzas that mull over the relation of the page of writing to the life of the world:

every dot of ink
becomes as large as an eyeball
what does it say about what a man thinks
nothing at all[16]

The "naked eyeballs" in Rich's poetry still do not lead to an entry into the person's actual being in Kolatkar's poetry because here, "what does it say about what a man thinks / nothing at all." In fact, much of Kolatkar's poetry is preoccupied with the fascinations and the treachery of the gaze and, along with that, the tantalizing yet never fully realizable relation of the literary page to the corporeal world.[17] Arun Kolatkar's poetry examines this chasm between the lived and the written through a collection of women's stories, legends, and news from different forms of narration (oral, literary, and visual archives) and from diverse languages and cultures of the world. *Bhijaki Vahi* makes the ultimately unsuccessful recovery of the women's voices and their realities the result of a failure of the act of representation itself as it tries out the different garbs of the book and the little magazine.

The most interesting intertextuality is the overarching idea of the gendered gaze and the visual sphere that finds expression in complex intersections of cultures, literatures, languages, and periods. In *Aso*,[18] Kolatkar translated into Marathi the fourth section of Ginsberg's long poem "Kaddish," part of which records the demented fears and illusions of Ginsberg's mother in a mental institution before she died:

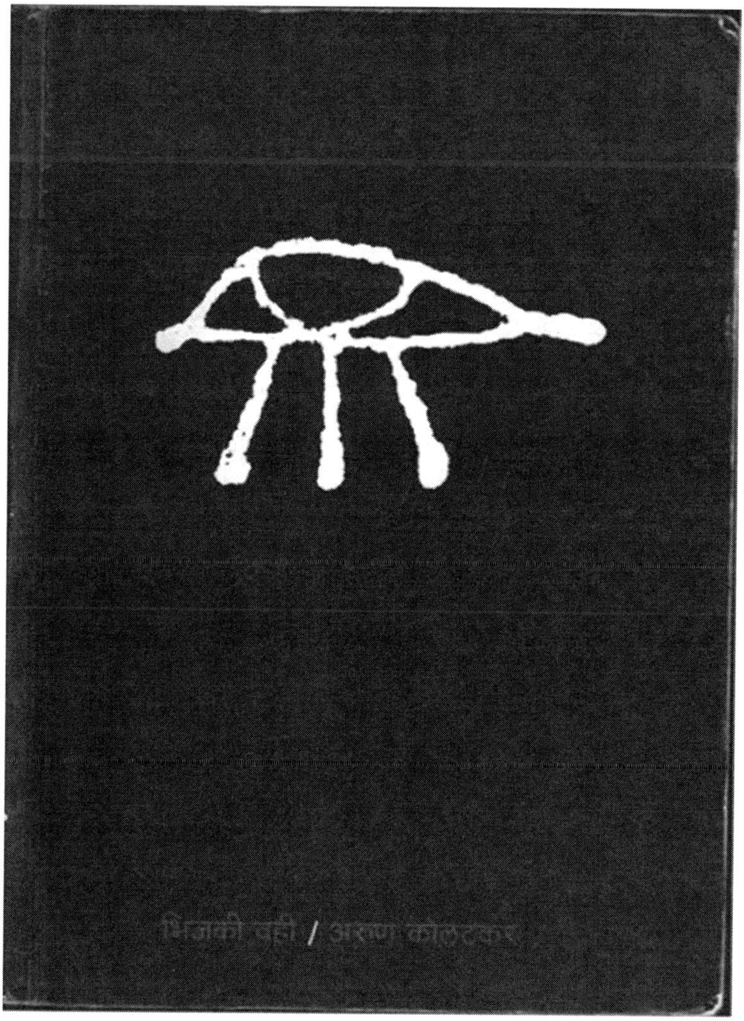

Figure 4.2. The cover page of *Bhijaki Vahi* (2003) that features a stylized weeping eye, which also alludes to the Egyptian "Eye of Horus" and the scarab beetle. Image reproduced with permission from Soonoo Kolatkar and Ashok Shahane.

with your eyes of Russia
with your eyes of no money
with your eyes of false China
with your eyes of Aunt Eleanor
with your eyes of starving India

with your eyes pissing in the park
with your eyes of America taking a fall
with your eyes of your relatives in California
with your eyes of M Rainey dying in an ambulance
with your eyes of Czechoslovakia attacked by robots
with your eyes going to painting class at night in the Bronx
with your eyes of the killer Grandma you see on the horizon
from your Fire-Escape
with your eyes running naked out of the apartment screaming
into the hall
with your eyes being led away by policemen into an ambulance[19]

The Marathi translation of this poem was published in 1963; forty-one years later, *Bhijaki Vahi*'s cover page, designed by Kolatkar, refers to this poem with its obsessive combination of the idea of vision, the voice of the hurt woman/women, and an incantation of the disasters of the world.[20] It is proof of the lasting impact of the little magazines on Kolatkar's work that near the end of his life, when he put together this book with the help of Ashok Shahane, he returned to several images from this early Ginsberg translation.

The apocalyptic sentiment of "Kaddish" is also replicated in Kolatkar's book, especially in the last poem, which lists the horrors of twentieth- and twenty-first-century India and of the world, while also asking for the stain of these atrocities to be washed away by the tears of the all-encompassing female figure.[21] However, this poem from *Bhijaki Vahi* also reenacts simultaneously the typically Marathi structure of the *pasayadan*, a prayer to the gods asking for succor in times of difficulty, a kind of poem that is most prominently associated with the thirteenth-century saint-poet Dnyaneshwar (1275–1296).[22] This form has been reinvented and reused by many poets, including several *sathottari* poets like Namdeo Dhasal, Narayan Surve, and Kolatkar. The Jewish prayer, Kaddish, merges with the Marathi/Hindu form of the literary prayer *pasayadan*, even though one is to be invoked at the death of a person while the other is uttered at the end of a successful project. This paradoxical cohabitation of death within the idea of poetic success is at the core of the thematics of the book (as will be discussed later in this chapter) and can be retrieved mainly by reverting to the pulsing structure of closure and continuity that is the legacy of the little magazines in *Bhijaki Vahi*.

The cover page of the book features a stylized image of a weeping eye, an ancient Egyptian religious symbol, the *wedjat*, or the Eye of

Figure 4.3. Arun Kolatkar with Allen Ginsberg, on his visit for the Festival of India to the United States in 1986. Image reproduced with permission from Soonoo Kolatkar and Ashok Shahane.

Horus (see figure 4.2).[23] Kolatkar's graphic cover image also alludes to the Egyptian scarab beetle considered sacred in ancient Egypt. But the choice of this image was an afterthought: according to Shahane, Kolatkar initially visualized the cover with Nick Ut's photograph of the fleeing Vietnamese girl Kim, her thin arms opened out in agony and crying for help; the figure of the girl's body would have been on the spine of the book with each arm seemingly holding the covers of the book together. It would have been a remarkable cover because it would have made the girl's body literally hold the pages of the book together; it would have materialized the word and the book in a striking manner. It would also have indicated the use to which women's bodies are put (they hold the meanings together) and the abuse that these bodies suffer (they are made to hold the meanings of the world). This idea was scrapped, however, because of the difficulty of dealing with copyrights of images, and Kolatkar settled on the ancient Egyptian hieroglyphic image of the Eye of Horus. This image has signified many things over time: for example, it is related to the story of Isis and Osiris, and it is also a symbol of healing and resurrection. In Kolatkar's own life, it echoes back to 1963 and his translation of "Kaddish" where the poet puts forth an image of transfixed vision in the face of the world's cruelties.

The relation of the image and the world is thus at the heart of this meditation on the gaze. The ethics of representation is also seen in the women's narratives, in the motif on its cover, and in the bracketing poems at the beginning and end. Even though the sequences themselves are discrete and separate narratives, there is a thin thematic thread that connects them all. The most obvious place to start identifying this interweave is the poetic sequence toward the end of the book, "camera," the poet's own statement about his writing practice. After recording the dispassionate documentation by the camera (which also stands for the poet's eye), the sequence ends with a poem that equates such documentation with a kind of death:

> one glance from you
> and Dad got cancer
>
> one glance from you
> and my wife
> started wasting away
> her hair started falling
>
> one glance from you
> and the cherry blossom tree
> in my garden
>
> brought all the way from Japan
> planted with such love
> and to see which people
> traveled long distances
> started its life-long sulk
>
> curse your evil-eye
> you black-faced one![24]

The association with nuclear bombing here (Japan, cancer, death) casts a malignant shade on the eye of the camera and of the poet. The most fascinating part of this poem is the last line, *buri nazarwale tera muh kala*, which loses so much in translation. It is in Hindi in this Marathi poem, and while I have been able to translate the meaning of the words here, it is impossible to convey the humor and pathos of the original because of the untranslatability of the social contexts of that utterance. This is a line seen on the backs of trucks in India, which most people interpret as gentle mockery because of its tone of female petulance that contrasts with the hypermasculinity of the truck drivers.[25] In her study of vehicular art in Kolkata, Swati Chattopadhyay points to the horizontal connections established by such vehicular art:

> From the garage where it is assembled, to bus stops, repair shops, bus terminuses (in most cases this just happens to be the street space or a patch of open ground at the end of the bus route), and the food stalls and workers' unions adjoining the bus terminus, [such vehicular artworks] constitute a network of unauthorized or semi-authorized spatial insertions along a planned artery that are essential for providing transportation services in the city.[26]

This arterial network of working-class spaces is not commensurate with the reference to cherry blossoms brought from Japan, since the people on this horizontal frame are not able to access such travel or acquisitions. Through the sheer manipulation of dialectical changes and linguistic details, Kolatkar manages to comment on multiple levels of the social world at the same time. Moreover, in this image of the evil eye that Kolatkar inserts into his own poem (*buri nazarwale tera muh kala*), there is also a playful yet dark pun: the curse (that the entity with the evil eye should have its face blackened) is also for the camera eye that has shutters, which implies that the camera routinely blackens its face, or shames itself, when it clicks a picture by momentarily shuttering its picture-taking eye. The ending of this poem, in this multiple pun, suggests a certain smiling acceptance of the inevitable, a lighthearted reference to our impotence in countering the wiles of the camera as well as the recording eye of the poet.

Susan Sontag is the reference for Kolatkar in this poem here, and she writes similarly about the camera in her famous book *On Photography*: "To photograph people is to violate them, by seeing them as they never see themselves, by having knowledge of them they can never have; it turns people into objects that can be symbolically possessed."[27] But while she distinguishes between the art of photography and of narration, Kolatkar merges both under the sign of the gaze. For Kolatkar in his poem, the violence is almost as much in the intellectual possession of the women as in their material abuse in the real world. The poet agrees with Sontag when she says that the knowledge acquired through photographs (and for Kolatkar, through all representation) is "knowledge at bargain prices—a semblance of knowledge, a semblance of wisdom; as the act of taking pictures is a semblance of appropriation, a semblance of rape."[28] Of course, Sontag does not mean it literally, as she explains: "The camera doesn't rape, or even possess, though it may presume, intrude, trespass, distort, exploit, and, at the farthest reach of the metaphor, assassinate—all activities that, unlike the sexual push and shove, can be conducted from a distance, and with some detachment."[29] But the gaze becomes sinister, in both Sontag's writing and in Kolatkar's poetry, precisely because of this seeming distance from its object.

The poet's eye, equated with the evil black eye of the camera, then, becomes aligned with the patriarchal world that has abused all the women in the narratives that Kolatkar has brought together in his book. The gaze and the eye become multiple and deliberately confusing: the eye of the camera as the recording eye of the poet is honest in its attempt to document the world and its people but greedy and violatory in its invasion of the women's lives through the gaze of representation. This confusion is further multiplied when the women in the poems look back at the reader (and the poet) and therefore try to retrieve the agency of the gaze. In another sequence on Picasso's girlfriend, "Dora," Kolatkar again evokes the dangerous character of viewing eyes. Describing the painting of the weeping Dora, the poet states:

> and from your eternally open
> impossible-to-close eyes
> there flows continuously the four-pointed tear
> in a stream of barbed wire
>
> it cannot be cut
> by the rusted wirecutter
> that are your jammed eyelids.[30]

The painful image of the "four-pointed tear" that must tear apart the delicate structure of an eye; the "jammed eyelids" that cannot be shut even if the person wants them shut; the image of the Holocaust and the barbed wire that hangs over this poem—all evoke the horrifying acts of surveillance perpetrated by the Nazi guards at the concentration camps. And the viewing and weeping eye of the woman that gazes back at the viewer is helpless in its inability to turn away because of the jammed eyelids; she is forced to witness the visual abuse of herself by the artist/poet/reader.

And that image of the jammed eyelids: where does that lead us but to the cover page of the book. The scarab beetle, revered religious symbol that wards off evil in ancient Egyptian belief, becomes the Susan Sontag-like devouring eye that *creates* the evil even as it documents the horrific exploitation of women around the world; the ancient Eye of Horus and the scarab beetle, both sanctified in the past, become the modern, debased eye of the poet, who should also be an insect, much like the Prufrockian lament ("I should have been a pair of ragged claws / Scuttling across the floors of silent seas"). The cover image is an eternally open eye, too, but the tears now could be either those of the women's lament or of self-frustration on the part of the poet. All of this comes together in one of the Nadezhda poems, where the poet blends together various connotations of seeing, writing, violence, and art in one piece. It is a nearly impossible task to unpack the multiply contradictory ways in which these poems attempt to understand the woman's burden of grief here, at her many years of living in dread, in exile with her husband in Stalin's Russia where her husband was a wanted man because of his rebellious poetry:

> Of the eighty-one years of her life, Nadezhda Mandelstam spent nineteen as the wife of Russia's greatest poet in this century, Osip Mandelstam, and forty-two as his widow. For decades this woman was on the run, darting through the back waters and provincial towns of the big empire, settling down in a new place only to take off at the first sign of danger.[31]

The desperate attempt to keep his renegade poems alive by memorizing them, the knowledge that all this effort had been for naught when Osip was sent to Siberia by Stalin, and the contrast of the lustful consumption of people's lives by the dictator versus the almost ascetic and self-denying life led by Nadezhda are captured in the poems on her life here. In one of the final poems in the Nadezhda sequence, the poet says:

> My eyes are simply
> quoting these tears
> without your permission
> Nadezhda
>
> I am not going to wipe them off
>
> These quotation marks
> standing in my two eyes

let them stay hanging there
forever[32]

The self-conscious reference to writing ("quotation," authorial "permission") makes this reference to weeping a complicated gesture. On the first level is Nadezhda, who quotes her husband when she rebelliously puts down on paper her memorized poems. The second level is the poet, who is quoting Nadezhda's grief when he retells their story. And an interesting substitution takes place here and then fails—in the first stanza, the poet's eyes are streaming with grief, but he says that his eyes are just containers for *her* tears; they are the quotation marks around her content. But these quote marks look exactly like the tears streaming from the eye on the cover, implying little distinction between the container and the contained. Does the eye on the cover belong to the poet or to Nadezhda or both? It is a tantalizing and unresolved question. The image-complex of the open eye, the barbed-wire stream from it in one poem, and the quotation marks hanging from its tender and sensitive inner flesh in another remind the reader of the famous Atwood poem:

You fit into me
Like a hook into an eye;
A fish hook
An open eye.[33]

The extreme violence in the last two lines of Atwood's poem can be juxtaposed with the extreme pain suffered by the women in *Bhijaki Vahi*. Hence this visually oriented artist-poet paradoxically prays for deliverance from this position by asking the female consciousness of the world, the *vishwatmaka*, to cleanse the eyes of their dirt:

Let all the dirt be washed away
from your eyes

all the galaxies, gutters, donkeys;
glorious heavens of angels; vultures;
gods, demons, Hindus, Mussalmans,
. . .
brotherhoods, family deals, all the mahabharats, crusades,

jihads
cities engulfed in flames . . . [34]

The woman is the deliverer from the rapacious gaze of the world of men.

STORIES OF WOMEN

In her essay "When a 'Long' Poem Is a 'Big' Poem: Self-Authorizing Strategies in Women's Twentieth-Century 'Long Poems,'" Susan Stanford Friedman shows that traditional histories never tell women's stories and neither are traditional genres of literature conducive to women's voices: "conventionally understood, 'history' is the diachronic narration of events and forces at work in the public sphere, precisely the domain from which women have been overwhelmingly excluded, precisely the arena upon which the epic has predominantly centered."[35] Therefore, the replacing of the one story or voice with the many implies not only an egalitarian worldview but also a feminist one, a delegitimization of linear structures in its exploration of alternate narratives and endings to the patriarchal stories. *Bhijaki Vahi* attempts to do both of these when it brings together the multiple stories of real women as well as those from legends and myths from various world spaces and times together in this massive book (393 pages) of Marathi poems.

In these poems, the women's stories play with the notion of the real and the represented on many levels, and the reader is left with a hazy notion of the woman's world: it is both the "real" world and that which can never be reached by the reader's eye. Realism and fiction, the material and the textual, the narrated and the lived all collide and tangle in these women's stories. Here are two examples from *Bhijaki Vahi* of the rewriting of world stories, one from the productive world of the real (Maimun) and the other from Greek mythology (Cassandra). Maimun was a young Muslim girl from Haryana, India, who was repeatedly raped for challenging the caste rules of her society, and Cassandra is the prophetic daughter of the Trojan king Priam and queen Hecuba. There is very little historical connection between these two women other than the abuse and rejection they have suffered at the hands of men. Kolatkar makes them both believable in the Marathi context through the language and structure of his poems that make the voices in these poems sound like one's next door neighbors in Bombay.

Maimun was a nineteen-year-old Muslim girl in rural Haryana in northern India from the butcher caste of the Kureishis who dared to step outside the "caste rules" of her community and marry an older man, Idris, from the higher caste of the land-tilling Meos. To punish her for this transgression, the men in her village repeatedly gang raped her and her cousin stabbed and cut her up. Idris managed to find her again, and with the help of the police they decided to return to the village, where the police were attacked by a village mob and, according to some accounts, the village headman again raped Maimun. There are no verifiable accounts of what happened next, but the activist and writer Syeda Hameed states, "We heard reports that Idris had gone to the Gulf for a while and then opened a shop in east Delhi. Then one day, I saw a familiar face in a newspaper, Idris with his two children. That's when I came to know that Maimun had been killed by her brother."[36] There are news clippings of this horrific event among Kolatkar's unpublished manuscripts, and they served as the basis of the documentary poem sequence that he wrote in *Bhijaki Vahi* titled "Maimun."

This sequence is one of the shortest, with only three poems forming the whole unit, but it is hard-hitting in its angry denunciation of the religious blindness of all communities, Hindu as well as Muslim. Kolatkar deliberately mixes religious and communal markers in these poems: he employs a heavy Urdu-laced Marathi diction (*khushnaseeb*, *gulbadan*) to indicate the Muslim background of the couple while also referencing Hindu/Marathi religious customs such as the *satyanarayan* in the same poems.[37] The woman is a Muslim girl from Haryana who belongs to a broadly Hindi-speaking region. By delivering this story in the dialect of everyday Marathi of Bombay, Kolatkar extends the blurring of religious and sectarian lines to include all Maharashtrian women and shows that the penalties for such transgressions are enforced with deadly consequences for the interlopers all over.

In "Maimun," the first poem surprisingly addresses Laila (of a previous poetic sequence, and the legendary equivalent of Juliet in the Middle Eastern and North Indian love story of Laila and Majnun). The poetic persona tells Laila here, who suffers in her own separate long poem in *Bhijaki Vahi*, that she is lucky to not be Maimun instead. The poem then goes on to delineate in gory detail the narrative of Maimun's supposed transgression and the subsequent rape and abuse. Throughout, Laila is addressed as *khushnaseeb* (fortunate) because the poet says to Laila, if you were Maimun, "you would have" been dragged out of your house by your own people and raped by them one by one.

The entire poem is structured on the phrase "you would have been," a conditional form that *implies* what actually transpired (in this village of Haryana in northern India) in the act of saying what did not happen to Laila. In this sequence, the much-narrated literary Laila stays untouched as compared to the flesh-and-blood raped and tortured Maimun, but the poem makes sure that reader is not comforted by this thought. "Laila," which appears earlier, is the story of the star-crossed lovers Majnun and Laila. There, the "real," corporeal Laila is disregarded by Majnun, who is mesmerized by his own popular image of the hopelessly enamored lover and lost in his own "imagination" of a perfect Laila. The "real" Laila is the unseen one in that eponymous long poem, so the "Maimun" poems seem to up the ante, so to speak, on the invisibility of women in this hall of mirrors that is the book's representation of women's narratives.

The second poem in the "Maimun" sequence examines the notion of *samudayik balatkar* (communal rape or gang rape, as translated from Marathi). The poetic voice compares the communal acquiescence demanded by the gang rape to something similar expected in public religious celebrations, "like the communal Ganesh festival / or the *satyanarayan puja* or collective sequential chanting of prayers," with a demand for conviction that what is happening is for the public good.[38] The anger of the poet toward this inhumanity is expressed through the enormity of the impropriety of comparing a popular religious celebration with gang rape. The third poem in "Maimun" is in the voice of the butcher cousin who slashed the young girl for the sake of family honor. This is a picture of a hardworking, business-wise, ethical man who takes pride in his butchering skills: "the skinned goat hanging on the hook / and the sister who has abandoned all communal propriety / abandoned all shame / my knife does not differentiate."[39] This underscores the previous poem's theme about the horrifying effect of righteousness in communal settings.

In "Maimun," the central character never speaks in her own voice, whereas in "Cassandra," the woman speaks and speaks but no one listens to her warnings. This long poetic sequence consists of fourteen poems, some which are themselves sequences of multiple poems. They are haunting statements made in the voice of Cassandra that catalogue the unseeing rush to oblivion by the city of Troy and its denizens even as Cassandra wails out her prophecies of doom that everyone disregards:

> it will be a full moon night
> and the town will wear a shining armor

and a helmet of fire
and in place of the horsehair plume
will be swaying a moon-covering
trail of smoke
and up in the sky
the prickling stars will also shut their eyes[40]

These poems display some of the striking poetic tools used by Kolatkar throughout the book. For instance, repetition in its various forms is a common structuring tool in many Kolatkar poems and it is in spectacular presentation here. In the first poem, Cassandra prophesies helplessly the destruction of the buildings, the homes, and the people of Troy, and the poem ends with a repeated "so what should I do if not cry?":

prostitutes or concubines
that is what will become of these princesses
concubines of the greek of the greek of the greek
i will also be abused by agamemnon
i will be abused i will be abused
and hector's child
will be grabbed brutally from his mother's side
and they will whirl him overhead round and round[41]

The entire poem repeats phrases at the ends of lines and this echoes the style of delivery of poor women in temple courtyards or in the street who claim to be under a spell such that they can see people's futures. Therefore, at the end when Cassandra says, "*mag radu nako / tar karu tari kay mi kay karu / mi kay karu*" (then not to cry / is not what i can do / what can i do), the lines exhibit the fruitless anguish of the prophetic woman who can see but cannot stop the destruction while simultaneously making the exotic Greek Cassandra a common, poor Marathi woman who goes into a trance in the temple precincts in order to eke out a living. In another poem, Kolatkar has Cassandra narrate her humiliating encounter with the god Apollo, who, according to one telling, spat into her mouth when she refused his advances; as a result, her words would be prophetic but unheeded. Cassandra states with disgusted defiance how Apollo used her as a spittoon, thus providing another example of patriarchal punishment suffered by the women in the book because of their defiance of social expectations.

"Maimun," "Cassandra," and "Laila" and the rest of the poems in the book are registered in a dialectical spoken Marathi that differs in tone and vocabulary from the middle-class language or the traditionally literary Marathi. These poetic sequences from all over the world and all across history are held together by the use of a strikingly colloquial register of Marathi that one associates with the working classes of Bombay; these are poems that are sonorous yet speak in the language of the urban street. The deliberate disjunction of working-world language and the more sophisticated content of the narratives (that reveals a more "cultured" and wide-ranging knowledge of the world) unsettles simplistic understandings of the unprivileged and of the idea of the "world" and the "local." In his interview with Eunice de Souza, Kolatkar complained about the typical literary language of much of Marathi poetry: "there is a gap between the daily life and the remote imagery used by some of the best poets. To the ordinary man, this is as remote as Greek imagery."[42] In his own poetry, Kolatkar divests that Greek world of its exclusivity and brings it to the Bombay streets through his language. The mixing of the dialect of the street encounter and the subject of sophisticated knowledges acquired through formal education means that disparate worlds collide on the streets of Bombay. The seemingly less-educated women of Kolatkar's poetry seem to share the street space of Bombay with legendary, famous, and mythical women from the world because of their shared experience of abuse and rejection. The women of these poems speak in a vocabulary and intonation that are out of joint with their social status in modern-day India. For example, the address to the river Nile, in "Isis," is made in a dialect of Marathi that is immediately identifiable as not belonging to the educated urban middle and upper classes.[43] The river Nile is addressed in the familiar diminutive of "*Nailey*"/"*Nailitley*," and the word *pishi* (instead of *vedi*) is used to denote "crazy"; both usages denote either a rural or an inner-city urban lifestyle.[44] Similarly, the present continuous form of the verb "to run" in standard Marathi is *dhavat ahes*, but in the poem Kolatkar uses the more rural/urban-poor inflection of *dhavtyes*. The same holds true for the past tense of "to imagine" or "to feel": Kolatkar uses the more street-smart *vatlavata* instead of *vatla hota*. Moreover, the dialect implies, at the very least, a vernacular, non-anglicized, and hence not "modern" upbringing—one that would not allow these women to even know who Isis is or where the Nile is located.[45]

By this ingenious interplay of Marathi dialects (the rural or urban poor versus the urban middle class), Kolatkar restages and reinterprets the linguistic, cultural, and social gap between the Anglicized Indians (who are generally seen as more affluent and more likely to be familiar with Greek and Egyptian mythology)[46] and those of the Marathi vernacular world of Bombay (who are perceived as less privileged in cultural and social contexts). Moreover, through this surprising juxtaposition of incommensurate dialects and thematic references, Kolatkar not only domesticates the world to his Maharashtrian space[47] but enlarges the significance of these overlooked, unheard, semi-/nonliterate voices by showing that their concerns are not foreign to those of the so-called great Western narratives.[48]

THE END IS THE BEGINNING: PASTS, PRESENT, AND TUKARAM

The representation of women's stories from diverse viewpoints, the poet's anguish about his patriarchal privilege of voice and gaze, and the concern with the material of the textual all converge in the final epigraph of the poem. The epigraph echoes the same complex of interconnected concepts of representation and corporeality even more directly when it reverts to the *bhakti* reference to Tukaram's poems in the book's title, *Bhijaki Vahi*:

> Do not let this book stay dry
> May my book soak
> and the ink splurge
> let the letters melt
> and let my poems become pulp
> and may its residue be found in the milk
> of the buffaloes that graze by the river.[49]

Because they came from the impoverished working class, many *bhakti* saint-poets violated both caste and linguistic prohibitions in claiming a direct relation to God, and they used the regional dialect to express that relationship (which, in Tukaram's case, was Marathi). In thus rebelling against the traditional mode of religious expression—Sanskrit—such *bhakti* poetry "undoubtedly defied Sanskrit's monopoly in interpreting and ordering the world, and articulated the idea of the equality of all *bhaktas* [devotees]."[50] Tukaram, who belonged to a lower caste, faced severe repercussions for continuing this socially interdicted practice and was challenged by the learned brahmin Rameshwarbhat to prove his godly abilities. He was ordered to leave his village and his *pothi* (collection of *abhangas*, or devotional songs) was thrown into the river Indrayani. The poems/songs are supposed to have resurfaced after thirteen days, however, without any physical blemish despite the act of drowning them. Even today, at Dehu, his native village, the devotees preserve one *pothi* that they choose to believe is that same *bhijaki vahi* (the soaked notebook) of Tukaram.

When Kolatkar asks for his own book to drown in the river and become his own *bhijaki vahi*, then one can almost believe the tongue-in-cheek statement he makes about his relationship with the *bhakti* poet elsewhere: "I'll create such confusion / that nobody can be sure about what you wrote and what I did," writes Kolatkar in his unfinished work titled "Making love to a poem."[51] Kolatkar contemporizes Tukaram in his own poetry by reflecting a similar concern for the spoken idiom, an engagement with the corporeal world, the depiction of quotidian life, and the attack on hypocrisy of institutionalized religion. And yet the difference is also made crystal clear by Kolatkar; he does not want to profess any larger-than-life poethood for himself by claiming an inviolable status for his own work. Rather, if Tukaram's poetry floated to the surface as is because of its divine qualities, Kolatkar instead asks for his own soaked notebook, drenched with the tears of innumerable women's stories, to be drowned and destroyed and reworked into the elements of the material world so that it can "become pulp" and "its residue be found in the milk / of the buffaloes that graze by the river." He thus locates intolerance and literary creation as invariable parts of the living practices of the everyday and asks for disappearance and yet also reincarnation as a useful part of a material practice.

Here is one of the many semantic conjunctures of the work: the demand for the end of the world in the last poem matches the prayer in the epigraph that begs for a destruction of the book as a material object (and with it, words as black marks on the page). At the end, then, the reader is forced to consider the possibility that this text might be more than a discrete collection of narratives; it might be an amalgamated telling of a long poem-like book. The desire for the destruction of the gaze then uncovers the unity of the book. This alternation between the theme of unity (of the written text of poems) and the destruction (of the intrusive and violating eye of the poet) is matched by the oscillation of the identity of this work between the conventional book and the little magazine. Uncovering the structural play of these forms, between the ephemeral and the monumental, the visual and the corporeal, the poet and his subjects, and finally between patriarchal privilege and the articulation of women's abuse, helps underline the thematic interchange between destruction and material creation that forms the core of this work.

The crux of these oscillations happens in the epigraph and the cover image of the book, which prove to be a concentrated bundle of contradictory thematic impulses. Inspired by Tukaram's own *bhijaki vahi*, and yet knowing that he can never compete with Tukaram and his stature, the poet's wish is to become material (and not merely intellectual) residue, paper pulp that will be ingested by the buffaloes and then be integral to the milk they produce. Note the urge to disappear, to melt, and to transform into the milk with which only females are capable of nourishing the world. And the image of buffaloes also connotes the hardened, weary worker in the poor, burden-carrying, unromanticized animal. The image conflates the powerlessness of the women with that of the underprivileged, the poor.[52] As Ramanujan points out in his essay "On Women Saints," "in the lives of the bhakti saints 'the last shall be the first': men wish to renounce their masculinity and to become women; upper-caste males wish to renounce pride, privilege, and wealth, seek dishonour and self-abasement, and learn from the untouchable devotee."[53] In his desire to become residue, Kolatkar thus performs a complicated turnaround to reach Tukaram again.

This idea of purging and re-forming that pervades the content and format of the book is necessarily connected with the politics of class and gender that is the core project. But the real issue of the book is the poet's battle with representation, with the symbolic power it vests in the eye that gazes, the voice that narrates, and the inability of bridging the impossible chasm between the written page and the lived life. In this case, the male poet who gazes and writes cannot give adequate voice to the lives of the beleaguered women in his poems. Even Kolatkar's unpublished manuscripts show a similar concern with the poet's own ethical stance. He wants to know "what lies behind man's inhumanity to man" so "i tore the newsprint i looked beyond / and all i saw was the crack in my own wall."[54]

What makes this attempt at recording the women's stories so poignant and sincere is the repeated admission by the poet of his own failure in the project. By asking for a literal melting of his own pages, Kolatkar expresses his wish to give up his patriarchal power of the gaze and the privileges of the self that in his poetry are equated with power over the weak. And the eye on the cover stays open and watches and weeps. While it is the Eye of Horus that stands for protection, here the eye only documents its own failures, and the unity of the cover and the bookending poems strain to hold together the divergent and multifarious stories of the different women within the book. What the covers of the book (and the bracketing poems at the beginning and the end) perform is the *malfunction* of the poetic project, which is to document, to acknowledge, and in the end, to hold the narratives of the women of the world together in one voice. It barely hangs together in the end, just like a loosely structured little magazine edited by someone with a powerful "vision." And locating the ephemeral nature of the little magazine form and the antagonistic stance of these magazines within the heart of *Bhijaki Vahi* shows us the "self-enclosed yet unclosable" nature of this book.

CHAPTER 5

Material Modernisms of Small Press Publishing in *Jejuri*, *Kala Ghoda Poems*, and *Sarpa Satra*

Intelligence, give me
The exact name of things!
Let my word be
The thing itself,
Newly created by my soul.
—NISSIM EZEKIEL

The *sathottari* Bombay poets who wrote in Marathi and English were virulently opposed to the romanticization of the world and therefore shunned conventional images of nature in their poems. And yet, as one sees in Kolatkar's poetry, images from nature are present everywhere and they represent something real and material more than something artificial or institutional or fake. But Kolatkar does not essentialize nature in any neo-romantic rapture. Rather, images of nature emerge in places where there is a rupture, where they themselves create a rupture. In *Jejuri*, *Kala Ghoda Poems*, and *Sarpa Satra*, nature is pitted against the falsity of institutionalized religion but also against the institutionalized mode of representation, and the images of nature show an unbridgeable fissure in the lives of the women represented there. The poet and his modes of representation fall on the side of the artificial, while the natural and the material fall on the side of the real and the unreachable. And in the end, the tactile page of the text and the physical construct of the book become both nature (because they are the real and material) and the artistic means of expression of the poet, and therefore the barrier that divides the natural from the artistic and the artificial—it leaves the reader in an interpretational dilemma about how to view and read the page and the poetry.

The fungible signification of the page, contradictory in its dual freeing and imprisoning impulse, is related to the persistent concern of the *sathottari* poets to capture and document the life of the city in poetry. The much-revered "workers' poet" in Marathi, Narayan Surve, illustrates this perfectly in his ghazal-style poem titled "Trying to protect the flame":

> Anyone can decorate their lives by lying
> Not that we also did not get such invitations, it isn't that either
>
> So many seasons passed by whistling at me
> Not that the words did not look up momentarily, it isn't that either
>
> The priest hides the meanings and has us just banging the cymbals
> There are so many who ask us to translate our lives, it isn't that either
>
> There are many businesses ready to buy our integrity
> Not that there aren't the self-righteous ready to pawn their brains, it isn't that either
>
> Trying to protect the flame in such a dishonest light
> Not that one did not steady oneself while almost falling, it isn't that either[1]

Each stanza indicates the process of enunciating this unspeakable truth of the everyday: the honesty to the world, the hard labor involved, the refusal to heed the cant of the establishment, and the insistence on a vision of integrity to the self and the moment, all in an attempt to capture the flickering sense of that ever ready-to-disappear flame of the present. And the refrain of "it isn't that either" indicates that fleeting, difficult-to-verbalize sense of contemporaneity that is beyond even this hard work put in by the poet. Surve tries to seize that present through the jumble of registers, dialects, and languages in many of his poems; Kolatkar tries to reach there through the liminalities of the word and the materiality of the page and book.

Arun Kolatkar studied art at J. J. School of Arts in Bombay and worked as a celebrated graphic designer at MCM advertising agency;

not surprisingly, the visual arts are an essential part of his education, his career, and his thematic in his many books. In his poetry, there is a concern with the implications of the gaze and a close study of how the eye works with the mind. Kolatkar's poetry is not enamored of the eye's practices; rather, it is bewitched by them and simultaneously horrified by the seduction of that "visual honey."[2] To quote Garrett Stewart about the material art of "book work," "that's its wit, its flair, its tonic charge, its edge, say, its conceptualism. . . . Say, its work."[3] No reader can therefore comprehensively account for Kolatkar's poetry without referencing the material constructs of the page and the book that contribute a separate and substantial current of meanings to the textual thematics. Kolatkar's material imagination allows him to interrogate both the reader and his own poetic self: How can these marks on the page that we call words be true to the complex, terrible, yet purposeful lives led by the homeless and the poor in the streets of Bombay? How does one make the words "stick" to the reality of the frustratingly contradictory world? As Jonathan Culler asks elsewhere, how can a man read "as a woman"? This idea suffuses all of Kolatkar's work, but we will examine *Jejuri*, *Kala Ghoda Poems*, and *Sarpa Satra* as exemplars of such poetics here. These poems force readers to question their own act of visually reading the book: "Why were they looking? What were they looking at? What pleasures, or anxieties in looking had to be managed? Who could look and who could not?"[4]

THE PAGES OF *JEJURI*

Since the English *Jejuri* won the Commonwealth Poetry Prize in 1977, there have been many analyses of the book of poems; it is the most widely read of all Kolatkar's books.[5] And yet few have looked at *Jejuri* "as a spatial apparatus of fold and hinge, a material aggregate of paper and ink."[6] Most of the book is frequently treated as a transparent medium for the semantic content of the words. I will show here, however, that the book reveals complicated material maneuvers of the page and the visual line/stanza that are indispensable in grasping the overall import of the long poem that pits the world of nature against the dominant regimes of both religion and technological modernity.

Jejuri, the location of the eponymous book of poems, is an age-old place of pilgrimage for Marathi Hindus in Maharashtra and houses many places of worship for the god Khandoba. Kolatkar's book of poems takes the reader on a journey to Jejuri where the book negates with equal force the hypocritical traditionalism of religious practices in this temple town and the fetishizing of the modern technological and instrumental rationalism. The publication of this poem demonstrates how Clearing House and Pras Prakashan were able to provide the space and resources of the book combined with the freedom to experiment with the publication format of the book. The poetic sequence demonstrates vividly the split ground on which this modern Indian poetic persona stands: there is no unadulterated, precolonial traditional past that he can have access to, nor can he wholeheartedly embrace the alienating, postcolonial, modern-urban *sathottari* present.

This divided perspective, or double vision, that is the signature of Kolatkar's writing can be seen throughout the book, but we can look at just one constituent poem, "Between Jejuri and the Railway Station," and examine its impact. This poem figures as an important part of the symbolic focus of the poetic sequence; *Jejuri* in its five publications spanned thirty-four years: the first one, in English, appeared in *Opinion Literary Quarterly* in 1974; the second was an English book published in 1976; the third was a *New York Review of Books* edition published in 2005; the fourth was included in the posthumous *Collected Poems in English* (published by Bloodaxe in the U.K.) in 2009; and a fifth appeared in Marathi, titled *Jejuri*. Through a reading of the politics of the page of the first two versions of *Jejuri*, it is evident that there is a significant development of the pointed texture of meanings in the Clearing House/Pras publications[7] as opposed to the version that appeared in *Opinion Literary Quarterly.*

Jejuri features the journey of the poetic speaker through the various shrines of Jejuri and his increasing alienation from the urban dystopia and rural traditionalism and hypocrisy. When the poet reaches the edge of the town, as shown in "Between Jejuri and the Railway Station," he is like the needle "in a trance" "that has struck a perfect balance between two equal scales," not able to lean toward either side since both seem equally repugnant to him.[8] The narrative arc takes the speaker to the outskirts of Jejuri and near the railway station (representing the modern world of technology), which is represented in the last six poems of the book. This precarious balance between two negatives—the deadened traditions of institutional religion and the sterilized technological modernity represented by the railway system—emerges out of the nexus of several elements: first, the placement of the poem on the page; second, the placement of the poem in the particular sequence of the book; and finally the poem's relation to the images on the cover of the book. Together, through this merger of the embodied and the conceptual, Kolatkar *re-creates* the iconoclastic experience of breaking the straight-laced and rigid traditionalisms in poetry as well as in life.

First the words and images themselves: the poem critiques the counterfeit religiosity of the town priests by splitting the text into two halves, the first of which shows the inflexible institutionalization of religion in its stone walls and the blind adherence to ritual that religion requires. Kolatkar indicates the lack of humanity and flexibility in this religious traditionalism through the repetition of numerical attributes that indicate mindless quantification:

You leave the little temple town
with its sixty three priests in their sixty three houses
. . .
with its three hundred pillars, five hundred steps and eighteen arches.
You pass the sixty fourth house of the temple dancer
who owes her prosperity to another skill.[9]

The intransigence of this ritualism covers up the hypocritical abuse of the believers and the poorer inhabitants of the town, as is seen in the highlighting of the temple dancer's profession (a euphemism and a cover for prostitution in many cases). The poem deepens this critique through the schematization of the poem on two opposing pages in the book. The verso and recto here create visual markers of the multiple and complex parallelisms across the two pages.

The location referenced on the verso is in contradistinction to the one on recto: the age-old temples of inflexible stone versus the open unstructured field with the fowl ranging free. Not only that, but the top half of the verso (the religious duplicity of the temple town) thematically clashes with the top half of the recto (the innocent and exhilarating dance of the birds). It is impossible to ignore the scattering of the type on this page, "up & down" instead of a straight line, just like the fowl in the field, which also seem to symbolize some unquantifiable remainder of joy and freedom (see figure 5.1).[10] And just as the poetic persona stands "between" the temple town and the railway station in the journey here, looking back at his experience in Jejuri and thinking ahead to his impending train travel back to Bombay, the poem also splits itself between this act of looking back and looking ahead: the bottom half of both pages of the poem refer to the modernity of the railway station that is the final destination of this reading act (because the six poems on the railway station appear after this particular poem in the book). It is also the irreversible chronology of the newly independent nation, which seems to be rushing headlong into the embrace of the instrumental modernity represented by the railway station.

Kolatkar deals with the symbolic and realistic aspects of the railway station in the last six poems of the book. There, the life of this modern space, the railway station (its activities, the memorable characters on the platform), is described in a language of faith that is curiously reminiscent of life in the traditionalist temple town. In other words, the railways stand for the modern post-independence world, and the poet doubts the fetishization of this brave new world as much as he rejects the old, defunct one of temples and ritual. The point of Kolatkar's book is that in the case of the railway station and its accessory elements, the veneer has changed (from traditionalism to modernity), but the impulse of people toward blind faith has not; technological prowess and scientific precision is the new religion in the modern world. Therefore, as the poetic persona stands here on a no-man's-land, between two negated spaces, one placed previous to this poem in the book (the temple town) and the other ahead of it (the railway station), he sees in front of him the riotous dance of the fowl in the fields, cocks and hens jumping up and down for no apparent reason. This scene from nature is the affirmation in the poem: of the breaking down of the inflexible rigidities on both sides, of an excess and a joy that is seen in the breakdown of the rigor of the line on the page. "Between Jejuri and the Railway Station" stands between the two poetic sequences (of traditional religion at the beginning of the book and of blind belief in modern technology in the poems at the end of the book) just as the poet himself stands in a quandary between two time periods in the history of the nation, the old and the modern, and between two options for himself, the rural/religious and urban/technological.

In this version of the Clearing House/Pras editions, if one looks at the way the lines are organized on the verso in the opening section of this poem, they resemble the structure of a pillar in an Indian temple. The wild dance of the cocks and hens on the right visually breaks the hard, stone-columned structure of words on the left, and the polar opposition of the two is emphasized and reiterated in the visual lineation of this text. It is well-known in the study of page design that "white space

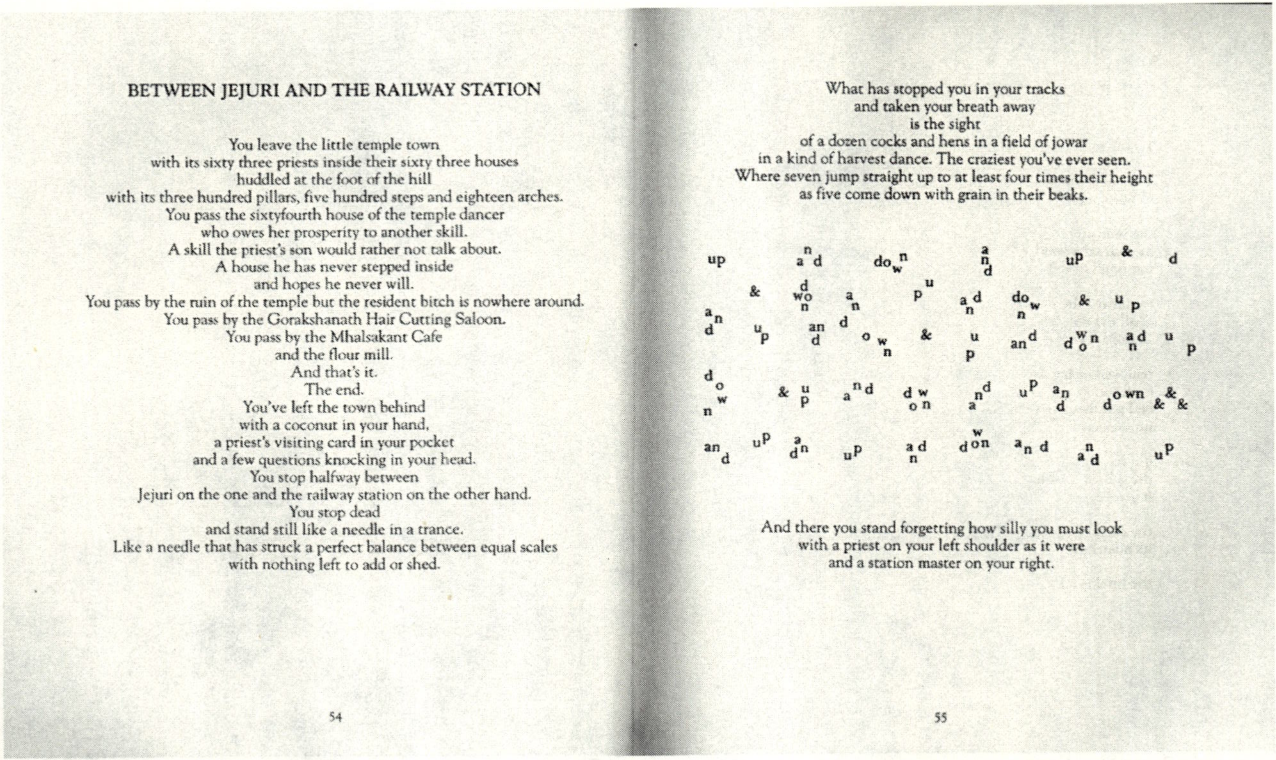

BETWEEN JEJURI AND THE RAILWAY STATION

You leave the little temple town
with its sixty three priests inside their sixty three houses
huddled at the foot of the hill
with its three hundred pillars, five hundred steps and eighteen arches.
You pass the sixtyfourth house of the temple dancer
who owes her prosperity to another skill.
A skill the priest's son would rather not talk about.
A house he has never stepped inside
and hopes he never will.
You pass by the ruin of the temple but the resident bitch is nowhere around.
You pass by the Gorakshanath Hair Cutting Saloon.
You pass by the Mhalsakant Cafe
and the flour mill.
And that's it.
The end.
You've left the town behind
with a coconut in your hand,
a priest's visiting card in your pocket
and a few questions knocking in your head.
You stop halfway between
Jejuri on the one and the railway station on the other hand.
You stop dead
and stand still like a needle in a trance.
Like a needle that has struck a perfect balance between equal scales
with nothing left to add or shed.

54

What has stopped you in your tracks
and taken your breath away
is the sight
of a dozen cocks and hens in a field of jowar
in a kind of harvest dance. The craziest you've ever seen.
Where seven jump straight up to at least four times their height
as five come down with grain in their beaks.

And there you stand forgetting how silly you must look
with a priest on your left shoulder as it were
and a station master on your right.

55

Figure 5.1. "Between Jejuri and the Railway Station," *Jejuri* (Bombay: Clearing House, 1976), 22–23. Image reproduced with permission from Soonoo Kolatkar and Ashok Shahane.

is not mere residue. It is an active force. It marshals type into clear and meaningful units or scatters it like grapeshot. It directs or misdirects our attention."[11] Kolatkar, too, scatters the type like "grapeshot" on the recto in order to direct our attention to the breaking of the linear inflexibility of tradition on the verso. This excess on the recto, visual and symbolic, is the ephemeral moment devoid of institutionalized significance, or of any prejudged meanings, and representing something beyond the past and future. This moment of scattered type "hinges on itself" like the crucial butterfly that flutters and disappears at the center of the book.[12] And the thematic is as much a part of the placement of the line on the page, or the breaking of that line, and of the manipulation of the white space on the page as it is of the words and images of what is seen traditionally as content.

In order to see the deliberate placing of this poem, it is instructive to compare this version with the previous publication of the poem in the last issue of the little magazine *Opinion Literary Quarterly* (*OLQ*), published by A. D. Gorawala and edited by Kersy Katrak and Gauri Deshpande in 1974. The entire poetic sequence appears on pages 1–25 of the little magazine and the poem, "Between Jejuri and the Railway Station," is on pages 22–23.[13] The most obvious difference between the *OLQ* version and the iconic one in the Clearing House/Pras edition is that in the *OLQ* issue, where the poem is split across two pages, the separation of content across the two pages is dictated by the page length of the magazine. It is therefore part of the sequential logic of the magazine rather than the internal necessities of the page and the poem. Moreover, in the *OLQ*, the lines of the poem are left-justified and the ocular reference to the stone pillars in the book version is consequently missing. The complex visual parallelisms across the two pages achieved in the book version are absent in the magazine version because the poet did not have control over the page space in the little magazine to stretch his poetic statement.[14]

The same can be said about the other thematic center of *Jejuri*, "The Butterfly"; this poem is analyzed in detail in chapter 6. Suffice it to note here the placement of the poem on the pages of the *OLQ* versus its appearance in the Clearing House and Pras editions. The poem appears at the top of page 10 in the *OLQ*,[15] with the next poem, "The Scratch," immediately following it on the second half of the magazine page. While the use of the white space on the page is equally striking even in the *OLQ*, the impact of this poem is significantly lessened because of the appearance of multiple poems together on the same page: the

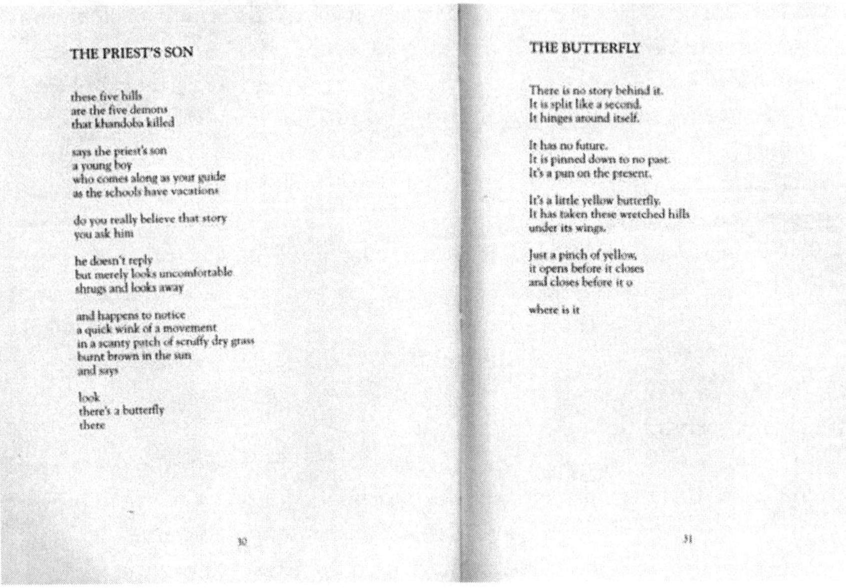

THE PRIEST'S SON

these five hills
are the five demons
that khandoba killed

says the priest's son
a young boy
who comes along as your guide
as the schools have vacations

do you really believe that story
you ask him

he doesn't reply
but merely looks uncomfortable
shrugs and looks away

and happens to notice
a quick wink of a movement
in a scanty patch of scruffy dry grass
burnt brown in the sun
and says

look
there's a butterfly
there

30

THE BUTTERFLY

There is no story behind it.
It is split like a second.
It hinges around itself.

It has no future.
It is pinned down to no past.
It's a pun on the present.

It's a little yellow butterfly.
It has taken these wretched hills
under its wings.

Just a pinch of yellow,
it opens before it closes
and closes before it o

where is it

31

Figure 5.2. "The Priest's Son" and "The Butterfly," *Jejuri* (Bombay: Clearing House, 1976), 30–31. Image reproduced with permission from Soonoo Kolatkar and Ashok Shahane.

evanescent butterfly that vanishes off the page at the end of the poem in a surprised "O" is not given enough room to register its disappearance because of the amount of print matter on the *OLQ* page. In contrast, in the Clearing House/Pras edition, the poem is placed on page 31, opposite and after the poem "The Priest's Son" on page 30. The two poems that face each other encapsulate visually the larger theme: the opposition of the stone religious monuments with the delicate, ephemeral butterfly, the dead against the living, the eternal against the transient moment.

Let us look closer at the Clearing House/Pras version (see figure 5.2). At the top of the verso is the following exchange between the traveling urban poetic speaker and the young priest's son: "these five hills / are the five demons / that Khandoba killed."[16] This is the supposed story of the sacred hills, "says the priest's son / a young boy," to which the poetic voice asks, "do you really believe that story" on the verso. That skepticism about the religious tale is visually manifested for the reader in the juxtaposition of that question on the left with "The Butterfly" on the recto: "There is no story behind it. / It is split like a second. / It hinges on itself." Visually, you read the question, "do you really believe that story," and then move to the next page that starts with the statement "There is no story behind it." The butterfly refutes the tall stories told of the temple complex, Jejuri, and this opposition is underlined by the symmetry of the presentation on facing pages.

There is a similar synchrony between the ending of the two poems on the facing pages: the first poem ends with "look / there's a butterfly / there," which sequentially leads to the poem on the butterfly on the next page. But this indicative "look" on the previous page is matched on the following page by the poetic eye that tries to follow that directive to locate the butterfly:

> Just a pinch of yellow
> it opens before it closes
> and closes before it o
> where is it[17]

If the bottom of the previous page demands you notice the fleeting creature, the following page makes it disappear, and the reader, along with the poet, is left asking, where is it? Thus the two pages debate each other visually as well as textually; it is the placing of the poems in the book that generates these additional semantic layers of significance and reenacts the fleeting hold of the real by the text at every reading. In that sense, the dance of the fowl, the breakdown of order on that page, and the brief glimpse and the subsequent disappearance of the butterfly represent the positive statement of the real and the significant. This is in contrast to both the world of institutionalized religion and the world of technological and consumerist progress to which these poems are visually juxtaposed and to which they are placed in opposition; the cracking of the forced rectilinearity of the poetic line allows the workaday world to make a brief epiphanic appearance.

In addition, *Jejuri* is bookended by images of similarly opposing worldviews: the front cover has a traditional stone image of the god Khandoba with his wife Mhalsa,[18] paralleling the first set of poems in the book that concentrate on the religious heritage of the place, Jejuri. The back cover, on the other hand, pictures two railway lines meeting at a point in the horizon in a large setting sun (see figure 5.3).[19] It parodies the contemporary misplaced faith in modernity by using the same traditional shape of the stone image but replaces the gods with the image of post-independence progress seen in the railway lines. Because the front and back covers have similar religious references in depicting

Figure 5.3. On the left and right, the front and back covers of *Jejuri* (Bombay: Clearing House, 1976). Image reproduced with permission from Soonoo Kolatkar and Ashok Shahane.

the traditional *tak* (the carved images in stone), the cover images code the blind and unthinking acceptance of traditional religion and modern technology as two sides of the same unquestioning urge to abandon doubt and opt for certainty.[20] In the book, the oppositions multiply visually and textually so that the book creates a dizzying array of two-sided statements with the reader (and the poet), left standing with the ghosts of tradition and modernity perched on each shoulder.

The separate interpretative emphases that emerge from the different material formats of the poems and the book illustrate the importance of deciphering the integral layering of the material and the semantic in Kolatkar's poetry. This reveals why the poet was dedicated to the philosophy of independent small publishing; it gave him control over the design and layout of the poem and allowed him to make that a semantic element in the poem's reading experience. In Kolatkar's unpublished papers he wrote that he hoped for

> A spell to protect / prevent a poem
> your poems from
> an anthologist's
> evil eye.
> & to ward off
> a publisher

hoping to make a
quick buck
from the text books
racket.[21]

Even in these incomplete thoughts the poet is resoundingly clear about his writerly politics: no popularity through textbooks prescribed in academic spaces, and especially no big publishers. He addresses his writing as "poor poems" when contemplating such housing in mass publications for them. To that end, Kolatkar stayed with his small publishing/little magazine friends. Kolatkar's collaborations with Clearing House and Pras Prakashan created singular opportunities for Kolatkar to make his poetry "a materially oriented act of imagination where 'meaning' is most fully constituted not as a conception but as an embodiment."[22]

THE YELLOW BAND OF *KALA GHODA POEMS*

All the books by Kolatkar exhibit the desire to cross-breed the intellectual with the material. Another example is in *Kala Ghoda Poems* (2004), where Kolatkar employs multiple material ways of encoding the poetic world into the book. The book comprises discrete poetic sequences, unequal in length, some single, others made of multiple poems, with the largest comprising thirty-one poems. The poems are all located in the space of Kala Ghoda, the triangular "square" near the popular Fort area in South Bombay and the place where the homeless and the poor congregate, pass through, or ply their dubious trades in the heart of the upper-middle-class neighborhood. Kolatkar used to sit in a now-defunct eatery, Wayside Inn, and watch the crowds of the homeless live their lives in public: the janitor at the nearby Jehangir Art Gallery, the grandmother who takes care of her grandson and bathes him in full view of all, the drug pusher, the prostitute, and the street sweeper. They all live in the book of poems as distinct characters and they, and the poems that house them, have discrete lives in the book. Therefore, the book is arranged chronologically and spatially so that the space of these pages reflects the varied activity of the space of the Kala Ghoda area in Bombay where the poems open with early dawn and end past midnight. But within this nominal structure of one day and one spatial location, there is a diverse, teeming multitude that threatens to spill out of the frame. The book gives them that temporary habitation just as the trisland does.[23] The inhabitants of the Kala Ghoda traffic island, as also of the book of poems, are contingent presences, coming in and going out according to the needs of their job, their daily schedule, and their resting spaces. In keeping with this contingent life of the location, *Kala Ghoda Poems* also works best as a *provisional* book, one ready to disappear or break apart at any moment, like the momentary gathering of the motley crowd of homeless people at the Kala Ghoda trisland who gather to eat idlis from the itinerant idli vendor.

To hold these poems together, then, Kolatkar employed several visual devices and materialisms that establish an extralinguistic connection between these separate poetic sequences. He placed the longest sequence of thirty-one poems, "Breakfast at Kala Ghoda," at the center of the book to indicate the importance of the meal in the lives of these poor people, the spatial centrality of the Kala Ghoda trisland in their lives, and the thematic focus of the book of poems. But there is a more intriguing element of book design in *Kala Ghoda Poems* that in fact works as a subterranean intertextual reference: it not only threads the poetic sequences within the book into one whole, it also binds *Kala Ghoda Poems* to the previous book, *Jejuri*, and through that to the Marathi folklore studies of Durga Bhagwat, the famous intellectual and one of Kolatkar's friends. It is thus one important and clear example of how closely English and Marathi works dovetailed with each other in influence and allusion.

In *Kala Ghoda Poems*, each new sequence of poems is marked visually by a band of sunflower- or butterfly-yellow color that runs three-fourths of the breadth of the page at the top (see figure 5.4). Ashok Shahane, the publisher of Pras books, has related how Kolatkar insisted on having the yellow band, almost like a banner, despite the substantial addition to the production cost it would entail. Kolatkar was adamant about appending this unexpected note of bright yellow to the otherwise black and white pages, a startling explosion for the reading eye. The most obvious echo of this yellow is with the *Jejuri* poems and the yellow butterfly that flits out of the pages and into the real world there. It stands for the ordinary reality of everyday, as opposed to the decaying tradition of the stone temple.[24] The yellow of the butterfly in *Jejuri* runs from that first book right into *Kala Ghoda Poems* (see figure 5.4); one valorizes the lives of the poor and homeless while the other prizes the value of the reality of the mongrel bitch and her pups in the poems, who stand in for similar dispossession:

> A mongrel bitch has found a place
> for herself and her puppies
>
> in the heart of the ruin.
> May be she likes a temple better this way.[25]

The "bitch" and her pups are the rightful residents of these stone temples, just as the "barefoot queen of the crossroads," the street-living prostitute, has a right to live her life in the public trisland of Kala Ghoda. The homeless in *Kala Ghoda Poems*, and especially the pi-dog who opens the book, could have walked right out of the ruined stone temple of Jejuri (1976) and into this book of poems of 2004.

These images of the quotidian world, but especially that of the yellow butterfly, are central to Kolatkar's aesthetic. The poet makes this clear in his interview with Eunice de Souza:

> Durga Bhagwat has an essay called "Absence of Butterflies", which she takes as symptomatic of all Marathi poetry, maybe even of Sanskrit and all Indian poetry. She was referring to the lack of physical observation and detail. There are a lot of mythical birds and beasts in Indian poetry but not ordinary things. Usually an ordinary thing appears only as a symbol of some higher spiritual meaning. Sparrows and crows have rarely appeared in Marathi poetry but it is full of mythical Sanskrit birds, the *chatak* and the *chakor*, for instance.[26]

Kolatkar refers here to the substantial study of folklore published by the Marathi anthropologist and translator Durga Bhagwat, *Lokasahityachi Ruparekha*. In this book, Durga Bhagwat takes stock of folk literature from all over India, in its various forms like fairy tales and proverbs, and its distinctive characteristics as well as its absences. The last section of the book focuses on the connections between folk literature and "high" literature in terms of worldview, imagery, and language. She finds that nature imagery is coded into certain meanings in these texts:

> The *purana*s have made immortal the eternally simple beauty of the *tulasi* plant. . . . Termites, ants have been declared as useful for religious rituals. They have celebrated the life-threatening dance of the moth around the flame in poetry but this nature seems limited because of the absence of butterflies.[27]

Bhagwat shows how, since the days of the Sanskrit epic poetry of Mahabharata and the Ramayana, the epic poets have detailed documentation of such creatures of the forest as the black beetle, the dragonfly, and the ants—but no butterflies. In fact in some folk cultures, like that of the Nagas, butterflies are the souls of the dead in the society and are therefore associated with decay. Bhagwat decries the lack of attention to the real world in Indian literature and notes that the formalized and coded nature of writing in traditional Indian literature meant that the real world was shut out of the domain of all art. In other words, she sees the emergence of the butterfly in Indian literature as a challenge to reified and immovable literary traditions and its presence as an indicator of the appearance of a realistic, sensory depiction of the world.

Kolatkar's butterfly in *Jejuri* works in a similar fashion; he contrasts its delicate ephemerality with the rigid stone pillars of the temples and the institutionalized religious practices within.[28] The fulcrum on which Kolatkar's poetics pivots is the representation of the ordinary reality of the workaday world and the connection between the mongrel bitch (from *Jejuri*) and the pi-dog (from *Kala Ghoda Poems*), or the dancing fowl and the butterfly (from *Jejuri*) and the barefoot queen, the ogress, the idli vendor, and the drunk giving the "shit sermon" (from *Kala Ghoda Poems*)—the connecting link is that visual band of yellow that binds all of them as representations of the unfussy, unglamorous real and the "now" of life in Bombay. The pages of *Kala Ghoda Poems* create a visual and textual bridge across Kolatkar's English and Marathi poetry, as well as across the works of Kolatkar and others, like Durga Bhagwat, of his generation.[29] The cross-identification of the yellow (between the two books of poems by Kolatkar, and backwards into Durga Bhagwat's folklore study) constructs a textual synchrony that tries to capture that elusive *sathottari* contemporaneity through such material pointers on the page.

There is one final materialism that enhances the humor and wit of the book's contents and is a good indicator of the overarching theme: the cover illustration of *Kala Ghoda Poems* and the titles of the various poetic sequences. The cover image is a photograph commissioned by Kolatkar: he wanted yellow flowers there, in some fashion or the other. Kolatkar collaborated with the photographer to digitally alter the image so that one of the yellow flowers is straddling the line between the white border of the cover and the gray inner box that shows the street pavement. It lies half outside and half inside the designated image. Similarly, just as when Kolatkar insisted on having the yellow band running across

Figure 5.4. "The Potato Peelers," *Kala Ghoda Poems* (Mumbai: Pras Prakashan, 2004), 132. The gray band along the title is a bright sunflower yellow in the book. Image reproduced with permission from Soonoo Kolatkar and Ashok Shahane.

the top of the page of each new poetic sequence in the book, he also insisted on having the font of some of the titles of the poetic sequences bestride the border of the yellow band—the serif of the "T" in "The Potato Peelers" visually slips into the adjoining white of the page while the rest of the title is highlighted in yellow (see figure 5.4).[30] This element of the design is barely visible to the reader and yet is present there as a miniscule, witty pointer by the border-crossing poet.[31]

The idea of marginal existence lies at the heart of Kolatkar's writing. In his unfinished poem "Making Love to a Poem," he notes that "Some of the finest poetry in India, or indeed in the world, has come from a sense of alienation. . . . It is the central experience of a lot of *bhakti* poetry for instance / it's at the bottom of a lot of Dalit poems / it has given us poems like 'Cold Mountain' / folk poetry where women sing of their lot."[32] That alienation is visually represented by the flower on the boundary of black and white on the cover and the letters of the titles of poetic sequences in *Kala Ghoda Poems*; they hint at limits and the possibility of crossing them.

Both of these design changes reflect a persistent concern of Kolatkar's writing: the relation of art to life, the thing to the word. Kolatkar remained skeptical of the power of representation, whether in words or in visual art, and what can and should be contained within the frame of art was a question he asked in different ways throughout his writing career. Other poets and artists of the period also desired the unity of word and experience: "Intelligence, give me," wrote Ezekiel, "The exact name of things! / Let my word be / The thing itself, / Newly created by my soul."[33] The painter F. N. Souza, who wrote "Nirvana of a Maggot," stated even more memorably that

> What I'd want to do is to suspend my vocal "cords" on the nib of my pen, like a mouthful of food on the end of a fork; to throw away my voice like a ventriloquist's but over a page; to emit sounds with gummed backs like postage stamps which stick firmly on paper; to make the split point of my pen the sensitive middle of a seismograph, as I can easily do when I draw.[34]

The yearning to make the words "stick" to the experience was not uncommon; what was different in Kolatkar's work was the repeated declaration of the failure of such a project. In her essay called "Reading Art," Mieke Bal asks, "Is seeing a form of sightseeing, of seeing sites, seeing aside; is it tourism, objectifying and appropriating, exploitative and consumerist; and on the side, lateral, misfiring, looking away?"[35] Kolatkar answers that question in his work with an embattled "yes."

The frame of art is the boundary that marks the out from the in, and Kolatkar experimented with the idea in different ways in his writing. In one of his unfinished poems, Kolatkar muses on how ineffective and heartless all writing can be:

> i'm afraid, people like you and i
> i was looking at a picture
> of a man being lynched
> i'm just an innocent bystander
> i'm not taking any sides
> i'm not picking any fights
> i will not give my name
> and even my head's outside the picture frame[36]

The poet attacks his own role as impassive documenter of the real, even if that real world is as brutal as he describes it here. As Susan Sontag states,

> To take a picture is to have an interest in things as they are, in the status quo remaining unchanged (at least for as long as it takes to get a "good" picture), to be in complicity with whatever makes a subject interesting, worth photographing—including, when that is the interest, another person's pain or misfortune.[37]

Figure 5.5. Back cover, *Kala Ghoda Poems* (Mumbai: Pras Prakashan, 2004). Image reproduced with permission from Soonoo Kolatkar and Ashok Shahane.

The artist's ivory tower is being dismantled in this poem as Kolatkar attacks his own dispassionate-viewer/invisible-voyeur's perspective on events and people. Every book of poems by Kolatkar contains at least one such self-referencing poem that questions the boundaries of art and life. The frame (of the gaze, of art, of poetry) brutalizes almost as much as the war in Vietnam in the sequence "Kim" in *Bhijaki Vahi*, where the young girl Kim, fleeing naked from the napalmed village behind her, runs away from the bombs right into the jaws of the camera's/artist's eye. Kolatkar seems to imply that what is captured by writing and all art is not the real but the spectacular.

Within this context, Kolatkar's insistence on pushing one yellow flower to the edge of the frame on the cover of *Kala Ghoda Poems* (as well as to move a miniscule fragment of the font of the poem's title outside the yellow band inside the book) suggests his continued statement about the mixed spaces of the real and artful.[38] It is the images from nature—the cocks and hens in *Jejuri*, the butterfly in the same text, and the flowers on the cover of *Kala Ghoda Poems*—that create the breach in the ranks, the ones that challenge the perimeter of art and of the page (see figure 5.5). Kolatkar's artful textual planning of this image can be seen in the hidden ways in which the real name of the flower (called "copper-pod" or "the rusty shield bearer") is repeatedly woven into the text[39] and the cover image is referenced in the poem "A Game of Tigers and Sheep." These images do not represent escapes into the natural world or a refuge from the urban dystopic Bombay; they are not merely the traditional repositories of innocence. Rather, they stand for the ordinary physicality of the everyday, the untrappable quotidian of the world outside of art that the poet seeks to materialize into the white space of the page, the black marks of ink, and the material object of the book.

THE POISONOUS TAIL OF REPRESENTATION: *SARPA SATRA*

The thematic of complicated representations also appears in *Sarpa Satra* (2004). The book of poems that is titled *Sarpa Satra* is a problematic entity: as a book in English, it holds together the poems that retell a section of the Indian epic *Mahabharata*. But in Marathi, it stands as a poem sequence, a subset of *Bhijaki Vahi*, a larger book of poems.[40] Reading the long poem "*sarpa satra*" as an independent set of poems generates additional and separate semantic confluences in the book. I will examine how *Sarpa Satra* re-presents the older story told in the *Mahabharata* and then show how the construct of the separate book performs the reinterpretation and consequently the singularity of this reformulation.

The *Mahabharata* is constructed with the framework of tellings and retellings in its schema, where the so-called author, Vyasa, narrates the story to Vaishampayana, who renarrates it to Janmejaya, the remaining descendant and the great-grandson of the five Pandavas who are the protagonists of the poem. Within this outer story is the main plot: the five Pandava brothers fight the "just" war in *Mahabharata* and regain their lost kingdom, of which they had been deprived by their wily cousins, the one hundred Kauravas led by the cunning Duryodhana. The eighteen-day battle that is fought near the end of the narrative wreaks havoc all around because the Pandava brothers have to kill their own uncles, teachers, cousins, and friends in this battle of the righteous. The *Mahabharata* has many narrative subplots and characters, and one of them is the "*sarpa satra*," the story of the snake sacrifice performed by King Janmejaya in which he empties the forest of all snakes because one snake had killed his father (the poem goes on: "you'd naturally assume first / that the man was joking. / And after you realise he's not"). Kolatkar starts with this in his book, where the capricious killing of all snakes by Janmejaya evokes an earlier, equally irrational killing of animal life in the Khandava forest in the *Mahabharata*. Written with the specter of the 1992 Babri Masjid riots in Bombay[41] hanging over the city, and published two years after the planned killings of Muslims in Gujarat in 2002, Kolatkar shows that the chain of violence in history and modern times is interlinked and continuous.[42]

The second section of Kolatkar's poem is in the voice of Jaratkaru, the snake woman who addresses her son, Aastika, and laments the mindless destruction of life, property, and the planet as whole:

> Surging with sap
> and bursting with gum and resins,
> that forest had been
>
> God's own laboratory on earth
> where life had been allowed to express itself
> with complete abandon.
>
> It contained five thousand
> different kinds of butterflies alone
> and a golden squirrel found nowhere else.[43]

The reader's eyes perk up at the familiar sight of the butterfly in this poem. It is the central trope that marks Kolatkar's value system and the unifying intertextual thread that sews the various books of poems together: from Durga Bhagwat's anthropological explorations, the butterfly emerges briefly in the English and Marathi *Jejuri*, its bright yellow color shines on the top of each set of poems in *Kala Ghoda Poems*, and it is burned down in the religious forest fires of the *Sarpa Satra*.

On the surface, Kolatkar's poem is a retelling, like so many others before it, of the culturally central Indian tales in the *Mahabharata*. But his book is also an attack on and demolition of the epic poem's foundational support of the caste and class structures of India. The *Mahabharata* narrates the lives of kings and princes, the institutionalized and wealthy people; characters like the untouchable Eklavya or the tribal snake woman Jaratkaru are minimized not only through the narrative that does not give them voice but also through the poem's construction in Sanskrit, a language whose use was prohibited to the lower castes.

But Kolatkar's *Sarpa Satra* goes even beyond that to castigate the poet himself when it rebukes the author of the epic poem, Vyasa:

an old man
who saw it as no part of his business
. . .
as a whole nation destroyed itself
and, instead of being
ashamed

of the whole saga
and his own role in it,
or trying to forget it all,

quietly set out
to put down the whole wretched chronicle
in black and white

and in polished verse
to the eternal shame
of posterity.[44]

Kolatkar, the poet, is writing a poem about Vyasa's own poem that tells the story of the destruction of the forests and its creatures, and Kolatkar berates Vyasa for continuing to merely write instead of actively participating in the process of eradicating this evil from the world. But clearly that is also what Kolatkar, the poet, is doing himself: writing *Sarpa Satra* in the shadow of the riots in the city and the nation. This self-reflexive reprimand to the writer and his craft (which is therefore a self-admonishment) is part of a repeated set of motifs that run through Kolatkar's work. In *Bhijaki Vahi*, the poet prays in frustration for his book to melt into a pulp and be destroyed, and he is disgusted with the ineffective nature of his craft; in *Kala Ghoda Poems*, "poets" share space with "arseholes" on the streets of Bombay, and the poet puts himself in the group of voyeurs who gape at the half-dressed female squatter at the public crossroad; in *Jejuri*, the poetic line explodes into nonlinear individuated script letters, thus destroying the very text of the poem in a protest against the deadening nature of texts; and in his unpublished manuscripts, Kolatkar has multiple references to the poisons of the gaze even as he himself feeds that gaze with beautiful creations in the book covers and in other visual treats for the reader. The "cat of the visual" purrs and licks the poet's eye in one place; in another, the poet refers to the impenetrable barrier of representational practices that refuse to allow the reality of the world through; the written word and the clicked picture, aspects of the poet's own skill set, are useless in revealing the source of "man's inhumanity to man":

> i came up against a solid wall / phalanx
> of sixty five dots per square inch
> but learn nothing at all
> about what goes on inside a man   *20 people think*[45]
> while a third is being lynched
> each determined to shield[46]

In another manuscript the speaker goes on to examine those "sixty five dots per square inch" of the newsprint report:

> examine a face under a magnifying glass
> your doubts are resolved your questions are clinched
> by the sixty five dots per square inch
> is all you learn about his thoughts
> does that answer your question
> what lies at the back
> of man's inhumanity to man
> is the falling plaster, the crack[47]

Given this refusal to glorify his own poetic calling, when Kolatkar condemns the poet Vyasa for "put[ting]down the whole wretched chronicle / in black and white / and in polished verse," the reader is forced to turn back the pages to the cover of the book, which features the reared head of the letter "S" that starts at the top of the front cover in white against black and stretches to the bottom of the back cover, mimicking the snakes sacrificed in the narrative. Even as Kolatkar protests the unconscionable killing of Muslims in the riots, he is simultaneously pointing in frustration to the ineffective nature of his own intervention.

The cover image of *Sarpa Satra* is memorable for the stark contrast of black and white,[48] but it also references the condemnation within the book of the other poet's "black and white" output (i.e., Vyasa's *Mahabharata*), and suddenly the story of the *Mahabharata* becomes the story of futile writing versus material activism. The poet rejects his own vocation, which seems to him to be unengaged with the pain of the world. The black and white front cover adds a new narrative focus to the poem by implicating the poet because of his writing, which is marked as futile and unimpactful by the poem itself.

But there is more that is added to this rejection of representation's predatory grasp: the bottom of the back cover features the tail of the black and white "S" of the front cover—only the erect tail is a prominent bloody red. Thus figured, the tail looks strikingly like a large flame, possibly of the fire that burned all the animals in the forest (see figure 5.6). The image of the upper body of the upright snake and the lower extremity transformed into the red flame indicates the eternal conjoining of the two—the innocence of the snake and the viciousness of the red flames; where one is there, the other follows. This red flame/tail is repeated in the last three pages of the book that are stark black (with no text on them) except for this rising flame at the bottom of each page (see figure 5.7). The red tail that is the flame visually tropes the theme of the narrative that places the snakes in the fire (the book seems to be burning itself here), and the graphic cover underscores the extremity of the violence that is described on the pages inside the book. The last three black pages that are slit through with the rising red flame perform a double semantic maneuver: on the one hand, they graphically picture the burning of the blameless snakes and are a comment on the senseless violence in contemporary India; on the other hand, the flames on the pages could also be seen as destroying the book itself, the sign of the writer's craft that Kolatkar finds so ineffectual. What he says about Vyasa, the purported author of the *Mahabharata*, is also directed at his own self:

> And the heart sinks
> when you realize that someone
> like the great Vyasa himself
>
> looks upon the event,
> essentially,
> as a not-to-be-missed opportunity
>
> to unleash his self-indulgent epic
> on an unsuspecting world[49]

The repeated references to the writer and his vocation make the book's graphics a double-edged sword that cuts the writer himself as he critiques

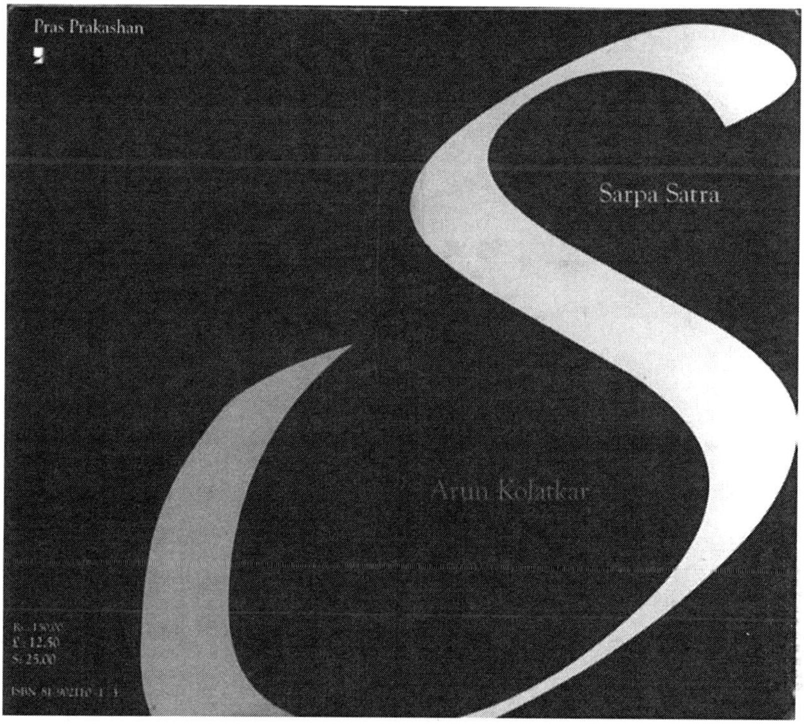

Figure 5.6. The front and back cover of *Sarpa Satra* (Mumbai: Pras Prakashan, 2004). Note the tail of the snake, which is bright red on the original cover, that also mimics the red flames that destroy the snakes. Image reproduced with permission from Soonoo Kolatkar and Ashok Shahane.

the deadened sympathies of modern India for its marginal communities. The poem ends with a list of the various fires from legends and throughout history that have burned and continue to scorch human endeavors:

> Though sooner or later
> these celebrations of hatred
> come to an end
>
> like everything else,
> the fire—the fire lit for the purpose—
> can never be put out.
>
> The fire that Aurva got up,
> for example,

Figure 5.7. The last two pages of *Sarpa Satra* where the tail of the serpent is a bright red against the black page in the book. Image reproduced with permission from Soonoo Kolatkar and Ashok Shahane.

to avenge the massacre of the Bhrugus,

still burns at the bottom of the sea,
where he threw it
at the instance of his ancestors.
And the fire that Parashara produced
for the destruction
of rakshasas

still rages, they say,
in the great forest beyond
the Himalayas . . .

and there, to this day,

they say, it continues to consume

rakshasas
rocks
trees

There is a startling reference in the last lines here ("rakshasas / rocks / trees") to Wordsworth's poem "A Slumber Did My Spirit Seal"; the poem ends with the death of the blameless Lucy:

No motion has she now, no force;
She neither hears nor sees;
Rolled round in earth's diurnal course,
With rocks, and stones, and trees.[50]

The paradoxical duplication of immortality as unrelenting death in Wordsworth's poem is recast here in the interplay of the "eternal" verities of the *Mahabharata* and the shocking indiscriminate murder of Muslims in Bombay committed in its name.

The unrelenting fire of violence is visually reproduced in the red flames at the end of the book, the fire that is both deadly and vicious because it kills all lives into eternity: "trumpeting elephants," "half-cooked turtles," bears, gazelles, crabs, and all others. But there is more: the red tongues of the flame sparking up on the completely black pages have also destroyed the black-on-white text of the poems, the ineffectual legacy of the poet, and they thus leave the reader with a complicated sense of a cleansing in both its genocidal and purificational senses. This graphic burning of the book coincides with the final prayer at the end of *Bhijaki Vahi* where the poet asks for a deluge that will wash away all mankind's hatreds and viciousness, a destruction of the world as is because it is infected with the diseases of so many hatreds:

Let all the dirt be washed away
from your eyes . . .

the torture chambers, mass graves, corpse silos, gas
chambers from here
the destructions sarpa satras final solutions ethnic cleanings ri-
ots murders from here [51]

If Kolatkar asks for a deluge to destroy the world and to pulp his book in *Bhijaki Vahi*, here in *Sarpa Satra*, the book graphically enacts such destruction—destruction of the Bombay world through the repeated cycles of violence but also the burning of its own self—through its last pages.

Thus the material presence of the page and the book signifies a paradoxical allegiance to the "real" and also a disavowal of it. It is both the natural because it is physical as opposed to the intellectual and also the representational tool and therefore the distancing element from the natural. And the poet himself delivers a colossal critique of the petty and large hatreds of the society he lives in even as he acknowledges the impediments of "rage, power, ego, pride / or any of the other / common diseases of the eye"[52] that invariably accompany his vocation as a poet.

CHAPTER 6

The Rough Ground of Translation in the Marathi and English *Jejuri*

At the moment I find myself at the crossroads, unless "confused" is the word I want. About which one I should tackle first. Get back to the Marathi version, or continue with the English. What I may end up doing is quite likely this: break the book down into two, or perhaps even three manageable chunks, treat them, as three books, each one anywhere between sixty to eighty thousand words, and finish them, one at a time, in both the languages more or less simultaneously.

—BALWANT BUA PROPOSAL, KOLATKAR PAPERS

Kolatkar already had a coterie reputation in the 1970s, and he became well-known after the publication of the English *Jejuri* when it won the Commonwealth Poetry Prize in 1977. Among other things, in 1977 Homi Bhabha declared the arrival of Indian poetry with the publication of *Jejuri*;[1] the Marathi little magazine *Rucha* brought out a special issue on Kolatkar in 1977, and the English little magazine *Kavi* devoted a section of its January 1978 issue to Kolatkar.[2] However, when the English *Jejuri* came out in book form in 1976, there were some critical reviews of it in Marathi by eminent writers like P. S. Rege[3] and Bhalchandra Nemade. "Why should someone who was born in Kolhapur, who studied in a Marathi school, and who is essentially a Marathi poet write in English?" asked Nemade, who concluded that "in order to stand out in the framework of an alien tongue, Kolatkar had to disavow the realities of home."[4] Kolatkar was accused of exoticizing his own culture in return for foreign recognition, and these charges were based on the language of the poetry, English, which was seen as fueling this alienating drive in the work. Others more approving of this work wondered what would emerge if there were a Marathi version of this book of poems.[5] Dilip Chitre, friend and admirer of Kolatkar, and supporter of his English usage, even declared a Marathi *Jejuri* unviable. "Take the famous example of *Jejuri*," said Chitre:

> even Kolatkar could not have conceived it in Marathi. Its ironic objectivity is a property of Kolatkar's poetic ideolect, and he is using his other language—*as the language of the other* in a spiritual sense as well. Of course it is possible to translate *Jejuri* into Kolatkar's mother tongue, which is Marathi. But in this case the mother will be found lacking the stepmother's brilliant craft and crooked wit. The very theme of *Jejuri* will collide head on with the Marathi poetic tradition moulded by Bhakti. In English it has got a traffic lane of its own within a wide mainstream of modernity. By choosing to write *Jejuri* in English Kolatkar has avoided a nasty cultural accident.[6]

The Marathi *Jejuri* was published in 2011,[7] and this changes the literary situation of reading the text; it demands a review of both books in conjunction and an evaluation as to whether the "nasty cultural incident" happened. The comparative reading retroactively transforms the writing act from being seen as a mere pandering to the West to an articulation of a new, bilingual way of writing and living, somewhere between the extremes of Anglocentric elitism and a parochial linguistic regionalism. By setting the two languages adjacent to each other in his work, and by showing the multiple bridges across but also the inevitable slippage between them, Kolatkar presents the nature of Bombay's everyday life in the work of his writing.

In this chapter, I will first chart the path of bilingualism and translational practice in its social and political context in Mumbai, followed by the history of publication of the two books of poetry, separated by thirty-five years and two languages. The heart of the chapter is a close reading of the corresponding poems in the two languages, side by side, in order to show the slippery nature of the translational practices, and through which I question the efficacy of the concept of "translation" as it is currently understood, and whether the term suffices to describe the complex to and fro across languages that one sees in Kolatkar's poetry.[8]

THE POLITICS OF LANGUAGE IN MAHARASHTRA

Language issues are inextricably entwined with the events happening in the political sphere and the presence of bilingualism, and the proliferation of translations is linked to changes in this power structure. In the post-independence period, the establishment of linguistic states, by means of violent agitation in the case of Maharashtra, the creation of the Sahitya Akademi to encourage a linguistic exchange between the various literatures in India, and the thrust of chauvinistic political parties like the Shiv Sena (and its contemporary offshoot, Maharashtra Navanirman Sena [MNS])[9] toward a monolingual Marathi identity for the state are the interwoven and invisible backdrop for the day-to-day linguistic practices of people in Bombay/Mumbai.[10] Kolatkar's opposition to such a chauvinistic and destructive worldview is clearly seen in his book *Sarpa Satra* (2004) and in poems like "*Takhta*" ("The Alphabet"),[11] where he interweaves the concerns of language and religion to show the rigidity and hollowness of such parochial claims. The claim here is that Kolatkar's bilingual texts of poetry can also be seen as a response and opposition to such external impositions of monoglossia. The language of the fight for the separate state of Maharashtra in the years immediately before or after 1960 (when the calls for strike and rebellion were still fresh) included a collation of the vocabulary of class warfare through the Communists who participated in the agitation[12] and the language of linguistic nationalism that the Communists shared with the Samyukta Maharashtra Parishad, the organization leading the call for a predominantly Marathi state. Kolatkar's works in English in this context and his writings about the working class using the language of the street, should be read as interjecting in this debate and creating new ways of speaking about these issues.

A second context for situating Kolatkar's Marathi *Jejuri* is the contestation in the literary world, between the region, the nation, and the global world, as evinced through language, style, and reference. Writers and critics have tried various means of identifying regional specificities, the native or the local, the non-metropolitan identities, in the midst of the monolithic globalization of the modern world. In the Indian literary world, one of the persistent differences highlighted in this regard is between what is seen as regional language literatures and English writing. The regional writers have, not incorrectly, been concerned about the disappearance of the regional language literatures in the onslaught of the global power of English, and they have tried to stem the tide by targeting English writing and translation as that of the "outsider." The argument has old roots—even Gandhi and Tagore argued about the comparative advantages of writing in a regional language as opposed to English.[13] Since then, there have been numerous articles attacking the "sellout" of the regional writer to the temptations of the English language.[14] And there have been vigorous rebuttals of such accusations by English writers like Adil Jussawalla and Arvind Krishna Mehrotra, who counter this with enough evidence to show that English writing is as much one of the threads in the Indian literary fabric as the writing of other regional literatures.

This dispute is not a straightforward one, as can be seen in the continuing contestations, even within what would be considered Indian writing in English. The larger argument here is about what is deemed the local and therefore authentic—there is no consensus, even among the writers in other languages or among the writers of Indian English. Kolatkar's *Jejuri* (in two languages) needs to be seen as part of this debate of the difference of the "local." What Kolatkar does by writing two texts, in Marathi and English, which dance around and over the idea of "translation," is what Dipesh Chakrabarty advocates as the mode of writing subaltern histories in *Provincializing Europe*. It is to "[produce] out of seeming 'incommensurabilities' . . . neither an absence of relationship between dominant and dominating forms of knowledge nor equivalents that successfully mediate between differences, but precisely the partly opaque relationship that we call 'difference.'"[15]

THE TEXTUAL HISTORY

It is in this complex framework that one needs to understand the publication of Arun Kolatkar's Marathi *Jejuri* in 2011 by his friend and publisher Ashok Shahane, more than three decades after Kolatkar published his first book with the same name but in English,[16] to the delight of the literary world.[17] In between is a career of writing in both languages—Kolatkar's English corpus includes *Kala Ghoda Poems* (2004), *Sarpa Satra* (2004), *Jejuri* (in English, published posthumously by New York Review of Books in 2005), *The Boatride and Other Poems* (published posthumously in 2009), and *Collected Poems in English* (published posthumously in 2010); his other Marathi publications consist of *Arun Kolatkarchya Kavita* (1977), *Bhijaki Vahi* (2003), *Chirimiri* (2003), *Dron* (2004), and *Arun Kolatkarchya Char Kavita* (2006).

The publishing history of the two *Jejuri* texts is a fascinating story in itself. Kolatkar's first poem in English was published by Nissim Ezekiel in 1955. Thus he had two decades of writing in English behind him when it came to writing the poems that became the English *Jejuri*.[18] The very first appearance of material from that volume consisted of the poem "A Low Temple," which appeared separately in a little magazine, *Dionysus*, edited by Shrinivas Pradhan and Abraham Benjamin. Kolatkar had handed over the manuscript of the entire English sequence of *Jejuri* to them, and they selected this poem for separate publication. In the process, they also misplaced the manuscript. What we have as the English *Jejuri* today was a rewriting undertaken by Kolatkar several years after Pradhan and Abraham informed him that they had misplaced the original manuscript.[19]

The Marathi *Jejuri* also had its beginning in the late 1960s. Individual poems from the sequence were written either concurrently with, or shortly after, the poems in English. As Kolatkar says, "While I was working on the English group, I felt suddenly at one point that one of the poems I had to write in Marathi. I left it aside. I might use it eventually when I finish translating *Jejuri* in Marathi or do a Marathi version."[20] Kolatkar worked on the Marathi sequence intermittently, leaving it incomplete and unfinished at his death. Ashok Shahane was prompted to publish this draft set of Marathi *Jejuri* belatedly and with alacrity when confronted in February 2010 by an unexpected development: a Marathi scholar, L. S. Deshpande, sent him a book manuscript of Kolatkar's Marathi translations of the English *Jejuri*, even dedicating the book to Shahane and Mrs. Kolatkar, and asked permission to publish it a mere fortnight later (the publication date on the manuscript read "March 2010"). Shahane and Soonoo Kolatkar immediately approached a lawyer and sent a "cease-and-desist" letter to Deshpande, asking for written assurance that the book would not be published. Concerned that other unauthorized attempts to publish the Marathi translations might follow, Shahane (with Mrs. Kolatkar's permission) put together his version of a Marathi *Jejuri*, drawing upon the surviving Kolatkar manuscripts at hand.

In 1976 after *Jejuri* was published, many Marathi critics took note of this English book by a poet whom they saw as essentially Marathi, and some of the critical attention was negative. R. S. Kimbahune, for example, declares this poem a failure because of the language in which it is written:

> To sum up, the failure of *Jejuri* as a poem becomes historically important in the context of Indo-Anglian poetry. For it achieves on the level of linguistic resourcefulness and much-coveted virtues of lucidity and precision and spells out the limits beyond

> which the use of a foreign language proves unwise. The linguistic achievements of *Jejuri* end where the creative use of one's own language begins.[21]

Starting with his very first book, therefore, Kolatkar was dogged by questions about the ethics of both bilingualism and translation.

Kolatkar has described his prolific bilingualism in a variety of metaphors. Most of them occur in a manuscript titled "Making love to a poem," which was reproduced posthumously by Mehrotra as an appendix to *The Boatride and Other Poems.* The list of images for this bilingual writing comprises incest,[22] "psychological double bookkeeping,"[23] "cultural schizophrenia," and "a cultural bypass operation."[24] Kolatkar also referred to self-translations as "equivalents,"[25] a term that underlines the degree of freedom he wished to access in deciding how a translation might depart from the original. He also affirmed that "Whenever I have written a version in both languages, I like to think of them as two original poems in two different languages rather than one a translation of another."[26] However, in Kolatkar's practice, the two poetic worlds were not that distinct or unrelated. Such a declaration implies a strategy of stepping back from admitting to the secondariness that is inevitable when translating from a source to a target language. It also suggests the abandonment of the criterion of fidelity in relation to the primary language. Specific pairs of original poem and corresponding equivalent poem could belong anywhere on a continuum stretching all the way from scrupulous self-translation to free adaptation.

The reader can attempt to comprehend the complex wayfaring across two languages and texts by looking at specific poetic pairs from the two texts to see just how the transfer of meaning takes place. We will look at three sets of poems: (1) poems that seem like reasonably faithful translations but that nevertheless show separation in structure and effect: "Heart of Ruin" and "*padaka deul*" ("The Temple in Ruins"); (2) poems that replicate ideas and structures but not in the same place in the book or in the same poem, namely the two sets of parallel poems, in the two books, that form the core of the *Jejuri* texts: the poem on the butterfly that forms the center (in material and symbolic terms) of both books, and "Between Jejuri and the Railway Station" in the English *Jejuri*, a poem that provides a summation of sorts of the walking trip of the poetic persona around the temple town; and (3) poems that are clearly related but cannot be said to be translations even when they share the same images and themes: the "extra" poem in the Marathi text (titled "???" by Shahane because it lacked a title in the manuscript), which corresponds, in a way, to numerous other poems in both the Marathi and the English texts and seems like a source poem for them. Through such comparison, we will see how Kolatkar shows a healthy respect for the linguistic and literary traditions of both languages and, in fact, deliberately smudges the footprints on this road of exchange so that the reader stays unaware of the direction of travel in each case.

DOUBLE BOOKKEEPING: POEMS SIDE BY SIDE

Our first pair of poems is "Heart of Ruin" and "*padaka deul*" ("The Temple in Ruins"). The poem describes the occupancy of the ruined temple by a bitch and her puppies,[27] which is treated as an ironically apt change of guard from defunct gods to derelict strays, a metonymy for the spiritual dereliction evoked by the sequence as the basic affective quality of the contemporary shrine. The English poem has a more metaphorical and affective title than does the Marathi version, and it is more systematically designed in terms of structure. It starts with the collapsing of the temple roof over the god Maruti's head, a feature of the dilapidation that the poem returns to as to a refrain, "Maybe he/she/they like a temple better this way." The poem also conveys a feeling of barely suppressed anger at the institutionalized or fetishized aspect of traditional idol worship, and this frustration finds expression in the punning "bitch" and her puppies, at once a mere reference to a female dog and a swear word indicative of a complex of negative associations. This element has no equivalence in the Marathi version, which uses the more mundane and pitying phrase *bevarshi kutri* ("unclaimed/unwanted female dog"). Admittedly, there are other "rough" terms in the Marathi poem, for example, *devacha bap* ("god's father") and *tangadisarakhe* ("like the legs," with legs referred to rudely, as in "shanks"), but they do not build up to a focused quality as do some of the more convincing evocations in the Marathi book.

The refrain "Maybe he/she/they like a temple better this way" also gives the poem rhythmic vigor and definition; it provides a structure of incremental expectation to the poetic statement, which becomes a series of non-identical iterations. Thus Maruti, the bitch, and her puppies appear equated because the refrains connect them, rendering them at a subliminal level as types of the abandoned outcast, an especially, even bitterly ironic fate for once sanctified inhabitants of a formerly hallowed place. Besides the refrain, the poem shows an economy of internal balances that creates a sense of structure, leading to the ambivalent closure of:

> *No more* a *place of worship* this place
> is *nothing less* than the *house of god.*[28]

The double negatives of the syntax seem to want to have it both ways, paradoxically: this is no more a place of worship, says the first line; and this is yet nothing less than the house of god, says the second, in apparent contradiction. One way of resolving the contrariness is to distinguish between worship and godhead. The sheer fact of the dilapidation observed everywhere by the narrator suggests that worship has declined or died in the here and now; but the point asserted, somewhat surprisingly in the final line (given the overall impression of nonchalance concerning matters of the spirit throughout the English volume), is that god persists in being here, even though his worshipers have gone. Thus we have a very interesting resolution: godhead remains in the place, though the disrepair is proof that worship has decayed. This becomes not the declaration of indifference attributable to a Kolatkar portrayed as agnostic, atheist, cynic, or skeptic but a Kolatkar far more precise in delineating the difference between values embodied and values cherished. Godhead, unlike beauty, exists not simply, purely, or primarily in the eyes of the (absent) beholder as worshiper.

The Marathi version loses the equipoise of this deliciously suspended ambivalence. In Marathi, a different kind of closure is attempted:

pujaryani deul khali kartach	as soon as the priest vacates the temple
ithha dev nahi devacha bap rhayla ala ki	it is not god but god's father who has come to stay here
deul padlyacha dukhha nahi	there is no grief over the ruin of the temple
dev sokawto	but for the fact that god gets out of hand[29]

The Marathi phrase "not god but god's father" (*dev nahi devacha bap*) has a certain colloquial vigor because it hints at the act of swearing at one's father and therefore has the raw energy of street language—the tone marks the stray dogs as a crude but lively replacement for the defunct, elitist gods. And the last two lines reference a popular Marathi idiom, *mhatari melyacha dukkha nahi pan kal sokawato* ("there is no grief over the death of the old woman but for the fact that time/fate runs amok").[30] That idiom is reworked here so that the poem seems to end in the slightly disapproving voice of the middle-class person who looks unfavorably on the lower-class replacement of the previous, more acceptable gods: the issue is not that the temple is in ruins but that the ruin has been populated by the strays (i.e., the new god has gotten out of hand). The poet has reworked the balance and repetition of "less/more" in the English poem into an unambiguous image of higher/lower in terms of class. The English poem only tangentially hints at the hierarchical nature of the substitution that the Marathi poem makes explicit. The Marathi poem uses more colloquialisms, more of the spoken language here, while the English poem is more finely balanced and structured, thus showing how, within the general correspondence between two poems (where the second grows out of the first), there is still scope for cultural differences in allusion, evocation, and overall affect.

Let's look now at the poems on the butterfly, which hover around a set of similar themes but articulate them in different spaces. These poems are central to both books in a double sense, as they are located in the exact middle of the sequence and present a kind of gnomic poetics for the entire volume in either language.[31] "The butterfly" appears at the center of the English *Jejuri*,[32] indicating the importance of this poem to the general thematic structure of the book. It also forms the cover page of the Marathi *Jejuri* for the same reason (there is a spectacularly eye-catching poem in Marathi on the same theme: see figure 6.1). Such a comparison will also demonstrate how difficult, even pointless, it is to decide if the Marathi volume works not as well as, as well as, or better than the English predecessor. The English poem is compact, brief, and densely packed:

> It's a little yellow butterfly.
> It has taken these wretched hills
> under its wings.
>
> Just a pinch of yellow,
> it opens before it closes
> and it closes before it o
> where is it?[33]

It focuses on a butterfly near the temple, pointed out by the priest's son when he is asked about the legend of the five hills and the five demons of Jejuri. The fragility, transience, and delicacy of the butterfly are then consciously pitted against the hard stone walls of the institutionalized religion that is embodied in the temples of Jejuri. The English poem illustrates the transience of the butterfly through the brevity of the words on the page, and the poem ends in a shock of "o" (the exclamation of surprise, as well as the truncated version of the word "opens") as the butterfly vanishes from the page and our view. The poem is not able to capture the reality of the butterfly for more than an instant. The poem thus highlights the inability of the word to capture the world in any real sense, and the black marks of the words melt into the white expanse of the page.

In contrast, the Marathi poem "*Phulapakharu*" ("The Butterfly") fills the page.[34] In fact, in the drafts, the original poem spanned two pages, with the bottom part of one page mimicking the shape of the hills and the other page mimicking the zigzag path of the butterfly's flight. Here, the poet tries out a different method of expressing the vitality of the butterfly. The page is covered with a transverse, fluctuating pattern of words that mobilizes print typography to simulate the erratic flight of the butterfly as it flits across the page. The significant departure in Marathi is that the butterfly actually appears and seems to stay longer on the page than it does in the English version. And yet read together, the two poems demonstrate a common thematic preoccupation: the disjunction amid conjuncture between outer and inner reality, between the world and the words we make of it. If in English the butterfly disappears before being caught and fixed by our gaze, in Marathi it escapes the imprisonment of the reading eye. It does so by having the letters that make up words disperse across the page in a seemingly disarrayed manner. The reader needs to crane his/her neck and turn the page round and round in order to make sense of the Marathi poem.

This joy of "excess" (as Kolatkar termed it in his 2004 interview with Gowri Ramnarayan) that spills across and almost off the page is highly original in Marathi and similar to the play of typography evoking the dancing fowl in the English poem "Between Jejuri and the Railway Station," which we encounter toward the end of the English book (see figure 5.1). There, too, the poem dramatizes the theme of the uncontainable, inexpressible joy of being seen in the up-and-down dancing of the cocks and hens that is mimicked by the words on the page, which bob up and down. There we also find the same inability to express the extent of this delight of and in the simple, and there too we find the poet eager to disrupt the accepted forms of staid typography through which sense is ordinarily communicated. Kolatkar's inexpressible joy in "Between Jejuri and the Railway Station" gets transferred to "*Phulapakharu*"; the theme stays constant, but the placing and presentation (see figure 6.1) in the Marathi book are changed.

The textual strategies used in the English poem have been transferred to the Marathi poem on the butterfly, thus shuffling, if you

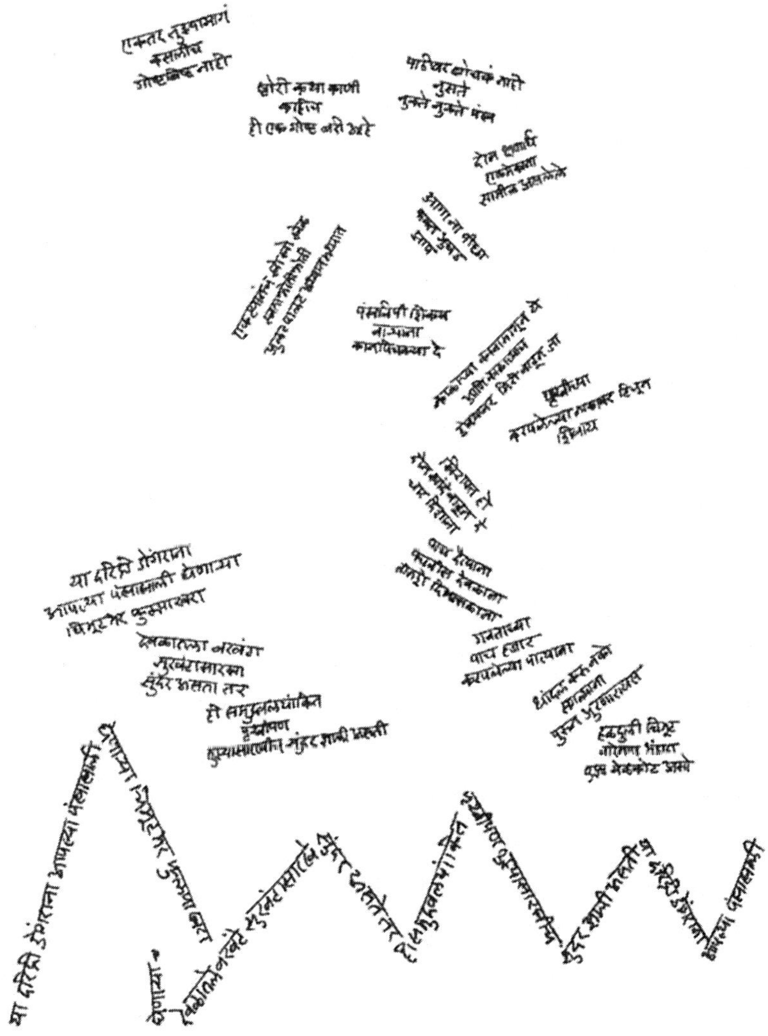

Figure 6.1. "*Phulapakharu*" ("The Butterfly") from the Marathi *Jejuri* (Mumbai: Pras Prakashan, 2011). Image reproduced with permission from Soonoo Kolatkar and Ashok Shahane.

will, the writing energies in English to Marathi, and from a different poem in English to the Marathi poem on the butterfly, even while keeping intact the thematic motive behind such textual disruption. The poem "*Phulapakharu*" then seems like an agglomeration of the themes behind the two English poems ("The Butterfly" and "Between Jejuri and the Railway Station"). And yet none of these poems exactly

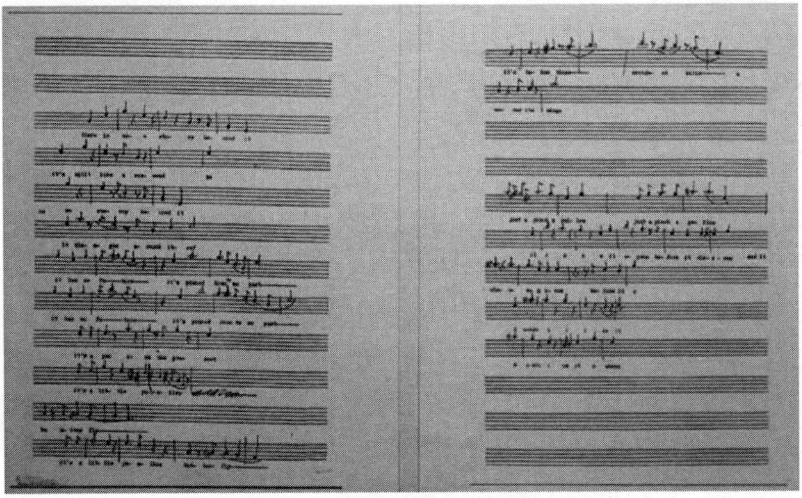

Figure 6.2. A musical score written by Kolatkar for the poem "The Butterfly" (Kolatkar Paper). Image reproduced with permission from Soonoo Kolatkar and Ashok Shahane.

duplicates the other. Their difference exemplifies the act of self-translation as an opportunity for a fresh "take": doing the same thing but with a huge difference

And now let's look at the third set, where the poems in the two books clearly point to each other but cannot be "translations" of each other. There is the untitled poem in Marathi, "???," for which there is no corresponding text in the English volume.[35] The poem contains the central images for five other, longer poems that appear in both the English and the Marathi editions: "The Doorstep," "A Low Temple," "The Reservoir," "The Water Supply," and "The Door." For instance, the concluding image of "The Water Supply" (that of the grindstone lying unused under the water faucet) figures as one stanza in this poem, where the poem explicitly asks how the stone finds itself in such an unusual, misplaced location, a question that is only implicit in the other poem:

> lying by the roadside this stone
> previously of the grinding mill
> ends up under the crooked faucet

how come[36]

Compare this to the concluding image of "The Water Supply" in the English *Jejuri*:

> without ever learning
> what chain of circumstances
> can bring an able bodied millstone
> to spend the rest of his life
> under a dry water tap.[37]

Or in the case of "The Reservoir":

> There isn't a drop of water
> in the great reservoir the Peshwas built.
>
> There is nothing in it.
> Except a hundred years of silt.[38]

The entirety of this poem appears as one stanza in the composite poem, where again the question "if you ask" is explicitly highlighted:

> if you ask
> about the tank built by the Peshwas
> there is only the silt
> of two centuries there[39]

Each stanza in "???" (except stanza 4) contains a question of some sort: "how come," "for how many years," "so what's the problem?" The poem takes some of the main images that are treated at greater length in the longer poems and makes explicit the radical, foundational doubt in all of them. It also makes explicit the inner connection between the other longer, separate poems listed in the right column above. This can also be treated as a seed poem or a set of jottings, corresponding in part to images from several separate poems in the English volume and the Marathi volume, and it is impossible to decide which way the translating practice has gone in this case: from the English poems to the Marathi seed poem, to the Marathi longer poems, or from the Marathi seed poem, to the longer English poems and then to the Marathi longer poems.[40] This confusion about the direction of linguistic travel is further reinforced by Kolatkar's own testimony about his writing elsewhere in his corpus:

> "Irani Restaurant Bombay": while doing it in English I overtook the Marathi version by adding one more stanza. The last stanza (in the English version) is absent in Marathi. To anyone reading it in both languages, it would appear as if the English version was the more complete one. "Teeth" is an interesting case. In a way, I wrote it first in Marathi or started writing it, and although I have the rough drafts lying around somewhere to this day, in the hope of getting back to it, I never completed it. After completing the English poem, I took up the theme in Marathi again. More than once. But every time I found a new variation and came up with 3 different poems in Marathi. I won't be surprised to find more Marathi poems coming out of it when I go back to it, or so I keep promising myself.[41]

Kolatkar could have said similarly about the crisscrossing of the translating pathway in several poems in *Kala Ghoda Poems*,[42] in the long poem "*sarpa satra*" in Marathi in *Bhijaki Vahi*, and the book *Sarpa Satra* in English, or about his massive unpublished project on Balwant Bua for which he has a Marathi book of poems that reference the Bua stories, a proposal of six stories written in English (1986), and a huge corpus of some 1,200 pages in Marathi prose, still unpublished.[43]

NO MORE A PLACE FOR TRANSLATION?

What this study of the three sets of poems shows is that the category of translation is too all-encompassing to be of any use when talking about specific acts of bilingual crossings in this manner. It seems like a portmanteau concept for a number of distinct writing acts. The better way to understand this would be by applying a concept like Wittgenstein's theory of resemblances. Wittgenstein deconstructs the notion of essentialism with reference to language and suggests that we understand language acts as a set of family resemblances,[44] where there is no one central copy, even if one notices connections and resemblances between family members. Another image he suggests is that of spinning thread: "we twist fibre on fibre. And the strength of the thread does not reside in the fact that some one fibre runs through its whole length, but in the overlapping of many fibres."[45] A similar notion can be applied to the act of self-translation or transcreation here. It is difficult to say which text is the original among Kolatkar's *Jejuri* poems in English and Marathi (although consensus has it that most of the *Jejuri* poems in English came first—most, but not all). There is also evidence of a deliberate and consistent practice by the poet of writing in both languages simultaneously, or of using the notion of "translation" to apply very liberally to his various comings and goings in the poetry of each language. It is clear that "translation" is a mere hold-all word for types of creative activity in which "secondness" is not to be equated with "secondariness" because it, too, entails the same kind of creative energy that occurs in a so-called original with no template to follow.

But Kolatkar goes a step further. Critics like Harish Trivedi have questioned the "balance of payment (or indeed the balance of cultural power)" in the transactions across languages, especially with the metropolitan power of English.[46] It is similar to the argument made against Kolatkar and Chitre by Nemade in *Tikasvayamvara*, where the two poets were berated for their capitulation to the temptations of the English language. But Kolatkar's *Jejuri* resists such simplified readings. The two books of poems are largely similar, but not completely identical—in each book there are poems that do not appear in the other; there are loose transferences of content, sometimes a close match, at other times not; and in more ways than one, Kolatkar disperses any clarity about the direction of transference of content in the two books. Paul De Man notes that:

> The translation . . . shows in the original a mobility, an instability, which at first one did not notice. [In a translation] the original work is not imitated or reproduced but is to some extent put in motion, de-canonised, questioned in a way which undoes its claim to canonical authority.[47]

Kolatkar's writing, sometimes simultaneous bilingual transcreation, sometimes translation, could be seen as a way, then, of questioning theories of origin, of interrogating authority by instigating such mobility across linguistic lines. And if the transfer of content across linguistic borders is seen as a colonial trade,[48] then Kolatkar deliberately makes one wonder who is the buyer and who is the seller in this context—there is no way of tracking the movement of the transfer; moreover, there are two separate texts in both languages on the same subject, so that the question of linguistic preference becomes moot.[49] It is parallel to the kind of "Indian" translating consciousness that G. N. Devy[50] and Ayappa Panikar capture in their work on translation in India. In fact, Panikar describes the "Indian" translating consciousness in similar terms in his essay "The Anxiety of Authenticity": "Could we suggest that the translation of a work is like its daughter, born of it, but still different—reflecting such a change in taste and attitude?"[51]

By dethroning the concept of "the original" and the "secondary" in his bilingual poetry, Kolatkar throws into doubt the notion of an essential regional or national identity even as he highlights major regional and national poetic influences in his own work. This writer's position on language and translation parallels the work of both the Marathi and English little magazines in Bombay: the Marathi littles rejected the monolingual push of the political formation of Maharashtra even as the magazines also insisted on a re-formed Marathi habitation; the English little magazines resituated English among the Indian languages by living beside the other languages in the same literary spaces.[52] On the spectrum of bilingual poetry, where the Shiv Sena stands for one extreme of threatening monolingual identity and the Anglicized rejection of so-called regional linguistic backwardness stands at the other extreme, Kolatkar disperses all straightforward lines between home and abroad through his bilingual pages.

There is too much Wittgensteinian nebulousness in his influences (for example, the sources for the poems in his Marathi volume *Bhijaki Vahi* include Native American stories, Russian literature, South Indian folklore, contemporary news from Bihar, the Bible, and modern European art), too much of the West and the non-West even in his Marathi poems, and too much back-and-forth from English to Marathi in his bilingual poetry for it to be pinned down in any one manner. Arvind Krishna Mehrotra shows this succinctly when he demonstrates the disparate influences on Kolatkar's poem that begins with "*maine manager ko bola*":

> So there it is, your Indian poem. It was written in a Bombay patois by a poet who otherwise wrote in Marathi and English. It then became part of two literatures, Marathi and Indian English, but entered the latter in a translation made in the American idiom, one of whose sources . . . was an American translation of a 19th-century Roman poet.[53]

And yet this is not Rushdie's chutneyfication here either. Rather, it is a somewhat dangerous place described by that other multilingual expert, A. K. Ramanujan, about his own work:

> When I write in Kannada, I'd *like* all my English, Tamil, etc. to be at the back of it; and when I write in English I *hope* my Tamil and my Kannada, like my linguistics and anthropology, what I know about America and India, are at the back of it. It's of course only a hope and not a claim. I'm less and less embarrassed of keeping these doors open even when it's dark outside and it's 3 a.m. inside.[54]

Like Ramanujan, Kolatkar writes poetry in both languages even as he keeps the door open between them for any traffic. We need a more nuanced term than "translation" (or maybe a range of related words) to deal with such bilingual forays across languages that destroy our monolingual sense of writing and of life because, as Wittgenstein reminds us, "it is not always an advantage to replace an indistinct picture with a sharp one. . . . Isn't the indistinct one often exactly what we need?"[55]

Kolatkar's bilingual writing presents a different notion of literature than the one projected by later nativist writers like Nemade.[56] In one of his essays, Amit Chaudhuri suggests that Kolatkar provides an alternative lineage to Salman Rushdie for modern Indian writers in English.[57] I suggest that Kolatkar also provides an alternative literary lineage in Marathi to the one that is designated by Nemade's work today. In fact, this place of distinction—from both Rushdie and Nemade—is the indefinable space of mediation that retains the distinctness of the two linguistic spheres while admitting the predominance of neither. The smooth certainties of binaries are dismantled and Kolatkar stands somewhere in between, on uncertain territory, as if heeding Wittgenstein's statement:

> We have got onto slippery ice where there is no friction and so in a certain sense conditions are ideal, but also, because of that we are unable to walk. We want to walk: so we need friction. Back to the rough ground![58]

The Marathi *Jejuri*, seemingly only a "translation" of the English text, brings us back to a consideration of the friction of languages and texts and gives us sturdy footholds to examine the intricate, unsimple relations of the regional languages and English in Indian poetry.

Epilogue: No Singular Truths

In the genre of poetry, *Bombay Modern* offers an alternative locus for scholarly study to that of fiction in South Asian and postcolonial studies. *Bombay Modern* reads *sathottari* poetry as textual concatenations of the rhythms of publishing, of literary gatherings, of translation practices of the new nation, of the bilingual and multilingual energies unleashed by the Samyukta Maharashtra agitations and the Ambedkar movement, and of the global literary, artistic, and popular cultural movements and events that seeped into the membrane of Bombay. It shows how the poem becomes the unit of the modern rhythm of post-independence Bombay.

Through its emphasis on material practices of reading and a bilingual method of interpretation, *Bombay Modern* asks for an expanded ring of interpretation and a double vision of literary history. This book draws the circle around the bilingual life of Bombay, with a circumference that goes well beyond the accepted boundaries of the conventional mapped line of the city. It also presents the *sathottari* period in poetry to illustrate how familiar categories (of modernism, translation, little magazines) materialize in contingent and local processes, an alternative modernism that constantly fluctuates between the global and the local.

In an unpublished draft from the Kolatkar Papers, the poetic speaker talks about himself in the context of the world's literary figures: "I was born the year Hart Crane killed himself / Nine years after *Ulysses* was burnt / three years after Auden published his first collection." This awareness of global writing worlds is an important element of Kolatkar's poetry and of the writing of the rest of his contemporaries. But in the unpublished Kolatkar Papers I also found another fragment that states a somewhat different sentiment:

> eliot pound both hard found
> dante donald hall
> spender goethe take my poets
> you can take them all
> take my poets yeats and goethe
> . . .
> if your old guitar is still around
> will you trade it for my ~~yeats and~~[1] ezra pound

Kolatkar likes to do this—he likes to shatter idols, even his own. This fragment shows that the poet does not leave any myth standing and will not allow any pedestal to stay intact. In an early Marathi poem from *Arun Kolatkarchya Kavita*, this time using religious idols as the metaphor, the poet says:

> *an tuze ganapati*
> *sod majhya dolyat*
> *rangena ubhe raha mhanava*
> *sagalyancha visarjan karanaray*[2]

The short poem refers to the big annual festival of Ganesha/Ganapati in Bombay where idols of Ganesha are installed under public canopies, and at the end of the seven- to ten-day festival the idols are taken out in a noisy procession on the road to the beach where they are slid into the seawater accompanied by loud chants. In this poem, "*Ganapati*," Kolatkar's speaker asks the world to "bring your ganeshas" (*an tuze ganapati*) and to glide them presumably in the rivers of his eyes (*sod majhya dolyat*). The speaker says he will take care of the queued ganeshas (*rangena ubhe raha mhanava*) and bid them all a ritual good-bye by drowning them (*sagalyancha visarjan karanaray*); his irreverent eye will take in and dislodge all unquestioned dogmas. The attempt in *Bombay Modern* is to uncover that other story of Kolatkar and of *sathottari* poetry, to take down the dogma of easy global cosmopolitanisms within which all discussions of modern Indian poetry is framed, and to show the transregional joints of both English and Marath poetry.

The book calls for a double vision of literary history, like that of A. K. Ramanujan's poem: "Adjust my single eye, rainbow bubble / so I too may see all things double."[3] It asks for a focus on close readings and individual writers but also an engagement with the larger multilingual world of material practices that by turn enables, hinders, and cathects the individual texts of literature; it proposes a study of the multilingual world's literature through a non-singular literary methodology that addresses multiple languages and their social and material histories as contexts for each text. And the book asks for a dual focus on the textual and the material processes that constitute the meaning-making universe of the book.

Very often, an individual writer is read in isolation, from his cohort, his period, his surroundings and canonized as a unique appearance in the literature of a region. *Bombay Modern* draws the line beyond the poet as an individual writer to include the messy material locations of his writing and the complex interactions with people, events, and experiences of his time and place. Simultaneously, it also insists on respecting "the verbal complexities, formal particularities, and aesthetic intricacy of the poetic text while analyzing the ideologies and social meanings that are condensed in and propelled by these linguistic and rhetorical choices."[4] The *sathottari* poem is not read as a mere vehicle of social comment in this book; there is an emphasis on close readings even as the interpretative process uncovers embedded social worlds in the word. As Rachel Blau Du Plessis convincingly argues, the reading method should aim at "understanding how poetic mechanisms (placement on a line, form of a stanza, specific imagery, genre allusions in a title, and so on) express particular historical moments, ideological materials, and debates."[5] Therefore, the book looks closely at the words of the poem, but also the surface of the page, the illustration on the cover, the context of its writing and publication, in order to decipher the sociality of this poetic text.

This effort starts with the belief that bilingual readings of literature can reveal new pathways of interpretation, a new methodology of understanding Indian modernisms that far too often are parsed only in one language and only in the words on the page. As Dilip Chitre reminds us, "[The bilingual writers] are not only Anglo-Marathi but basically Bombay poets in one sense or another. There is something in this polyglot city's culture that drives some people to write in two languages and belong to two cultures simultaneously."[6] *Bombay Modern* attempts to understand that polyglot culture that gets encoded in the poems of the *sathottari* poets. In documenting the bilingual grammar of the poems of this period and of Kolatkar's own poetry, it aims to concretize the otherwise vague attributions of a happy and easy hybridity of this urban space. There needs to be a locus-based study of modernities because while "cultural form, social practices, and institutional arrangements surface in most places in the wake of modernity, at each national and cultural site, those elements are put together (reticulated) in a unique and contingent formation in response to local culture and politics."[7] That alternative modernism of *sathottari* Bombay is the burden of this book.

That typical crosshatch of languages, politics, and culture of any location can be seen in many other works by Arun Kolatkar in addition to the ones that are centrally featured in the chapters here. I necessarily leave the task unfinished: there are other books of poems by Kolatkar that are lightly handled here but that deserve closer scrutiny (*Chirimiri*, *Dron*, *Arun Kolatkarchya Kavita*, *Arun Kolatkarchya Char Kavita*, *The Policeman*).[8] Each one of these can provide more critical knowledge about the work of multiple languages and the complex interweave of the social and the literary. The book also presents just a few of the creative exchanges between Kolatkar and his contemporaries: his work interacts with that of many visual artists, with the world of advertising (which was an intimate part of the poet's own life as well that of several of his friends), and with newspapers (Kolatkar evinces a strong documentary impulse in his poetry and in his literary habits).[9] He was closely aware of the innovations of American blues and jazz music as well.

The possibilities of material and bilingual literary analysis are not restricted to Kolatkar's poetry or to the Bombay *sathottari* poets. There are others, like Jayanta Mahapatra and A. K. Ramanujan, who engage different linguistic tools in their writing: Mahapatra in his bilingual Oriya/English contexts and Ramanujan in his multilingual involvement in English, Kannada, and Tamil. The print culture from which their works emerge and the multiple linguistic environments that they belong to can prove to be a rich ground for future literary analyses.

There is also a continuum of literary practices between the poets of this generation who actively pursued translation as a form of writing and those who practice bilingual writing methods. Chapter 3 examines this rich movement across multiple languages in the anthologies, little magazines, and the writing of the Bombay poets, showing that even when not writing in two languages like the bilingual poets, others like Nissim Ezekiel, Adil Jussawalla, R. Parthasarathy, Gieve Patel, and Arvind Krishna Mehrotra insisted on a translingual consciousness of Indian poetry through their focus on translation. Jussawalla notes this urge toward a comparatist view in his heartfelt talk given at the 7th ACLALS conference in Singapore in June 1986, titled "Being There: Aspects of an Indian Crisis." Referring to the Hindi writer Nirmal Verma and himself, an English poet, Jussawalla said,

> We'd share the hope that the only way to be a responsible writer was to be true to oneself and to what one saw; that we were responsible to those who came after us—to bear witness to what the official lie or the censor or Time was always trying to wipe out. If we agreed on that, then we might find our strategies with two languages—whether we were writing poetry or prose—not very different. We might find both our languages—his Hindi, my English—in their currently accepted forms in daily commerce—wholly inadequate to fill out the poetic and fictional worlds of our witnessing.[10]

Jussawalla continues in this speech what he started in his path-breaking anthology, *New Writing in India*, in 1974. He was one of the first to aggressively pursue the documentation of a localized idiom of the modern Indian world. As he said in his introduction,

> In the best Indian writing . . . there [is] an assured use of indigenous forms [and] the content is . . . very much the product of local stresses and strains, the dialectics of a particular socio-economic situation [and] the Western reader is more likely to be annoyed by a certain contrariness in the Indian's attitude to fundamental issues like war, sex, and poverty, than be contemptuous of the similarities with his.[11]

In his 1986 ACLALS talk as well, Jussawalla is on the same mission: to forge a common literary project with writers in other languages, like Nirmal Verma in Hindi, for an idiom that would speak truthfully of the world in which they lived. It is not an easy task and neither Jussawalla's nor Kolatkar's poetry offers easy solutions for it.

Bombay Modern opens with an enigmatic poem by Kolatkar that refuses to spill its heart of meanings out into public view. The book ends with yet another one, from the unpublished drafts of poems in the folder for *Kala Ghoda Poems*, where Kolatkar tries out a version of an image that appears in multiple forms in the published version.[12] The poem perhaps refers to the barefoot queen of the crossroads,[13] the self-assured, practical woman living in the streets under the gaze of the thousands of people who pass by each day watching her perform private acts in public. They probably judge her in many ways: as destitute, beggarly, pitiable, dirty. And in this unfinished poetic fragment, the poet seems to be trying out his response to such blatant acts of monologic interpretation of the other's life through the pigeons' behavior:

a boundless circle of pidgeons[14]
in its search of a common centre
narrows down at her feet
each pidgeon takes what it holds in its beak
to be the absolute truth
and radiates to the nearest roof

and goes off at a tangent
to the nearest roof

The "pidgeons" are unaware of the vastness and complexity of the world from which they pick individual grains and clutch at them as the only truth about the world. But the poet is painfully conscious of the contrary—he tries to capture the moment through words, through visual design, through musical scores, through a material rendering of the textual, all in the hope of getting beyond that "phalanx / of sixty five dots per square inch"[15] that is the printed page and which shields the poet and his reader from the world of experience.

Therefore, no singular truths will work for Kolatkar or his readers. Perhaps that could also serve as a reading methodology for literary studies in India, one that will heed the variegated linguistic, visual, and material blocks that go into the construction of a poetic text.

Notes

INTRODUCTION

1. Arun Kolatkar and Arvind Krishna Mehrotra, *The Boatride & Other Poems* (Mumbai: Pras Prakashan, 2009), 61.

2. Vilas Sarang, "Mother Tongue, Other Tongue," *New Quest* 139 (2000): 104–8.

3. Arvind Krishna Mehrotra, "The Emperor Has No Clothes," in *The Vintage Book of Modern Indian Literature*, ed. Amit Chaudhuri (New York: Vintage, 2004), 456–77. This essay was first published in 1980 in *Chandrabhaga*.

4. Bruce King, "Modern Indian and American Poetry: Some Contacts and Relations," *Indian Journal of American Studies* 15, no. 1 (1985): 5–17. This was an early documentation of the international connections of modern Indian poetry.

5. Dipesh Chakrabarty, *Provincializing Europe: Postcolonial Thought and Historical Difference* (Princeton, NJ: Princeton University Press, 2000), 28.

6. Dilip Chitre, "A Home for Every Voice," in *Indian Poetry: Modernism and After*, ed. K. Satchidanandan (Delhi: Sahitya Akademi, 2001), 2.

7. See Margery Sabin, *Dissenters and Mavericks: Writings About India in English, 1765–2000* (Oxford: Oxford University Press, 2002); and Eric Pullin, "'Money Does Not Make Any Difference to the Opinions That We Hold': India, the CIA, and the Congress for Cultural Freedom, 1951–58," *Intelligence and National Security* 26, no. 2–3 (2011): 377–98. Also see chapter 3 for details about the Indian Committee for Cultural Freedom.

8. The issues of *Shabda* were cyclostyled in the office of the mercurial political figure and then union activist George Fernandes because one of the editors, Ramesh Samarth, used to work there.

9. There were little magazines like *Kavi India* that continued into the 1980s, but there were few of these significant independent ventures at that time.

10. Loren Glass, *Counterculture Colophon: Grove Press, the Evergreen Review, and the Incorporation of the Avant-Garde* (Stanford, CA: Stanford University Press, 2013). Glass looks at the workings of the Grove Press and its efforts to normalize the so-called obscenity of the literature of the period as a "vulgar modernism" of the time.

11. For more on the idea of *sathottari* as it was conceived in Marathi poetry, see T. S. Kulkarni, *Svatantryottara Marathi Kavita, 1961–80* (New Delhi: Sahitya Akademi, 1994); R. G. Jadhav, ed., *Marathi Vangmayacha Itihas*, vol. 7, part 2 (Pune: Maharashtra Sahitya Parishad, 2010); R. G. Jadhav, *Sathottari Marathi Kavita Va Kavi* (Aurangabad: Saket Prakashan, 1997); the introduction to Chandrakant Patil and N. D. Mahanor, eds., *Punha Ekada Kavita* (Pune: Neelkanth Prakashan, 1982); and the introduction to Chandrakant Patil, ed., *Drushyantar: Swatantryanantarchi Marathi Kavita* (Delhi: National Book Trust, 2007).

12. Sachin Ketkar, "Globalization and New Marathi Poetry," http://www.museindia.com/viewarticle.asp?myr=2005&issid=3&id=69.

13. Laetitia Zecchini, *Arun Kolatkar and Literary Modernism in India: Moving Lines* (London: Bloomsbury, 2014). Zecchini's book on Arun Kolatkar is an excellent book-length analysis of Kolatkar's English poetry but, as she notes in her preface, she does not read Marathi and therefore the larger part of Kolatkar's oeuvre still remains to be critically analyzed in its own context. Her book on Kolatkar also presents a different monolingual approach as opposed to the bilingual readings in *Bombay Modern*.

14. Vinay Dharwadker, "The Modernist Novel in India: Paradigms and Practices," in *A History of the Indian Novel in English*, ed. Ulka Anjaria (New York: Cambridge University Press, 2015), 103–18.

15. The poet Krishnaji Keshav Damle wrote under the pen name of Keshavsut (son of Keshav).

16. See Philip Engblom, "Keshavsut and Early Modernist Strategies for Indigenizing the Sonnet in Marathi," *Journal of South Asian Literature* 23 (1988): 42–66. Engblom shows how Keshavsut adapted the English sonnet to Marathi poetic forms: "It was a slow, gradual process of trial and error, in which accommodations had to be made both for the formal constraints of his English models . . . as well as for established Marathi convention" (62).

17. T. S. Kulkarni even sees the same double bind of romanticism and realism in both of the poets when he points to the nature poetry of Mardhekar as opposed to his starkly physical, brutally honest critique of society's hypocrisy in other poems (*Svatantryottara Marathi Kavita*, xviii–xi).

18. Philip Engblom, "Bombay Modernisms: English and Marathi Versions in the Poetry of Nissim Ezekiel and Bal Sitaram Mardhekar," *Bombay Literary Review* 2, no. 1 (1990): 31–48.

19. I look at these complex differences as well as collaborations between the two generations in "Little Magazines, Bilingualism and Bombay Poetry," in *History of Indian Poetry in English*, ed. Rosinka Chaudhuri (Cambridge: Cambridge University Press, forthcoming). For a different evaluation of Ezekiel's and Mehrotra's modernisms and their little magazines, see Emma Bird, "'It's missing': *damn you, Missing Person* and the Material History of the Postcolonial Poem," *Postcolonial Text* 9, no. 4 (2014).

20. Kolatkar coined the term "trisland" in *Kala Ghoda Poems* (Mumbai: Pras Prakashan, 2004) to indicate that the Kala Ghoda space is a triangle with rounded corners.

21. See chapter 1 for a discussion of these informal gatherings of like-minded people in Bombay that led to the new writing of the *sathottari* period.

22. Nitin Dadrawala, "*Koslachya mukhaprushtha sambandhi. . udaharan-artha 23 varshanantar,*" *Loksatta*, December 1, 2013, http://www.loksatta.com/lokrang-news/50-years-of-kosala-novel-and-its-cover-page-281891/.

23. Nemade started a little magazine, *Vacha*, in 1968, but even though it was printed in Aurangabad, the copies were sent to readers in Bombay, writers in the magazine were predominantly from the urban areas, and there was a close relation between the writers in the two spaces of Aurangabad and Bombay.

24. See his famous poem "Bharatmata": it starts and ends in Bombay even though it moves across the central Indian towns of Allahabad and Bhillai in the intervening stanzas.

25. Qtd. in Anjum Hasan, "'Your Missing Person': Clearing House and the Bombay Poets," *Caravan* (November 2010): 66.

26. Ibid. Arundhati Subramanium, a poet from the next generation of Bombay poets, also makes a similar point when insisting on a Bombay/Mumbai "literary scene": "The Mumbai scene is about a web of allegiances, acknowledged and unacknowledged; about debts and apprenticeships, conscious and unconscious." See Arundhati Subramanium, "End of the Road for Mumbai's Poetry Scene?" *DNA India*, January 13, 2007, http://www.dnaindia.com/mumbai/report-end-of-the-road-for-mumbai-s-poetry-scene-1074255.

27. Chitre called Bombay "the city of [Kolatkar's] destiny and his poetic *habitat*." Dilip Chitre, "Remembering Kolatkar" (blog, now defunct, accessed December 10, 2007).

28. Ash Amin and Nigel Thrift, *Cities: Reimagining the Urban* (Cambridge: Polity, 2002), 8.

29. Ibid.

30. Salman Rushdie, *The Moor's Last Sigh* (London: Vintage, 1995), 350.

31. Dilip Chitre, *An Anthology of Marathi Poetry, 1945–65* (Bombay: Nirmala Sadanand, 1967); King, "Modern Indian and American Poetry"; Arvind Krishna Mehrotra, *Partial Recall: Essays on Literature and Literary History* (Hyderabad: Orient Blackswan, 2012); Amit Chaudhuri, *Clearing a Space: Reflections on India, Literature and Culture* (Witney, England: Peter Lang, 2008); Zecchini, *Arun Kolatkar.*

32. Tukaram, Muktabai, Janabai, Namdev, and other Marathi saint-poets. See Kolatkar's translations of this poetry published in *Vrischik* (September–October 1970); Philip Engblom, "Marathi Poetry in English Translation," *Journal of South Asian Literature* 17, no. 1 (Winter/Spring 1982): 115–32; and *Boatride*, 157–93.

33. Both chart the working-class world of Bombay, albeit in different parts of the city and through different poetic structures. See Surve's poem "Mumbai" (in Vinay Lal, *The Oxford Anthology of the Modern Indian City: The City in Its Plenitude* [New Delhi: Oxford University Press, 2013], 41) where he documents the contrast

between the street sweepers and the rich upper classes; Kolatkar also writes their lives in *Kala Ghoda Poems* but in a more ironic and less overtly ideological vein.

34. Meera Kosambi, "British Bombay and Marathi Mumbai: Some Nineteenth Century Perceptions," in *Bombay: Mosaic of Modern Culture*, ed. Sujata Patel and Alice Thorner (Bombay: Oxford University Press, 1995), 3–24.

35. In his 1967 introduction to *The Anthology of Marathi Poetry*, Dilip Chitre was the earliest reader/poet to note the complex connections between Euro-American literature and modern Indian poetry in Marathi.

36. Gyan Prakash, *Mumbai Fables* (Princeton, NJ: Princeton University Press, 2010), 2.

37. Francesca Orsini, "How to Do Multilingual Literary History? Lessons from Fifteenth- and Sixteenth-century North India," *Indian Economic & Social History Review* 49, no. 2 (2012): 225–46.

38. Engblom, "Bombay Modernisms," 31. My book makes a distinction between the generation of the post-1960 and those who came before (like the poets B. S. Mardhekar and P. S. Rege, for instance) based on their poetics and their publishing worlds. Therefore, even while acknowledging the connection between Mardhekar's *bhakti*-inspired poetry and Kolatkar's Tukaram-influenced writing, I differentiate between the initial modernism of Mardhekar and the second-level modernist writing strategies of a poet like Kolatkar. After all, the opposition to Mardhekar's poetics was one of the rallying cries of this cohort of poets. See Ashok Shahane, "*Ajakalachya Marathi vangmayavar 'ksha' kiran*" ("An X-Ray of Contemporary Marathi Literature"), in *Napeksha* (Mumbai: Lokvangmaya Griha, 2008), 3–30.

39. Ramachandra Guha, "The Rise and Fall of the Bilingual Individual," *Economic & Political Weekly* 44, no. 33 (August 15, 2009): 39.

40. Orsini, "How to Do Multilingual Literary History?" 20.

41. See Dharwadker, "The Modernist Novel in India"; Rajeev Patke, *Postcolonial Poetry in English* (Oxford: Oxford University Press, 2006); and Engblom, "Marathi Poetry"; see also "Bombay Modernisms."

42. A. K. Ramanujan, Vinay Dharwadker, and Stuart H. Blackburn, *The Collected Essays of A. K. Ramanujan* (New Delhi: Oxford University Press, 1999), 333.

43. *Boatride*, 228.

44. In a letter dated March 16, 1976, in the Clearing House Papers, Jussawalla asked Mehrotra to go first in the publishing queue for the Press Collective because "Arun would like to have time to prepare the manuscript for his Marathi work too, so that it can be published as a book about the same time as Jejuri." The Marathi book *Arun Kolatkarchya Kavita* was published a year later in the end, but the letter shows that Kolatkar was determined to be, and determined to be perceived to be, a bilingual right from the beginning.

45. Vilas Sarang, "Fullstoppers and Semi-colonials," *New Quest* 143 (2001): 94.

46. See Jahan Ramazani, *The Hybrid Muse: Postcolonial Poetry in English* (Chicago: University of Chicago Press, 2001).

47. R. B. Du Plessis, "Social Texts and Poetic Texts: Poetry and Cultural Studies," in *The Oxford Handbook of Modern and Contemporary American Poetry*, ed. Cary Nelson (Oxford: Oxford University Press, 2012), 65.

48. Laura Moss, "'The Plague of Normality': Reconfiguring Realism in Recent Postcolonial Theory," *Jouvert* 5, no. 1 (Fall 2000), english.chass.ncsu/jouvert/v5i1/moss.htm.

49. Geeta Kapur, "When Was Modernism in Indian/Third World Art?" *South Atlantic Quarterly* 92, no. 3 (Summer 1993): 473–514, reprinted in *When Was Modernism? Essays on Contemporary Cultural Practice in India* (New Delhi: Tulika Press, 2001).

50. See Priyamvada Gopal, *The Indian English Novel: Nation, History, and Narration* (Oxford: Oxford University Press, 2009); Ulka Anjaria, *Realism in the Twentieth-Century Indian Novel: Colonial Difference and Literary Form* (New York: Cambridge University Press, 2012); and Toral Jatin Gajarawala, *Untouchable Fictions: Literary Realism and the Crisis of Caste* (New York: Fordham University Press, 2013).

51. Meenakshi Mukherjee, "The Anxiety of Indianness: Our Novels in English," in *Mapping Cultural Spaces: Postcolonial Indian Literature in English*, ed. Nilufer E. Bharucha and Vrinda Nabar (New Delhi: Vision, 1998), 99–100.

52. Chakrabarty, *Provincializing Europe*, 149–79.

53. Note that Chakrabarty does include poetry in his study of the social construction of genres in West Bengal and in India.

54. Marathi poet Namdeo Dhasal says that "those writers who were producing literature under the banner of realism were themselves probably unaware that their writing was realistic." Namdeo Dhasal and Dilip Chitre, *Namdeo Dhasal, Poet of the Underworld: Poems, 1972–2006* (Pondicherry: Navayana, 2007), 165.

55. Nissim Ezekiel, *Hymns in Darkness* (New Delhi: Oxford University Press, 1976), 9.

56. Arvind Krishna Mehrotra, *Nine Enclosures* (Bombay: Clearing House, 1976), 46.

57. Ibid., 25.

58. Patil, *Drushyantar*, 150. The Marathi poem is "*Majhya priya kavite*" as follows: "*mala nahi basavayacha vegle bet / majhya priya kavite, tu chalat rha samanyatla samanya / mansansobat thet tyache bot pakadun.*" The translation is mine.

59. Qtd. in Mangesh Narayan Kale, "IFA Project on Little Magazines" (unpublished manuscript), 284.

60. Vijay Tendulkar, introduction to *Golpitha* by Namdeo Dhasal (Bombay: Neelkanth Prakashan, 1975), 6.

61. Namdeo Dhasal, "Arsefucker's Park," trans. Chitre in *Namdeo Dhasal, Poet of the Underworld*, 100.

62. Shanta Gokhale, "Words, Pistol Shots," *Outlook Magazine*, July 2, 2007, http://www.outlookindia.com/article/Words-Pistol-Shots/234978.

63. Vilas Sarang, "*Marathi sahityatil tinpani khel*" ("The Three-Card Game of Poker in Marathi Literature"), in *Sarjanashodh ani lihita lekhak* (Mumbai: Mauj Prakashan, 2007), 70–72.

64. Clearing House Papers.

65. Jerome J. McGann, *The Textual Condition* (Princeton, NJ: Princeton University Press, 1991), 12–13.

66. Stephen Bann, *Concrete Poetry: An International Anthology* (London: London Magazine, 1967), 15.

67. Chapter 1 examines this material turn in the little magazines and chapter 2 examines the influence of the concrete poetry movement on the publishing as well as the poetry of the writers of this period.

68. See chapter 2 for Mehrotra's concrete poem published in *Vrishchik* 2, and R. K. Joshi's poems in Patil and Mahanor, *Punha Ekada Kavita*.

69. R. K. Joshi, *Rawa* 10 (November 1972).

70. McGann, *The Textual Condition*, 12.

71. Ibid., 56.

72. Ibid., 13.

73. Ibid., 14.

74. George Bornstein, *Material Modernism: The Politics of the Page* (Cambridge: Cambridge University Press, 2001), 179.

75. Clifford Siskin, "Textual Culture in the History of the Real," *Textual Cultures* 2, no. 2 (2007): 121.

76. Maurice Rickards, *Collecting Printed Ephemera* (New York: Abbeville Press, 1988), 16–17.

77. Kolatkar Papers.

78. Kolatkar Papers. The English translation is mine. The words are spaced as in the original draft (including the word that is struck out).

79. Arvind Krishna Mehrotra, "Being Here," review of *Maps of a Mortal Moon* by Adil Jussawalla, *Caravan*, April 1, 2014, http://www.caravanmagazine.in/books/being-here.

80. For a more detailed study, see chapter 1 and the section "The *Katta* of Modern Indian Poetry."

81. "It was a modernism dominated by men. As the trajectory from Lawrence to Miller to Burroughs economically illustrates, Grove's battle against censorship began with a quintessentially high modernist preoccupation with adulterous women—inaugurated by *Madame Bovary* and *Ulysses*—and ended up with the highly homosocial and increasingly homosexual preoccupations of late modernist figures such as Burroughs and Jean Genet. All of Genet's novels take place within homosocial institutions and networks—reform schools, prisons, the criminal underworld—and his overwrought stylization and spiritualization of these milieus helped provide a cultural consecration for the boy gang as a dissident literary community in the United States" (Glass, *Counterculture Colophon*, 123). Also see Michael Davidson, *Gays Like Us: Citing Masculinity in Cold War Poetics* (Chicago: University of Chicago Press, 2004).

82. Eunice de Souza cites in dismay the patriarchal comment made by an academic regarding her work and her role in this period: "A very strange, even grotesque version of these facts appeared in a review by an academic in a prestigious paper. 'She has had the advantage,' he writes, 'of getting to know, rather intimately, her contemporaries, poets who helped shape her poems, offering suggestions and putting her on the right track'" ("On a Wing and a Prayer," *Mumbai Mirror*, June 17, 2010).

83. Ashok Shahane, interview by Anjali Nerlekar, 2010.

84. Shri Pu., as Mr. P. Bhagwat (1923–2007) was called in the Marathi literary world, was an editor beloved by many, and even among the little magaziners, editors and writers like Ashok Shahane continued to have high personal regard and respect for the man even as they excoriated the institutional space taken up by *Satyakatha*. This exchange with Gauri Deshpande and many such anecdotes show that one needs to separate the vitriol directed against the magazine from the respect for the editor and that Shri Pu. did indeed have a large and expansive vision as far as literature and the arts were concerned.

85. This is from the introduction by Vidya Bal to the book *Katha Gaurichi* ([Mumbai: Mauj Prakashan Griha, 2008], 7), a compilation of articles on Gauri Deshpande that were first published in a special issue of the Marathi periodical *Milun Saryajani* that was published four months after Gauri Deshpande died in 2003. In it is the publication of a series of correspondence by mail between Gauri Deshpande and Shri Pu. Bhagwat of *Satyakatha*.

86. Santan Rodrigues, editorial, *Kavi* 1 (1976): 1–2.

87. Chakrabarty, *Provincializing Europe*, 144.

88. Lakshmibai Tilak is the accomplished author of *Smritichitre* (Pictures of the Mind), an autobiography that is considered one of the earliest statements of women's agency and literary abilities. For more on Lakshmibai Tilak, see Meera Kosambi, *Crossing Thresholds: Feminist Essays in Social History* (Delhi: Permanent Black, 2007).

89. Shahane, "*Ajakalachya Marathi vangmayavar 'ksha' kiran*," 25.

90. Girish Karnad talks about the fruitful period of the 1970s when Satyajit Ray, Mani Kaul, and others frequented the Film and Television Institute of India (FTII) in his 2013 interview with the *Times of India*. Also, see the histories of the first years of the FTII, started in Pune in 1960, where there was a rich interchange of ideas and influences between the Marathi, Bengali, Kannada, and Malayalam filmmakers, as well as those from other regional film industries.

91. Gauri Deshpande also worked a lot with women's periodicals, like *Milun Saryajani*. Most women's periodicals largely came after the first decade of the *sathottari* period of the little magazines as did a majority of the Dalit periodicals, and they uncover and extend radically the political fight that was covert in the writings of the little magaziners.

92. Eunice de Souza, *Women in Dutch Painting* (Bombay: Praxis, 1988), 29.

93. Alix Shulman, "Women Writers of the Beat Generation," *Moody Street Irregulars* 28 (1994): 3.

OVERVIEW

1. My translation. Qtd. in Vasant Abaji Dahake, *Marathi Sahitya: Itihas Ani Sanskriti* (Mumbai: Popular Publishers, 2005).

2. Since the inception of the state of Maharashtra in 1960, there have been border disputes with the neighboring state of Kannada-speaking Karnataka

about towns like Belgaum (which have sizable populations from both linguistic communities, Marathi and Kannada). And there have been periodic outbursts of public demands in Maharashtra such as "Belgaum should become part of united Maharashtra" (*Belgaum Maharashtra jhalach pahije*), starting with a violent agitation in 1969.

3. According to his friend Avinash Gupte, Kolatkar even visited the environs of this priest's home, just to make sure he was not apocryphal. Pralhad Jadhav notes this incident in his article on Kolatkar in *Loksatta* (May 30, 2003), 4, http://webcache.googleusercontent.com/search?q=cache:bNVS9QTX8koJ:www.loksatta.com/daily/20040530/lm03.htm+&cd=1&hl=en&ct=clnk&gl=us.

4. In India, especially in rural spaces, *lotas* are also used to carry water to wash oneself after defecating.

5. Arun Kolatkar, *Arun Kolatkarchya Kavita* (Mumbai: Pras Prakashan, 1977), 32. The translation is mine.

6. The little magazine has no dates and there is some confusion about the year it was launched. Several Marathi and English scholars have dated the first issue of *Aso* to 1962. But Shahane and Nemade are certain that it was 1963, after the publication of the landmark novel *Kosla* by Bhalchandra Nemade in the same year and after Ginsberg's visit to India the previous year. According to Shahane, "We had promised 12 issues in a year, but the press went on delaying them & we overran the timetable. Then came the idea of six-a-year in a new format." The graphic designer and poet R. K. Joshi was also part of the designing of the new format where they "experimented with direct linocuts (in place of metal blocks) for the cover" (Ashok Shahane, email communication with Anjali Nerlekar, September 27, 2014).

7. For instance, on October 11, 1955, the Communists protested against the national government's States Reorganisation Commission report by burning it in a bonfire and with a strike of six hundred thousand people in November of the same year. Several died in the ensuing police action and three hundred people were hurt.

8. Arun Kolatkar, "Interview," *Indian Literary Review* (August 1978): 4–10, quote on p. 9.

CHAPTER 1

1. Eric Bulson, "Little Magazine, World Form," in *The Oxford Handbook of Global Modernisms*, ed. Matt Eatough and Mark Wollaeger (New York: Oxford University Press, 2013), 268.

2. See Bruce King, *Modern Indian Poetry in English* (Delhi: Oxford University Press, 2001); and Dahake, *Marathi Sahitya*.

3. Such images of conventionally ugly creatures abound in other writings, too. Manohar Oak and Arun Kolatkar also use uncommon and non-beautiful images to reinforce the ordinary realism of their writing. In the folder titled "Loose ends," Kolatkar records one wonderful image that captures his writing project: "*vyutapattichi varula . . . mungikhad manala ghaltat bhural*" ("my pangolin mind is enthralled by the anthills of etymology"). Manohar Oak

uses the image of the toad in the following poem: *dagadaatlya bedki sarkha vyakul / mala pavasacha gana gayachay*" ("Like the toad under the rock / I want to sing the song of rain"). Perhaps both these poets reveal the influence of the modernist Marianne Moore in their selection of such unusual creatures.

4. Dilip Chitre, *Travelling in a Cage* (Bombay: Clearing House, 1980), 55.

5. Steven Clay and Rodney Phillips, *A Secret Location on the Lower East Side: Adventures in Writing, 1960–1980: A Sourcebook of Information* (New York: New York Public Library, 1998), 10.

6. "Strategy" refers to the techniques of power, of the panoptical, and the overseeing vision. "Tactics," on the other hand, refers to the "clandestine forms taken by the dispersed, tactical, and makeshift creativity of groups of individuals already caught in the nets of the 'discipline'" (Michel De Certeau, *The Practice of Everyday Life*, trans. Steven Rendell [Berkeley: University of California Press, 1984], xiv). For an application of De Certeau to the interpretation of Kolatkar's poetry, see Anjali Nerlekar, "The Cartography of the Local in Arun Kolatkar's Poetry," *Journal of Postcolonial Writing* 49, no. 5 (2013): 609–23.

7. It is true that important little magazines in Marathi (like *Vacha*) moved out of Bombay and into the periphery of places like Aurangabad, expressly stating the desire to create a non-urban, non-metropolitan poetics. And yet many of the readers and subscribers of *Vacha* were from Bombay and the writers in this magazine kept close connections with Bombay's literary scene. In the second decade of the little magazines, when the Dalit movement separated itself from the little magazine movement, there was a more determined and concerted effort to move out of Bombay.

8. The Marathi and English poets and critics alike refer to the transient publications of this period as little magazines, and they do not necessarily differentiate between the bibelot, or an ephemeral publication, and the little magazine. I will abide by their categorization of the little magazines, and when I am referring to them, they will include both *Poetry India* (which is like any Western little magazine in appearance and content) and *Tornado* and *Timba* (which would be classified as bibelots in Anglo-American literary magazine taxonomy).

9. Bulson, "Little Magazine, World Form," 268.

10. Ibid.

11. This started as a little magazine and, in its first avatar, published five issues in 1969 and six issues in 1972. But after that, the editor, Chandrakant Khot, decided to make it an annual Diwali issue and focused each issue on one selected genre of writing (letters, the diary, and so on) or on one theme. In this form, it survived for twenty-four years until 1996, when Khot shut it down because of a lack of funding (despite its immense popularity). Satish Kalsekar and Arun Shevte published an anthology of select content from these issues of the magazine in 2012: *Nivadak Abakadaee* (Mumbai: Lokvangmaya Griha, 2012).

12. Such definitions are not easy. In 1942, Alan Swallow compared the little magazines to the "moon; changeable, often short-lived, apparently shining in the indirect light of literature and holding in their devotees a desire which is

insatiable" (qtd. in Mary Biggs, "Small Publishing: A Review Article," *Library Quarterly* 52, no. 1 [January 1982]: 61.

13. Robert Scholes and Clifford Wulfman, *Modernism in the Magazines: An Introduction* (New Haven, CT: Yale University Press, 2010), 56.

14. For a discussion of the rebelliousness of format, see Vasant Patankar, "*Aniyatkalikanchi sankalpana ani itihas*," *Navakshar Darshan* 5, no. 2 (2001): 5–11. This is a special issue on little magazines.

15. And yet it carried an advertisement for the issues of *damn you: a magazine of the arts* (edited by Arvind Mehrotra, Alok Rai, and Amit Rai), which declared itself "India's first avant mimeo" and claimed an editorial policy that was "open as hell" and ended with the exhortation to "support little magazines everywhere" (*Poetry India* 2, no. 1 [January–March 1967]: 8).

16. Santan Rodrigues started *Kavi* in 1976; the magazine was temporarily shut down after its fifth issue, but it came back in 1978 as *Kavi India* and continued well into the 1980s.

17. David Bennett, "Periodical Fragments and Organic Culture: Modernism, the Avant Garde, and the Little Magazine," *Contemporary Literature* 30, no. 4 (Winter 1989): 482.

18. This antipathy toward numbers can also indicate a rejection of the market economy in which the poets find themselves entangled. See Vasant Gurjar, "Tally Clerk," *Atta* 3; see also Anil Bandekar, "*Ekhada stand, ek ranget ubhe raha, chi pati*" ("One Bus-Stand, One Board, Please Queue Here"), *Vacha* 3 (1968): 37–38.

19. Mehrotra's *damn you* declared its cost thus on most of its issues: "Price: anything commensurate with your dignity—and ours also."

20. A review of the little magazine *Tornado*, started by Pavan Kumar Jain in Bombay (1967–71), states that "the magazine, we are told, has no subscription rates. Like many of our sadhus it lives on kind gestures of soft souls" ([review of *Tornado*], *Free Press Bulletin*, March 21, 1968). In *Poetry India* 1, no. 3 (1966): 6, there is a page of acknowledgments where the editor thanks all who contributed toward the making of the little magazine. Along with the bigger sources of funding, including the painters M. F. Husain and Akbar Padamsee, who donated the money from the sale of one their paintings each, there are thanks expressed to "a hundred subscribers who collected four other subscriptions each, when requested to do so."

21. Ashok Shahane, interview by Anjali Nerlekar, 2011. Also see Shahane, "*Bal Thakur an makhar*," *Anubhav* (Diwali 2013): 140–44, where he narrates in detail the closing down of the magazine *Rahasyaranjan* and the birth of *Aso* in Pune.

22. Qtd. in Loss P. Glazier, *Small Press: An Annotated Guide to the Literature* (Freemont, CA: Ruddy Duck Press, 1985), 8.

23. Kiran Nagarkar and Shubha Slee, *Seven Sixes Are Forty-Three* (Oxford: Heinemann, 1995), 170.

24. Shahane, "*Ajakalachya Marathi vangmayavar 'ksha' kiran*," 28. The translation is mine. This essay was first presented in English at a conference arranged by the Congress for Cultural Freedom in Bombay and subsequently translated and published in the Marathi magazine *Manohar* in 1963.

25. Qtd. in Allen De Loach and Allen Ginsberg, "Little Mags/Small Presses and the Cultural Revolution: [A Panel Discussion Moderated by] Allen De Loach," *Intrepid* 21/22 (1972): 112.

26. Dipesh Chakrabarty, "Adda, Calcutta: Dwelling in Modernity," in *Public Cuture* 11, no. 1 (1999): 109–45.

27. Ibid., 119.

28. See Len Fulton, "Anima Rising: Little Magazines in the Sixties," *American Libraries* 2, no. 1 (January 1971): 29, where Fulton quotes d. a. levy's self-description "poeteditorpublisher" and says that "this is an agglutination which Levy himself coined, and it more or less summarizes what Levy and much of American concrete was about." For more on the relation between concrete poetry and *sathottari* Indian poetry, see chapter 3.

29. Pradeep Nerurkar, "*Little Magazine ani Raja Dhale*," special issue on Raja Dhale, *Khel* 23 (2012): 55.

30. In his article on Bal Thakur, Shahane describes the *katta* that formed around the magazine where Shahane worked, *Rahasyaranjan*, and then, when he moved to Pune, a second "quorum," as he refers to it, was reached around his creation of the little *Aso*. See Shahane, "*Bal Thakur an makhar*."

31. See Nerlekar, "Cartography" for a detailed analysis of the long poem.

32. Arun Kolatkar, "Breakfast at Kala Ghoda," in *Kala Ghoda Poems* (Mumbai: Pras Prakashan, 2004), 87.

33. This poem is further discussed in Nerlekar, "Cartography."

34. Beginning in the early 1960s, this group of writers and readers met every Thursday afternoon (which was Shahane's day off from his printing press job) at the Wayside Inn at Kala Ghoda, Bombay, to chat and discuss and exchange ideas. That practice continues to this day, though the Wayside Inn is now closed and the meeting place has moved a few times to various small restaurants in the area, like the Military Café and Stadium Café. Amit Chaudhuri writes about this briefly in his introduction to the *New York Review of Books' Jejuri* edition and refers to it in Amit Chaudhuri, *Real Time: Stories and a Memoir in Verse* (London: Picador, 2001), 179–82.

35. This essay, originally delivered as a seminar presentation in English as "Literature and Commitment," was soon translated and published in Marathi in *Manohar* in 1963 before appearing in other little magazines and finally being collected in Shahane's anthology of essays, *Napeksha* (2008).

36. Shahane, "*Ajakalachya Marathi vangmayavar 'ksha' kiran*," 28. As late as 2013, with the fiftieth anniversaries of Shahane's landmark essay and the even more momentous novel in Marathi, *Kosla* (Cocoon) by Bhalchandra Nemade, in several interviews and articles Shahane and Nemade recounted anecdotes of the *sathottari* writing world and the process of writing these texts. And fifty years later, it is now on record that these two path-breaking texts of modern Marathi literature (one, the essay that was the unofficial manifesto of the period; the second, a novel

that changed the course of Marathi literature with its experimentation with language) were both collaborations, to a certain extent, between Shahane and Nemade. The two figures of Marathi literature, friends for over fifty years and literary conspirators against the establishment, seem to have jointly dealt the crucial blows to the edifice of tradition in the *sathottari* period.

37. There is an oft-quoted list by Kolatkar (made years later) that also constructs such an eclectic community of writers from all over the world and across time. Kolatkar presented this list in one of his rare interviews, and one of the first, with Sunil Karnik in the *Rucha* special issue on Kolatkar in 1977. It was a combative exchange where the poet was clearly not eager to respond to questions:

> Want me to give you a list? Whitman, Mardhekar, Manmohan, Eliot, Pound, Auden, Hart Crane, Dylan Thomas, Kafka, Baudelaire, Heine, Catullus, Villon, Dyaneshwar, Namdev, Janabai, Eknath, Tukaram, Wang Wei, Tu Fu, Han Shan, Ramjoshi, Honaji, Mandelstam, Dostoevsky, Gogol, Isaac Bashevis Singer, Babel, Apollinaire, Breton, Brecht, Neruda, Ginsberg, Barthes, Duras, Joseph Heller, Enzensberger, Gunter Grass, Norman Mailer, Henry Miller, Nabokov, Namdev Dhasal, Patte Bapurav, Rabelais, Apuleius, Rex Stout, Agatha Christie, Robert Sheckley, Harlan Ellison, Bhalchandra Nemade, Durrenmatt, Aarp, Cummings, Lewis Carrol, John Lennon, Bob Dylan, Sylvia Plath, Ted Hughes, Godse Bhatji, Morgenstern, Chakradhar, Gerard Manley Hopkins, Balwantbua, Kierkegaard, Lenny Bruce, Bahinabai Chaudhari, Kabir, Robert Johnson, Muddy Waters, Leadbelly, Howlin' Wolf, John Lee Hooker, Leiber and Stoller, Eisenstein, Truffaut, Woody Guthrie, Laurel and Hardy. (Trans. and qtd. in Engblom 2001, 399)

Also compare this list with the artist Bhupen Khakhar's list, "Notes on the Visual Sources of My Painting," *Vrischik*, no. 1 (1969), where Khakhar lists common calendar art, advertisements, and Hindi film images along with temple art and colonial photographs.

38. In fact, Kolatkar wrote a long poetic sequence in *Kala Ghoda Poems* titled "The Rat-poison Man's Lunch Hour" that features the walls of the Wayside Inn extensively; see Kolatkar, *Kala Ghoda Poems*, 134–41. Also see his poem "*Irani*" in Marathi (*Arun Kolatkarchya Kavita*, 56–57), and its English version, "Irani restaurant Bombay," *Boatride*, 53. In the endnote to the poem, Mehrotra states that Kolatkar had "combined the interiors of three or four restaurants to create the one described in the poem" (*Boatride*, 243).

39. See Sarang, "*Marathi sahityatil tinpani khel*" where Sarang says, "Often in Bombay, one finds a gang of young men, mostly vagrant, sitting in a group by the roadside. If you venture closer, you will see a game of three-card poker in full swing. Any Mumbaikar will tell you that it is dangerous to linger in such company for too long. The *sathottari* poets started the trend of playing the three-card game of poker on the streets of the literary world" (71). He predicts that while this age of the roadside vagrants is ending in Marathi literature, a similar rebellion is likely to explode again if there is too much fetishizing of the rational and of the academic modes of writing.

40. Jack Spicer, *The Collected Books of Jack Spicer*, ed. Robin Blaser (Santa Barbara, CA: Black Sparrow Press, 1980), 61.

41. R. K. Joshi also designed Allen Ginsberg's poster-poem, "September on Jessore Road," first published by Ashok Shahane in Bombay; see figure 1.5.

42. Patil and Mahanor, *Punha Ekada Kavita*, 129.

43. Dilip Chitre, "At My Age and of My Age," *The Hindu*, January 4, 2009, http://www.thehindu.com/todays-paper/tp-features/tp-literaryreview/at-my-age-and-of-my-age/article662159.ece.

44. Dilip Chitre, *As Is, Where Is: Selected English Poems, 1964–2007* (Mumbai: Poetrywala, 2007), 81.

45. Kolatkar, *Kala Ghoda Poems*, 28.

46. Ibid.

47. Walter Benjamin's famous description of the modern writer/artist as a ragpicker is well-known: "And if we want to visualize him just for himself, in the solitude of his craft and his endeavor, we see: a ragpicker at daybreak, lancing with his stick scraps of language and tatters of speech in order to throw them in his cart, grumbling, stubbornly, somewhat the worse for drink." See Walter Benjamin, *Illuminations* (New York: Schocken Books, 1998), 114. But here it is not just the poet who is the cultural ragpicker that is on display; rather the actual ragpicker is made poetic and meaningful. See Chaudhuri, *Clearing a Space*, and Zecchini, *Kolatkar*, for more detailed discussions.

48. *Poetry India* 2, no. 2 (1967).

49. See King, "Modern Indian and American Poetry"; Mehrotra, "The Emperor Has No Clothes"; and Zecchini, *Arun Kolatkar.*

50. Mehrotra, *Partial Recall*, 59.

51. See Chitre, *An Anthology of Marathi Poetry*, p. 5, where Chitre writes in the introduction that "[the 'paperback revolution'] unleashed a tremendous variety of . . . influences [that] ranged from the classical Greek and Chinese to contemporary French, German, Spanish, Russian, Italian. The intellectual proletariat that was the product of the rise in literacy was exposed to these diverse influences. A pan-literary context was created."

52. See Mehrotra, *Partial Recall*, 59.

> The dual lives we led, of ambitious terrestrial students and rebellious subterranean poets, continued to run side by side and on the whole peacefully, one part of us concentrating on the campaigns of Alexander the Great, the Punic Wars, the rise of the Guptas, the significance of the opening scene in *Macbeth*, and the other reading the *Village Voice* and declaiming "Under-wear" ("Women's underwear holds things up / Men's underwear holds things down") and "America" ("America when will you send your eggs to India") from *Penguin Modern Poets* 5. According to the date below my signature in the title page, I had bought the book in August 1965. That September we had brought out the first issue of *damn you*.

53. King, "Modern Indian and American Poetry."

54. "*Kay danger wara sutlay*" in Kolatkar's Marathi book of poems, *Arun Kolatkarchya Kavita*, is an explicit comment on and a reconstitution of Bob Dylan's famous song "Blowin' in the Wind." In his interview in the *Indian Literary Review*, Kolatkar said, "I am completely taken up by the rock and the music of the last ten–twenty years that has come out of America" (10). Also see Mehrotra's introduction in *Boatride*, 29, for Kolatkar's affinity with the American Blues. Kolatkar wrote several songs in this style and even had his

friend Avinash Gupte take a demo of these songs to the United States. Kolatkar's songs feature in the original longer documentary on the poet by Dilip Chitre, and the lyrics feature in the "Words for Music" section in *Boatride*. And Naresh Fernandes writes about the same in "Beat Poets," *Time Out* (September 23–October 6, 2005): 24–25.

55. A generation of rock musicians emerged during this period, and there were creative and novel fusions of genres when Bombay rocker Nandu Bhende (son of veteran Marathi theater personality Atmaram Bhende) performed an iconic role in *Teen Paishyacha Tamasha* (the Marathi adaptation of Brecht's *The Threepenny Opera*).

56. See Engblom, "Bombay Modernisms," where he presents a provocative comparison of Ezekiel's and Mardhekar's modernism, and the modernisms in English and Marathi poetry: "What flies in the face of common expectation is that a Modernist 'dislocation' affected Marathi poetry considerably earlier than Indian English poetry" (41).

57. See Neera Adarkar and Meena Menon, *One Hundred Years, One Hundred Voices: The Millworkers of Girangaon: An Oral History* (Calcutta: Seagull Books, 2004); Rajnarayan Chandavarkar, *History, Culture and the Indian City: Essays* (Cambridge: Cambridge University Press, 2009); and Prakash, *Mumbai Fables*.

58. Laura Doyle and Laura A. Winkiel, *Geomodernisms: Race, Modernism, Modernity* (Bloomington: Indiana University Press, 2005), 1.

59. Ezekiel discovered a lot of new poetic talent throughout his years as editor of various magazines. In the introduction to *The Boatride & Other Poems* by Arun Kolatkar, Mehrotra notes that Ezekiel gave Kolatkar his first publishing break by printing his poem "The Renunciation of a Dog" in the inaugural issue of his magazine *Quest* in 1955.

60. For instance, *Kala Ghoda Poems* (2004) and *Boatride* (2009).

61. There are other such collaborations across the English-Marathi writing worlds. In a letter dated February 10, 1969, Ezekiel wrote to Jussawalla that his plays "*Marriage Poems* and *Nalini* were staged in Marathi at the Jai Hind College January 28 and 29. The shorter play was universally liked, other aroused mixed feelings" (Adil Jussawalla Papers). Later, Ezekiel also collaborated with Vrinda Nabar to translate the work of Marathi poet Indira Sant into English (*Snake-skin and Other Poems of Indira Sant*, trans. Nissim Ezekiel and Vrinda Nabar [Bombay: Nirmala Sadanand Publishers, 1975]).

62. King, *Modern Indian Poetry*, 19.

63. In the first issue of *Aso*, Shahane published Ginsberg's letter to Shakti Chattopadhyaya in English, and he also published Sudhir Kolatkar's translation of Gregory Corso's poem "Second Night in NYC After 3 Years."

64. In *Indian Journals*, Allen Ginsberg has a corresponding entry against "Bombay 29 April 1962": "Shankara said existence is a wet dream *The Century of Verses #36*"; see Allen Ginsberg, *Indian Journals, March 1962–May 1963: Notebooks, Diary, Blank Pages, Writings* (San Francisco: Dave Haselwood Books, 1970). In this context, the reference to Shankaracharya in Shahane's poem is even more irreverent.

65. *Timba*, May 1968.

66. The 18/23-inch poster-poem was designed by poet and designer R. K. Joshi, partly with 3-inch wooden letter types that were lying around; it was printed on letterpress by Shahane at Mohan Mudranalaya. On the poster it says: "PRICE—AS MUCH AS YOU CAN WILINGLY PART WITH / PROCEEDS TO GO TO REHABILITATION OF BANGLA DESH REFUGEES." Ironically, when Shahane visited the liberation War Museum in Dhaka, Bangladesh, many decades later, he found to his surprise a reproduction of this very poster being sold as a marker of the turbulent struggle.

67. There is an amusing story that Ashok Shahane tells about the time Allen Ginsberg and Peter Orlovsky visited Bombay and Sham Lal, then editor of *Times of India*, threw a party to welcome the Beats to Bombay. Knowing of Ginsberg's partiality for vernacular poetry (see the Naropa audiotapes of the Indian poets' visit to the Naropa Institute in Colorado in 1986 when Kedarnath Singh, Arun Kolatkar, and Ashok Vajpeyi read their poetry in Marathi and Hindi on the American stage in front of Ginsberg and the other Beat writers), Sham Lal had arranged for a reading of Urdu poetry at his residence. After the reading, Ginsberg stood up and composed a poem on the spot: "Whenever I go out, I put on my belt / because I own everything that lies below it." Shahane is not entirely certain whether the word was "below" or "under," but the implication of the bodily reference was clear and apparently several listeners were offended. For more on the Beats in India, see Deborah Baker, *A Blue Hand: The Beats in India* (New York: Penguin, 2008); Zecchini, *Kolatkar*; R. Parthasarathy, "Meeting Allen Ginsberg," *Writers Workshop Miscellany* 11 (1962): 65–66; and Ginsberg, *Indian Journals*. Also see figure 1.4 for an image of Ginsberg's dedication on his *Collected Poems* to Kolatkar and Shahane.

68. Aniket Jaaware, "Eating and Eating with the Dalit: A Reconsideration Touching upon Marathi Poetry," in *Indian Poetry: Modernism and After*, ed. K. Satchidanandan (New Delhi: Sahitya Akademi, 1998), 279.

69. Gajarawala, *Untouchable Fictions*, 281.

70. "Panther self-representation also tied into the longstanding politics of the street, which had been defined by demonstrations, strikes, and tense relations between trade unions and the police in central Bombay" (Anupama Rao, *The Caste Question: Dalits and the Politics of Modern India* [Berkeley: University of California Press, 2009], 198).

71. Nishikant Thakar notes the importance of the little magazines in the development of the signature Dalit literature, but he connects the two on the basis of chronology and history. See also the introduction to Patil, *Drushyantar*, 22–24.

72. It first started as *Asmita* in 1967 in interior Maharashtra, in Aurangabad, but later changed to *Asmitadarsha*.

73. See Ganesh Devy, introduction to Sharankumar Limbale, *Akkarmashi* (The Outcaste), trans. Santosh Bhoomkar (Delhi: Oxford University Press, 2003), 13–26. Devy makes a general claim that the beginnings of the Dalit protest found space for expression in the little magazines.

74. Raja Dhale, interview, *Lokaprabha*, December 14, 2012, http://www.lokprabha.com/20121214/cover01-video.htm.

75. See Homi Bhabha, *The Location of Culture* (London: Routledge, 1994), 83–84, for an earlier reading of this stanza that mainly emphasizes the hybridity of the postcolonial shown in the poem; see also Ramazani, *The Hybrid Muse.*

76. Kersy Katrak, "Pseuds, Plagiarists & Poets," *Gentlemen* 5 (June 1982): 38.

77. Lawrence Bantleman, review, *The Century*, December 31, 1966, 15. Mehrotra's magazines certainly demonstrate a different visual and periodic publishing ethic than does Ezekiel's *Poetry India* (1966–67); they are more avant-garde in both aspects and more rebellious in their overt attitude. But there is greater similarity between the contents of the two sets of little magazines and they seem to be invested in a similar vision of establishing Indian writing in English as part of the larger landscape of Indian literatures in other languages. See Anjali Nerlekar, "Melted Out of Circulation: Little Magazines and Bombay Poetry in the 60s and 70s," in *History of Indian Poetry in English*, ed. Rosinka Chaudhuri (Cambridge: Cambridge University Press, forthcoming 2015).

78. This was a collection of the best writing published in one of the influential littles of the 1970s, *Vagartha*, which was edited by Meenakshi Mukherjee from Delhi from 1973 to 1979.

79. Bharat Iyer, "An Interview with Arvind Krishna Mehrotra," *Eclectica* 17, no. 1 (January–February 2013), http://www.eclectica.org/v17n1/iyer.html. As this book goes into publication, Emma Bird's exciting work on English little magazines has appeared in print. See Bird, "It's Missing."

80. Arvind Krishna Mehrotra, Keki Daruwalla, Vilas Sarang, Saleem Peeradeena, Gauri Deshpande, and R. Parthasarathy, all poets themselves, brought out anthologies of Indian poetry in English, while in Marathi, poets like Bhalchandra Nemade, Satish Kalsekar, Chandrakant Khot, Raja Dhale, N. D. Mahanor, and Chandrakant Patil either anthologized the poems or published books of poems of their contemporaries. In addition, Adil Jussawalla wrote a striking preface to *Three Poets*, and Kolatkar designed the covers for the books by Jussawalla, Gieve Patel, Mehrotra, Eunice de Souza, Nagarkar, and many others.

81. Rodrigues, editorial, 1.

82. Vijaya Rajadhyaksha, "*Aniyatkalike*," *Rajadhyaksha* (1981): 183–98; originally published in *Samaj Prabodhan Patrika* (January/February 1975). Rajadhyaksha is a prominent critic and writer in Marathi; she won the Sahitya Akademi award in 1993 for her critical study of B. S. Mardhekar's poetry.

83. See http://ekregh.blogspot.com/.

84. Rafik Suraj, *Laghuniyatkalikanchi Varnanatmak Suchi* (Mumbai: Lokvangmaya Griha, 2011). While this is an important first bibliography, it is noticeably incomplete and sometimes erroneous. For instance, it lists an incorrect year for *Atharva*, the little magazine started by Ashok Shahane, which had only one issue before it closed down.

85. *Abhiruchi*, in its second period in Bombay, comes to mind here because of its important cultural and literary influence on the writers of the time.

86. This appeared in *Yeru* (1969), and the essay formed an entire issue of the little magazine. Dhale's piece garnered a lot of attention (positive and negative), and he was briefly jailed for the so-called antinational sentiments expressed in the essay.

87. Bandekar, "*Aniyatakalikanmadhil kavita.*" *Navakshar Darshan* 5, no. 2 (2001): 38.

88. Nerurkar, "*Little Magazine ani Raja Dhale*," 62. See *Navakshar Darshan* 5, no. 2 (2001) for an interview of Raja Dhale. Also see the special issue of *Khel* (vol. 23 [2012]) that has a wide-ranging interview as well as surveys of Dhale's work.

89. Satish Kalsekar, interview by Anjali Nerlekar, 2010.

90. "Isn't linguistic awareness at the root of all activism?" asked Nemade, when confronted with this critique (Bhalchandra Nemade, interview by Anjali Nerlekar, 2013).

91. Bhalchandra Nemade, "*Kavi lok*" ("The Poets"), in *Meladi: Dekhani ani Nantarchya Kavita* (Mumbai: Popular Prakashan, 1991), 30. The translation is mine.

92. Samuel Taylor Coleridge, *Biographia Literaria, or, Biographical Sketches of My Literary Life and Opinions* (New York: American Book Exchange, 1881), 539.

93. Qtd. in De Loach and Ginsberg, "Little Mags/Small Presses," 111.

94. Arvind Krishna Mehrotra, "Between Bricks and Madness," in *Nine Enclosures* (Bombay: Clearing House, 1976), 12.

CHAPTER 2

1. "Prakashan" is the Marathi equivalent of "publishing house."

2. Mehrotra, *Partial Recall*, 60.

3. Glazier, *Small Press*, 5.

4. The name "small press" itself is one of several that early practitioners and readers used to describe such renegade operations. As noted in Len Fulton, *The Psychologique of Small Press Publishing* (New Brunswick, NJ: Graduate School of Library Service, 1976), 2:

> Nona Bakhtin, an editor of the *New York Times Book Review*[,] calls them "the little presses," both in genuine sympathy . . . and in a kind of acknowledgement of corporate publishing's sense of mercantile hierarchology [*sic*]. You once saw the term "underground" too, little used now, ridiculous when it is, even a bit sophomoric when it was used somewhat meaningfully ten years ago. You also hear "private press"—an eighteenth-century term used by those galloping headlong into the nineteenth. "Independent" is the term I am coming to like more and more because it is not loaded with implications for that greatest of all American virtues, *size* . . . I seem to continue to use the word "small" out of habit, and I suppose that is presently the most familiar to everyone.

5. Eunice de Souza, *Talking Poems: Conversations with Poets* (New Delhi: Oxford University Press, 1999), 126–27.

6. De Souza, "On a Wing and a Prayer."

7. See M. L. Rosenthal and Sally M. Gall, *The Modern Poetic Sequence: The Genius of Modern Poetry* (New York: Oxford University Press, 1983); Margaret Dickie, *On the Modernist Long Poem* (Iowa City: University of Iowa Press, 1986); and Susan Stanford Friedman, "When a 'Long' Poem Is a

'Big' Poem: Self-Authorizing Strategies in Women's Twentieth-Century 'Long Poems,'" *Lit* 2, no. 1 (1990): 9–25.

8. Kolatkar Papers.

9. Spicer, *The Collected Books of Jack Spicer*, 61.

10. Kolatkar Papers.

11. Mchale describes this as a feature of postmodernist poetry in the United States; see Brian Mchale, "Telling Stories Again: On the Replenishment of Narrative in the Postmodernist Long Poem," *Yearbook of English Studies* 30 (2000): 250–62. As shown in the introduction, these periodizations do not apply as closely once they cross borders. There are coterminus transatlantic modernist works that feature what might seem to be anomalous stylistic features when seen from a universalizing perspective. I choose to go by the broader term "modernisms" to describe them all.

12. Clearing House Papers.

13. This splitting of the poems within the sequence was a herald of larger issues in relation to *Jejuri*'s manuscript. See chapter 6 for a description of the lost and found manuscript of this long poem. The Jejuri sequence was also published in its entirety in Kersy Katrak and Gauri Deshpande's *Opinion Literary Quarterly* in 1974. There were limitations, however, of even this publishing exercise as opposed to its appearance in book form with Clearing House in 1976, as shown in chapter 6.

14. There were also several anthologies of poetry that appeared during this period, but while that helped make the work of the poets visible, these anthologies were also consumed by intrapoetic disagreements that brought notoriety to some of the collections. For instance, Jussawalla did not include Parthasarathy in Penguin's *New Writing in India* (1974), and in retaliation, Parthasarathy did not include Jussawalla's poetry in his own Oxford anthology, *Ten 20th Century Poets* (1976). There is also a bitter literary quarrel fought by Mehrotra and Parthasarathy in the pages of *Chandrabhaga*, the little magazine run by the poet Jayanta Mahapatra. See Mehrotra, "The Emperor Has No Clothes," first published there and later collected in Mehrotra, *Partial Recall*, 147–95.

15. Fulton, "Anima Rising," 26.

16. Sujit Patwardhan owns the Mudra printing press in Pune that has printed the majority of books published by Shahane at Pras Prakashan. He is known for his fine sense of the printing craft and used to run a small little magazine of his own called *Motif*, which focused on the art of printing, and he was a close associate of many *sathottari* writers.

17. Sujit Patwardhan, email correspondence with Anjali Nerlekar, August 4, 2013.

18. Chaudhuri, *Clearing a Space*, 224.

19. This is from a now defunct blog started by the late Dilip Chitre that began documenting his long association with Arun Kolatkar. The blog was left unfinished because of Chitre's own health concerns and has now vanished from the web. A Marathi translation of the blog can be found at ekregh.blogspot.com. The area he sketches out here is the space mapped by Arun Kolatkar's *Kala Ghoda Poems* as the place where the beggars of Bombay jostle with the imposing colonial architecture described here.

20. Chitre adds to the memories in "Remembering Kolatkar":

> It was in Mumbai that Arun met many aspiring artists—among them the now widely acclaimed members of the Bombay "Progressive Artists" group of the 1950s. His long association with Rampart Row and the "Kala Ghoda" square began at that time:
>
> Just round the corner was the University of Bombay and its Rajabai Tower. This is still, architecturally, the most British and European part of the city. Arun's favourite restaurant for five decades—*The Wayside Inn*—was also located here. His *Kala Ghoda Poems* are "centred" here.
>
> Two of his friends in his student days in Bombay were Ambadas (the now internationally famous Indian painter who is a naturalized citizen of Norway) and the maverick, self-taught artist Bandu Waze who was perhaps the most original and daring abstract painter with immense energy, talent, and conviction that many of his academically cultivated colleagues lacked.
>
> The Jehangir Art Gallery and The Artists' Aid Fund Centre on Rampart Row were the only galleries in downtown Bombay in the 1950s.
>
> Two other galleries that came up were Keku and Khorshed Gandhi's *Gallery Chemould* and Kali Pundole's *Pundole Art Gallery* next to *Pyrkes Restaurant* at Flora Fountain.
>
> The Club' or The Artists' Aid Fund Centre on Rampart Row where members of the Bombay Progressive Artists Group and some who were not members of that group assembled every day, hoping for a buyer to turn up. . . .
>
> It is here that Arun first saw Darshan Chhabda and was smitten by her.

This was towards the end of 1953.

21. McGann, *The Textual Condition*, 149.

22. Ibid., 12–13.

23. The Emergency also appears in the indirect reference to it in Kolatkar's Marathi poem "*kala rumal*" in *Arun Kolatkarchya Kavita* (144–45), where the poet asks the reader to take a strip of black cloth and cover his eyes, presumably referring to the violation of rights happening in the political world at the time.

24. Sunil Karnik, "*Granthanirmitiche 'Shahane' kavatik*," *Divyamarathi*, July 10, 2011, http://divyamarathi.bhaskar.com/news/MAG-granthanirmiti-by-sunil-karnik-2251309.html.

25. Qtd. in Ashok R. Kelkar, "The Being of a Poem," *Foundations of Language* 5, no. 1 (February 1969): 27.

26. De Loach and Ginsberg, "Little Mags/Small Presses," 106.

27. Mike Weaver, "Concrete Poetry," *Visible Language* 6 (1976): 294.

28. Bann, *Concrete Poetry*, 15.

29. As Len Fulton put it, "If concrete poetry in the United States, Canada and England is, in part at least, bound into the mimeograph movement of the mid-sixties, that movement in its turn is bound centrally into the entire small press movement. I call 1965 the year of 'peak activity' for the mimeos" ("Anima Rising," 31).

30. King reads the shape of this poem on the page as "a bomb, skyscraper or phallic symbol" (*Modern Indian Poetry*, 185).

31. R. K. Joshi was a visually oriented poet; this passion is reflected in his later life in his career as a calligrapher and the originator of the "Mangal" script for the online transcription of Devanagari script (for Marathi, among

other languages). He was also a close associate of Shahane and part of the group that helped in the creation of the little magazine *Aso*. For more of his poems and more concrete poems in Marathi, see Patil and Mahanor, *Punha Ekada Kavita*.

32. R. K. Joshi designed the layout for the little magazine *Rawa* and published his own poetry in it, in addition to editing the special issue in 1972. His phrase "*aksharkar ashya kavita*" describes his project well in Marathi. The word for an artist, *chitrakar*, is *chitra* (picture) + *-kar* (artisan/maker). Joshi co-opts the structure of that word for his concrete poetry project when he describes his own writing as *aksharkar ashya kavita*, "poems like those of the wordsmith."

33. Rafik Suraj makes a brief mention of this poem in *Laghuniyatkalikanchi Varnanatmak Suchi*, 18.

34. Among the many names considered for the new press were "The Impulse," "The Touch and Go," "The Off Chance," and "The Suchmuch Press"; in Hindi, "suchmuch" means "truly" or "the real," and this name would pun on the English combination of such + much.

35. The Newground Press has an interesting relation to Clearing House Press in that it was a continuation of the collective experiment started by the Clearing House four (Jussawalla, Mehrotra, Kolatkar, and Patel) two years earlier. Moreover, the initial list of poets likely to be published by Clearing House included all the later Newground poets: Eunice de Souza, Melanie Silgardo, and Santan Rodrigues.

36. See Melanie Silgardo, Raul D'Gama Rose, and Santan Rodrigues, *Three Poets: Melanie Silgardo, Raul D'Gama Rose, Santan Rodrigues* (Bombay: Newground, 1978), 6:

> Nissim Ezekiel's cyclostyled batches of his own poems (including *Hymns in Darkness*) and his publishing Gieve Patel's first book, *Poems*, in 1965; Arvind Krishna Mehrotra's cyclostyled copies of his Bharatmata (1966) and his publishing other poets in his magazines, *ezra* and *damn you*; the book of poems published by P. Lal, the books published by Pritish Nandy, Dilip Chitre's printed copies of his *Ambulance Ride* (1972); Santan Rodrigues's cyclostyled copies of his *I Exist* (1973); K. D. Katrak and Gauri Deshpande's first publishing of *Jejuri* by Arun Kolatkar in their *Opinion Literary Quarterly* (1974); and the books published by Clearing House (1976) run by Arun Kolatkar, Arvind Krishna Mehrotra, Gieve Patel and myself.

37. There is the short-lived but excellent Three Crown series from Oxford University Press in the 1970s/1980s, which, under the stewardship of the poet R. Parthasarathy, brought out important books of poems that have also added significantly to the canon of Indian poetry in English today: Nissim Ezekiel's *Hymns in Darkness* (1976), R. Parthasarathy's *Rough Passage* (1977), Keki Daruwalla's *The Keeper of the Dead* (1982), Jayanta Mahapatra's *Life Signs* (1983), and A. K. Ramanujan's *Selected Poems* (1976). However, this publishing venture is not representative of the time in that there were not many or enough such large publishers willing to publish poetry books, and Clearing House and Pras Prakashan as small publishers are chosen for a closer study here as representative examples of what was happening during this period.

38. Adil Jussawalla has also served over the years as one of the unofficial archivists of the contextual literature of the *sathottari* English poetry.

As Mehrotra remarked in an interview in 2012, "We all do collect works or fugitive publications. But as far as the works of others go, the collection of Adil Jussawalla is extraordinary." See Gayatri Jayaraman, "Noah's Archive," Poetry, *Mint*, June 30, 2012, http://www.livemint.com/Leisure/TuhTZtoaM-rmgevNh7lvLHJ/Poetry—Noah8217s-archive.html. Jussawalla has been very generous in sharing this archive. As he says, "I have no copyright over anything that is here. When scholars and other poets who know about it come to me for their research, I hand it over, and then the relationship between the works is between them" (ibid.). Also see the introduction by Jerry Pinto to the collection of Jussawalla's prose writings over the years in Jerry Pinto, ed., *Maps for a Mortal Moon* (New Delhi: Aleph Book Company, 2014). Jussawalla's essays from the little magazines also serve as a collection of memories of the people, experiences, and places of the *sathottari* years, recorded in his impeccable prose. This rich collection of texts and documents, along with Arvind Mehrotra's vast archive, is now preserved at the Cornell Library South Asia Collection.

39. In his notes from the period, Jussawalla writes: "THE POET: would have to see his book through the press and be responsible for the design of his book. Alternatively, he'd be responsible for finding someone to do it for him. Uniformity in the series is probably out as this isn't a scheme for a collective; but the poet would have maximum control over this product" (Clearing House Papers).

40. See Fulton, "Anima Rising," for a reference to these little magazines. Earlier, in spring 1968, the American magazine *Intrepid* brought out a special Indian poetry issue that included the poets of the Hungry generation in Bengal as well as the Bombay poets, Mehrotra among them.

41. Jussawalla notes that the initial idea was to have a larger group of poets who had their own manuscripts and who would form a larger collective: "We had been discussing the idea for a while, the problem of all the manuscripts that we had lying around and which weren't getting published because there were no publishers. When the group finally coalesced into the four of us, I could feel that there was some considerable heartburn among other poets" (Clearing House Papers).

42. Jussawalla, Clearing House Papers.

43. Jussawalla to Vilas Sarang, November 1, 1976, Clearing House Papers.

44. Jussawalla agonized over the abandonment of his half-finished novel at this time, as his letters show, and put in an incredible amount of effort, along with Mehrotra, into not just the editing of manuscripts but also the packaging, mailing, and publicizing of the books of the collective.

45. In Jussawalla's notes, there is a list of poets under "ideal beginning" (first Arun Kolatkar/Arvind Krishna Mehrotra/Adil Jussawalla, then Eunice de Souza/Raul D'Gama Rose/Santan Rodrigues, then Darius Cooper/ Saleem Peeradina/Nissim Ezekiel) and another under "likely beginning" (first Eunice de Souza/Raul D'Gama Rose/Adil Jussawalla, then Nissim Ezekiel/Arun Kolatkar/Dilip Chitre). In the end the actual sequence of publications matched neither list.

46. Hasan, "'Your Missing Person,'" 64–65.

47. Clearing House Papers.

48. This has lasted until today: Arvind Krishna Mehrotra and Adil Jussawalla remain the closest of friends and this relation has been acknowledged in print at various times: Mehrotra dedicates *Nine Enclosures* to Kolatkar, *Distance in Statute Miles* to Jussawalla, and *Middle Earth* to both; and Kolatkar thanks Jussawalla and Mehrotra at the beginning of *Kala Ghoda Poems*.

49. R. Parthasarathy also sent his book of poems, *Rough Passage*, as an entry and received an honorable mention that year. Many other literary reasons make 1976 "the most significant year for Indian English poetry since the period 1965–6," as Bruce King says. "It saw the appearance of the first four books from Clearing House, the start of the Oxford University Press New Poetry in India series, two new books by Jayant Mahapatra, the special Nissim Ezekiel issue of the *Journal of South Asian Literature*, and the first signs of a new, younger generation of poets in the shape of Santan Rodriguez's first book in the start of *Kavi*" (*Modern Indian Poetry*, 34).

50. Jussawalla to Mehrotra, August 20, 1977, Clearing House Papers.

51. See Janet Powers Gemmill, "Fine Poetry in Fine Wrappings," review of Clearing House books, *Journal of South Asian Literature* 16, no. 2 (Summer/Fall 1981): 207: "One should undoubtedly disregard the appearance of a book when evaluating its contents, but in the case of a new series of Indo-English poetry, published by Clearing House in Bombay, that's hard to do."

52. Jussawalla to Mahapatra, June 16, 1980, Clearing House Papers.

53. Mehrotra to Jussawalla, March 8, 1975, Clearing House Papers.

54. See chapter 7 for a discussion of how the line dictum by Kolatkar was not implemented in the *New York Review of Books* edition of *Jejuri* (published in 2005).

55. Jussawalla to Gieve Patel, June 6, 1976, Clearing House Papers.

56. Gieve Patel, *How Do You Withstand, Body* (Bombay: Clearing House, 1976), 12.

57. Ibid., 18.

58. Ibid.

59. This cover almost did not get made. Gieve Patel wanted a blank, imageless cover for his book because in an earlier conversation with Ezekiel, Ezekiel had stated that any book that wants itself to be taken seriously would not have images on the cover. Patel decided initially to adopt that principle but later realized his mistake and approached Kolatkar with a request to design a cover that would convey the lightness as well as the solidity of the body and was very pleased with the result (interview by Anjali Nerlekar, New York, 2011).

60. Arvind Krishna Mehrotra, *Distance in Statute Miles* (Bombay: Clearing House, 1982), 12.

61. In an interview I conducted with Mehrotra in 2010 in Allahabad, he said he did not know of this hidden portrait on the cover until many years after the book was published.

62. Parthasarathy, a redoubtable poet of this period himself, published several important books of poems, and the correspondence between Jussawalla and Mehrotra (Clearing House Papers) shows the simultaneous engagement

of both the presses with the writing scene of Bombay at that time, but Three Crowns cannot be seen as training its editorial eyes only on Bombay.

63. In an interview I conducted with Shahane in 2008 in Mumbai, he said that Raghu Dandavate, the Marathi poet and one of his close associates, described Pras Prakashan as "*dostonki shayari*" (the poetry of friends).

64. Thanks to Mangesh Narayan Kale for this information.

65. On one of my visits to Shahane's residence in Malad, Bombay, in 2007, he asked me if I was leaving for Pune right away, and when I said yes, he asked if I would deliver a dozen books of Arun Kolatlar's *Chirimiri* to International Book House in Pune, which stocked these books. This unconventional delivery by hand seems to be a standard means of operation for Shahane.

66. Ashok Shahane, interview by Anjali Nerlekar, Mumbai, June 2008.

67. Among the unpublished manuscripts left by Kolatkar is a massive draft of a biographical text based on the life of Balwant Bua, singer, petty worker, follower of Tukaram, and Kolatkar's muse for much of his Marathi poetry, especially the poems in *Chirimiri*. In 1986, as a result of David Davidar's encouragement, Kolatkar sent Penguin a book proposal of six stories of the English version of this work. Part of that proposal, a story titled "Sticky Fingers" that was first narrated in Marathi in the poem "Tomato" in *Chirimiri* and features thematically on the cover of that book, is now published in *Granta* 130 (2015).

68. Kolatkar Papers.

69. See chapter 2 for more on the literary *kattas* in Bombay (the equivalent of the *adda*, as it is called in Bengali and Hindi) of which Shahane was a leading figure. In fact, a few writers and scholars have speculated about the reason for the Thursday afternoon meeting of friends of which Kolatkar was a part for three decades (see Amit Chaudhuri, introduction to *Jejuri*, by Arun Kolatkar [New York: New York Review of Books, 2005]), but it is not widely known that they chose Thursday to meet because that was Shahane's day off from Mohan Mudranalaya. Thursday continues to be the day of the *katta*, even though some of the original participants, like Arun Kolatkar and poet Raghu Dandavate, have passed away.

70. Mehrotra, *Partial Recall*, 91.

71. Ashok Shahane, interview by Anjali Nerlekar, June 2010.

72. One should add 78 to the year in order to get the conventional year format.

73. The following is a partial list of the books published by Pras, secured from various library catalogs in Bombay. It is sizable for a one-man publishing project, and the list provided here does not include second and third reprints of books first published by Pras: *Jejuri* (2nd ed., Arun Kolatkar, 1977); *Arun Kolatkarchya Kavita* (Kolatkar, 1977); *Kula Vruttanta* (Vrindavan Dandavate, 1977); *Majhi Kahani* (Ustad Allauddin Khan, 1978); *Antarvedhi* (Manohar Oak, 1978); *Isam* (Gaurkishor Ghosh, 1979); *Samudra* (Vasant Gurjar, 1979); *Drusthchakra* (Vrindavan Dandavate, 1980); *Ghardar* (Madhu Sabane, 1980); *Meladi* (2nd ed., Nemade, 1981); *Sisyphus ani Belacqua* (Sarang, 1982); *Mayalu* (Vrindavan Dandavate, 1982); *Vasechi Na* (Raghu Dandavate, 1983); *Chavya* (Dilip Chitre, 1983); *Daha by Daha* (Dilip Chitre, 1983); *Khel*

(Namdeo Dhasal, 1983); *Pravasi Kshan* (Ramesh Samarth, 1994); *Avashesh* (Rekha Athalye, 2003); *Varshav* (Suresh Kadam, 2003); *Vadhvel* (Raghu Dandavate, 2003); *Chirimiri* (Kolatkar, 2003); *Bhijaki Vahi* (Kolatkar, 2003); *Dron* (Arun Kolatkar, 2004); *Kala Ghoda Poems* (Kolatkar, 2004); *Sarpa Satra* (Kolatkar, 2004); *Arun Kolatkarchya Char Kavita* (Kolatkar, 2006); *The Boatride & Other Poems* (Mehrotra/Kolatkar, 2009); *Jejuri* (in Marathi, Arun Kolatkar, 2010); and *Dubuk* (Raghu Dandavate, 2011). The covers of many of these books have been created by the graphic artist Bal Thakur, others by Vrindavan Dandavate and Arun Kolatkar. See Shahane's article in *Anubhav* for details about the collaboration between Shahane and graphic artist Bal Thakur.

74. Arun Kolatkar, *Bhijaki Vahi* (Mumbai: Pras Prakashan, 2003), 98.

75. Ibid.

76. Ibid., 99.

77. See Avadhoot Dongare, "*Darvarshicha ath jun, Kim ani Kolatkar*," http://ekregh.blogspot.in/2013/06/blog-post_8.html for another example of the use of white space, in the poetic sequence on the Vietnam War's "Kim." Dongare interprets the blank space there as the poet's attempt to articulate a "real" apology to the little girl beyond the words of the text.

78. It is interesting to note that Clearing House Press also fought valiantly against the big publishers and their disregard of copyright in the 1970s and tried to get the poets their due in terms of reproduction fees for their poems. See the Clearing House Papers for their struggle with Vikas publishing and with Oxford University Press, and see Lata Dabholkar, "*Shahanyani dakhavali swamitvahakkachi 'sakal,'*" *Loksatta*, October 7, 2013, http://epaper.loksatta.com/169284/indian-express/07-10-2013#page/1/2, for details of Shahane's case against *Sakal*.

79. Ashok Shahane, phone interview by Anjali Nerlekar, New Jersey, 2013.

CHAPTER 3

1. Rajadhyaksha, "*Aniyatkalike*," 195.

2. See Sheldon Pollock's edited collection, *Literary Cultures in History: Reconstructions from South Asia* (Berkeley: University of California Press, 2003), which demonstrates how most regional Indian languages launched their literary traditions on translations of older, often Sanskrit texts. Similarly, most European vernacular literary traditions are connected to the translation of the Bible.

3. Dilip Parameshwar Gaonkar, "On Alternative Modernities," in *Alternative Modernities*, ed. Dilip Parameshwar Gaonkar (Durham, NC: Duke University Press, 2001), 15–16.

4. V. S. Naipaul, *East Indians in the Caribbean: Colonialism and the Struggle for Identity: Papers Presented to a Symposium on East Indians in the Caribbean, the University of the West Indies, June, 1975* (Millwood, NY: Kraus International Publications, 1982), 7.

5. Emily Apter, "Translation at the Checkpoint," *Journal of Postcolonial Writing* 50, no. 1 (2014): 72.

6. Vinay Dharwadker, "Some Contexts of Modern Indian Poetry," *Chicago Review* 38, no. 1/2 (1992): 218; see also Engblom, "Marathi Poetry in English Translation."

7. Arvind Krishna Mehrotra, ed., *The Oxford Anthology of Twelve Modern Indian Poets* (Delhi: Oxford University Press, 1992), 1.

8. Qtd. in Hasan, "'Your Missing Person,'" 67.

9. Initially, an acronym for "Poets, Essayists, Novelists," later expanded to "Poets, Playwrights, Editors, Essayists, Novelists."

10. King, *Modern Indian Poetry*, 9. *Quest* was one of the many literary projects funded by the Indian Committee for Cultural Freedom, as well as a covert operation of the U.S. government, and it also supported the publication of Chitre's *An Anthology* as is noted in the footnote to the Mardhekar translations in Ezekiel's *Poetry India*. This was part of the Cold War politics with regard to the United States, and Prime Minister Nehru is supposed to have been very upset by the activities of the committee. The committee supported many such regional language projects around the newly created nation, and this relation deserves its own separate and lengthy study. See Sabin, *Dissenters and Mavericks*; and Pullin, "'Money Does Not Make Any Difference to the Opinions That We Hold.'"

11. Qtd. in Eunice de Souza, "'Indianness' and the Critic in a Post-Colonial Structure," *Bombay Review* 1 (1989): 35.

12. There were many others, too: Mehrotra's little magazine *fakir* was created with the deliberate purpose of featuring translations, and the first (and only) issue of the magazine showcased Chitre's translations of Tukaram's Marathi poetry (1968). *Tornado* (edited by Pavankumar Jain, 1967–71) published translations from Gujarati, original artwork from subsequently renowned artists like Bhupen Khakhar, and original poetry in English together.

13. Rodrigues, editorial, 1.

14. M. Asaduddin, "Translation and Indian Literature: Some Reflections," *Translation Today* 3, no. 1 (2006): 12.

15. Prabodhan Thackeray is the pen name of Keshav Sitaram Thackeray, one of the leaders of the Samayukta Maharashtra agitation that demanded the separate linguistic state of Maharashtra.

16. Along with its anti–South Indian strategy, the Shiv Sena ("the army of Shivaji") also attacked the left-backed trade unions in the city in order to gain a foothold in local politics. In 1967 they attacked union offices, disrupted their meetings, and assaulted individuals affiliated with them. In 1970 the followers of the Shiv Sena attacked and murdered Krishna Desai, who was at that time a Member of the Legislature.

17. Gerard Heuze, "Populism, Religion, and Nation in Contemporary India: The Evolution of the Shiv Sena in Maharashtra," *Comparative Studies of South Asia, Africa and the Middle East* 20, no. 1 (2000): 5.

18. Engblom, "Bombay Modernisms," 41.

19. In the essay "*Ajakalachya Marathi vangmayavar 'ksha' kiran*," Shahane both praises and criticizes Mardhekar's poetry. Mardhekar is seen as the

best of an insipid generation of writers and his poetry is criticized for making a virtue of obscurity.

20. Lawrence Venuti, "Translation, Community, Utopia," in *The Translation Studies Reader* (London: Routledge, 2000), 477. Also see Steven Yao, *Translation and the Languages of Modernism: Gender, Politics, Language* (New York: Palgrave, 2002): "It embodied a comprehensive textual strategy for negotiating between the demands of transmission and transformation, between the authority of tradition and the demands of innovation, between the endowments of the past and the imperatives of the present" (22).

21. Similarly, Kolatkar makes an indirect reference to Mardhekar's notorious poem on rats (*Pipat mele olya undir* ["rats in a wet barrel died"]) when he writes about "an obscure poet munching on Welsh rabbit / and thinking of rats dying in a wet barrel" (Kolatkar, *Kala Ghoda Poems*, 137).

22. See Saleem Peeradina, *Contemporary Indian Poetry in English: An Assessment and Selection* (Bombay: Macmillan, 1972); Adil J. Jussawalla, ed., *New Writing in India* (Harmondsworth, England: Penguin, 1974); R. Parthasarathy, *Ten Twentieth-Century Indian Poets* (Delhi: Oxford University Press, 1976); Mehrotra, *The Oxford Anthology*; and Arvind Krishna Mehrotra, *A History of Indian Literature in English* (New York: Columbia University Press, 2003).

23. Adil Jussawalla, "Being There: Aspects of an Indian Crisis," *Bombay Review* 1 (1989): 21.

24. Mehrotra, *The Oxford Anthology*, 2.

25. Zecchini, *Arun Kolatkar.*

26. See Aijaz Ahmad, *In Theory: Classes, Nations, Literatures* (London: Verso, 1992).

27. Also see the poem "Tukaram in Heaven; Chitre in Hell" (*As Is, Where Is: Selected English Poems, 1964–2007* [Mumbai: Poetrywala, 2007], 61–65): "Tukaram in heaven, / Chitre in hell, / Sing the same song / Centuries apart."

28. See the epigraph of *Bhijaki Vahi* and of *Boatride* where Kolatkar addresses Tukaram in his unfinished drafts:

> I'm not gonna pan off your poems as mine
> Salo Malo tried that
> Salo Malo tried to pass off your poems as his
> that didn't work
> I'll try to pass off mine as yours
> I'll create such confusion
> that nobody can be sure about what you wrote and what I did. (*Boatride* 234)

Kolatkar collected various editions of Tukaram's *abhangas*, and Bhalchandra Nemade has his father's collection of Tukaram's works in which Kolatkar had made notes in 1961 (when Nemade, Shahane, and Kolatkar met regularly at the Asiatic). There are pieces of paper in the book where Kolatkar has copied stanzas that deeply affected him.

29. John S. Hawley shows how the idea of a *bhakti* movement belongs to the twentieth century even though the work of the saints themselves has a deep, rooted past. See the introduction to *A Storm of Songs: India and the Idea of the Bhakti Movement* (Cambridge, MA: Harvard University Press, 2015), 1–12.

30. Veena Naregal, *Language, Hierarchy and Identity: Emergence of the Public Sphere in Colonial Western India* (Delhi: Oxford University Press, 2001).

31. Sheldon Pollock, "Literary History, Indian History, World History," *Social Scientist* 23, no. 10/12 (1995): 112–42.

32. "One result of the identification of *bhakti* as Maharashtra dharma, and therefore a religious source of Maratha inspiration, was the overdetermination of a complex and diverse set of spiritual interventions into a generalized and politicized ideology of religious community" (Prachi Deshpande, *Creative Pasts: Historical Memory and Identity in Western India, 1700–1960* [New York: Columbia University Press, 2007], 133). See also Naregal, *Language, Hierarchy and Identity.*

33. Chaudhuri, *Clearing a Space*, 41.

34. See Christian Novetzke's notion of the "publics" created by the *bhakti* performances in *Religion and Public Memory: A Cultural History of Saint Namdev in India* (New York: Columbia University Press, 2008).

35. Naregal, *Language, Hierarchy and Identity*, 268.

36. Janabai (c. 1270–1350 C.E., the dates associated with Namdev) was the devotee and servant of Namdev, another *bhakti* saint-poet, and is one of the five women seen as saint-poets associated with the Western Maharashtrian *bhakti* movement originating in Pandharpur. As an orphan and servant, she, too, falls outside the pale of the brahmin establishment and has about three hundred poems/*abhangas* to her credit.

37. Vitthal is considered to be a manifestation of Lord Vishnu and is the reigning deity of the Western Maharashtrian Varkari movement associated with the *bhakti* saints. Starting out as a pastoral god, he is now worshiped more broadly by the Marathi and Kannada followers, and others from Andhra Pradesh and Tamil Nadu. The most important temple of Vitthal is in Pandharpur in Maharashtra, and *Chirimiri* and the Balwant Bua stories reference this location.

38. Dilip Chitre, *Says Tuka: Selected Poetry of Tukaram* (New Delhi: Penguin, 1991), 75.

39. Susan Bassnett and André Lefèvre, *Translation, History, and Culture* (London: Pinter Publishers, 1990), 11.

40. For instance, Kolatkar himself took pains to distinguish even between his own poems that could otherwise broadly be categorized as about "religion." Differentiating between his poems in *Chirimiri* (that refer to the temples of Pandharpur) and the poems in *Jejuri*, which locate the writing in the temples of the town of Jejuri, Kolatkar stated, "The difference between Jejuri and Pandharpur is that you go to Jejuri for your self-interest, because you want something from the god. You go to Pandharpur just to sing and dance" (Eunice de Souza, "Being Bilingual Is a Strain, Says Arun Kolatkar," *Economic Times*, September 11, 1977, 5).

41. See Tony Triglio, *Allen Ginsberg's Buddhist Poetics* (Carbondale: Southern Illinois University Press, 2007), 85–86; and Erik Mortenson, *Capturing the Beat Moment: Cultural Politics and the Poetics of Presence* (Carbondale: Southern Illinois University Press, 2011), 53–83.

42. Adil Jussawalla, *Land's End: Poems* (Calcutta: Writer's Workshop, 1962), 12.

43. Gita Mehta, *Karma Cola: Marketing the Mystic East* (New York: Simon and Schuster, 1979), 6.

44. Dharwadker, "The Modernist Novel in India."

45. See Baker, *A Blue Hand*.

46. Prakash, *Mumbai Fables*, 220.

47. In 1955, Prime Minister Nehru proposed a three-way division of the region that included the states of Maharashtra, Gujarat, and Bombay, but there was a series of prolonged protests against this move by the Central Government. See Usha Thakkar and Nagindas Sanghavi, "Political Currents in Maharashtra: Language and Beyond," in *Reorganisation of States: Culture, Identity and Politics in India*, ed. Asha Sarangi and Sudha Pai (New Delhi: Routledge India, 2011), 148, 149; and Prakash, *Mumbai Fables*, 225.

48. See Prakash, *Mumbai Fables*. A decade later in 1969, the writers of the little magazine movement in Bombay organized a bonfire (similar to the earlier one though on a smaller scale in terms of people who attended the event) to symbolically burn an issue of the Marathi *Satyakatha* as a rejection of its institutional status and power in the world of Marathi literature. It would also be fascinating to compare these events with Kolatkar's much-loved and beautifully crafted poem "Fire," which also repeats this act of burning on another front, translated in Vinay Dharwadker, "Twenty-Nine Modern Indian Poems," *TriQuarterly* 77 (Winter 1989–90): 119–228:

> this fire   fififire
> it's the bonfire of   holi
> a running fence   I'm a fleeing fence
> it's holi   it's holi   it's holi
> a broken window   I'm a broken door
> it's holi   it's holi   it's holi
> a limping chair   I'm a crawling table
> it's holi   it's holi   it's holi
> a flying cupboard   I'm a raiding larder
> it's holi   it's holi   it's holi

49. Sudipta Kaviraj, *Imaginary Institution of India: Politics and Ideas* (New York: Columbia University Press, 2010), 141.

50. Apter, "Translation at the Checkpoint," 72.

51. In Suresh Dalal, "The Translation of Poetry and the Translator," *Rucha* 7, no. 10 (1976), the note on the essay says that the journal *Kavyavishwa* published three hundred translations of world poetry and that this is a reprint of the introduction by Suresh Dalal to that magazine (103).

52. See the introduction to *Counterculture Colophon* where Loren Glass describes the manner in which Grove Press launched the imprint as an experiment analogous to the avant-garde literature in its rapidly expanding catalog. In a 1958 circular to booksellers, boldly headed "An Experiment," Grove notes the industry's concern "over the shrinking market for new, original fiction" and attributes the shrinkage to "the wide gap between the prices of original hardbound fiction and paperback reprints." The circular proposes that the

imprint will "bridge that gap." . . . A mere six months later, Grove ran an ad in the *New York Times Book Review* trumpeting its Evergreen Originals imprint as "an experiment in book publishing that worked." (28)

Among these books were the Kerouac best sellers that the poets in Bombay were eagerly reading.

53. Arun Kolatkar, *Jejuri* (Mumbai: Pras Prakashan, 1976), 17.

54. Karuna Mantena, "The Ideas of Indians," *Caravan*, March 1, 2013, http://www.caravanmagazine.in/books/ideas-indians.

55. The goal of the Akademi was to create "a national organization to work actively for the development of Indian letters, to set high literary standards, to foster and co-ordinate literary activities in all the Indian languages and to promote through them all the cultural unity of the country" (*Sahitya Akademi Annual Report, 1954–57* [New Delhi: Sahitya Akademi], appendix 1).

56. Sukumar Sen, *History of Bengali Literature* (New Delhi: Sahitya Akademi, 1971), v.

57. One of the best books on this subject is by Rosemary George, *Indian English and the Fiction of National Literature* (New York: Cambridge University Press, 2013). George analyzes the Akademi's attempt to create the fiction of national literature that ignored the chasms of caste and class in the desire for a unified literature. Also see Rashmi Sadana, "At the Sahitya Akademi," in *English Heart, Hindi Heartland: The Political Life of Literature in India* (Berkeley: University of California Press, 2012), 94–115.

58. Nadig, *Aso*, 166. Even if Adiga's politics do not coincide in any exact manner with the *sathottari* worldview in Bombay, here too, as in the earlier example of Mardhekar, translating the text reinvents the context and changes the interpretation of the poem.

59. Big, institutionalized journals like *Satyakatha* in Marathi were the initial spaces where the *sathottari* writers (Dilip Chitre, Ashok Shahane, and many others) debuted their translations before moving on to their little magazines.

60. Eunice de Souza, "Interviews with Four Indian English Poets," *Bombay Review* 1 (1989): 84.

61. Chaudhuri, *Clearing a Space*, 115.

62. Arvind Krishna Mehrotra, "Bharatmata," *Poetry India* 2, no. 2 (1967): 16.

63. Ibid., 22.

64. In fact, there is a letter from Ezekiel to the young Jussawalla (dated December 20, 1965, Adil Jussawalla Papers), still a student then in England, that shows that at one point Ezekiel wanted to expand the idea of "regional" beyond the national to also include Pakistani writing:

> Dear Adil,
>
> The poems of Adrian Husain that you sent me, I am returning separately by sea mail. I was sorry to hear that he did not want them used in *Poetry India* because he is a Pakistani, and there was this trouble with Pakistan recently.
>
> As a matter of fact I was trying to get some Pakistani poems as soon as the idea of the journal was mooted. So far I have had no success.
>
> I hope you will send me any new poems you have written.

With regards,

Yours sincerely,
Nissim Ezekiel
Editor

65. Arvind Krishna Mehrotra, *Songs of Kabir* (New York: New York Review of Books, 2011).

66. Mary John, "Reframing Globalization: Perspectives from the Women's Movement," *Economic & Political Weekly* 44, no. 10 (March 7, 2009): 48.

67. Nivedita Menon, "Thinking Through the Postnation," *Economic & Political Weekly* 44, no. 10 (March 7, 2009): 71.

68. Kedar N. Singh, Arun Kolatkar, Ashok Vajapeyi, Reed Bye, Anne Waldman, and Bob Rosenthal, *Naropa Institute, Indian Poets, May 20, 1986*, sound recording, http://archive.org/details/Reading_of_Indian_poets_May_1986_86P060.

69. *Boatride*, 87. *The Boatride & Other Poems* has an English translation of this poem by the poet himself and this was also one of the several poems that Kolatkar read in Naropa in Marathi (which was simultaneously read in English by Anne Waldman). Kolatkar was in the habit of writing much of his work in two languages. See chapter 6 for a detailed discussion of this practice of self-translation and bilingual writing.

70. Singh et al., *Naropa Institute, Indian Poets, May 20, 1986.*

71. Maurice Blanchot and Susan Hanson, "Everyday Speech," *Yale French Studies* 73 (1987): 15.

72. Sukanta Chaudhuri, "The Translator as Sceptic," in *Translation and Understanding* (New Delhi: Oxford University Press, 1999), 43.

73. Ibid.

OVERVIEW

1. See Zecchini, *Arun Kolatkar*, for a complete biography of the poet and for details about the relationship between Darshan Chhabda and Arun Kolatkar.

2. In the Balwant Bua proposal, Kolatkar describes the life and stories of the hardnosed, eternally positive Balwant Bua, who took a bunch of prostitutes to the pilgrimage site of Pandharpur temple where the god Vitthal resides : "He [Balwant Bua] talks about the whorehouses of Bombay, about the people who frequented them, their peculiarities, and the perversions they practiced; about the prostitutes themselves—not the ritzy kind, but their humbler sisters—and how he came to be soothsayer, entertainer, bhajansinger, treasurer, bridge partner, attarwalla, spiritual guide, client and close friend, all rolled into one, to a whole lot of them. How he went to Alandi with some of them, and was thrown out of a dharmashala by the scandalized trustees; and how he went on a pilgrimage to Pandharpur with a flock of them, and what fun they had there."

3. "You could have mistaken him for a hick; but he was city-born, city-bred, and street-smart; and he was an instant hit with me, became my favourite bhajansinger, the moment he started singing, accompanying himself brilliantly on a pair of cymbals" (Balwant Bua book proposal).

4. See *Boatride*, 131–56.

5. Kiran Nagarkar, "Arun Kolatkar: Some Memories" (Unpublished manuscript).

6. Adil Jussawalla mentioned this about the Q&A after the posthumous screening of the documentary on Kolatkar (on January 23, 2005, at the Kala Ghoda festival in Bombay) when someone asked Chitre what Kolatkar's reaction had been to this film.

In his unpublished drafts in the folder titled "Loose Ends: Late fifties/early sixties" (Kolatkar Papers), Kolatkar muses on this reticent behavior in his writing: "I write because I cannot talk / get tonguetied," and he goes on to thematize it in different ways:

> my tongue is swollen
> when I choked on my tongue
> —
> speech has ceased
> —
> It's Rushdie's paap."

7. *Rucha* (1977): 95 The translation is mine.

8. *Boatride*, 143.

9. Ibid., 219.

CHAPTER 4

1. There has not yet been a full-length study of *Bhijaki Vahi* in English, although there have been analyses of *Sarpa Satra*, a breakaway section from *Bhijaki Vahi* that was published as a separate book in English in 2004. There are several scholars who refer to *Bhijaki Vahi* briefly (in English, Dharwadker, Mehrotra, Patke, Zecchini, and a few others), but none performs a close reading of the book.

2. The continuities between the different books of poems and across different languages (Marathi and English) can be seen by the presence of a parallel list of women near the end of *Kala Ghoda Poems*. There, in the poem "Man of the Year," Kolatkar lists another diverse series of women: "Malati, Niloufer, Anjali, Shanta / Alpana, Kalpana, Shirin, Zarine, Sylvia, Maria / Harlene, Yasmine, Nina, Kamala, Mona, Lopa" (157). This modern-day list of women complements the women in *Bhijaki Vahi*, most of whom are from older narratives and events.

3. In his essay "Death of a Poet," Arvind Krishna Mehrotra states that Kolatkar wanted to write many more such poetic sets on different legendary women but that "he has not been able to find a way into the story, by which he meant a new perspective on it that would make it different from a retelling. He faced a similar problem with Hypatia of Alexandria, which he solved by making St. Cyril, who is thought to have had a hand in her murder, the poem's speaker" (*Partial Recall*, 102).

4. Shahane states that reading Adil Jussawalla's copy of *The Satanic Verses* (which was banned in India) is what triggered this wide-ranging poetic travel across the religions of the world.

5. Kolatkar's vast library of books is now located at the Bhandarkar Oriental Institute in Pune, and it reveals the voracious reading habits of the poet, who consulted a long list of instructions on how to make papyrus/paper in Egypt in addition to analyses of Egyptian culture and history when writing the poems on Egyptian characters in *Bhijaki Vahi*. The collection also includes a large number of books on the history of Islam in India and in the world, with particular texts from Indian Islamic culture and literature; a great number of books on the women named in *Bhijaki Vahi* (Nadezhda Mandelstam, Hypatia, and Helen, among others); and a long list of books about women in history and the labels attached to them. Here is a sampling of books from that section: *Whores in History*, Nickie Roberts; *The Clever Adulteress, Stories of Jain Literature*, ed. Phyllis Granoff; *Witchcraze*, Anne Llewellyn Barstow; *History's Mistresses*, Paula Weidegger; *Salem Witchcraft*, Charles Upham; *A Handbook on Witches*, Gillian Tindall. There is also a selection of books on violence and riots in post-independence India and around the world, with books on the Babri Masjid riots in Bombay and war in the Balkans.

6. Kolatkar, *Bhijaki Vahi*, 393.

7. The newspaper clippings in Kolatkar's papers about the Idris/Maimun episode in the 1990s and the fact that he wrote the opening poem, "*tipa*" (tears), in the early 2000s show that the book was a compilation of years of work and thinking, and individual poetic sequences were written over the course of two decades.

8. Bennett, "Periodical Fragments and Organic Culture," 481.

9. Kolatkar designed the cover of *Dionysus* (1965), and he submitted his poetry for publication in that magazine as well as the littles started by Mehrotra, Bhupen Khakhar, and Gauri Deshpande. Kolatkar was involved with the creation, design, and circulation of little magazines throughout his career and was associated with the publication of what is widely seen as the first *sathottari* literary little magazine in Marathi (*Shabda*). Ashok Shahane, the publisher of all of Kolatkar's work, notes how Kolatkar was approached by Oxford to publish his *Jejuri* after the first edition by Clearing House sold out. Kolatkar, then still an up-and-coming poet, held to his ideas of poetry and asked that his poems be published with the integrity of the longest line kept intact on the page. When OUP could not guarantee this, Kolatkar refused the offer and chose to publish with Pras Prakashan, which at the time was an unknown and very small press. See also Chaudhuri, *Real Time*, where Chaudhuri recounts Kolatkar's reluctance to publish with bigger presses.

10. For details regarding the book version, see the section "The Poisonous Tail of Representation: *Sarpa Satra*" in chapter 5.

11. Kolatkar, *Bhijaki Vahi*, 16.

12. For another contemporary example of the use of this formal feature of *pasayadan*, see "*Golpitha*" in Dhasal and Chitre, *Namdeo Dhasal, Poet of the Underworld*.

13. Kolatkar, *Bhijaki Vahi*, 391.

14. De Souza, *Talking Poems*, 19.

15. Adrienne Rich, *Later Poems Selected and New: 1971–2012* (New York: W. W. Norton, 2013), 43.

16. Kolatkar Papers.

17. See the Marathi poem "*Khekade*" ("The Crabs") in his early collection, *Arun Kolatkarchya Kavita* (125–28), also in English in *Boatride* (89–91). Even there, the poet meditates on the infidelities of the gaze and imagines the eyeballs being eaten by the crabs that have emerged from the poet's head.

18. Kolatkar, *Aso*, 1963, 154–55.

19. Allen Ginsberg, *Kaddish and Other Poems, 1958–1960* (San Francisco: City Lights Books, 1961), 34–35. Ginsberg visited India and met Shahane and Kolatkar in Bombay in 1962; Kolatkar met with Ginsberg again on his visit to the United States for the Festival of India in 1986. See figure 4.3 for a rare picture of the two poets together. Ginsberg also gave him a signed copy of his *Collected Poems* (inscribed for both Shahane and Kolatkar) with a question, "When'll we meet again?" (see figure 1.4).

20. In his afterword to the text, on the back cover, Ginsberg states that his poem is a response to seeing "my self my own mother and my very nation trapped desolate our worlds of consciousness homeless and at war" (Ginsberg, *Kaddish*).

21. The poem refers to the Kaddish, the Jewish prayer service that is performed upon the death of person and that lists the losses and states the love of God despite these setbacks. Ginsberg uses that form and title of "Kaddish" to document his troubled mother's ailments and her life, as well as to express his grief about his mother's discomposed state of mind and his country's history of war and violence.

22. *Pasayadan* is the final prayer in the *bhakti* poet Dnyaneshwar's commentary on the Bhagavad Gita in Marathi, called *Dnyaneshwari*. In this *pasayadan*, the poet Dnyaneshwar lists what constitutes a good deed and a good person and asks for the world to be graced with such people. Kolatkar's poem is the *pasayadan* in reverse because it asks for the obliteration of the "jihads" and the murders and the people who commit these acts.

23. In the Kolatkar Papers, there is a page of graphics that shows the various designs of "the weeping eye" that Kolatkar tried out. Almost every one of them has something poisonous or negative about it—one has snakes coming out of it, another has lightning striking through it, etc. (see figure 4.1). An interesting coincidence is the older cover of a book published by Ashok Shahane/Pras Prakashan, *Antarvedh* (Manohar Oak, 1978). The cover features an open eye of a woman, but this is a photographic image of verisimilitude, as compared to the graphic image by Kolatkar that refers to Egypt, and to Susan Sontag's study of the photographer's gaze.

24. Kolatkar, *Bhijaki Vahi*, 329.

25. "The graphics and writings on buses and the activities with these spaces may appear to be minor, even frivolous, interventions in public space, hardly political. But it is through these minor acts and signs that a large majority of the city residents navigate, occupy, make sense of, and momentarily defy their location in the city" (Swati Chattopadhyay, *Unlearning the City: Infrastructure in a New Optical Field* [Minneapolis: University of Minnesota Press, 2012], 165–66). She even mentions a common saying that appears all over Indian towns and cities: "The most common image [on the vehicles] is a

masklike 'monster' face. An unpropitious image, it is meant to ward off the evil eye. Often accompanied with written warnings against the jealous gaze—*buri nazar wale tera muh kala* (shame on you who gives the evil eye) or with old shoes or brooms hanging from the rear bumper—the sign and the object compel you to see but suggest that you look away" (183–84).

26. Ibid., 178.

27. Susan Sontag, *On Photography* (New York: Farrar, Straus & Giroux, 1973), 14.

28. Ibid., 24.

29. Ibid., 13.

30. Kolatkar, *Bhijaki Vahi*, 285.

31. Joseph Brodsky, "Nadezhda Mandelstam (1899–1980)," *New York Review of Books* 28, no. 3 (March 5, 1981): 3–4.

32. Kolatkar, *Bhijaki Vahi*, 81.

33. Margaret Atwood, *Power Politics* (Toronto: Anansi, 1971), 1.

34. Kolatkar, *Bhijaki Vahi*, 391.

35. Friedman, "When a 'Long' Poem Is a 'Big' Poem," 727. Also see Kolatkar's interview with Eunice de Souza (1999) where he questions a unitary understanding of history: "What is history? While reading it one doesn't know. It's a floating situation, a nagging quest. It's difficult to arrive at any certainties. What you get is versions of history, with nothing final about them. Some parts are better lit than others or the light may change, or one may see the object differently" (19–20). Also, in his unpublished drafts, among the Kolatkar Papers, are further musings on official histories:

Impatient with fiction   works of fiction   I've no time for fiction
I try to take refuge   in   history   the best disguise for truth   fine feathers of truth
natural   clothes that truth feels
costume   most comfortable in
the only kind of fiction I can take   read
is history   is shelved under "history"

36. Syeda Hameed, quoted in Saira Kurup, "Four Women India Forgot," *Times of India*, May 7, 2006, http://timesofindia.indiatimes.com/home/sunday-toi/special-report/Four-women-India-forgot/articleshow/1519056.cms?referral=PM.

37. The news reports also mentioned that the communities in Haryana retained some of the Hindu communal customs despite their conversion to Islam, so the mixed vocabulary seems particularly apt.

38. Kolatkar, *Bhijaki Vahi*, 218. Here one cannot help but be reminded of the now famous play by Vijay Tendulkar, *Ghashiram Kotwal* (1972), in which the religious invocations during the puja are sung to the tune of the lowly, more sexualized dance/song form of the *lavni*, and vice versa. This transposition allows the dramatist to make a succinct yet biting comment on the seamless movement between the sacred and the profane in modern society and on the hypocrisy of its orthodox beliefs.

39. Kolatkar, *Bhijaki Vahi*, 221.

40. Ibid., 100.

41. Ibid., 96.

42. De Souza, "Interviews," 82.

43. In his famous poem on Karl Marx, Narayan Surve writes about him in the colloquial Marathi of Bombay and shows both the striking millworker and Marx as equally familiar with Goethe's work.

44. Kolatkar, *Bhijaki Vahi*, 59–60.

45. Elsewhere, in the section titled "Helen" (*Bhijaki Vahi*, 177–80), the poet states how there need not be a Homer for myths to start collecting around a story, nor need there be a Helen to start a war. The ordinary women from Maharashtra, and by implication all over the world, can be both the source of myths and the victims of war.

46. Nissim Ezekiel, *Collected Poems, 1952–1988* (Delhi: Oxford University Press, 1989). Ezekiel has a biting image of this class in his poetry:

> This, she said to herself
> As she sat at the table
> With the English boss,
> Is IT. This is the promise:
> The long evenings
> In the large apartment
> With cold beer and Western music,
> Lucid talk of art and literature,
>
> And of all "the changes India needs." (133)

47. See Ramnarayan's interview with the poet, where he accepted the deliberateness of this artistic choice: "I'm dragging non-Marathi themes, feelings and traditions into Marathi. . . . Language should be capable of expressing not just what's in your lane or village, but happenings anywhere in the world" (Gowri Ramnarayan, "No Easy Answers," *The Hindu*, September 5, 2004, http://www.hindu.com/lr/2004/09/05/stories/2004090500110100.htm).

48. The story of Isis is not properly Western, but the manner in which that myth is used in Euro-American literature makes it inaccessible to most readers with only vernacular reading/speaking abilities. For more on the domesticating of the West, see Anuradha Dingwaney and Carol Maier, eds., *Between Languages and Cultures: Translation and Cross-Cultural Texts* (Delhi: Oxford University Press, 1996): "Lawrence Venuti, acknowledging Sciermacher, . . . distinguishes between the translator who chooses a 'domesticating method, an ethnocentric reduction of the foreign text to target language cultural values, bringing the author back home' and the translator who chooses a 'foreignizing method, an ethnodeviant pressure on these values to register the linguistic and cultural difference of the foreign text, sending the reader abroad'" (7).

49. This appears at the beginning of the text as well as on the back cover.

50. Naregal, *Language, Hierarchy and Identity*, 268.

51. *Boatride*, 234.

52. A related image of the bullocks appears to be a common one in the language of rural women, as Sharon Kemp notes: "Discussing their lives, women say, 'We work like bullocks,' and quote a saying common in this area,

'bāikānā āni bailānā jāsta kām astānā pan nāv mātra purusāce hote' ('Women and bullocks do more work, but the man is named [or praised]')." Sharon Kemp, "Women as Bullocks: A Self-Image of Maharashtrian Village Women," in *Images of Women in Maharashtrian Society*, ed. Anne Feldhaus (Albany: State University of New York Press, 1998), 217.

53. Ramanujan, Dharwadker, and Blackburn, *The Collected Essays of A. K. Ramanujan*, 271.

54. Kolatkar Papers.

CHAPTER 5

1. Narayan Surve, *Majhe Vidyapeeth* (Pune: Popular Prakashan, 1992), 54.

2. Kolatkar, *Bhijaki Vahi*, 309.

3. Garrett Stewart, *Bookwork: Medium to Object to Concept to Art* (Chicago: University of Chicago Press, 2011), xvi.

4. Griselda Pollock, "Beholding Art History: Vision, Place and Power," in *Vision and Textuality*, ed. Stephen Melville and Bill Readings (Durham, NC: Duke University Press, 1995), 41.

5. Here is a sampling of the many detailed readings of *Jejuri*: Bhalchandra Nemade, "Arun Kolatkar: Bilingual Poet," in *Tikasvayamvara* (Aurangabad: Saket Prakashan, 1990), 117–26; R. S. Kimbahune, "From Jejuri to Arun Kolatkar," *New Quest* (January–February 1980): 27–32; Shubhangi Raykar, ed., *Jejuri: A Commentary and Critical Perspectives* (Pune: Prachet Publications, 1995); Sudesh Mishra, *Preparing Faces: Modernism and Indian Poetry in English* (Adelaide: Flinders University of South Australia, 1995); Philip Engblom, "Arun Kolatkar: Reading *Jejuri* and *Arun Kolatkarachya Kavita* in Tandem," *New Quest* 146 (October–December 2001): 389–409; Patke, *Postcolonial Poetry in English*; Emma Bird, "Re-reading Postcolonial Poetry: Arun Kolatkar's *Jejuri*," *Journal of Commonwealth Literature* 47 (2012): 229–43; Vinay Dharwadker, "Arun Kolatkar's Historical Imagination," in *Marginalized: Indian Poetry in English*, ed. Smita Agarwal (Amsterdam: Rodopi, 2014), 151–82; and Zecchini, *Arun Kolatkar*.

6. Stewart, *Bookwork*, xvi.

7. In 1976, *Jejuri* was first published by the Clearing House Collective that consisted of Adil Jussawalla, Arvind Krishna Mehrotra, Arun Kolatkar, and Gieve Patel. The book won the Commonwealth award in 1977 and was sold out in its limited edition. Like most small presses, Clearing House struggled to stay afloat and continue publishing, and it was not possible for the collective to publish second editions at that point. In 1978, Ashok Shahane's Pras Prakashan stepped in to fill the breach and has kept this book and all others in continuous publication since then. Shahane and Kolatkar retained the graphic format first used in the Clearing House edition.

8. Kolatkar, *Jejuri* (1976), 54.

9. Ibid., 22.

10. Mehrotra remembers that when Kolatkar handed him the early version of *Jejuri* in 1974, the long poem did not have the dance of the "cocks and hens" in the field in the form of the scattered words on the page; rather, there was just one line regarding the birds. The visual dimension of the dispersed words mimicking the dancing birds came later with the publication of the poem by *OLO* and later by Clearing House. This also demonstrates the extraordinary facility the poet accessed by having a resource like the small press at his disposal.

11. Harold Evans, "Harold Evans on Newspaper Design and Typography," *Motif* 1 (January 1995): 23.

12. Kolatkar, *Jejuri* (1976), 31.

13. Note there is a single typo of the word "sily" on page 23, an error uncharacteristic of most Kolatkar publications; he meticulously proofread and designed them whenever possible.

14. Kersy Katrak and Gauri Deshpande were prescient in publishing this whole poetic sequence. Given the financial strain under which the little magazine operated (this was its last issue of a run of just four issues), one cannot blame the editors but instead praise their foresight in recognizing the poetic value of this text. The point here is that what the little magazines could not afford or offer, despite the small publishing context, the small presses made possible in cases like that of Clearing House Books and Pras Prakashan.

15. *Opinion Literary Quarterly* 1, no. 4 (1974): 10.

16. Kolatkar, *Jejuri* (1976), 30.

17. Ibid., 31.

18. Khandoba is a martial god who is the guardian of the Kunbi group of castes in Western Maharashtra. Beginning as a local deity of the *dhangars*, the nomadic shepherds, he has become adopted as the incarnation of Lord Shiva and is more widely worshiped now. In the image on *Jejuri*, he is pictured in his traditional figuration with a sword in hand and astride his horse. Mhalsa is one of the several wives of the martial god and the one most often pictured in the songs of Khandoba. She represents the high-caste connection of the god, while other wives represent his relation to the lower castes. See Gunther Sontheimer, "All the God's Wives," in *Images of Women in Maharashtrian Literature and Religion*, ed. Anne Feldhaus (Albany: State University of New York Press, 1996), 115–34.

19. A belated note: when he was working as a graphic designer, Kolatkar created a similar image in the 1960s when he designed the cover for a report on the underground rail system proposed at the time. See Aarefa Johari, "Mumbai Had a Plan for an Underground Railway in 1963—50 Years Before It Cleared Metro 3," *Scroll* (October 14, 2015), http://scroll.in/article/748882/mumbai-had-a-plan-for-an-underground-railway-in-1963-50-years-before-it-cleared-metro-3. There, the rail lines travel into the heart of a large orb (indicating the earth), placed at an angle to the center. Here the orb is centered above the rail lines and represents the sun. Does the *Jejuri* cover (and its critique of modernity) show an evolution of Kolatkar's view from his earlier illustration? Or is there a subtle comment embedded even in the cover design of the 1960s? This role of advertising in Kolatkar's creative work, along with its myriad contradictions, deserves a separate study.

20. Ashok Shahane tells of an additional detail regarding the cover and Kolatkar's rejection of traditional ritualism through the public signifying elements of his poetry. As a graphic artist, Kolatkar designed his own covers and his own books, and in the case of *Jejuri*, he drew these cover images on the tinfoil wrapper of an empty cigarette box of his friend Royan—an ultimate gesture of private rejection of what traditional Hindu religion represents, because smoking and drinking are seen as disrespecting the acts of faith in such religious locations.

21. Kolatkar Papers.

22. McGann, *The Textual Condition*, 58. For Kolatkar's interest in print culture, see his collection of books at the library of the Bhandarkar Oriental Research Institute in Pune, where among the many books stored are *Scribes and Sources* (A. S. Osley) and *Book Culture and Textual Transmission in Sung China* (Susan Cherniak).

23. In *Unlearning the City*, Chattopadhyay studies subaltern urban practices like street cricket that transform the street space from one of passage to that of impromptu tenancy.

24. On the front cover of *Jejuri* (2005) is a scene from the temple precincts where people are celebrating a festival: they are covered with yellow and there is yellow powder being thrown in the air. That is the ritual *bhandara* that is thrown in the air at religious ceremonies at Jejuri. The editors at the *New York Review of Books* decided to use this literal cover for the posthumously published edition, but the symbolic aspect of the yellow color is also present in the *Jejuri* poems, where Kolatkar deliberately uses it to signify multiple and contradictory effects in his text. See Rajeev Patke, *Modernist Literature and Postcolonial Studies* (Edinburgh: Edinburgh University Press, 2013).

25. Kolatkar, *Jejuri* (1976), 16.

26. De Souza, *Talking Poems*, 2.

27. Durga Bhagwat, *Lokasahityachi Ruparekha* (Pune: Varada Books, 1977), 505.

28. Other *sathottari* writers and poets also featured the butterfly in their work. See Jussawalla, *Land's End: Poems*; and in Marathi, Sadanand S. Rege, *Veḍya Kavita* (Mumbai: Popular Prakashan, 1980).

29. Durga Bhagwat championed a cosmopolitan and worldly *sathottari* local that looked at regional translations, international art and literature, and a selective Maharashtrian past to create a sense of the contemporary place and time in Bombay.

30. Kolatkar, *Kala Ghoda Poems* (2004), 132. Also see Zecchini, *Kolatkar.*

31. The cross-references multiply with this color—the yellow also recalls Van Gogh's sunflower yellow with the explicit allusion to his painting *The Potato Peeler* here. The reference to canonical global art within the bounds of the street life of the Bombay poor monumentalizes the discarded lives and demands a significance for them; on the other hand, the stray end of the serif of the title that stands outside the yellow band and the thematic connection to the butterfly through the yellow band together give a fleeting character to the same lives.

32. *Boatride*, 223.

33. Ezekiel, *Collected Poems, 1952–1988*, 127.

34. Adil Jussawalla and Eunice de Souza, eds., *Statements: An Anthology of Indian Prose in English* (New Delhi: Orient Longman, 1976), 111.

35. Mieke Bal, "Reading Art?" in *Generations and Geographies in the Visual Arts: Feminist Readings*, ed. Griselda Pollock (London: Routledge, 1996), 27.

36. Kolatkar Papers.

37. Sontag, *On Photography*, 12.

38. See Kolatkar, *Kala Ghoda Poems*, 72:

> The rusty shield-bearer
> neutral till then
> paradrops a winning flower
> —yellow
> And irrelevant—
>
> on the checkerboard.

Zecchini also talks about Kolatkar's fascination with frames but she reads it exactly opposed to this interpretation in *Bombay Modern*: her reading suggests Kolatkar's stepping out of the frame as a defiant act that breaks established social constraints. Instead, *Bombay Modern* presents such references as a conflicted admission by the poet that, try as he might, he is *unable* to break the final unbreakable mold of representation.

39. Kolatkar, *Kala Ghoda Poems*, 28, 72.

40. The two versions of the long poem are not exactly the same and, as in the case of *Jejuri*, it is an interesting exercise to do a close reading of the two versions and examine the translation issues that emerge.

41. The Bombay riots of January 1993 took place amid the politics of urban conflagration in the year after the demolition of the Babri Masjid in Ayodhya. Tensions between the Hindu and Muslim communities reached a flashpoint when a Hindu family was burned to death by unknown persons. The local political party, the Shiv Sena, vowed to take revenge and took to the streets. Violent Hindu mobs, often led by Shiv Sena activists, burned Muslim establishments and killed Muslim people indiscriminately. At the end of the riots, which spanned several days, the death toll was more than eight hundred, mostly Muslim residents of Bombay. See Jim Masselos, *Indian Nationalism: A History* (New Delhi: Sterling Publishers, 1993); and Thomas Blom Hansen, "Shiv Sena, the City, and Communal Populism," in *The Oxford Anthology of the Modern Indian City: The City in Its Plenitude*, ed. Vinay Lal (New Delhi: Oxford University Press, 2013), 30–45.

42. I was fortunate to meet Arun Kolatkar at Military Café in the summer of 2004, just before the publication of the book, and also at the publication party in July 2004. When I asked him at the NCPA why he had decided to republish just this section of *Bhijaki Vahi* in English, Kolatkar said to me, "Because I think this is an important statement to make today!"

43. Arun Kolatkar, *Sarpa Satra* (Mumbai: Pras Prakashan, 2004), 43.

44. Ibid., 36.

45. This is in Kolatkar's handwriting in the unfinished typescript of the poem.

46. Kolatkar Papers.

47. Ibid.

48. Kolatkar is said to have insisted on the particular deep black shade that is evident on the cover and discarded many others in his search for the perfect pitch-black.

49. Kolatkar, *Sarpa Satra*, 35.

50. William Wordsworth, "A Slumber Did My Spirit Seal," in *The Collected Poems of William Wordsworth* (Chatham, Kent: Wordsworth Pocket Editions, 1994), 187.

51. Kolatkar, *Bhijaki Vahi*, 391.

52. Kolatkar, *Sarpa Satra*, 65.

CHAPTER 6

1. Homi Bhabha, "Indo-Anglian Attitudes," *TLS: Times Literary Supplement*, February 3, 1978, 136.

2. The cover of this issue is a silhouette of Kolatkar with a long mane and distinct moustache, along with an announcement of his Commonwealth Award.

3. P. S. Rege (1910–1978) is considered one of the great poets of the modernist period in Marathi along with B. S. Mardhekar. He was revolutionary in his frank yet lyrical exploration of the body and of sexuality in poetry and was a well-respected literary figure during this period in 1977.

4. Bhalchandra Nemade, *Tikasvayamvara* (Aurangabad: Saket Prakashan, 1990), 123, 126. In her short piece on Kolatkar written soon after he won the award, Eunice de Souza writes: "I asked him [Kolatkar] if he remembered the ham-handed piece a young woman . . . had written on him. She had denounced him for his ironic attitude to his subject. . . . He remembered. In fact, he said, after that piece he had wanted to write a new bio-data for himself, all about how he lived in a colonial mansion in Jejuri and took pot shots at passing peasants" ("Being Bilingual," 5).

5. See Namdeo Dhasal, "*Arunchya kaviteche june nave valan*" ("The Old and New Turns of Arun Kolatkar's Poetry"), *Shabda* (Diwali 2005): 100–104; Vilas Sarang, "Self Translators," *Journal of South Asian Literature* 16, no. 2 (1981): 33–38; and Satish Tambe, *Lekha-Jokha* (Mumbai: Lokavangmaya Griha, 2007).

6. Dilip Chitre, "Vague Targets, Some Thoughts on Indian English Poetry and (Of Course) Poetry in General," *Bombay Literary Review* 1 (1991): 30.

7. See Anjali Nerlekar, "The Rough Ground of Translation and Bilingual Writing in Arun Kolatkar's *Jejuri*," *Perspectives: Studies in Translatology* 21, no. 2 (2013): 226–40. There I stated that the Marathi *Jejuri* was published in 2010. The book came out at the end of December 2010, and my article was written soon after. The publication date on the book is 2011, however, so that date is used here.

8. For a close look at the formation of the Sahitya Akademi and the role of translations in post-independence Indian nationalism, see chapter 3.

9. Raj Thackeray, nephew of Shiv Sena leader Bal Thackeray, formed this breakaway political group in 2006, which contemporized the grievances and stances of the older party by retaining the ethnic chauvinism in a new garb. For a detailed understanding of the "linguistic localism" of this political party,

see Suhas Palshikar, "In the Midst of Sub-democratic Politics," *Economic and Political Weekly* 7 (2010): 12–16.

10. See chapter 3 for a detailed discussion of the creation of the Maharashtra state and the relation of the little magazine movement and its focus on translation with the political creation of the monolingual state.

11. For a detailed reading of this poem, see Dharwadker, "Twenty-Nine Modern Indian Poems"; and Patke, *Postcolonial Poetry in English*.

12. Prakash, *Mumbai Fables*, 226.

13. See Ramachandra Guha, "What Gandhi Owed to Tagore," *The Hindu*, September 28, 2008, http://www.thehindu.com/todays-paper/tp-features/tp-sundaymagazine/what-gandhi-owed-to-tagore/article1437661.ece.

14. Some prominent ones from the last few decades include: Harish Trivedi, "The Politics of Postcolonial Translation," in *Translation: Its Theory and Practice*, ed. Avadesh Singh (New Delhi: Creative Books, 1996), 46–55; Mukherjee, "The Anxiety of Indianness"; Kimbahune, "From Jejuri to Arun Kolatkar"; P. S. Rege, "Jejuri," *Rucha* 1, no. 2 (1977): 76–78; and Nemade, *Tikasvayamvara*. Nemade's polemics as a critic need to be separated from his sensibilities as a novelist and a poet. Nemade was a close associate of Arun Kolatkar, more so of his publisher and friend Ashok Shahane, and in 2013 when the Marathi daily *Sakal* approached Nemade to do an anniversary piece on his famous novel *Kosla* (Cocoon), Nemade rejected the offer because the newspaper was simultaneously involved in denying the copyright of Kolatkar's poetry to his wife and his publisher. In his criticism, Nemade adopts extreme nativist positions, but his novels, especially *Hindu* (2010), demonstrate a vast imaginative range that is more radically inclusive than many other works of today. For reviews of the groundbreaking novel *Hindu*, see Prachi Deshpande, "Pasts in the Plural: A Review of Bhalchandra Nemade's *Hindu: Jaganyachi Samruddha Adagal*," *Studies in Humanities and Social Sciences* 17, no. 1/2 (2010): 211–20.

15. Chakrabarty, *Provincializing Europe*, 17.

16. I am not including the 2005 edition here because the contrast here is between the first English text of *Jejuri* (1976) and the first Marathi text (2011).

17. Even Salman Rushdie, much later, stated in the acknowledgments to *Satanic Verses* that the character Bhupen Gandhi is in fact partly modeled on Kolatkar. Bhupen Gandhi states that his poetry is about "herds of legends, with sacred cowbells tinkling, grazing on hillsides" (Salman Rushdie, *Satanic Verses* [New York: Random House, 1988], 536). Rushdie also refers to *Jejuri* in his notorious introduction to the *Mirrorwork* anthology; see Salman Rushdie and Elizabeth West, *Mirrorwork: 50 Years of Indian Writing, 1947–1997* (New York: H. Holt and Company, 1997), xiii.

18. Kolatkar wrote the poems after a journey to Jejuri in 1964 with his brother and the Marathi poet Manohar Oak (the "Manohar" addressed in some of the book's poems).

19. Mehrotra remembers that Kolatkar completed the second full version of the English *Jejuri* in 1974; Kersy Katrak was its first reader. Kolatkar then showed it to Mehrotra. The poem "Between Jejuri and the Railway Station" did not have the destruction of the linear script in the dance of the fowl then;

it must have been added subsequently when Kolatkar submitted this long sequence to *Opinion Literary Quarterly* for publication.

20. Arun Kolatkar, "Arun Kolatkar, Interview by Darryl D'Monte," *Debonair* 6, no. 10 (October 1977): 10.

21. Kimbahune, "From Jejuri to Arun Kolatkar," 32.

22. *Boatride*, 222.

23. Ibid., 229.

24. Ibid., 231.

25. Ibid., 220.

26. Ibid., 221.

27. Dogs are a prominent part of the Beat literary works in the United States, the most prominent of which is a poem by Ferlinghetti ("Dog"), who has a "realist tale to tell." In Indian literature, Adil Jussawalla also has a poem on the dog in his book *Missing Person* (1976), and Kolatkar has a version of the realist dog in *Kala Ghoda Poems* (2004).

28. Kolatkar, *Jejuri* (1976), 10; emphasis added.

29. Kolatkar, *Jejuri* (2011), 17; my translation.

30. Thanks to Ashok Shahane for pointing out this connection.

31. The concept of this butterfly clearly persisted in the poet's mind for a while, something he sources to Durga Bhagwat's essay "Absence of Butterflies" (see chapter 5). Kolatkar also tried his hand at putting the poem to music (see figure 6.2); the yellow of this ordinary butterfly colors the titles of poems in *Kala Ghoda Poems*, and the butterfly appears and is burned in the forest fires in *Sarpa Satra*.

32. Kolatkar, *Jejuri* (1976), 31.

33. Ibid.

34. Kolatkar, *Jejuri* (2011), 30–33.

35. Its inclusion by Shahane indicates the difficulty he had in deciding between preserving and publishing almost every significant scrap of manuscript material and keeping to an idea of coherence in a set of poems that were not finalized for book publication by the poet.

36. Kolatkar, *Jejuri* (2011), 21.

37. Kolatkar, *Jejuri* (1976), 18.

38. Ibid., 40.

39. Kolatkar, *Jejuri* (2011), 21.

40. This poem was the example used by Nemade to show how Kolatkar's English poetry is less effective than his Marathi version; it is also the poem used by Vilas Sarang to show how the two versions are each excellent in their own language. Sarang was one of the earliest to discuss Kolatkar's bilingualism and the complexity of self-translations. See Sarang, "Self-Translators," and Sarang, "Mother Tongue, Other Tongue."

41. *Boatride*, 221.

42. There are several drafts of poems in Marathi in the folder for *Kala Ghoda Poems*.

43. One of the stories from the proposal appeared in *Granta* 130 in January 2014.

44. Ludwig Wittgenstein, *Philosophical Investigations* (New York: Macmillan, 1973), 32.

45. Ibid.

46. Trivedi, "The Politics of Postcolonial Translation," 46.

47. Paul De Man, *The Resistance to Theory* (Minneapolis: University of Minnesota Press, 1986), 82.

48. See Gayatri Chakrabarty Spivak, "Translating into English," in *Nation, Language, and the Ethics of Translation*, ed. Sandra Bermann and Michael Wood (Princeton, NJ: Princeton University Press, 2005), 93–110; Trivedi, "The Politics of Postcolonial Translation."

49. Also see chapter 5, where I show that the English *Jejuri* has origins in the Marathi folklore study by Durga Bhagwat and how that connection also extends to the pages of *Kala Ghoda Poems* (2004).

50. G. N. Devy, "Indian Literature in English Translation," in *In Another Tongue: Essays on Indian English Literature*, ed. G. N. Devy (Frankfurt: Peter Lang, 1993), 117–33.

51. Ayappa Panikar, "The Anxiety of Authenticity," in *Translation: Its Theory and Practice*, ed. Avadesh Singh (New Delhi: Creative Books, 1996), 45. For another text that instantiates this free-form mode of translation in the same group of poets, see Mehrotra, *Songs of Kabir.* See also M. Asaduddin, "Lost/Found in Translation: Qurratulain Hyder as Self-Translator," *Annual of Urdu Studies* 23 (2008): 234–49, for a detailed analysis of Qurratulain Hyder's bilingual work.

52. See chapters 2 and 3 for multilingualism and little magazines.

53. *Boatride*, 359.

54. C. Kulashreshtha, "Interview," in *Uncollected Poems and Prose*, ed. A. K. Ramanujan, M. Daniels-Ramanujan, and K. Harrison (Delhi: Oxford University Press, 2001), 47.

55. Wittgenstein, *Philosophical Investigations*, 73, 34.

56. In the *sathottari* period, Nemade was not the kind of nativist that he is portrayed as today: he published translations of Mallarmé in his little magazine, *Vacha*; he collaborated with Shahane closely on publishing *Aso*, where the Beats figured prominently; and his own first novel, *Kosla*, reveals a distinct influence of J. D. Salinger. It is his critical pronouncements that are polemical on the matter of the native versus the foreign.

57. Amit Chaudhuri, introduction to *Jejuri*, xxv–xxvi.

58. Wittgenstein, *Philosophical Investigations*, 46.

EPILOGUE

1. These words are scratched out in the original draft.

2. *Arun Kolatkarchya Kavita*, 138.

3. A. K. Ramanujan, *The Collected Poems of A. K. Ramanujan* (Delhi: Oxford University Press 1995), 226.

4. Du Plessis, "Social Texts and Poetic Texts," 66.

5. Ibid., 65.

6. Chitre, "Vague Targets," 34.

7. Dilip Parameshwar Gaonkar, introduction to *Alternative Modernities*, ed. Dilip Gaonkar (Durham, NC: Duke University Press, 2001), 15–16.

8. Similarly, there are other omissions because of the lack of space: important Marathi poets like Bhalchandra Nemade, Dilip Chitre, Vasant Dattatraya Gurjar, Vasant Abaji Dahake, and Manohar Oak also need extended study in this context.

9. Some of these multilingual and interdisciplinary contexts will be explored in an upcoming special issue, "The Worlds of Bombay Poetry," ed. Anjali Nerlekar and Laetitia Zecchini (2016).

10. Jussawalla, "Being There," 22.

11. Jussawalla, *New Writing in India*, 20.

12. In *Kala Ghoda Poems*, in the poem-sequence titled "The Shit Sermon," there is an image of the words from the drunk man's mouth rising up like a flock of ravens and circling the air before alighting on top of the Victorian Gothic buildings around this South Bombay location. That image of the circling birds moves from down to up as opposed to the pigeons in the draft that swoop from up above to the street below.

13. This is because the latter half of this fragment refers to the woman's sari and shows how the woman's sari envelops the space around it, a theme that was reprised in the published version in poem 3 of the sequence, "The Barefoot Queen of the Crossroads." Here is the fragment in the draft:

air   the mutant of her sari
that inherits the preoccupations
of her flesh
folds of her flesh
skin-sari-space continuum
space is the mutant of her sari
and her sari of her flesh

as the looms of her flesh produce it
her endless sari is consumed by ~~flesh~~ space
the transmutation
of flesh into sari and sari
into space

I have retained the spaces between words and the strikethrough as in the Kolatkar draft.

14. The draft has pigeons spelled as "pidgeons" consistently.

15. Fragment, Kolatkar Papers.

Bibliography

PRIMARY SOURCES

Private Papers and Print Material Held in Personal or Small Collections

Clearing House Papers (correspondence between Adil Jussawalla and Arvind Krishna Mehrotra, compiled by Jerry Pinto)
Vrindavan Dandavate's little magazines collection
Adil Jussawalla Papers
Satish Kalsekar's little magazines collection
Arun Kolatkar book collection and newspaper clippings from Bhandarkar Oriental Research Institute, Pune
Arun Kolatkar Papers
Arvind Krishna Mehrotra Papers
Bhalchandra Nemade Papers

Little Magazines

Abakadaee
Anuwad
Aso
Atharva
Atta
Bharud
Bombay Duck
Bombay Literary Review
Chakravarti

damn you
Dionysus
ezra
Fakta
Katta
Kavi
Khel
Motif
Navakshar Darshan
Opinion Literary Quarterly (*OLQ*)
Poetry India
Rawa
Rucha
Shabda
Timba
Tornado
Vacha
Vagartha
Vidroha
Vrishchik
Yeru

SECONDARY SOURCES

Adarkar, Neera, and Meena Menon. *One Hundred Years, One Hundred Voices: The Millworkers of Girangaon, An Oral History*. Calcutta: Seagull Books, 2004.

Ahmad, Aijaz. *In Theory: Classes, Nations, Literatures*. London: Verso, 1992.

Amin, Ash, and Nigel Thrift. *Cities: Reimagining the Urban*. Cambridge: Polity, 2002.

Anjaria, Ulka. *Realism in the Twentieth-Century Indian Novel: Colonial Difference and Literary Form*. New York: Cambridge University Press, 2012.

Apter, Emily. "Translation at the Checkpoint." *Journal of Postcolonial Writing* 50, no. 1 (2014): 56–74.

Asaduddin, M. "Lost/Found in Translation: Qurratulain Hyder as Self-Translator." *Annual of Urdu Studies* 23 (2008): 234–49.

———. "Translation and Indian Literature: Some Reflections." *Translation Today* 3, no. 1 (2006): 1–19.

Ashcroft, Bill. "Urbanism, Mobility and Bombay: Reading the Postcolonial City." *Journal of Postcolonial Writing* 47, no. 5 (2011): 497–509.

Atwood, Margaret. *Power Politics*. Toronto: Anansi, 1971.

Baker, Deborah. *A Blue Hand: The Beats in India*. New York: Penguin, 2008.

Bal, Mieke. "Reading Art?" In *Generations and Geographies in the Visual Arts: Feminist Readings*, ed. Griselda Pollock, 25–41. London: Routledge, 1996.

Bal, Vidya, V. M. Gitali, and Vandana Bhagavat. *Katha Gaurichi*. Mumbai: Mauj Prakashan Griha, 2008.

Bandekar, Anil. "*Ekhada stand, ek ranget ubhe raha, chi pati*" ("One Bus-Stand, One Board, Please Queue Here"). *Vacha* 3 (1968): 37–38.

Bandekar, Pravin. "*Aniyatakalikanmadhil kavita*." *Navakshar Darshan* 5, no. 2 (2001): 36–51.

Bann, Stephen. *Concrete Poetry: An International Anthology*. London: London Magazine, 1967.

Bantleman, Lawrence. Review. *The Century*, December 31, 1966, 15.

Barthes, Roland. "The Death of the Author." In *Image-Music-Text*, trans. Stephen Heath, 146–48. New York: Farrar, Straus and Giroux, 1977.

Bassnett, Susan, and André Lefèvre. *Translation, History, and Culture*. London: Pinter Publishers, 1990.

Beasley, Rebecca. "Modernism's Translations." In *The Oxford Handbook of Global Modernisms*, ed. Matt Eatough and Mark Wollaeger, 551–70. New York: Oxford University Press, 2013.

Belgrad, Daniel. *The Culture of Spontaneity: Improvisation and the Arts in Postwar America*. Chicago: University of Chicago Press, 1998.

Benjamin, Walter. *Illuminations*. New York: Schocken Books, 1998.

Bennett, David. "Periodical Fragments and Organic Culture: Modernism, the Avant Garde, and the Little Magazine." *Contemporary Literature* 30, no. 4 (Winter 1989): 480–502.

Bermann, Sandra. "Working in the 'And' Zone: Comparative Literature and Translation." *Comparative Literature* 61, no. 4 (2009): 432–46.

Bhabha, Homi. "Indo-Anglian Attitudes." *TLS: Times Literary Supplement*, February 3, 1978, 136.

———. *The Location of Culture*. London: Routledge, 1994.

Bhagwat, Durga. *Lokasahityachi Ruparekha*. Pune: Varada Books, 1977.

Bhagwat, Vidyut. "Bombay in Dalit Literature." In *Bombay: Mosaic of Modern Culture*, ed. Sujata Patel and Alice Thorner, 113–25. Bombay: Oxford University Press, 1995.

Biggs, Mary. "Small Publishing: A Review Article." *Library Quarterly* 52, no. 1 (January 1982): 59–65.

Bird, Emma. "'It's missing': *damn you, Missing Person* and the Material History of the Postcolonial Poem." *Postcolonial Text* 9, no. 4 (2014). http://postcolonial.org/index.php/pct/article/viewArticle/1757.

———. "Re-reading Postcolonial Poetry: Arun Kolatkar's *Jejuri*." *Journal of Commonwealth Literature* 47 (2012): 229–43.

Blanchot, Maurice, and Susan Hanson. "Everyday Speech." *Yale French Studies* 73 (1987): 12–20.

Bornstein, George. *Material Modernism: The Politics of the Page*. Cambridge: Cambridge University Press, 2001.

———, ed. *Representing Modernist Texts: Editing as Interpretation*. Ann Arbor: University of Michigan Press, 1991.

———. "Textual Scholarship and Diversity: Which Needs Affirmative Action More?" *Textual Cultures: Texts, Contexts, Interpretation* 3, no. 1 (2008): 65–76.

Bray, Joe, and Ruth Evans. "Definitions of Textual Culture." *Textual Cultures: Texts, Contexts, Interpretation* 2, no. 2 (2007): 1–130.

Brodsky, Joseph. "Nadezhda Mandelstam (1899–1980)." *New York Review of Books* 28, no. 3 (March 5, 1981): 3–4.

Bulson, Eric. "Little Magazine, World Form." In *The Oxford Handbook of Global Modernisms*, ed. Matt Eatough and Mark Wollaeger, 267–87. New York: Oxford University Press, 2013.

Chakrabarty, Dipesh. "Adda, Calcutta: Dwelling in Modernity." *Public Culture* 11, no. 1 (1999): 109–45.

———. *Provincializing Europe: Postcolonial Thought and Historical Difference*. Princeton, NJ: Princeton University Press, 2000.

Chandavarkar, Rajnarayan. *History, Culture and the Indian City: Essays*. Cambridge: Cambridge University Press, 2009.

Chandra, Shefali. *The Sexual Life of English: Languages of Caste and Desire in Colonial India*. Durham, NC: Duke University Press, 2012.

Chattopadhyay, Swati. *Unlearning the City: Infrastructure in a New Optical Field*. Minneapolis: University of Minnesota Press, 2012.

Chaudhuri, Amit. *Clearing a Space: Reflections on India, Literature and Culture*. Witney, England: Peter Lang, 2008.

———. Introduction to *Jejuri*, by Arun Kolatkar, xxv–xxvi. New York: New York Review of Books, 2005.

———. *Real Time: Stories and a Memoir in Verse*. London: Picador, 2001.

———. "The Sideways Movement: The Rare Critical Confidence of Arvind Krishna Mehrotra." *Caravan*, September 1, 2012. http://www.caravanmagazine.in/books/sideways-movement.

Chaudhuri, Sukanta. "The Translator as Sceptic." In *Translation and Understanding*, 23–44. New Delhi: Oxford University Press, 1999.

Chaudhuri, Supriya. "Modernisms in India." In *The Oxford Handbook of Modernisms*, ed. Peter Brooker, Andrzej Gasiorek, Deborah Parsons, and Andrew Thacker, 942–60. Oxford: Oxford University Press, 2010.

Chitre, Dilip. *An Anthology of Marathi Poetry, 1945–65*. Bombay: Nirmala Sadanand, 1967.

———. *Arun Kolatkar*. DVD. New Delhi: Sahitya Akademi, 2010.

———. "Arun Kolatkar, Primarily a Poet." *The Little Magazine* 2/3:50–53.

———. *As Is, Where Is: Selected English Poems, 1964–2007*. Mumbai: Poetrywala, 2007.

———. "At My Age and of My Age." *The Hindu*, January 4, 2009. http://www.thehindu.com/todays-paper/tp-features/tp-literaryreview/at-my-age-and-of-my-age/article662159.ece.

———. *Ekun Kavita*-1. Mumbai: Popular Prakashan, 1992.

———. *Ekun Kavita*-2. Mumbai: Popular Prakashan, 1995.

———. "A Home for Every Voice." In *Indian Poetry: Modernism and After*, ed. K. Satchidanandan, 1–12. Delhi: Sahitya Akademi, 2001.

———. "An Introductory Footnote from the Editor's Desk." *New Quest* 162 (October–December 2005): 4–7.

———. "Losing Contemporaries." *New Quest* 157–58 (July–December 2004): 5–6.

———. "Poem 10." Translation of B. S. Mardhekar's poems. *Poetry India* 1, no. 1 (January–March 1966): 58.

———. "Remembering Kolatkar." Blog, now defunct. Accessed December 10, 2007.

———. *Says Tuka: Selected Poetry of Tukaram*. New Delhi: Penguin, 1991.

———. "Translation: Problems of a Paralysed Republic." *New Quest* 154 (2003): 45–49.

———. *Travelling in a Cage*. Bombay: Clearing House, 1980.

———. "Vague Targets, Some Thoughts on Indian English Poetry and (Of Course) Poetry in General." *Bombay Literary Review* 1 (1991): 29–36.

Clay, Steven, and Rodney Phillips. *A Secret Location on the Lower East Side: Adventures in Writing, 1960–1980: A Sourcebook of Information*. New York: New York Public Library, 1998.

Clifford, James. *Routes: Travel and Translation in the Late Twentieth Century*. Cambridge, MA: Harvard University Press, 1997.

Coleridge, Samuel Taylor. *Biographia Literaria, or, Biographical Sketches of My Literary Life and Opinions*. New York: American Book Exchange, 1881.

Culler, Jonathan. *On Deconstruction: Theory and Criticism After Structuralism*. London: Routledge, 1983.

Dabholkar, Lata. "*Shahanyani dakhavali swamitvahakkachi 'sakal.'*" *Loksatta*, October 7, 2013. http://epaper.loksatta.com/169284/indian-express/07-10-2013#page/1/2.

Dadrawala, Nitin. "*Koslachya mukhaprushtha sambandhi. . udaharanartha 23 varshanantar.*" *Loksatta*, December 1, 2013. http://www.loksatta.com/lokrang-news/50-years-of-kosala-novel-and-its-cover-page-281891/.

Dahake, Vasant Abaji. *Marathi Sahitya: Itihas ani Sanskriti*. Mumbai: Popular Publishers, 2005.

Davidson, Michael. *Gays Like Us: Citing Masculinity in Cold War Poetics*. Chicago: University of Chicago Press, 2004.

De Certeau, Michel. *The Practice of Everyday Life*. Trans. Steven Rendell. Berkeley: University of California Press, 1984.

De Loach, Allen, and Allen Ginsberg. "Little Mags/Small Presses and the Cultural Revolution: [A Panel Discussion Moderated by] Allen De Loach." *Intrepid* 21/22 (1972): 106–39.

De Man, Paul. *The Resistance to Theory*. Minneapolis: University of Minnesota Press, 1986.

Derrida, Jacques, and Eric Prenowitz. *Archive Fever: A Freudian Impression*. Chicago: University of Chicago Press, 1996.

Deshpande, Prachi. *Creative Pasts: Historical Memory and Identity in Western India, 1700–1960*. New York: Columbia University Press, 2007.

———. "Pasts in the Plural: A Review of Bhalchandra Nemade's *Hindu: Jaganyachi Samruddha Adagal*." *Studies in Humanities and Social Sciences* 17, no. 1/2 (2010): 211–20.

De Souza, Eunice. "Being Bilingual Is a Strain, Says Arun Kolatkar." *Economic Times*, September 11, 1977, 5.

———. "'Indianness' and the Critic in a Post-Colonial Structure." *Bombay Review* 1 (1989): 35.

———. "Interviews with Four Indian English Poets." *Bombay Review* 1 (1989): 71–84.

———. "On a Wing and a Prayer." *Mumbai Mirror*, June 17, 2010.

———. *Talking Poems: Conversations with Poets*. New Delhi: Oxford University Press, 1999.

———. *Women in Dutch Painting*. Bombay: Praxis, 1988.

Devy, G. N. "Indian Literature in English Translation." In *In Another Tongue: Essays on Indian English Literature*, ed. G. N. Devy, 117–33. Frankfurt: Peter Lang, 1993.

Dhale, Raja. Interview. *Lokaprabha*. December 14, 2012. http://www.lokprabha.com/20121214/cover01-video.htm.

———. Interview by Mangesh Narayan Kale. Special issue on Raja Dhale. *Khel* 23 (2012): 7–15.

———. "*Satyakathechi satyakatha*." *Yeru*. 1969.

Dharwadker, Vinay. "Arun Kolatkar's Historical Imagination." In *Marginalized: Indian Poetry in English*, ed. Smita Agarwal, 151–82. Amsterdam: Rodopi, 2014.

———. "The Historical Formation of Indian-English Literature." In *Literary Cultures in History: Reconstructions from South Asia*, ed. Sheldon Pollock, 199–267. Berkeley: University of California Press, 2003.

———. "Indian Writing in English Today: A View from 1994." In *Twayne Companion to Contemporary World Literature*, 686–90. New York: Twayne, Thomson Gale, 2003.

———. "Literary Criticism, Modern Marathi Verse, and the Early Poetry of Mangesh Padgaonkar." *Journal of South Asian Literature* 19, no. 2 (1984): 91–110.

———. "The Modernist Novel in India: Paradigms and Practices." In *A History of the Indian Novel in English*, ed. Ulka Anjaria, 103–18. New York: Cambridge University Press, 2015.

———. "Print Culture and Literary Markets in Colonial India." In *Language Machines: Technologies of Literary and Cultural Production*, ed. Jeffrey Masten, Peter Stallybrass, and Nancy Vickers, 108–33. New York: Routledge, 1997.

———. "Some Contexts of Modern Indian Poetry." *Chicago Review* 38, no. 1/2 (1992): 218–31.

———. "Twenty-Nine Modern Indian Poems." *TriQuarterly* 77 (Winter 1989–90): 119–228.

Dhasal, Namdeo. "*Arunchya kaviteche june nave valan*." *Shabda* (Diwali 2005): 100–104.

———. *Golapitha*. Pune: Nilakant Prakashan, 1975.

Dhasal, Namdeo, and Dilip Chitre. *Namdeo Dhasal, Poet of the Underworld: Poems, 1972–2006*. Pondicherry: Navayana, 2007.

Dickie, Margaret. *On the Modernist Long Poem*. Iowa City: University of Iowa Press, 1986.

Dingwaney, Anuradha, and Carol Maier, eds. *Between Languages and Cultures: Translation and Cross-Cultural Texts*. Delhi: Oxford University Press, 1996.

Doctor, Vikram. "Flamboyant Adman: Remembering Kersy Katrak." *Economic Times of India*, January 9, 2008. http://articles.economictimes.indiatimes.com/2008-01-09/news/27694215_1_ad-agency-mcm-jwt.

———. "Inscrutable Warrior." *Economic Times of India*, October 6, 2004. http://articles.economictimes.indiatimes.com/2004-10-06/news/42809617_1_jj-school-kersy-katrak-new-agency.

Dongare, Avadhoot. "*Darvarshicha ath jun, Kim ani Kolatkar.*" http://ekregh.blogspot.in/2013/06/blog-post_8.html.

———. "*Napeksha . . . Ashok Shahane.*" http://napekshaashokshahane.blogspot.com/.

Doyle, Laura, and Laura A. Winkiel. *Geomodernisms: Race, Modernism, Modernity*. Bloomington: Indiana University Press, 2005.

Du Plessis, R. B. "Social Texts and Poetic Texts: Poetry and Cultural Studies." In *The Oxford Handbook of Modern and Contemporary American Poetry*, ed. Cary Nelson, 53–70. Oxford: Oxford University Press, 2012.

Dwivedi, Sharada, Rahul Mehrotra, and Umaima Mulla-Feroze. *Bombay: The Cities Within*. Bombay: India Book House, 1995.

Engblom, Philip. "Arun Kolatkar: Reading *Jejuri* and *Arun Kolatkarachya Kavita* in Tandem." *New Quest* 146 (October–December 2001): 389–409.

———. "Bombay Modernisms: English and Marathi Versions in the Poetry of Nissim Ezekiel and Bal Sitaram Mardhekar." *Bombay Literary Review* 2, no. 1 (1990): 31–48.

———. "Keshavsut and Early Modernist Strategies for Indigenizing the Sonnet in Marathi." *Journal of South Asian Literature* 23 (1988): 42–66.

———. "Marathi Poetry in English Translation." *Journal of South Asian Literature* 17, no. 1 (Winter/Spring 1982): 115–32.

Evans, Harold. "Harold Evans on Newspaper Design and Typography." *Motif* 1 (January 1995): 23–24.

Ezekiel, Nissim. *Collected Poems, 1952–1988*. Delhi: Oxford University Press, 1989.

———. *Hymns in Darkness*. New Delhi: Oxford University Press, 1976.

———. *Poetry India* 1–6. Bombay: Parichay Trust, January–March 1966 to April–June 1967.

Ezekiel, Nissim, and Meenakshi Mukherjee. *Another India: An Anthology of Contemporary Indian Fiction and Poetry*. New Delhi: Penguin, 1990.

Fernandes, Naresh. "Beat Poets." *Time Out* (September 23–October 6, 2005): 24–25.

Friedman, Susan Stanford. "Planetarity: Musing Modernist Studies." *Modernism/Modernity* 17, no. 3 (2010): 471–99.

———. "When a 'Long' Poem Is a 'Big' Poem: Self-Authorizing Strategies in Women's Twentieth-Century 'Long Poems.'" In *Feminisms: An Anthology of Literary Theory and Criticism*, ed. Robyn Warhol and Herndl Price, 721–38. New Brunswick, NJ: Rutgers University Press, 1991.

Fulton, Len. "Anima Rising: Little Magazines in the Sixties." *American Libraries* 2, no. 1 (January 1971): 25–47.

———. *The Psychologique of Small Press Publishing*. New Brunswick, NJ: Graduate School of Library Service, 1976.

Gajarawala, Toral Jatin. *Untouchable Fictions: Literary Realism and the Crisis of Caste.* New York: Fordham University Press, 2013.

Gaonkar, Dilip Parameshwar. "On Alternative Modernities." In *Alternative Modernities*, ed. Dilip Parameshwar Gaonkar, 15–16. Durham, NC: Duke University Press, 2001.

Gemmill, Janet Powers. "Fine Poetry in Fine Wrappings." Review of Clearing House books. *Journal of South Asian Literature* 16, no. 2 (Summer/Fall 1981): 207–14.

George, Rosemary. *Indian English and the Fiction of National Literature.* New York: Cambridge University Press, 2013.

Ginsberg, Allen. *Indian Journals, March 1962–May 1963: Notebooks, Diary, Blank Pages, Writings.* San Francisco: Dave Haselwood Books, 1970.

———. *Kaddish and Other Poems, 1958–1960.* San Francisco: City Lights Books, 1961.

Glass, Loren. *Counterculture Colophon: Grove Press, the Evergreen Review, and the Incorporation of the Avant-Garde.* Stanford, CA: Stanford University Press, 2013.

Glazier, Loss P. *Small Press: An Annotated Guide to the Literature.* Freemont, CA: Ruddy Duck Press, 1985.

Gokhale, Shanta. "Words, Pistol Shots." *Outlook Magazine*, July 2, 2007. http://www.outlookindia.com/article/Words-Pistol-Shots/234978.

Gopal, Priyamvada. *The Indian English Novel: Nation, History, and Narration.* Oxford: Oxford University Press, 2009.

Guha, Ramachandra. "The Rise and Fall of the Bilingual Individual." *Economic & Political Weekly* 44, no. 33 (August 15, 2009): 36–42.

———. "What Gandhi Owed to Tagore." *The Hindu*, September 28, 2008. http://www.thehindu.com/todays-paper/tp-features/tp-sundaymagazine/what-gandhi-owed-to-tagore/article1437661.ece.

Gurjar, Vasant. "Tally Clerk." *Atta* 3.

Hansen, Thomas Blom. "Shiv Sena, the City, and Communal Populism." In *The Oxford Anthology of the Modern Indian City: The City in Its Plenitude*, ed. Vinay Lal, 30–45. New Delhi: Oxford University Press, 2013.

Hasan, Anjum. "'Your Missing Person': Clearing House and the Bombay Poets." *Caravan* (November 2010): 62–69.

Hawley, John S. *A Storm of Songs: India and the Idea of the Bhakti Movement.* Cambridge, MA: Harvard University Press, 2015.

Heuze, Gerard. "Populism, Religion, and Nation in Contemporary India: The Evolution of the Shiv Sena in Maharashtra." *Comparative Studies of South Asia, Africa and the Middle East* 20, no. 1 (2000): 3–43.

Iyer, Bharat. "An Interview with Arvind Krishna Mehrotra." *Eclectica* 17, no. 1 (January–February 2013). http://www.eclectica.org/v17n1/iyer.html.

Jaaware, Aniket. "Eating and Eating with the Dalit: A Reconsideration Touching upon Marathi Poetry." In *Indian Poetry: Modernism and After*, ed. K. Satchidanandan, 262–92. New Delhi: Sahitya Akademi, 1998.

Jadhav, R. G., ed. *Marathi Vangmayacha Itihas.* Vol. 7, part 2. Pune: Maharashtra Sahitya Parishad, 2010.

———. *Sathottari Marathi Kavita va Kavi*. Aurangabad: Saket Prakashan, 1997.

James, Henry, and Morris Shapira. *Selected Literary Criticism*. New York: Horizon Press, 1964.

Jayaraman, Gayatri. "Noah's Archive." Poetry. *Mint*, June 30, 2012. http://www.livemint.com/Leisure/TuhTZtoaMrmgevNh7lvLHJ/Poetry—Noah8217s-archive.html.

Johari, Aarefa. "Mumbai Had a Plan for an Underground Railway in 1963—50 Years Before It Cleared Metro 3." *Scroll* (October 14, 2015). http://scroll.in/article/748882/mumbai-had-a-plan-for-an-underground-railway-in-1963–50-years-before-it-cleared-metro-3.

John, Mary. "Reframing Globalization: Perspectives from the Women's Movement." *Economic & Political Weekly* 44, no. 10 (March 7, 2009): 46–49.

Joshi, Keshav. *Satyakatha-Sahitya Suchi*. Nagpur: Keshav Joshi, 1997.

Joshi, R. K. *Vacha* 3 (1968): 65.

Jussawalla, Adil. "Before and After." Interview by Vivek Narayanan and Sharmistha Mohanty. *Almost Island* (Monsoon 2012): 1–45.

———. "Being There: Aspects of an Indian Crisis." *Bombay Review* 1 (1989): 20–27.

———. Introduction to *New Writing in India*, ed. Adil Jussawalla, 17–35. Harmondsworth, England: Penguin, 1974.

———. *Land's End: Poems*. Calcutta: Writer's Workshop, 1962.

———. *Missing Person*. Bombay: Clearing House, 1976.

———, ed. *New Writing in India*. Harmondsworth, England: Penguin, 1974.

———. Preface to *Three Poets: Melanie Silgardo, Raul D'Gama Rose, Santan Rodrigues*, ed. Melanie Silgardo, Raul D'Gama Rose, and Santan Rodrigues, 5–6. Bombay: Newground, 1978.

———. *The Right Kind of Dog*. Chennai: Duckbill Books, 2013.

———. *Trying to Say Goodbye: Poems*. Mumbai: Almost Island Books, 2011.

Jussawalla, Adil, and Eunice de Souza, eds. *Statements: An Anthology of Indian Prose in English*. New Delhi: Orient Longman, 1976.

Jussawalla, Adil, and Jerry Pinto. *Maps for a Mortal Moon: Essays and Entertainments*. New Delhi: Aleph Book Company, 2014.

Kale, Mangesh Narayan. "IFA Project on Little Magazines." Unpublished manuscript.

Kalsekar, Satish, and Arun Shevte, eds. *Nivadak Abakadaee*. Mumbai: Lokvangmaya Griha, 2012.

Kapur, Geeta. "Revelation and Doubt: *Sant Tukaram* and *Devi*." In *Interrogating Modernity: Culture and Colonialism in India*, ed. Tejaswini Niranjana, 19–46. Calcutta: Seagull, 1993.

———. "When Was Modernism in Indian/Third World Art?" *South Atlantic Quarterly* 92, no. 3 (Summer 1993): 473–514. Reprinted in *When Was Modernism? Essays on Contemporary Cultural Practice in India*. New Delhi: Tulika Press, 2001.

Karnad, Girish. "Re-presenting 'India.'" *The Hindu*, August 19, 2001. www.thehindu.com/thehindu/2001/08/19/stories/1319067g.htm.

Karnik, Sunil. "*Granthanirmitiche 'Shahane' kavatik*." *Divyamarathi*, July

10, 2011. http://divyamarathi.bhaskar.com/news/MAG-granthanirmiti-by-sunil-karnik-2251309.html.

———. *Prashna Uttare*. Interview with Arun Kolatkar. *Rucha* 2 (December 1977): 92–96.

Katrak, Kersy. "Pseuds, Plagiarists & Poets." *Gentlemen* 5 (June 1982): 35–40.

Kaviraj, Sudipta. *Imaginary Institution of India: Politics and Ideas*. New York: Columbia University Press, 2010.

Kelkar, Ashok R. "The Being of a Poem." *Foundations of Language* 5, no. 1 (February 1969): 17–33.

Kemp, Sharon. "Women as Bullocks: A Self-Image of Maharashtrian Village Women." In *Images of Women in Maharashtrian Society*, ed. Anne Feldhaus, 217–39. Albany: State University of New York Press, 1998.

Ketkar. Sachin. "Globalization and New Marathi Poetry." http://www.museindia.com/viewarticle.asp?myr=2005&issid=3&id=69.

Khakhar, Bhupen. "Notes on the Visual Sources of My Painting." *Vrischik*, no. 1 (1969).

Kimbahune, R. S. "From Jejuri to Arun Kolatkar." *New Quest* (January–February 1980): 27–32.

King, Bruce. "Modern Indian and American Poetry: Some Contacts and Relations." *Indian Journal of American Studies* 15, no. 1 (1985): 5–17.

———. *Modern Indian Poetry in English*. Delhi: Oxford University Press, 2001.

Kolatkar, Arun. *Arun Kolatkarchya Char Kavita*. Mumbai: Pras Prakashan, 2006.

———. *Arun Kolatkarchya Kavita*. Mumbai: Pras Prakashan, 1977.

———. "Arun Kolatkar, Interview by Darryl D'Monte." *Debonair* 6, no. 10 (October 1977): 9–13.

———. *Bhijaki Vahi*. Mumbai: Pras Prakashan, 2003.

———. *Chirimiri*. Mumbai: Pras Prakashan, 2003.

———. *Dron*. Mumbai: Pras Prakashan, 2004.

———. "Interview." *Indian Literary Review* (August 1978): 4–10.

———. *Jejuri*. Mumbai: Clearing House, 1976. Reprint, Mumbai: Pras Prakashan, 1977.

———. *Jejuri*. Mumbai: Pras Prakashan, 2011.

———. *Kala Ghoda Poems*. Mumbai: Pras Prakashan, 2004.

———. *Sarpa Satra*. Mumbai: Pras Prakashan, 2004.

Kolatkar, Arun, and Arvind Krishna Mehrotra. *Arun Kolatkar: Collected Poems in English*. Tarset: Bloodaxe, 2010.

———. *The Boatride & Other Poems*. Mumbai: Pras Prakashan, 2009.

Kosambi, Meera. "British Bombay and Marathi Mumbai: Some Nineteenth Century Perceptions." In *Bombay: Mosaic of Modern Culture*, ed. Sujata Patel and Alice Thorner, 3–24. Bombay: Oxford University Press, 1995.

———. *Crossing Thresholds: Feminist Essays in Social History*. Delhi: Permanent Black, 2007.

Kulashreshtha, C. "Interview." In *Uncollected Poems and Prose*, ed. A. K. Ramanujan, M. Daniels-Ramanujan, and K. Harrison, 41–51. Delhi: Oxford University Press, 2001.

Kulkarni, T. S. *Svatantryottara Marathi Kavita, 1961–80*. New Delhi: Sahitya Akademi, 1994.

Kumar, Akshaya. *Poetry, Politics, and Culture: Essays on Indian Texts and Contexts*. New Delhi: Routledge, 2009.

Kurup, Saira. "Four Women India Forgot." *Times of India*, May 7, 2006. http://timesofindia.indiatimes.com/home/sunday-toi/special-report/Four-women-India-forgot/articleshow/1519056.cms?referral=PM.

Lal, Vinay. *The Oxford Anthology of the Modern Indian City: The City in Its Plenitude*. New Delhi: Oxford University Press, 2013.

Limbale, Sharankumar. *Akkarmashi* (The Outcaste). Trans. Santosh Bhoomkar. Delhi: Oxford University Press, 2003.

———. Introduction to *Akkarmashi* (The Outcaste), 13–26. Trans. Santosh Bhoomkar. Delhi: Oxford University Press, 2003.

———. *Sathottari Marathi Vangmayatil Pravaha*. Pune: Dilipraj Prakashan, 2007.

Mahmud, Shabana. "*Angare* and the Founding of the Progressive Writers' Association." *Modern Asian Studies* 30, no. 2 (May 1996): 447–67.

Manohar, Yashwant. "*Marathitil little magazine ani bandhilaki*." In *Sahitya, Bandhilaki Ani Vidroha*, ed. Yashwant Manohar, 84–91. Aurangabad: Ananda Prakashan, 1987.

Mantena, Karuna. "The Ideas of Indians." *Caravan*, March 1, 2013. http://www.caravanmagazine.in/books/ideas-indians.

Masselos, Jim. *Indian Nationalism: A History*. New Delhi: Sterling Publishers, 1993.

McGann, Jerome J. *The Textual Condition*. Princeton, NJ: Princeton University Press, 1991.

Mchale, Brian. "Telling Stories Again: On the Replenishment of Narrative in the Postmodernist Long Poem." *Yearbook of English Studies* 30 (2000): 250–62.

Mehrotra, Arvind Krishna. *The Absent Traveller: Prakrit Love Poetry from the Gaathaasaptashatii of Saatvaahanan Haala*. New Delhi: Ravi Dayal Publisher, 1991.

———. "Being Here." Review of *Maps of a Mortal Moon*, by Adil Jussawalla. *Caravan*, April 1, 2014. http://www.caravanmagazine.in/books/being-here.

———. "Bharatmata." *Poetry India* 2, no. 2 (1967): 16–22.

———. "The Closing of the Bhasha Mind." *Biblio: A Review of Books* 17 (May–June 2012): 27–28.

———, ed. *damn you* 1–6. Allahabad: Ezra-fakir Press, 1965–68.

———. *Distance in Statute Miles*. Bombay: Clearing House, 1982.

———. "The Emperor Has No Clothes." In *The Vintage Book of Modern Indian Literature*, ed. Amit Chaudhuri, 456–77. New York: Vintage, 2004.

———, ed. *ezra* 1–5. Allahabad: Ezra-fakir Press, 1967–71.

———. *A History of Indian Literature in English*. New York: Columbia University Press, 2003.

———. *Middle Earth*. Delhi: Oxford University Press, 1984.

———. *Nine Enclosures*. Bombay: Clearing House, 1976.
———, ed. *The Oxford Anthology of Twelve Modern Indian Poets*. Delhi: Oxford University Press, 1992.
———. *Partial Recall: Essays on Literature and Literary History*. Hyderabad: Orient Blackswan, 2012.
———. *Pomes/Poemes/Poemas*. Baroda: Vrischik Publication, 1971.
———. "Sant Kabir, Rudyard Kipling, and Vernacular English." *Metamorphoses* 17, no. 2 (2009): 18–39.
———. *Songs of Kabir*. New York: New York Review of Books, 2011.
———. *The Transfiguring Places: Poems*. Delhi: Ravi Dayal Publisher, 1998.
———. "Translating the Indian Past: The Poets' Experience." *Journal of Commonwealth Literature* 49, no. 3 (2014): 427–39.
Mehta, Gita. *Karma Cola: Marketing the Mystic East*. New York: Simon and Schuster, 1979.
Menon, Nivedita. "Thinking Through the Postnation." *Economic & Political Weekly* 44, no. 10 (March 7, 2009): 70–77.
Mishra, Sudesh. *Preparing Faces: Modernism and Indian Poetry in English*. Adelaide: Flinders University of South Australia, 1995.
Mortenson, Erik. *Capturing the Beat Moment: Cultural Politics and the Poetics of Presence*. Carbondale: Southern Illinois University Press, 2011.
Moss, Laura. "'The Plague of Normality': Reconfiguring Realism in Recent Postcolonial Theory." *Jouvert* 5, no. 1 (Fall 2000). english.chass.ncsu/jouvert/v5i1/moss.htm.
Mukherjee, Meenakshi. "The Anxiety of Indianness: Our Novels in English." In *Mapping Cultural Spaces: Postcolonial Indian Literature in English*, ed. Nilufer E. Bharucha and Vrinda Nabar, 78–93. New Delhi: Vision, 1998.
Nagarkar, Kiran. "Arun Kolatkar: Some Memories." Unpublished manuscript.
Nagarkar, Kiran, and Shubha Slee. *Seven Sixes Are Forty-Three*. Oxford: Heinemann, 1995.
Naipaul, V. S. *East Indians in the Caribbean: Colonialism and the Struggle for Identity: Papers Presented to a Symposium on East Indians in the Caribbean, the University of the West Indies, June, 1975*. Millwood, NY: Kraus International Publications, 1982.
Nandy, Pritish. *Strangertime: An Anthology of Indian Poetry in English*. Delhi: Hind Pocket Books, 1977.
Naregal, Veena. *Language, Hierarchy and Identity: Emergence of the Public Sphere in Colonial Western India*. Delhi: Oxford University Press, 2001.
Nemade, Bhalchandra. "Arun Kolatkar: Bilingual Poet." In *Tikasvayamvara*, 117–26. Aurangabad: Saket Prakashan, 1990.
———. "*Halli lekhakacha lekhakrao hoto to ka?*" ("How Does the Writer Become Mr. Writer?") *Vacha* 6 (1968).
———. *Kosla*. Pune: Popular Prakashan, 1963.
———. "*Kavi lok*" ("The Poets"). In *Meladi: Dekhani ani Nantarchya Kavita*, by Bhalchandra Nemade, 30. Mumbai: Popular Prakashan, 1991.
———. *Tikasvayamvara*. Aurangabad: Saket Prakashan, 1990.
Nerlekar, Anjali. "*Adarallu Idu* ['This, Even in the Midst of That']: Girish

Karnad Talks About A. K. Ramanujan and His Own Dramaturgy." *South Asian Review* 26, no. 2 (2005): 217–36.

———. "The Cartography of the Local in Arun Kolatkar's Poetry." *Journal of Postcolonial Writing* 49, no. 5 (2013): 609–23.

———. "Little Magazines, Bilingualism and Bombay Poetry." In *History of Indian Poetry in English*, ed. Rosinka Chaudhuri. Cambridge: Cambridge University Press, forthcoming.

———. Review of Arun Kolatkar's *Kala Ghoda Poems*, *Modern Language Studies* 35, no. 1 (Spring 2005): 94–98.

———. "The Rough Ground of Translation and Bilingual Writing in Arun Kolatkar's *Jejuri*." *Perspectives, Studies in Translatology* 21, no. 2 (2013): 226–40.

Nerurkar, Pradeep. "*Little Magazine ani Raja Dhale*" ("Little Magazines and Raja Dhale"). Special issue on Raja Dhale, *Khel* 23 (2012): 53–74.

Novetzke, Christian. *Religion and Public Memory: A Cultural History of Saint Namdev in India*. New York: Columbia University Press, 2008.

Orsini, Francesca. *The Hindi Public Sphere, 1920–1940: Language and Literature in the Age of Nationalism*. New Delhi: Oxford University Press, 2009.

———, ed. *The History of the Book in South Asia*. London: Ashgate, 2013.

———. "How to Do Multilingual Literary History? Lessons from Fifteenth- and Sixteenth-century North India." *Indian Economic & Social History Review* 49, no. 2 (2012): 225–46.

———. "India in the Mirror of World Fiction." *New Left Review* 13 (January–February 2002). http://newleftreview.org/II/13/francesca-orsini-india-in-the-mirror-of-world-fiction.

Palshikar, Suhas. "In the Midst of Sub-democratic Politics." *Economic and Political Weekly* 7 (2010): 12–16.

Panikar, Ayappa. "The Anxiety of Authenticity." In *Translation: Its Theory and Practice*, ed. Avadesh Singh, 36–45. New Delhi: Creative Books, 1996.

Parthasarathy, R. "Meeting Allen Ginsberg." *Writers Workshop Miscellany* 11 (1962): 65–66.

———. *Ten Twentieth-Century Indian Poets*. Delhi: Oxford University Press, 1976.

Patankar, Vasant. "*Aniyatkalikanchi sankalpana ani itihas*." *Navakshar Darshan* 5, no. 2, special issue on little magazines (April–May 2009): 5–11.

———. *Arun Kolatkaranchi Kavita*. Mumbai: Lokvangmaya Griha, 2004.

Patel, Gieve. *How Do You Withstand, Body*. Bombay: Clearing House, 1976.

———. *Mirrored, Mirroring*. Madras: Oxford University Press, 1991.

Patil, Chandrakant, ed. *Drushyantar: Swatantryanantarchi Marathi Kavita*. Delhi: National Book Trust, 2007.

———. Editorial. *Vacha* 6 (1967).

Patil, Chandrakant, and N. D. Mahanor, eds. *Punha Ekada Kavita*. Pune: Neelkanth Prakashan, 1982.

Patke, Rajeev. "Arun Kolatkar." In *The Cambridge History of Indian Poetry in English*, ed. Rosinka Chaudhuri. New York: Cambridge University Press, forthcoming.

———. "Arun Kolatkar." In *The Routledge Encyclopedia of Modernism*, ed. Stephen Ross. London: Routledge, 2015.

———. *Modernist Literature and Postcolonial Studies*. Edinburgh: Edinburgh University Press, 2013.

———. "Poetry and the Experience of Urban Space in the Poetry of Arun Kolatkar." In *Cross/Cultures: Readings in the Post/Colonial Literatures in English*, ed. Cecile Sandten and Annika Bauer. New York: Rodopi, forthcoming.

———. *Postcolonial Poetry in English*. Oxford: Oxford University Press, 2006.

Pavar, G. M., and M. D. Hatakanangalekar. *Marathi Sahitya: Prerana va Svarupa, 1950–1975*. Mumbai: Popular Prakashan, 1986.

Peeradina, Saleem. *Contemporary Indian Poetry in English: An Assessment and Selection*. Bombay: Macmillan, 1972.

Pollock, Griselda. "Beholding Art History: Vision, Place and Power." In *Vision and Textuality*, ed. Stephen Melville and Bill Readings, 38–66. Durham, NC: Duke University Press, 1995.

Pollock, Sheldon. "Literary History, Indian History, World History." *Social Scientist* 23, no. 10/12 (1995): 112–42.

Pound, Ezra. "Small Magazines." *English Journal* 19, no. 9 (1930): 689–704.

Prakash, Gyan. *Mumbai Fables*. Princeton, NJ: Princeton University Press, 2010.

Prakash, Gyan, and Kevin M. Kruse, eds. *The Spaces of the Modern City: Imaginaries, Politics, and Everyday Life*. Princeton, NJ: Princeton University Press, 2008.

Pullin, Eric. "'Money Does Not Make Any Difference to the Opinions That We Hold': India, the CIA, and the Congress for Cultural Freedom, 1951–58." *Intelligence and National Security* 26, no. 2–3 (2011): 377–98.

Rajadhyaksha, Vijaya. "*Aniyatkalike*." In *Jivhar Swanandache*, 183–98. Mumbai: Dinapushp Prakashan, 1981.

Ramakrishnan, E. V. *Making It New: Modernism in Malayalam, Marathi, and Hindi Poetry*. Shimla: Indian Institute of Advanced Study, 1995.

Ramanujan, A. K. *The Collected Poems of A. K. Ramanujan*. Delhi: Oxford University Press, 1995.

Ramanujan, A. K., Vinay Dharwadker, and Stuart H. Blackburn. *The Collected Essays of A. K. Ramanujan*. New Delhi: Oxford University Press, 1999.

Ramazani, Jahan. *The Hybrid Muse: Postcolonial Poetry in English*. Chicago: University of Chicago Press, 2001.

———. *Poetry and Its Others: News, Prayer, Song, and the Dialogue of Genres*. Chicago: University of Chicago Press, 2014.

———. *A Transnational Poetics*. Chicago: University of Chicago Press, 2009.

Ramnarayan, Gowri. "No Easy Answers." *The Hindu*, September 5, 2004. http://www.hindu.com/lr/2004/09/05/stories/2004090500110100.htm.

Rao, Anupama. *The Caste Question: Dalits and the Politics of Modern India*. Berkeley: University of California Press, 2009.

Raykar, Shubhangi, ed. *Jejuri: A Commentary and Critical Perspectives*. Pune: Prachet Publications, 1995.

Rege, P. S. "Jejuri." *Rucha* 2 (1977): 76–78.

Rich, Adrienne. *Later Poems Selected and New: 1971–2012*. New York: W. W. Norton, 2013.

Rickards, Maurice. *Collecting Printed Ephemera*. New York: Abbeville Press, 1988.

Rodrigues, Santan. Editorial. *Kavi* 1 (1976): 1–2.

Rosenthal, M. L., and Sally M. Gall. *The Modern Poetic Sequence: The Genius of Modern Poetry*. New York: Oxford University Press, 1983.

Rushdie, Salman. *The Moor's Last Sigh*. London: Vintage, 1995.

———. *Satanic Verses*. New York: Random House, 1988.

Rushdie, Salman, and Elizabeth West. *Mirrorwork: 50 Years of Indian Writing, 1947–1997*. New York: H. Holt and Company, 1997.

Sabin, Margery. *Dissenters and Mavericks: Writings About India in English, 1765–2000*. Oxford: Oxford University Press, 2002.

Sadana, Rashmi. *English Heart, Hindi Heartland: The Political Life of Literature in India*. Berkeley: University of California Press, 2012.

Sahitya Akademi Annual Report, 1954–57. Appendix 1. New Delhi: Sahitya Akademi.

Sarang, Vilas. *Aksharancha Shram Kela*. Mumbai: Mauj Prakashan, 2000.

———. "Confessions of a Marathi Writer." *World Literature Today* 68, no. 2 (Spring 1994): 309–12.

———. "Fullstoppers and Semi-colonials." *New Quest* 143 (2001): 92–96.

———. *Indian English Poetry Since 1950: An Anthology*. Bombay: Disha Books, 1990.

———. "*Marathi sahityatil tinpani khel*" ("The Three-Card Game of Poker in Marathi Literature"). In *Sarjanashodh ani Lihita Lekhak*, 70–72. Mumbai: Mauj Prakashan, 2007.

———. "Mother Tongue, Other Tongue." *New Quest* 139 (2000): 104–8.

———. *Sarjanashodh ani Lihita Lekhak*. Mumbai: Mauj Prakashan, 2007.

———. "Self-Translators." *Journal of South Asian Literature* 16, no. 2 (1981): 33–38.

———. "Tradition and Conflict in the Context of Marathi Literature." *Indian Literature* 35, no. 5 (1992): 159–68.

———. "War Between the Bhasha Tribes and the Firangs." *New Quest* 146 (2011): 470–79.

Satchidanandan K., ed. *Indian Poetry: Modernism and After, a Seminar*. Delhi: Sahitya Akademi, 2001.

Scholes, Robert, and Clifford Wulfman. *Modernism in the Magazines: An Introduction*. New Haven, CT: Yale University Press, 2010.

Sen, Sukumar. *History of Bengali Literature*. New Delhi: Sahitya Akademi, 1971.

Shahane, Ashok. "*Ajakalachya Marathi vangmayavar 'ksha' kiran*" ("An X-Ray of Contemporary Marathi Literature"). In *Napeksha*, 3–30. Mumbai: Lokvangmaya Griha, 2008.

———. "*Bal Thakur an makhar.*" *Anubhav* (Diwali 2013): 140–44.

———. "*Marathitun lihun chuknare sahityikach jasta.*" *Loksatta*, October 27, 2013. http://www.loksatta.com/lokrang-news/todays-marathi-literature-233612/.

———. *Napeksha*. Mumbai: Lokvangmaya Griha, 2008.

Shankar, Subramanian. *Flesh and Fish Blood: Postcolonialism, Translation, and the Vernacular.* Berkeley: University of California Press, 2012.

Sheikh, Gulammohammed, and Bhupen Khakhar, eds. *Vrischik*. Baroda: Vrischik Publication, 1969–73.

Shirwadker, Vasant. *Sarva Surve.* Vasai, Thane: Dimple Publication, 1985.

Shrinivas, Pradhan V., and Abraham Benjamin, eds. *Dionysus* 1–3. Bombay: Alankar Printers, 1965.

Shulman, Alix. "Women Writers of the Beat Generation." *Moody Street Irregulars* 28 (1994): 3–9.

Silgardo, Melanie, Raul D'Gama Rose, and Santan Rodrigues. *Three Poets: Melanie Silgardo, Raul D'Gama Rose, Santan Rodrigues.* Bombay: Newground, 1978.

Singh, Brijraj. "Four New Voices." *Chandrabhaga* 1 (1979): 68–85.

Singh, Kedar N., Arun Kolatakar, Ashok Vajapeyi, Reed Bye, Anne Waldman, and Bob Rosenthal. *Naropa Institute, Indian Poets, May 20, 1986.* Sound recording. http://archive.org/details/Reading_of_Indian_poets_May_1986_86P060.

Siskin, Clifford. "Textual Culture in the History of the Real." *Textual Cultures* 2, no. 2 (2007): 118–30.

Sontag, Susan. *On Photography.* New York: Farrar, Straus and Giroux, 1973.

Sontheimer, Gunther. "All the God's Wives." In *Images of Women in Maharashtrian Literature and Religion*, ed. Anne Feldhaus, 115–34. Albany: State University of New York Press, 1996.

———. *Pastoral Deities in Western India.* Delhi: Oxford University Press, 1993.

Spicer, Jack. *The Collected Books of Jack Spicer.* Ed. Robin Blaser. Santa Barbara, CA: Black Sparrow Press, 1980.

Spivak, Gayatri Chakrabarty. "Translating into English." In *Nation, Language, and the Ethics of Translation*, ed. Sandra Bermann and Michael Wood, 93–110. Princeton, NJ: Princeton University Press, 2005.

Stewart, Garrett. *Bookwork: Medium to Object to Concept to Art.* Chicago: University of Chicago Press, 2011.

Stillwell, Alix. "Women Poets of the Beat Generation." *Moody Street Irregulars* 28 (1994): 3–9.

Subrahmanyam, Sanjay. "Recovering Babel." In *Invoking the Past: The Uses of History in South Asia*, ed. Daud Ali, 280–321. Delhi: Oxford University Press, 1999.

Subramanium, Arundhati. "End of the Road for Mumbai's Poetry Scene?" *DNA India*, January 13, 2007. http://www.dnaindia.com/mumbai/report-end-of-the-road-for-mumbai-s-poetry-scene-1074255.

Suraj, Rafik. *Laghuniyatkalikanchi Varnanatmak Suchi.* Mumbai: Lokvangmaya Griha, 2011.

Surve, Narayan. *Majhe Vidyapeeth.* Pune: Popular Prakashan, 1992.

Tambe, Satish. "*Ashayachya londhyat ghat bhuisapat.*" In *Lekha-Jokha*, 196–217. Mumbai: Lokavangmaya Griha, 2007.

Tendulkar, Vijay. Introduction to *Golpitha* by Namdeo Dhasal. Bombay: Neelkanth Prakashan, 1975.

Thakar, Nishikant. "*Laghuniyatkalikanchi chalval.*" In *Sathottari Marathi Vangmayatil Pravaha*, ed. Sharankumar Limbale. Pune: Dilipraj Prakashan, 2007.

Triglio, Tony. *Allen Ginsberg's Buddhist Poetics*. Carbondale: Southern Illinois University Press, 2007.

Trivedi, Harish. "The Politics of Postcolonial Translation." In *Translation: Its Theory and Practice*, ed. Avadesh Singh, 46–55. New Delhi: Creative Books, 1996.

Venuti, Lawrence. "Translation, Community, Utopia." In *The Translation Studies Reader*, 468–88. London: Routledge, 2000.

Weaver, Mike. "Concrete Poetry." *Visible Language* 6 (1976): 293–326.

Williams, Raymond, and Tony Pinkney. *The Politics of Modernism: Against the New Conformists*. London: Verso, 1989.

Wittgenstein, Ludwig. *Philosophical Investigations*. New York: Macmillan, 1973.

Wordsworth, William. "A Slumber Did My Spirit Seal." In *The Collected Poems of William Wordsworth*. Chatham, Kent: Wordsworth Pocket Editions, 1994.

Yao, Steven. *Translation and the Languages of Modernism: Gender, Politics, Language*. New York: Palgrave, 2002.

Zecchini, Laetitia. *Arun Kolatkar and Literary Modernism in India: Moving Lines*. London: Bloomsbury, 2014.

Index

Figures are indicated by "f" following page numbers.